Outstanding Dissertations in
LINGUISTICS

edited by
LAURENCE HORN
Yale University

DEFINITIONS

IMPLICATIONS FOR SYNTAX, SEMANTICS, AND THE LANGUAGE OF THOUGHT

ANNABEL CORMACK

Routledge
Taylor & Francis Group
New York London

First published 1998 by Garland Publishing Inc.

This edition Published 2011 by Routledge
711 Third Avenue, New York, NY 10017
2 Park Square, Milton Park, Abingdon, Oxfordshire OX14 4RN

First issued in paperback 2014

*Routledge is an imprint of the Taylor and Francis Group,
an informa business*

Copyright © 1998 Annabel Cormack
All rights reserved

Library of Congress Cataloging-in-Publication Data

Cormack, Annabel, 1939–
　　Definitions : implications for syntax, semantics, and the language of thought / Annabel Cormack.
　　　　p.　　cm. — (Outstanding dissertations in linguistics)
　　A slight revision of the author's thesis (Ph. D.)—University College, London, 1989.
　　Includes bibliographical references and index.
　　ISBN 0-8153-3131-2 (alk. paper)
　　1. Lexicography. 2. Definition (Logic) 3. Grammar, Comparative and general—Syntax. 4. Thought and trhinking.
5. Semantics. I. Title. II. Series.
P327.C67 1998
413'.028—dc21

98-28259

ISBN 13: 978-1-138-86837-3 (pbk)
ISBN 13: 978-0-8153-3131-5 (hbk)

Contents

Preface vii

Acknowledgments xi

1   Theoretical Preliminaries 3
    1.0   Introduction 3
    1.1   A little simple syntax 6
    1.2   Relevance theory 30
    1.3   The 'language of thought' hypothesis 36
    1.4   Model theoretic semantics 44
    1.5   The formal interpretation of definitions 56
    Notes 77

2   Dictionary Definitions 83
    2.0   Introduction 83
    2.1   Simple nouns 85
    2.2   Simple adjectives 94
    2.3   Elimination of simple nouns and adjectives 113
    2.4   Dictionary definitions—elimination and
           complements 130
    2.5   Problem definitions 151
    Notes 156

3   Text Definitions 163
    3.0   Introduction 163
    3.1   Characteristics of text definitions 165
    3.2   Interpretation of simple definitions 174
    3.3   Complex definitions with 'if' or 'when' 195
    Notes 222

4 Syntax: Conclusions, Problems, and Speculations 231

4.0 Introduction: argument structure in syntax and semantics 231
4.1 Distinctions between adjectives: c-selection and learnability 236
4.2 Syntactic mechanisms for θ-roles 262
Notes 291

5 The Language of Thought: Findings, Problems, and Speculations 301

5.0 Points of departure 301
5.1 Variables 302
5.2 The expressive power and the syntax of the language of thought 305
5.3 LF as the sole input to interpretation? 310
5.4 Conceptual adicity, s-selection and c-selection 313
5.5 How are definitions interpreted and used? 317
5.6 Conclusions 325
Notes 326

Bibliography 329

Index 339

Preface

> What! you have had wings for ten years, and you haven't flown yet!
> Poincaré, *Science and method*; addressed to the 'logisticians'

Apart from this preface itself, what follows is essentially my 1989 Ph.D. thesis, with the omission of the old preface and abstract, and the provision of an index. I have updated bibliographical entries, and added those works mentioned here. The only other changes are typographical, and the correction of typing errors.

As I look at it now, although much is out of date, and some analyses are unsatisfactory, there is also much that has not been discussed elsewhere, or not discussed from the perspectives I employed. In particular, I think that many of the questions I have raised, and some of my conclusions, warrant further work, which I hope may be stimulated by this publication.

The focus is on definitions, which were culled both from a variety of dictionaries (chapter 2), and from various text books (chapter 3). I consider on the one hand, the syntax and semantics of the definition itself, and on the other, how the information conveyed by the definition can be put to use in constructing an item in the mental lexicon. Both kinds of definition pose problems of interpretation and usability, involving semantics and pragmatics, and the text definitions in particular raise syntactic problems as well. I attacked the data using, and as necessary adapting, the theoretical tools of Principles-and-Parameters syntax (Chomsky 1986a), Fodor's (1975) Language of Thought hypothesis (backed up by model theoretic semantics) for meaning, and Relevance theory for pragmatics (Sperber and Wilson 1986). The first chapter discusses relevant elements of each of these tools. It was I think the confrontation of a corpus of data with all these theories simultaneously which was so exciting, and productive of interesting questions and hypotheses.

The analyses raise numerous new questions, and suggest some answers. It is argued that because phrases, as occurring in dictionary definitions, can be understood in isolation, 'NP movement' has to be reanalyzed as transmission of θ-roles. In chapter 4, these ideas are applied to a variety of adjectives which take propositional complements. I discuss in detail not only what lexical specification is needed to distinguish the various syntactic options for each kind of adjective, but how the child can determine what the specification for the lexical item is. For adjectives such as *ready*, I argue that the external argument obtains one θ-role directly (by virtue of external selection by the head adjective) and one indirectly (by virtue of θ-transmission from an internal position). The θ-transmission from the internal position corresponds to either raising, or *tough*-movement, with correspondingly different interpretations for *ready*.

The main interest of the text definitions is the interplay between object language and metalanguage. Most such definitions are to be construed as statements about the meanings of words of English, but the definiendum is used, not just mentioned, within the definition, despite the fact that its meaning is not known previously. It is argued that for such definitions to be understood, the syntax of the Language of Thought must be close to that of Natural Language in specifiable ways. For example, semantic types must be common to the two languages. There is also considerable involvement of pragmatics, with some interesting consequences, particularly to ensure that the interpretation conforms to the requirements on a well-formed definition.

Both syntax and semantics have developed considerably in the last ten years, with more syntacticians paying attention to semantic issues. It is obvious that had I been addressing the same questions now, my answers would often have been different. In particular, the discipline of the Minimalist program (Chomsky 1995) would have been salutary in limiting the options apparently available.

There has been a fair amount of work which is directly pertinent to my concerns in this thesis. I mention here the most relevant of this. I should have mentioned Bierwisch and Kiefer (1970) in relation to the general problems raised by definitions. In the discussion of section 1.4, it would have been useful to have been able to refer the reader to Larson and Segal (1995), and Heim and Kratzer (1998). Fodor's Language of Thought hypothesis, and in particular the status of its semantics, has been the subject of much discussion by philosophers including Fodor himself. Carruthers (1996) considers much of this. Jackendoff (1992, chapter 2), places Conceptual Semantics in relation to model theoretic semantics and Internalist theories of meaning (and see Zwarts and Verkuyl 1994). Grimshaw 1990 and Williams 1994 are major discussions of argument structure and its relation to syntax. The content of the lexicon has been investigated under various approaches, from the computational to the conceptual: Boguraev and Briscoe (1989), Pustejovsky (1995), Levin (1993), and Jackendoff (1990) all discuss substantial portions of the lexicon in some detail. Dowty's (1991) discussion of θ-roles is relevant to my section 2.4.3. Cinque's (1990) paper on ergative adjectives is relevant to section 4.1.2, and Stowell (1991) to the discussion of *stupid* in section 4.1.3. Rothstein (1991) discusses the (absence of) projection of minor categories (compare my 'quasi-projections' in section 1.1.2). Chomsky and Lasnik (1993) argue that PRO has Case (see my section 4.1.2). Jacobson's 1990 paper *Raising As Function Composition* is important in relation to my notion of θ-movement (my section 2.2.2 and chapter 4). Bošković (1994) argues that there can be some movement into θ-positions, and see also Vikner (1988) who invokes the 'addition' of θ-roles for some modals (relevant to section 4.1.3). Hornstein (1996), and Manzini and Roussou (1997) independently argue that PRO can be dispensed with (as I argue for heads such as *able* in section 4.1.3), and assimilate Control to Raising. The latter also argue, as I do, that Raising itself is not to be seen as the movement of a noun-phrase, but arises from a chain involving rather some licensing of the relevant noun-phrase (for Manzini and Roussou, this licensing arises from Aspectual projections).

I have pursued some of the concerns myself. In particular Cormack and Breheny (1994) discuses projection of minor categories, relating to section 1.1.2, and uses covert conjunction as an alternative to the 'adjunction is conjunction' analysis of section 2.1.3; and Cormack and Smith 1994 introduce the notion of a 'nil' semantic θ-role, which obviates the need for an empty specifier position, and further exploit the idea of covert conjunction. Cormack 1996 captures the θ-movement of chapters 2 and 4 using combinators instead of variables and coindexing; but I have yet to find a satisfactory analysis of the problems with *stupid* type adjectives first raised by Postal (1974). Cormack (forthcoming) explores the 'murky' status of specifiers mentioned in section 1.1.2.

I had intended to revise the thesis, but have been prevented by illness; I am grateful to Garland for accepting it in its present form. I would like to thank my two Ph.D. examiners, Deirdre Wilson and Elisabet Engdahl, for stimulating discussion, and for encouragement and advice. and Justin Cormack for proof reading and typographical expertise.

Acknowledgments

It pleases me to be able to thank those people who have one way or another enabled me to write this thesis. First, this is the appropriate time to thank Martin Davies (of Stirling University) and Dave Bennett (of SOAS), who persuaded me when I was a mathematics teacher that what I was trying to do was linguistics. Secondly, I would like to thank those who helped to turn me into a linguist; in particular Ruth Kempson at SOAS, and Deirdre Wilson and Neil Smith at UCL. Thirdly, I am grateful to the DES for financial support for nearly three years, and to the University of London for allowing time, and to its libraries for supplying books. Fourthly, I would like to thank everyone else: fellow students, visiting scholars, conference acquaintances, friends; linguists (including in particular Robyn Carston and Rita Manzini), psychologists, philosophers—for discussion, stimulation and enlightenment; my colleagues at Reading for making it possible for me to have a sabbatical term; the authors of the books and articles I have read (especially those whom I can no longer identify as the sources of my ideas). Those categories are not mutually exclusive. Finally, I thank Neil Smith, my supervisor. From the heady delight of his first year lectures to the awful illumination of his questions about this work, he has been a most excellent teacher. He has set standards which I fail to reach, but at the same time his encouragement has kept me from despair. I am grateful for his patience, kindness and generosity, and for all he has taught me. It has been a pleasure and a challenge to write for one who combines a limitless intellectual curiosity with a demand for responses which are interesting to questions which are significant; and so I offer Neil this inadequate thesis.

Definitions

CHAPTER ONE

Theoretical Preliminaries

> It is in expounding the first principles that we must avoid too much subtlety, for there it would be too disheartening, and useless besides. We cannot prove everything, we cannot define everything, and it will always be necessary to draw on intuition.
>
> Poincaré, *Science and Method*

1.0 Introduction

> I have often had occasion to criticise definitions which I advocate today. These criticisms hold good in their entirety; the definitions can only be provisional, but it is through them that we must advance.
>
> Poincaré, *Science and Method*

It appears that there are such things as definitions. They can be found in dictionaries, and they can be found in text books. They are useful and used: manifestly, these definitions have some special function to do with learning the uses or meanings of words. On the other hand, there is considerable doubt as to the status of definitions. It is said that few or no words are definable; that meanings are not decomposed into parts; that there are not special things properly called definitions, but just ordinary uses of language.

In this thesis, the naive idea of a definition will be pursued, in the expectation that the attempt to show how, syntactically and semantically, there could be such things, will shed some light on the darker areas of doubt, and will test the powers of the explanatory theories we have available.

I had better say straight away that I am not going to say anything about lexicography. That we assess whether one definition is better or worse than another seems to me to dispose of the objection that words are not definable. Perfection seldom is attainable.

At worst, if definitions as such turned out to be illusory, we could regard a so-called definition simply as a source of particularly concentrated lexical information, and inquire just what syntactic, semantic, encyclopedic, inferential, associative ... information could be conveyed, and how. Is a putative definition in any way different syntactically or semantically from the same string taken as a general statement? Does the apparent special status arise merely from heuristic considerations? What is the gap between a normal interpretation of a string, and what would be needed if it satisfied the formal criteria for a definition—and can this gap be filled by ordinary pragmatic processes? Such questions can be asked, and to some extent answered, whether or not it is agreed that 'there really are' definitions.

The aim is to investigate the function of definitions within a model of language and language processing based more or less on Fodor's 'Language of Thought' hypothesis, Sperber and Wilson's Relevance theory, and Chomsky's Government and Binding theory, with the aid of Model Theoretic Semantics as necessary. The hope is not only to explain what definitions are used for, but to throw some light on aspects of the three theories.

Almost every model of a grammar contains as one component a lexicon. Here, information concerning the use and meaning of a word is stored; each lexical entry contains phonological, syntactic and semantic information. A definition can be regarded as an utterance (written or spoken) designed to facilitate the acquisition or refinement of a lexical entry. If we further suppose that the lexical item must be associated with an appropriate concept, then presumably the definition must facilitate this association, too.

In what follows, I shall be considering on the one hand, the syntax and semantics of the definition itself, and on the other, how the information conveyed by the definition can be put to use in constructing a lexical entry. Both dictionary definitions, such as (i), and written definitions such as (ii) and (iii) from running text, will be considered:

i *perissodactyl* having an odd number of toes

ii A *proper fraction* is a fraction whose numerator is less than its denominator

iii Any number that can be shown as a rectangular pattern of dots is called a *rectangular number*

Theoretical Preliminaries

There are characteristic formats for definitions, and the very fact that an utterance is construed as a definition makes a difference to its interpretation. In particular, an object-language versus meta-language distinction may be imposed, and special inferences drawn.

I assume Chomsky's modular grammar, so a lexical entry for a verb, for instance, should contain information which directly or indirectly gives the subcategorization potential of the verb, and the theta-roles assigned by the verb. Similarly, assuming that the meaning is given in terms of a Fodorian 'Language of Thought', the semantics for the verb must contain information about the roles of semantic arguments. Either a complex representation of meaning or associated 'Meaning Postulates' must indicate the inferential roles associated with the lexical item. The relation between the syntactic and the semantic (language of thought) forms must be mediated at least partly compositionally; the tools of model theoretic semantics, Montague grammar and its extensions, will be used to explore this relation. The simplest hypothesis would be that categorial selection, θ-role assignment, and language-of-thought argument structure were in correspondence, and that the language of thought itself had a simple compositional semantics with respect to some model. Such simplicity unfortunately, but interestingly, is unrealistic. The question then arises as to what constraints there are on possible failures of correspondence; the examination of definitions considered as sources of information about argument structure of the various kinds suggests particular (partial) answers to the question.

In the following sections the various theories just mentioned are briefly discussed, as is the formal theory of definitions. The possible ways in which definitions might be construed using this explanatory apparatus are then set out. Chapters 2 and 3 apply the theories to data; and force some innovation. Chapters 4 and 5 discuss the theoretical consequences of the analyses offered, raise further questions, and suggest possible approaches to problems.

1.1 A little simple syntax

> Such is the primitive conception in all its purity. It only remains to seek in the different case what value should be given to this exponent in order to be able to explain all the facts.
>
> Poincaré, *The value of Science*

1.1.0 Introduction

I shall be assuming a modular, multi-level, 'principles and parameters' theory of universal grammar, more or less a simplified version of what appears in Chomsky's (1986a) *Knowledge of Language*. Aside from the setting of the parameters, it is argued that the knowledge we have of the grammar is innate; what has to be learned is the contents of the lexicon.

The sketch below is not intended to be expository; it is here merely to remind the reader of those parts of the theory which I shall make use of; because my data is relatively simple, much has been omitted and simplified.

1.1.1 Levels of representation

Syntactic structure is primarily a vehicle for representing relationships between elements, where those relationships form the basis for our understanding of the meaning relationships between the semantic reflexes of those elements. On this view, the elaborateness of the grammar is largely a consequence of the elaborateness of the relationships which must, by hypothesis, be coded in the level of LF, in relation to the relative paucity of the relationships encoded directly in the input string. The postulation of S-structure, with its potential for syntactic structure and empty categories, adds information so to speak to the PF string of words. But it would lose this information in an infinitude of ambiguity were it not for the constraints imposed by the modules of the grammar. The grammar can be seen as functional to the extent that the constraints contribute to the construction of LF, on the assumption that it is the structures of LF that bear semantic interpretation.[1]

The most obviously semantic information coded in LF is the distribution of θ-roles (thematic roles) in relation to predicates—which

Theoretical Preliminaries

NP takes agent and which patient role, for instance, in relation to the predicate *kiss*, in *John kissed Mary* or *John was kissed by Mary*. We find that θ-roles are distributed to chains, and that the chains need Case; Case is assigned under government, so the conditions on chains and on government are contributing essentially to interpretation. This is so even of a condition applying just at D-structure, since there are a number of principles ensuring that what is possible at one level is closely related to what is possible at another, in a particular analysis. Move-α itself, the projection principle and the uniformity principle in Case theory are such principles. Those parts of the grammar which are most directly related to semantic interpretation, such as θ-role assignment, are discussed in section 1.1.9 below.

The various modules of the grammar, and other overriding principles, act as well-formedness conditions on the several levels of representation. Each level of representation consists (as far as I am concerned) of lexical items, morphemes and features, and other items of syntactic vocabulary (such as brackets and labels) in some fixed linear order. The levels are connected with each other by transformations. The available transformations are movement (move-α), deletion, and insertion (including the insertion of indices). The process of comprehending a sentence involves constructing four levels of representation, LF, PF, S-structure and D-structure, all of which are as far as possible properly connected and satisfy the various well-formedness conditions applicable to them. This formulation exonerates the language processor from any responsibility to construct intermediate levels, say between D-structure and S-structure. Chomsky (1987) has argued that a proof that D-structure is not just a notational convenience depends on finding a situation where S-structure does not in itself bear all the evidence for D-structure and for a proper relationship between the two levels; an alien element has obliterated some trace, perhaps. Such a situation would require that the grammaticality is ascertained by checking the licensing of S-structure in relation to some intermediate representation, and the licensing of the intermediate representation in relation to D-structure. In this way the ESSENTIALLY transformational nature of 'move-α' between these levels could be demonstrated. For myself, I hope that convincing arguments are not forthcoming, for two reasons. One is that the 'notational convenience' and simplicity arguments that one would be left with if no such demonstration is forthcoming seem to me to offer possibilities for further exploration of notation and computation; and secondly the temporal ordering of movements presupposed (first you move this to here and then you move that to there) seem to be intuitively at least incompatible with the shift to licensing rather than rules which is otherwise pervasive in the syntactic parts of the grammar. At worst, it might be possible to annotate S-structure further so that the missing information relating to the intermediate representation was present. If the sentence is not fully grammatical, it may all the same be possible to construct four representations such that just one or two conditions have been violated; then it may still be acceptable and understood.

In the familiar inverted T- (or Y-) diagram, S-structure is the central node, to which the other levels are connected. In the direction of PF, we move to realization; I shall have nothing to say about this, and in general will simply assume (inaccurately) that PF gives a surface string, the lexical items of S-structure in the order of S-structure, but without any brackets, empty categories, indices or other ornamentation (if this were correct, PF would be obtained from S-structure using just deletion). LF on the other hand is more informative than S-structure, in that further movement and more indexing has taken place; it is the interface level for semantic interpretation, and so must represent the totality of the syntactic contribution to meaning. D-structure is not an interface level (unless as suggested in Chomsky 1990 it is the interface with the lexicon), but is logically prior to S-structure in that S-structure is transformationally derived from D-structure (perhaps entirely by move-α). Intuitively, D-structure is the level at which grammatical relations are seen in their 'pure' state; but within the theory the levels are individually defined by the well-formedness conditions set on them, and collectively by their proper relation to each other in each particular derivation.

I want to characterize the three grammatical levels rather generally, before discussing in a little more detail some of the modules and principles of the grammar.

D-structure is the simplest level, because the totality of symbols available for forming strings at this level does not include indices. The requirements of some of the modules (binding and bounding) are then vacuously met. The projection principle and perhaps θ-theory apply to all the syntactic levels. X-bar theory is usually considered to be proprietary to D-structure. I think that the conditions indicated define D-structure. Movement is plausibly considered to be not assumed (or used) unless forced—this would clearly reduce computational options usefully, if translated into a processing model. From D-structure to S-structure, movement is characteristically forced by the imposition at S-structure of Case theory (accounting, as is familiar, for passive and raising structures *i.e.* NP-movement), and for English, a '*wh*-scope requirement' (accounting for the fronting of non-exempt *wh*-phrases; to be discussed below).[2] Other movement is forced by the inability of various features or morphemes to stand alone without a lexical host (accounting for anything like affix-hopping or V-movement). I think it is these conditions which identify S-structure, provided we assume there is only forced movement. The problem is to characterize S-structure rigorously, given the existence of further movement at LF. The movement leading to LF (which I shall assume is restricted to QR) is forced by the requirement that every QNP (quantified noun phrase) binds a syntactic variable;[3] for languages like Japanese without the *wh*-scope requirement on S-structure, *wh*-movement would be forced at LF by this condition. If we do not assume that movement is forced, then something must actually prevent QR from taking place at S-structure. Possibly the relevant restriction is that landing sites for S-structure movement must be base-generated (not produced by adjunction).

Other modules impose well-formedness conditions on S-structure and LF: θ-theory and the projection principle already mentioned, and those modules referring particularly to indexing relations (bounding theory and binding theory). Chomsky argues that there are no parameters to be fixed for LF. We may expect that S-structure and LF share most of their properties, especially if what S-structure is is parametrized, where the relevant parameters serve to single out some particular level between D-structure and LF. Chomsky (1990) suggests that S-structure may be considered as the solution to the equations imposed by the three peripheral (interface) levels. Taken definitively, this would lead us to postulate that any conditions apparently applying just to S-structure within syntax must in fact belong to PF—Case theory, perhaps, then.

The description in terms of well-formedness conditions suggests a rather negative existence for grammatical strings: they are what falls through if everything possible has been dropped through a set of sieves.

Rather more positively, we can conceive of structures as consisting of various elements (sub-structures) each of which must be *licensed*. We might expect and require that every element should be licensed with respect to each module. Alternatively, a single structure is seen differently by each module, so that which elements are visible varies according to the module. For instance X-bar theory may be blind to all except brackets and category labels: lexical content might not be visible to this module. The notion of *visibility* has been introduced and used so far just for θ-role assignment: a chain is not visible for θ-role assignment unless it has Case. In effect, the chains that the θ-module can see are not identical to the chains that say the binding module can see. In particular, what is visible for θ-theory is conditional on the dispositions of the Case-module.[4] I think that the notion of visibility may be usefully extended further.

1.1.2 Categorial Structure

X-bar theory is a general theory of the internal construction of maximal projections, or if you like, a theory of the categories related to a head. Assuming a three level analysis, we have licensed COMPLEMENTS, which are sisters of X-zero under X'; and a SPECIFIER, which is a sister of X' under X". Complements and specifiers—and indeed any other independently introduced categories—must be maximal projections. (I shall frequently refer to complements as arguments, whether or not they are NPs, since the semantic role of a complement is to be an argument.)

It is clear that we need as well some theory of the distribution of maximal projections, unless this is all. And this is not all—there are missing structures for predication, and structures for modification, at least. Both these can be accommodated as adjunction structures; so we need a general theory of adjunction. For instance, predication in small clauses may be analyzed like this (following Chomsky 1986b):

Theoretical Preliminaries

1 i   I consider [$_{SC}$ John ridiculous]

  ii

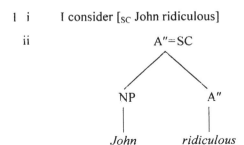

Here, the NP *John* is adjoined to the left of the A" *ridiculous*, and this sisterhood permits the predicate *ridiculous* to be predicated of its subject (external argument) *John*.

A typical modification structure is given for (2i) by (2ii):

2 i   [her [$_{N'}$ ridiculous hat]]

  ii

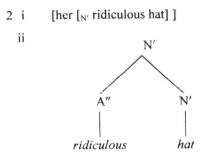

Assuming that these two structures are correct, we may take it that base-generated adjunction to at least X" and X' level is possible. Let us assume that base-generated adjunction of a Y" category is possible to a category of any level, including X-zero, for the moment.

Base-generated adjunction, and the subject-status of the NP in (1) might suggest that all subjects should be found in adjoined rather than specifier positions; Koopman and Sportiche (1985) and Manzini (1989) argue that subjects are indeed adjoined to VP, but only for some languages. These subjects will be moved to the pre-I position. The status of specifiers in general seems to me to be rather murky (as it is bound to, to someone with sympathy for extended categorial grammar), but for the most part I shall take what is offered by the standard theory. In chapter 4 I make some particular suggestions regarding specifiers.

It is important to note that an adjunction structure can be seen by any particular module with more or less structure (see section 1.1.6). That is, given (i), for instance, a module may effectively 'see' rather (ii):

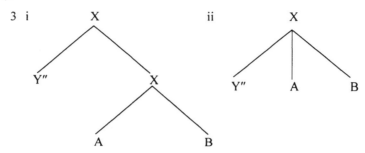

Intuitively, in (ii), the two instances of 'X', which are identical in (i), are actually identified.

We have not yet accommodated coordination and subordination. The arguments for constituent coordination seem to me to be overwhelming, now that we have semantics for this. (Non-constituent coordination is another matter, but fortunately it does not arise here.) Gazdar *et al.* (1985) argue for a combination of binary branching and multiple flat structures (see also Sag *et al.* 1985). They provide for examples like *no [man, woman or child]*. This would usually be considered to involve N or N' conjunction, and hence necessarily non-maximal categories. However on the DP analysis, what was an N' becomes an N''. But we may have instead examples such as

4 i   no [[brother, sister, or cousin] of mine]

Here the conjuncts must be non-maximal, if we take the *of mine* to be the complement of the conjuncts. Consider then the structure:

Theoretical Preliminaries

4 ii

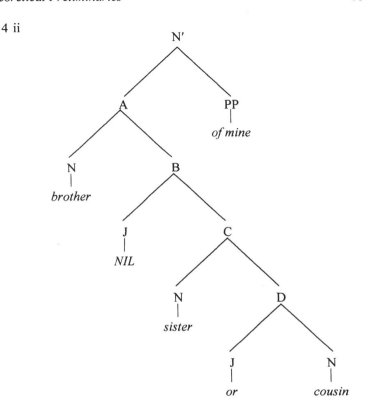

Gazdar *et al.* would have a flatter structure, with A = B = C, here. It is clear that this cannot be construed as falling under X' theory, as it stands, since the N nodes are non-maximal, nor under an adjunction theory where adjuncts must be maximal projections. The whole functions as an N, so for most purposes certainly, that is what A should be. On the other hand, so far as argument structure in the semantic sense is concerned, one might suppose that A was a projection of a head 'NIL', and C of the head *or* (both of category J for conJunction). We would suppose then that the whole was a J″. This conflict can be dealt with neatly in GPSG using feature-transmission. The feature system of GPSG is further developed than that of GB theory, and there is probably more than one line that might be pursued in adapting the GPSG analysis to a GB theory, assuming it to be correct. I shall make some tentative suggestions, which could be extended by adapting more of the GPSG solution.

If A, B, C and D are all N, we would have a non-standard adjunction structure; suppose this is licensed by the nonstandard 'heads' NIL and *or* which are of a defective category J. This category is so defective that it is relegated to the status of feature rather than category in the presence of any 'proper' category. Thus, for instance, node A is [N, J″], where the category visible out of the two is for almost all purposes the N. We have to allow this defective category to take "arguments" which are not maximal projections. Thus B is [N, J′], C is [N, J″], and D is [N, J′]. Let us call a defective projection like that of J a 'quasi-projection', with J the quasi-head. We may note that by category, A = B = C = D, so that the structure is capable of functioning as if it were a flat structure.

It is possible to conjoin items of distinct syntactic categories, and GPSG makes provision for this using an 'underspecified category'(see Sag *et al.* 1985). The need for this shows up in definitions like

5 *phl*ogistic of, like, or containing phlogiston

where we have categories P, A and V conjoined.

It may be that there are other 'minor' categories which would yield to being treated as quasi-projections. Some possibilities are discussed in later sections. We would expect them all to be semantically operators, given their yielding to full categories.

Finally, we need a structure for subordination, and in particular for connectives like *if*. There are good grounds for supposing that the connective is not like the conjunctions just discussed. There are various alternatives within what has been provided already and some of these are discussed in relation to definitions in chapter 3. For a sentence consisting of "P if Q", at least the following structures would appear to be licensed under the assumptions of X′ theory and adjunction theory:

Theoretical Preliminaries

6   (*if* as head of C-projection, I" in SPEC of CP)

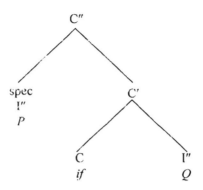

7   (adjunction of C" to I")

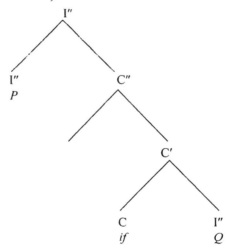

In chapter 3, section 3.3.1, I shall argue that (7) is the structure for subordination in the sentences which will concern us.

Chomsky (1986a, 161) states that the level at which X-bar theory applies is D-structure, because movement may produce structures which do not conform to the X-bar schemata. He also states that D-structures do conform to the X-bar theory. I have suggested above that we need base-generated adjunction (and the quasi-projections for coordination). If we require that D-structures are licensed by one of these schemata, then we will find that S-structure and LF will fall under the same schemata, so that something like Emonds' (1976) structure preserving principle is again operating. Let us suppose then that structures at all levels are licensed by the X-bar theory with the extensions indicated above.

1.1.3 Categories and features

As can be seen above, I am assuming that we have the full projections of the categories for I and C, as put forward in Chomsky 1986b. However, for expository convenience I shall sometimes refer to the I" as VP (but not as V") in the old style. There are the other major categories: A, V, P and N. With respect to this last, there has been a recent suggestion within GB theory (Abney 1987) that the head of a noun-phrase should be the determiner, so that we have a determiner-phrase, D", as the top node, with D taking N" as its complement, instead of N" as top node with (presumably) D" in specifier position.

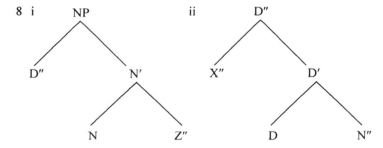

Note that if D" in (i) and N" in (ii) are fully expanded, the two trees produce directly the same string of potential categories *viz* (iii):

8iii   X" D Y" N Z"

Of course, these are bracketed differently under the two hypotheses. Until it becomes relevant, mainly in chapter 4, I shall use the more familiar NP structures of (i), referring to the maximal projection as NP rather than as N".

Theoretical Preliminaries 17

I have suggested a minor quasi-projection J in the previous section, for conjunctions. There are a number of categories such as those needed for the various traditional adverb categories that I have not discussed at all.

The system of features assumed within GB theory is informal. I shall assume anything I need to assume, borrowing from GPSG (see Gazdar *et al.* 1985). For example, it is commonly taken that some verbs such as *ask* may admit or require an embedded question as complement. If we take it that this is stipulated by assigning a feature to the subcategorization specification, then the complement may be CP[+WH]. This feature may be realized legitimately on either the specifier of CP (as a *wh*-phrase), or on the head of CP (as either a *wh*-complement such as *if*, or for root clauses by the presence of a V[+AUX] in C). I shall also assume (following GPSG) that lexical items may be used as features on complements, and that this requires that such an item appears in the SPEC or Head of the complement. For example, the adjective *opposite* may have a complement NP[P[*to*]]. Since *to* itself requires an NP argument, the structure induced is a PP, [*to* NP]; I assume that the whole of the structure associated with the feature *to* is invisible for the purposes of checking the gross subcategorization for an NP.

1.1.4 Movement

Movement is characterized by 'move-α', a shorthand for the idea that any category α may be moved—in principle, to any position. In fact, movement seems to be restricted to zero-level and maximal projections. X-zero movement must be 'head to head' movement; little use will be made of this in what follows.[5] Maximal projections, which in the most studied cases are NPs, move in three distinct ways. There is 'NP movement', movement to an A-position; and A-bar movement. A-bar movement is either to an existing but empty slot designated for maximal projections, such as specifier of C″; or it is adjunction to some maximal projection. A-positions are defined as positions to which a theta role could in principle be assigned (were the relevant lexical item suited to doing so) (Chomsky 1986a, 80; this has always seemed to me to be a somewhat odd definition—there is some discussion in my chapter 4). What is accounted for are the structures of passive, and raising. Movement to the specifier slot of the C-projection has replaced movement to COMP as the characterization of *wh*-movement. Adjunction is involved in QR, the movement of quantified nounphrases out of A-positions at LF. As noted above, none of this movement produces structures of a kind distinct from those needed at D-structure.

1.1.5 Indices

Further structure is given to representations by indices. The main indexing which will concern us is the coindexing of NPs under anaphoric dependency and the indexing consequent on movement.

The former is brought into being by the free indexing of every NP impossible coindexings are ruled out by the binding theory and (possibly outside the grammar) by inappropriate effects such as gender mismatch. Direct dependency (loosely referred to as coreference) gives rise to 'bound variable' interpretations of pronouns, for instance. Less direct dependency can account for the status of indefinite NPs in 'donkey sentences' (discussed section 3.5.1), and possibly for *wh*-NPs left *in situ* in multiple *wh*-questions.

The latter is an automatic concomitant of movement (or is definitive of it): a moved element leaves behind it a coindexed *trace*. The trace is usually an empty element, but possibly it may be realized as a resumptive pronoun. An element in an A-position and its traces form a chain, with (usually) a Case marked head and a θ-marked terminal position. These chains are said to form abstract representations of their heads (Chomsky 1986a, 96). An element that moves to an A-bar position changes its status: it becomes an operator (a binder) rather than an argument. The operator and its traces form an A-barchain; the term chain is used either just for A-chains, or for both kinds; and quite often to mean maximal chain in some obvious sense, though a subpart of a chain is a chain too (Chomsky 1986a, 96–98).

1.1.6 Structural relations

There are a number of structural relations which hold between a particular element and some domain or set of elements: the relation may hold jointly by virtue of properties of the particular element and

Theoretical Preliminaries

the structural configuration or other properties of its neighborhood. One such relation is that of domination. They are usually seen as defined relations—as part of the way we can describe things. If we were to include the notions of barriers (Chomsky 1986b) here, then we would be giving part of what otherwise falls under a module—the bounding module, mostly. Since most of what I talk about is fairly simple syntactically, I shall keep to the earlier formulations, and not use the apparatus of barriers.

The simplest domain is the c-command domain of an element. C-command (from 'Constituent-command') was introduced by Reinhart (1976) in the course of accounting for the possibility of the 'bound variable' reading of pronouns (as in *Everyone lost his temper*). For an element, say α, this is defined to be the set of elements dominated by the first branching node above α, but (usually) excluding those elements dominated by α. In terms of bracketed strings, and ignoring the possibility of non-branching nodes, in the string $[_\gamma[_\alpha ...] [_\beta...]]$, the node α c-commands β and everything in it; and the node β c-commands α and everything in it. It is thus closely related to the standard notion of logical scope: if α were an operator, then β would be its logical scope, and *vice versa*.[6] If what is dominated by α is NOT excluded, then in the string given, the 'domain' of α (or β) will be γ.

A variant of c-command is 'm-command' ('m' for 'maximal'). The definition (Chomsky 1986b, 8) follows that of c-command except that "first branching node above α" is replaced by "first maximal projection dominating α." However, matters are confused by the fact that the definition of 'dominate' may also be modified. The modifications affect only adjunction structures, where it appears that different modules of the grammar need distinct versions of 'dominate'. In an adjunction structure like (9i) below, the two nodes labeled 'X' are considered to be two 'segments' of a single category X.

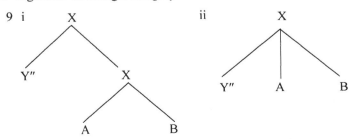

Following suggestions by May (see May 1985), Chomsky (1986b, 7) defines 'dominate' so that "α is dominated by β only if it is dominated by every segment of β." Under this definition, Y" is not dominated by X in (9i), whereas A is. The category X is asymmetric with respect to these two. The relation for the other pattern is given by 'exclusion' (ibid., 9): "α excludes β if no segment of α dominates β." Thus in (9i), Y" does 'not exclude' A, and A also does 'not exclude' Y". Hence the relation between Y" and A is identical with respect to the category X, and the effect is just as if the structure were as in (9ii)—the relation of 'non-exclusion' effectively flattens adjunction structures. May uses m-command and the modification of domination in his characterization of the logical scope potential of NPs in LF structures. This is discussed in section 3.5.1.

There are two other important relations: those of government and those of binding. The relation of government enters into the licensing conditions of more than one module. Government is a relation between a category and a set of other elements defined partly in terms of m-command. I follow here the definition of Chomsky (1986a, 162, but with the terminology of m-command). The category must be either a lexical category or one of their projections (N, V, A, P, NP, VP are listed by Chomsky) or the element AGR of INFL. One of these elements, a category α say, governs a maximal projection X" if and only if α and X" m-command each other. Then by definition α also governs the specifier and head of X". The effect will be for instance that heads govern their complements, that a subject is governed by AGR, that when an NP is governed then so is its determiner in the specifier position (or the SPEC of DP).

Binding is an asymmetric relation between two categories, rather than between an element and a domain. An element α binds an element β if and only if the two are coindexed and α c-commands β. An element which is not bound is free; an element is bound in a particular domain if it has a binder in that domain.

1.1.7 Binding, bounding, control and the ECP

Binding theory, bounding theory, control theory and the ECP all impose well-formedness conditions on structures with indices, and *a fortiori*, traces.

Theoretical Preliminaries

Binding theory is the module dealing with the permitted relations between an NP binder and an NP bindee where the latter is in some sense anaphorically dependent on the former. It thus imposes well-formedness conditions on chains, on operator binding of a variable, on the interpretation of pronouns and anaphoric expressions. The theory is sensitive to the status of the bindee. In Chomsky (1986a, 166 ff.) the three principles of the Binding Theory are given as:

(A) An anaphor is bound in a local domain
(B) A pronominal is free in a local domain
(C) An r-expression is free (in the domain of the head of its chain)

Anaphors include reflexive and reciprocal pronouns; pronominals include other pronouns. An approximation to the required local domains for (A) and (B) is the minimal governing category for the bindee in question. A governing category for α is a maximal projection containing both a subject and a lexical governor for α. The notion of r-expression is clear at the center but not always clear elsewhere. The central cases of r-expressions are referential expressions like *John, the child*, and variables (a trace bound by an operator). If all the conditions apply just to LF, then any quantified NP such as *every rabbit* will have been moved out of its A-position, (becoming an operator), so just these two kinds of r-expression will arise. If expletives are deleted at LF, then all overt NPs will be accounted for. Of the empty categories, *wh*-trace is a variable, and an r-expression, as noted. NP-trace is an anaphor; PRO is standardly both an anaphor and a pronominal, from which it follows that it cannot be governed.

Control theory deals with the circumstances under which PRO (the empty subject of gerundive and infinitival clauses) may be anaphorically dependent on some antecedent. I shall simply take it that there is such a theory; semantic interpretation makes it clear when there is anaphoric dependency, since otherwise we have the 'arbitrary' interpretation as in *It is forbidden* [PRO *to go there*].

Bounding theory puts restrictions on the kind or number of category boundaries which can intervene between a binder and a bindee. There are a number of principles enunciated, but they will not be discussed here since I have little (probably nothing) to say concerning this part of the theory. Bounding theory is vacuously satisfied at D-structure, must apply to S-structure, and is possibly supposed to be met at LF.

The ECP is described by Chomsky (1986a) as imposing "certain narrow identification conditions" on empty categories, specifically traces. In its simplest formulation it states that an empty category must be 'properly governed', where proper government means θ-government or antecedent-government (Chomsky 1986b). Antecedent government is simply government by a coindexed antecedent, so that a trace can fail to be antecedent governed only if there is some barrier to government of the trace by its nearest antecedent. But in this situation, the trace might instead be θ-governed, that is, governed by an element that θ-marks it; because it is a complement for instance. It is subjects and adjuncts that may fail to leave properly governed traces, then.

1.1.8 Case

Case is an abstract property assigned to NPs (and perhaps to SPEC and head inside); *Case theory* deals with how it is assigned. "If the category *a* has a Case to assign, then it may assign it to an element that it governs" (Chomsky 1986a, 187). Inherent Case is assigned at D-structure and realized at S-structure by morphological Case marking (residual in English) or alternatively at least for possessive Case by an empty preposition (*of*). Items of the lexical categories N, A, and P, as well as V, are (sometimes) capable of assigning Case, with for instance *picture* assigning genitive Case marked by *of* to *John* in [*picture* [*of John*]]. Inherent Case assignment by a category α can only be to an element θ-marked by α (at D-structure); Case realization can only be on an element governed by α (at S-structure). Structural Case is assigned by V, and by INFL if it has the feature [+AGR], and it is assigned at S-structure, with a requirement of adjacency (in English). It is not essentially associated with θ-marking, but as with inherent Case, it can only be assigned and realized under government. Nominative Case is assigned by INFL; V assigns objective (accusative) Case, normally to an adjacent complement NP. Exceptional Case marking, as in *John believes* [*her to be clever*], is accounted for, provided *believe* governs *her*, by the fact that *believe* DOES have objective Case to assign, as can be seen in [*John believes that fact*].

Theoretical Preliminaries

The condition that any lexical NP has to have Case, the 'Case filter' has been replaced by a condition on chains, which stipulates that a chain is not visible for θ-marking unless it has Case. The chain has Case if it has a Case-marked element in it—which is usually the head. This reformulation has the important consequence that there is no requirement on a non-argument NP to have Case, since it does not get θ-marked (morphologically, it must appear with a default Case or a Case acquired by agreement with the NP to which it is adjoined) (see Chomsky 1986a, 95). It appears that argument CP chains also need Case.

The visibility condition must clearly apply just to S-structure, or anyway not to D-structure, since no subject will have Case at D-structure. There is a uniformity condition, too, which is to apply at S-structure, although its function is to relate D-structure and S-structure inherent Case marking. This stipulates that "If α is an inherent Case-marker, then α Case-marks NP if and only if α θ-marks the chain headed by NP" (Chomsky 1986a, 194). The Case-marking in question is Case realization derived from Case-assignment at D-structure, and θ-marking depends on there being a θ-position in the chain, where this position is that assigned a θ-role at D-structure.

1.1.9 Semantic structure

The semantic component of the grammar (as opposed to semantics outside the grammar) deals with the recognition and distribution of such categories as predicate and argument, operator and variable, adjunct and modifier. It has to be related to the structures and categories already set up.

Let us start with the notions of predicate and argument. These are intended to correspond at least approximately to those same notions from predicate calculus. Heads, as defined within X-bar theory, are predicates in some sense, and they take as internal arguments their complements. A head together with its complements forms a maximal projection and this may itself be a predicate if it (still) has a θ-role to assign.[7] For example, a preposition usually requires an internal NP argument, and a prepositional phrase like *in the garden* is capable of being predicated of an NP such as *John* in an intuitively obvious way. The capacity of a head to take or require arguments is given in the lexicon, by means of a specification of what θ-roles the head disposes, and whether they are internal or external. Note that the current syntactic terminology usually uses 'predicate' only for maximal projections.

We may assume that the external role is specified compositionally so that it does in fact get assigned by the maximal projection of the head, though because the relation of head to external argument is normally transparent, we speak of it loosely as an external argument of the head. The problematic cases concern idioms, for instance, where the actual role is not necessarily predictable from the head, although the fact of θ-marking capacity is so predictable (consider *kick the bucket* as compared with *kick the doorstep*). There are also somewhat exceptional cases where an NP, which is normally an argument rather than a predicate, can function as a predicate, as in *I think [John a fool]*, which is similar in meaning and structure to *I think [John foolish]*. This requires special provision, semantically, and also syntactically in order to account for the fact that the argument NP (*John*) receives a θ-role.

What counts as an argument depends on what level of representation we are talking about. I will confine the discussion to NP arguments for the moment. At D-structure, any NP except an expletive may count as an argument. At S-structure and at LF, it is an A-chain that is an argument, where the chain is an abstract representation of the NP at its head. Trivially, we could see the NPs of D-structure as one-member chains. NPs in A-bar position are excluded from being arguments, then, but a chain headed by the trace bound by such an NP is an argument—the trace is a variable, and an argument. Since expletives are not subject either to *wh*-movement or to QR, there will not be any problem here. At LF, it is only chains headed by simple 'referential' expressions that are arguments—this is one way of forcing QR for quantified NPs. The permitted simple expressions will be definite NPs like *the rabbit* or *John*, and variables.

The well-formedness condition connecting θ-roles (from the lexicon) and arguments (as they appear in a structure) is the θ-criterion. A position to which a θ-role is assigned is a θ-position. The θ-criterion states that a chain has at least one and at most one θ-position (Chomsky 1986a, 133, 135), (where as mentioned above, the arguments are chains, including the one-member chains of D-structure). The θ-criterion must hold at LF (but see the Projection Principle below), and perhaps holds at other levels. The formulation above permits a single NP to receive two θ-roles at the single θ-position (Chomsky 1986a, 97). Consider

10   John left the room angry

John is the argument of two separate predications, one by the VP *left the room*, and one by *angry*, by each of which a θ-role is assigned, but there is a single θ-position involved. There is a uniformity condition stipulated on theta marking: if an element is θ-marked by any potential θ-marker, then it is θ-marked by every potential θ-marker (Chomsky 1986a, 97). This is to rule out structures like

11   *John seems [that it is raining] angry

The Projection Principle states that the subcategorization properties of a lexical item must be projected to every syntactic level (Chomsky 1981, 31). There is also a rule connecting subcategorized complements and θ-roles: subcategorization entails θ-marking. Consequently, θ-roles associated with internal arguments will always be realized, whereas on this formulation of the Principle, those relating to external arguments need not be. Stronger versions of the Principle have been proposed: we may for instance require that all θ-roles are projected.

Non-head predicates are constrained to find an argument through a general statement to the effect that predicates must have arguments. In this context, if a phrase IS an argument, it is absolved, even though it might be capable of being a predicate.[8] For instance, it is possible in principle for a verb to take a VP argument (Chomsky 1982, 18 footnote 13), although VPs are normally predicates. Conversely, every argument must be the argument of some predicate (head or otherwise). If predicates have arguments, then even though subjects are in principle optional, a non-argument VP will have to have an external argument if it has an external θ-role to assign. But the grammar requires all clauses to have subjects—that is, clausal non-argument VPs have syntactic subjects, even if these are empty or expletive *i.e.* are not arguments). This requirement is usually tacked onto the projection principle, with the two together being called the EPP (extended projection principle).

The fact that variables are arguments means that the construal of a clause with a variable in it is in the Tarskian style, rather than in the Russellian 'open sentence' style where variables are merely 'place-holders'. Semantically, such a clause is a proper sentence. The necessity for a binder for the variable has to be stipulated: every variable must be bound by an operator. Chomsky adds another condition here, stipulating that a variable must not only be bound, but must be 'strongly bound'. This is to exclude a variable's being bound solely by an operator which in some sense does not have sufficient content Chomsky characterizes the sufficiency as amounting to specification of either the range or the value of the variable. Typically, the empty operator is not a strong binder, whereas a *wh*-NP is.[9] In addition, we must have the converse relation: every operator must bind a variable. This last is not a requirement of logic, but is a consequence of the principle of Full Interpretation (FI), which says, roughly, that at every interpretive level, every element visible should have a non-trivial function or interpretation. The predicate-argument conditions will also be a consequence of FI. Given FI, we must look at every construction licensed, and ask what its function is.

Everything falling under X-bar theory, and extensions to chains, has been covered above. Of adjuncts, we have so far said nothing. They may be predicates, as is *angry* in (1) above, or they may be modifiers. A modifier should modify something: this will follow from FI. We should have a set of conditions on the structural licensing for these relations, but they are relatively little studied. A predicate must c-command its argument at LF, presumably. Williams' predication theory discusses possibilities, but in a somewhat different framework (Williams 1980). It has been suggested that adjuncts which are modifiers must be adjacent to the modified category or to its head (Sportiche 1988). So far as movement adjunction is concerned, the moved element if an NP will become an operator. Chomsky (1986b, 6) assumes that such adjunction is only possible to a maximal projection that is a non-argument. This is natural, but perhaps not necessary in every case, from the point of view of semantic interpretation.

1.1.10 The lexicon

We may understand the lexicon to be a list of lexical items together with phonological, morphological, syntactic and semantic information. Phonological information I will ignore for the most part. By semantic information here, I mean the sort of semantics I have been talking of above, relating to such things as θ-roles.

Theoretical Preliminaries

Besides the usual words (or morphemes), I take it that the lexicon contains information about the phonologically null elements of the grammar, or at least about the ones that can be base-generated. For instance, there is probably a phonologically empty version of *that*. There should be some general schema allowing that whole constituents (perhaps just XP) can be phonologically empty, to allow for ellipsis; this surfaces in our representations as [e]. In addition, there are the special phonologically null nouns (or NPs) PRO, pro and *O*. It is at least debatable whether pro is available in English; anyway, it does not concern me here. If PRO is not controlled (coindexed with a permitted antecedent) then it has an 'arbitrary' interpretation, as in *To laugh is salutary*. PRO is also supposed to have the curious property of inherent Case. The empty operator *O* is somewhat like a *wh* element, but it is missing the restriction to persons of *who*, to rabbits of *which rabbit*, and so on. There may be other items of this sort: Chomsky suggests (1986a, 168) that we may need an item, "an implicit argument similar to PRO in the DET position as the subject of *realization*," for a particular reading.

It looks as if for any word in the lexicon, a large amount of syntactic information must be recorded, and learned. It is obviously necessary to construct the theory in such a way that this is possible, both on the basis of the evidence available (in many cases, to a child), and in not imposing an undue burden. One mechanism for reducing the burden of learning is to have default values given, so that only deviations must be learned; another is to have correlations between different kinds of information; and a third is to establish (by learning or as a property of UG) regularities over the lexicon as a whole. There is evidence for all these, and for combinations such as 'conditional defaults', like the CSR (below). Much is as yet unclear about the organization of the lexicon, so the comments below are somewhat unsystematic.

It is reasonably clear that the lexical entry must contain semantic information of some kind. Suppose for the moment this is in terms of θ-roles such as agent, patient, theme, and so on (though I think these are best regarded as shorthand indicators of classes of inference rules). The kind or type of argument capable of taking on such roles (say animate object, agent, proposition, or whatever is needed here) is said to be s-selected (for 'semantic selected') by the item (Chomsky 1986a,

86 ff.). These arguments must be classified into internal (complement) and external (compositionally mediated) arguments, for syntactic and semantic purposes. Categorial selection (c-selection) by a head can be seen as connected by conditional default rules to s-selection. Chomsky suggests that if a head 's-selects a semantic category C, then it c-selects a syntactic category which is the "canonic structural realization of C" (CSR(C))' (p.87). To avoid confusion, I shall refer to the s-selection categories as types, and when discussing other aspects of semantics, they may be referred to as 'syntactic types'. Then the CSR of an agent is an NP, and of a proposition, a clause, for instance. Chomsky goes further than this, and suggests that the CSR of a proposition is in fact C'' (p.190) and not I'', so that the complement of an 'Exceptional Case Marking' verb is indeed the exception that has to be learned. C-selection is restricted to maximal projections, which, as noted above, may in principle include V''. A strong condition on argument types is that they must all be 'entity' or 'proposition'.

Morphologically related items of differing category may have identical s-selection properties. The noun *destruction* in one of its senses has just the same s-selection properties as the verb *destroy*, so that we have the familiar parallel between *the enemy's destruction of the city* and *the enemy destroyed the city*. A morphologically marked process like passivization can systematically change lexical properties (opinions differ as to exactly which). In the case of passivization itself, with respect to the internal arguments, it is sufficient that objective Case-marking is deleted ('absorbed'). In addition, a passive participle somehow becomes incapable of c-selecting an external argument, but it appears that the θ-role is assigned to an "implicit argument" which although not categorially realized is still capable of entering in to syntactic relationships. The classic example here is *The boat was sunk to collect the insurance* (see Chomsky 1986a, 119), where the suppressed agent of the sinking is also the agent of the intended collecting of the insurance, so that this latter must be a controlled rather than free PRO subject of the embedded clause. Structurally, such an implicit argument is taken to be 'present', perhaps in the passive morpheme. In general, if s-selection is connected with comprehension, it is likely that no s-selection can simply be abandoned, if it is not assigned a value by an overt syntactic category, but it is logically

Theoretical Preliminaries

possible that neither an explicit nor an implicit argument is present in any of the syntactic representations.

The ability of an item to govern another in a suitable configuration depends solely on the syntactic category of the item, so needs no special provision. The lexicon must however record the Case assigning properties of an item, if these do not follow from general principles. On general grounds, we will expect a verb having an NP complement to be able to assign the objective Case, for instance, though for noun heads, this is replaced by the genitive Case. The explanation for exceptional Case marking verbs like *believe* in terms of subcategorization for I" rather than C" permits Case assignment, but we will have to have in addition the fact that the verb has Case to assign despite having just a clausal complement, unless the Case assigning property is somehow held by some verb which is neutral as between the *believe* of *I believe her* and of *I believe that she is telling the truth*. This is possible if we regard the NP complement as a non-standard realization of the s-selection for a proposition (see Chomsky 1986a, 140, and page 88 for discussion in relation to *wonder* versus *ask*).

In addition to the actual category given by c-selection, features may be assigned, as mentioned in section 1.1.3. If such features are lexical, they can induce quite complex structures. For example, suppose *keep* has a propositional internal argument, realized as a small clause. Then the ordinary *keep* is subcategorized for say PP; the requirement that the whole have propositional, rather than predicational, status, forces the introduction of an adjoined NP. We have [*keep* [$_{AP}$ [*John* [$_{AP}$ *at home*]]]] for instance. For the idiom, we can impose as further features [*tabs*] and [*on*]. It will turn out that the minimal structure meeting the requirements imposed is a small clause with 'specifier' *tabs* and 'head' a PP[*on*] which itself must have *on* as its head; this will give us structures like [*keep* [*tabs* [*on Phil*]]].

1.2 Relevance theory

> For that there is no need to penetrate the mechanism of this equilibrium and to know how the forces compensate each other in the interior of the machine; it suffices to know that this compensation cannot fail to occur ...
>
> Poincaré, *The Value of Science*

Definitions are a special class of utterances; they are special in that they are construed in a characteristic manner. Any account needs a theory of pragmatics, then. Relevance theory, as propounded by Sperber and Wilson (1986), is a general theory of information processing, and in particular of utterance interpretation, which can provide a suitable framework within which to explain these particular construals.

It is possible that every construal of a statement as a definition could be accounted for by appeal to lexical or scopal ambiguity. In that case, given the scope of this thesis, pragmatics could be ignored: it would be enough to give an account of the possibility of such and such a meaning, without giving more than elementary indications as to how the meaning was selected. After all, definitions are often even labeled as such. But I shall be arguing that a simple ambiguity account is not correct, and consequently that we need a theory that allows that intended meaning may be constructed on the basis of, rather than just decoded from, the linguistic input. In the Sperber and Wilson theory, this is just what is to be expected.

A sketch of those parts of the theory and its constructs that I shall need follows. The underlying rationale and motivation can be found in Sperber and Wilson (1986). I shall simplify, possibly to the point of distortion.

Let us assume that lexical items correspond (in general) to *concepts*, and that concepts can be put together to form *propositions*. These are representations in the mind. The correct interpretation of an utterance consists in the identification of one or more propositions, which loosely correspond to 'what was meant' by the utterance. One or more of these will be the literal meaning of the utterance (its *explicature*); the rest will be contextual effects of various sorts, of which we shall be mostly concerned with *contextual implications*. An

Theoretical Preliminaries

utterance of "It is draughty with the door open" will have a literal meaning which includes some identification of the door; it will probably include among the contextual implications the proposition that the hearer should shut the door.

In general, pragmatic processing rather than just direct linguistic-semantic processing is needed in order to construct the explicature.[10] I shall be presupposing this step most of the time. Let us suppose (counterfactually, in almost every case) that the utterance leads directly to its explicature—it is totally explicit. Then pragmatic processing proceeds from this. There are two first-level kinds of processing involved. A limited set of propositions which form the immediate *context* must be accessed; and deductive processes are carried out over these together with the explicature to give the contextual implications. The propositions forming the context can come from a variety of sources: they can be remembered from immediately preceding conversation, derived as a result of perception of the surroundings, retrieved from memory, or simply invented (hypothesized); most probably some recognition of degree of belief in each must be recorded, but I shall ignore this complication. It is not supposed that this accessing of context is necessarily rational or algorithmically specifiable; it certainly varies from person to person and from time to time. However, at least some of it is mediated by the concepts derived from the utterance's words and (I assume) phrases. For concreteness, we can assume that one mechanism is association: for me, a sentence containing the words "Sophie" and "spider" is likely to result in the accession of the proposition that my daughter Sophie dislikes cobwebs, for instance, as this is readily accessible in my memory.

Something similar to association and pattern matching is presumably responsible for the invention or hypothesizing of propositions which appear in context. They appear under the pressure to make sense of what is already there, and so must form inferential links with it. The existing concepts and structures then in part at least determine the shape of the hypotheses. Consider for instance the interpretation of "I forgot my library ticket" in the following two mini-conversations:

1 A: Why are you so late?
    B: I forgot my library ticket

2 A: What did you get from the library?
  B: I forgot my library ticket

It is almost inevitable, automatic, and predictable, that in (1), A will hypothesize that B returned to fetch her library ticket, but that in (2), A will hypothesize that B did NOT return to fetch her ticket. In each case, the proposition hypothesized is one that A will need in order to construe B's reply as providing an answer to her question. The predictability is what B is relying on, in not providing an explicit answer.

Once some context propositions have been added to working memory, processing of these together with the utterance explicature takes place. This processing is regular and rule-governed. By hypothesis, it consists in forming the logical closure under a set of deductive rules of the whole set of propositions in working memory. The deductive rules are to be such that only a finite set of propositions results, and there are other restrictions imposed to prevent waste of time and space. Of the new propositions, those that are essentially new, inferentially derived from the interaction of the utterance-proposition and the context constructed, are the contextual implications. On the basis of what is now in working memory, more propositions can be added to the context, and other inferences drawn. There must also be provision for deleting material.

The central part of the theory relating to utterance interpretation is the assumption that the hearer recognizes that she has understood the utterance at the point when the weight of contextual implications adequately balances the effort expended in deriving these. The 'adequately' there is in recognition of the fact that we are prepared to put more effort into some understanding than others.[11] Of course, processing does not stop there; otherwise we would have nothing to say in return. The essence of the theory is that utterance understanding (like other apprehension) is driven by the necessity to select or attend to what is relevant in a context. The speaker who takes account of this will attempt to ensure that his utterance is worth attention, that it will be found to be relevant to the hearer, that the reward balances the effort. The hearer of an utterance then relies on the Principle of Relevance (Sperber and Wilson 1986, 158):

Theoretical Preliminaries

3 Every act of ostensive communication communicates the presumption of its own optimal relevance

We may assume, I think, that the initial processing of linguistic input, retrieving the structural description from the acoustic or written input, is relatively costly in terms of effort (and time), relative to the pragmatic processes of context construction and deduction. Even if natural language were capable of being fully explicit, it would then not follow that the most efficient means of communication would consist in an exhaustive statement of what is to be communicated. There are of course vast numbers of other reasons for not attempting explicitness; one of the nice things about relevance theory is its ability to describe in a principled way why verbal communication is in general astonishingly effective despite (or because of) inexplicitness.

The propositions are representations in what I shall assume is a Fodorian language of thought, with concepts as the words. The linguistic input will be a grammatical representation, (say a Chomskian LF) or rather something derived from this at least by substituting concepts for the lexical items (a level Sperber and Wilson still call logical form). It is clear within the theory that it is essential that linguistic structure be preserved at the propositional level, because the variety of ways one can say the same thing manifestly affects the way it is understood—we do not have active and passive just for variety in language. The input as a structure of concepts may turn out not to represent a proposition: notably it may lack any indication of essential temporal specification, but it may underdetermine the proposition intended in other ways too. The same principles which operate to generate contextual implications operate to produce a determinate proposition. That is, a hypothesis about the correct determination of what has been left undetermined is confirmed by its leading to an adequate number of contextual implications for minimal processing cost. Disambiguation falls under the same explanation as the resolution of underdetermination.

Sperber and Wilson propose some mechanisms for a processing device with the sorts of properties they argue for. I think these should be regarded as illustrative, rather than as essential parts of the theory, but it does help to have some mechanism in mind when thinking about the theory. The two suggested mechanisms I wish to comment on here are concerned with the deductive logic, and with the organization of the lexicon.

The deductive logic is modeled on so-called natural logic, rather than on axiomatic logic. Suppose a particular logic has five basic logical terms (connectives, and so on). In an axiomatic system, there will normally be one inference rule (*modus ponens*, to tell us how to use material implication), and a collection of axioms, usually reduced to as few as possible, which are sentences of the logical language deemed to be true, and which serve to constrain mutually the interpretations of the other four basic terms. In a system of natural logic, we would have no axioms, but instead the interpretation of each of the other terms would be constrained by inference rules.[12] The inference rules may be divided into introduction rules and elimination rules: for example for *&* we may have

$$4 \quad \text{i} \quad \frac{A \quad B}{(A \& B)} \qquad \text{ii} \quad \frac{(A \& B)}{B} \qquad \text{iii} \quad \frac{(A \& B)}{A}$$

where (4i) is an introduction rule, and (4ii) and (4iii) are &-elimination rules. It is intuitively clear that if I already know A and B, then I do not gain anything by adding '$A \& B$' to the list of things I know, and still less is it useful to add '$A \& A$'; and that if I were to use the rule (4i) I would waste time and space (assuming that the notation is effectively as in predicate calculus). Sperber and Wilson eliminate the introduction rules: there are none. (None, that is, in the logic which is used to do the kind of processing that has been described above).

It is argued that inferences that we make by virtue of meaning should all be captured by the same mechanism. That is, if because of the meaning of *spaniel* we can infer *John is a dog* from *John is a spaniel*, then this conclusion should be mediated by an inference rule rather than by an axiom (or meaning postulate, in Carnap's terms). In Sperber and Wilson (1986), a "giraffe-elimination rule" is suggested:

5 input: *(X—giraffe—Y)*

   output: *(X—animal of a certain species—Y)*

and a "yellow-elimination rule":

Theoretical Preliminaries

6   input: *(X—yellow—Y)*

    output: *(X—color of a certain hue—Y)*

The idea was to restate Fodor's adaptation of a meaning postulate (see the next section) as an inference rule: the forms above are to correspond to what Fodor in Fodor (1975) might have written as

   giraffe $\Rightarrow$ *animal*

   yellow $\Rightarrow$ *color*

The elimination rules in (5) and (6) are not sufficiently constrained as they stand, which is not surprising. The elimination rules (4ii) and (4iii) must be taken to have A and B ranging over strings each of which constitute a well-formed sentence in the logic.[13] An extension to accommodate say conjunction of verb phrases would necessitate putting more complicated restrictions on A and B, since semantic (inferential) information about A and B is needed, rather than just syntactic information, to capture the whole range of correct inferences. Essentially, it is necessary to ensure that *(A—B)* is an upward-entailing environment, as defined by Ladusaw (1979, 146). Similarly with (5) and (6): in fact the restrictions needed for (5) will be exactly the restriction needed if (4ii) were to be adapted to conjunction of nouns.[14] If this is done, then the phrase "*of a certain kind*" can be safely omitted so that the rule will have content closer to that of the related meaning postulate.[15] Alternative ways of giving these same meaning-relations will be discussed in the section 1.5.

The organization of the 'conceptual lexicon' is not unconnected with the system of natural logic proposed. It is suggested that a particular concept be associated with three kinds of information: logical, encyclopedic and linguistic. To take these in reverse order: the last will give for, say, the concept GIRAFFE the English word *giraffe*, and the usual grammatical entry for that word: syntactic and phonological information. The encyclopedic entry will consist of a set of propositions concerning giraffes: the things I think about giraffes in general and in particular. I assume it will also contain what I know about the English word *giraffe*, for instance its spelling, and whether the word is acceptable to a three-year-old. All this information is changeable over time. The logical entry gives the 'logical content' of a concept, and is to contain the inference rules involving giraffes such as that in (5) above. Encyclopedic and logical entries then are distinguished on the one hand by the fact that the former correspond to synthetic and the latter to analytic information, and on the other by the fact that the former are propositional in form while the latter are inference rules, recipes for active processing. It is possible for a concept to have nothing under any one or conceivably even two of the three headings, either properly or on account of ignorance.

The whole of the conceptual entry scheme is a suggestion for a mental filing system, so that for instance a useful inference rule can be readily activated when a particular English word is heard, or encyclopedic information immediately accessed. It is crucial to the theory that there may be made a sharp distinction between the necessary activation of the logical entry, and the optional accessing of encyclopedic information. A contrast between information stored in the form of inference rules and that stored propositionally seems to me to be not crucial—and I shall argue that it is improbable.

Finally, I should mention here that I have made some use of two particular ideas relating to interpretation. One of these is the 'focal scale' or set of 'ordered entailments' that can be associated with an utterance (Sperber and Wilson 1986, chapter 4 section 5; Smith and Wilson 1979, 158–189). The other is the 'interpretive use' (as opposed to literal use) of an expression (Sperber and Wilson 1986, chapter 4, sections 7 and 8). But here I have reverted to the simpler notion of 'mention', which suffices for my needs.

1.3 The 'language of thought' hypothesis

> Is it these associations (or at least those of them that we have inherited from our ancestors), which constitute this *a priori* form of which it is said that we have pure intuition? Then I do not see why one should declare it refractory to analysis and should deny me the right to investigate its origin.
>
> Poincaré, *The Value of Science*

1.3.1 Mental computation

A computational theory of mind is not necessarily a representational theory of mind. And a representational theory of mind does not necessarily have its representations in a language-like form. For

Theoretical Preliminaries

example, I could use a spring-balance to do addition sums, but as I carry on, the sums to be added are registered as changes of state, and are not represented by any actual state of the balance: we have computation without representation. Perhaps the mind performs computations like this.[16] Suppose instead I use Cuisenaire rods to perform my addition sums: then there is partial representation, but the representations of the numbers are in analogue form, not symbolic, and are not at all language-like. Perhaps mental computation is like this. But Fodor has argued that our internal thought processes are in fact carried out by manipulating representations which are sentences of an internal language, the 'language of thought'. Relevance theory too includes an assumption that there are computational, (but not necessarily algorithmically specifiable) information-based and representation-based processes, and logical (deductive) processes over representations.

I am not going to argue for Fodor's position, but rather take it as a starting point; all I shall do here is to indicate some of the issues involved, and sketch how I understand these.

If one starts out thinking about language and logic, it is natural to suppose that thought is carried out over symbolic representations. Nor has there been any serious alternative, until the recent revival of the connectionists and the opening up of unexpected and exciting possibilities in parallel distributed processing.[17] Suppose that what we naively think of as symbols are in some sense epiphenomenal in relation to the computational reality of subsymbolic, non-semantic units of thought. The success of the symbolic description surely means that those epiphemomena are robust (as the objects of the sensible world are robust despite atomic or subatomic probabilistic theory); we will not *in general* need to appeal to any lower level of analysis in order to produce descriptions and explanations. In particular cases, or for particular processes, it might turn out that we did need to make such an appeal, in order to account for the otherwise inexplicable. Wait and see.

So I am assuming representation. Does the representation have to be language-like? Again, if one starts off thinking about language, and is familiar with a logical calculus, it is natural to suppose that that sort of thing is what the mind might use. And there is no point at all in discussing strange-looking notational variants without very precise motivation. There are questions that can and should be asked, however, even if it is not always clear whether they could in principle be answered. Many of these have been raised by Fodor.

What do we mean by asking whether a certain calculus is a language? It appears that we should at least be asking whether it has a lexicon, a syntax and a semantics (and, presumably, realizations).[18] In addition, we will be asking whether it has certain of the properties of a *natural* language; what that means will of course depend on what we take to be the properties of a natural language, but also on which ones we take to be critical to language as such. For example, the artificial notations of mathematics in general seem to qualify as parts of a language. The internal representations of numbers larger than 9 according to standard notation are language like, the semantics depending on relative position. But a pre-zero system, where the semantics depended on an absolute position relative to some external framework (as on an abacus) arguably would NOT count as part of a language. The explorations of the next two chapters make certain demands on the internal calculus, which are consistent with its being language-like, and serve to constrain its properties a little. The investigation of natural language definitions sheds some light on the lexicon, and a little on syntax and semantics, it turns out. The work relates directly to some of the questions raised in Fodor's (1975) *The Language of Thought*, rather than to more recent concerns.

In *The Language of Thought*, Fodor was concerned (among other things) with the place of the internal language in giving a 'semantics' for a natural language. Much of the argument was directed against the advocates of 'real' rather than 'translational' semantics for natural language; ironically, in 1987 Fodor devotes a large part of his book *Psychosemantics* to worrying about how the internal system comes to have any sort of 'real' semantics. In the intervening decade, there have been shifts of emphasis, in particular in that propositional attitudes have come to be the central problem; and shifts in the impinging disciplines of linguistics and logic. I have nothing to say about propositional attitudes, but it seems to me that many of the questions raised earlier are just as interesting as they were then, and deserving of discussion now.

1.3.2 Fodor 1975

Fodor should be read, not least for entertainment. All I am offering here is a sketch of the apparatus (by now familiar) which Fodor sets up, in pages 59–156 of Fodor 1975. This is minimal in the sense that it is there only to do the job of explaining the possibility of the acquisition of new items of natural language vocabulary, and of some facts about the acquisition of concepts. It is not suggested that elaboration is not required, and indeed Fodor uses some evidence from for instance bound variable anaphora to uncover some of the properties that the language should have.

The minimal apparatus appears to consist at least of the following: an internal language with a large vocabulary (the primitive vocabulary); a logic defined over that vocabulary and the syntax; a repository for axioms or definitions. This last could include definitions of new (non-primitive) items of the vocabulary. It could also include statements of implication. It is obvious that there must be a logic; its moves are inferences. It does seem that Fodor intends his use of Carnap's 'meaning postulates' to add new inference rules to the logic, rather than for them to be added as implicational statements to the axioms. He talks of adding $\ulcorner F \Rightarrow G \urcorner$ to the inference rules (p.149); where under this assumption the sign '$\Rightarrow$' is an item of the metalanguage in which we as observers describe the logic (and not an item of the internal language). But he talks also of 'learning a meaning postulate'. Learning a meaning postulate adds another item to a stored list (p.150), so that there is a strong suggestion that (unless yet another language is involved) the meaning postulate should rather be expressed as a sentence of the internal language, with the '$\Rightarrow$' a part of that language. We also need "whatever combinatorial operations on elementary concepts are necessary to put 'airplane' together" (p.96); these too are presumably part of the internal language.

The strategy for learning new NL vocabulary is stated thus: "... if, as we have supposed, language learning is a matter of testing and confirming hypotheses, then among the generalizations about a language that the learner must hypothesize and confirm are some which determine the extensions of the predicates of that language. A generalization that effects such a determination is, by stipulation, a *truth rule*" (p.59).[19] Fodor continues most of the time to talk as if the language (in fact both languages, NL and the language of thought) only contained predicates, (and one-place predicates with the syntax of predicate calculus at that). The schema for a truth rule is given (following Davidson 1967) in a form only suited to such items in NL:

1   $F:$ ⌜Py⌝ is true (in L) iff x is G (p.59 footnote 5)

In this,[20] we are to substitute object language items inside the corners, and metalanguage terms outside. For 'Py' we must substitute a *sentence* whose subject is some name or other referring expression, and which has P as the predicate. For x we substitute an expression of the metalanguage which designates the individual referred to by y. G must be what it must (but it had better not include any reference to P). Later, this is given with 'iff Gx' on the right hand side, as:

2   ⌜Py⌝ is true iff Gx (example (1) of p.80)

It is notable that there is total disregard for the syntax of the natural language and of the metalanguage, here. The 'predicates' are apparently not necessarily simple, since we have for example *is a philosopher* (p.59, footnote 5). I suspect this is not an accident, for later (p.128) Fodor in discussing natural language definitions explicitly complains that 'definition in use' is an affront to his intuitions, having no psychological plausibility. In particular, he makes this claim of a definition of *or* produced by offering elimination of 'P or Q' in favor of '*not both (not P) and (not Q)*'. Despite recognizing that P and Q here are variables, he feels that the definition is treating P *or* Q 'as an idiom'. Presumably what he wants is a definition of *or* alone, without the variables P and Q. I think he is simply mistaken, here. It is quite surprising that he countenances the truth rule schema at all, since it has to incorporate the 'substitutional variable' on each side, for predicates. If the truth-rule schema is to be extended to what "we can loosely call 'relational' expressions," (which seem to be many-place predicates), like *or*, then I should have thought Fodor's (1975) intuition was likely to be further affronted. Meaning postulates however may apparently unexceptionably look just like 'definitions in use' (p.149, footnote 35). In the next section I attempt to clear up some of the confusion.

From considering such schemata as F, Fodor deduces that it is not possible to learn any predicate P in a language L without already understanding some coextensive predicate G, or slightly less brutally,

Theoretical Preliminaries

the metalanguage must be "rich enough to express the extensions of the predicates of L" (p.82). Of this conclusion, Fodor says that it is so outrageous as to incline him to view it "as a reductio ad absurdum of the theory that learning a language is learning the semantic properties of its predicates, except that no serious alternative view to that theory has ever been proposed." He goes on to draw the conclusion that "there is a sense in which there can be no such thing as learning a new concept" (p.95), where by 'concept' he apparently means whatever it is that corresponds to a possible predicate of a language (so, 'airplane' and 'cow' are concepts), and hence, presumably to a word or phrase or combination of such in the internal language.

This talk of concepts I find thoroughly confusing. (In fact I'd like to excise it). In his footnote 31, p.95, the terms 'concept' and 'predicate' are reasonably sharply distinguished. Here "we identify learning a concept C with learning that $(x) Cx$ iff Fx .... C and F are coextensive concepts." But

> ... to learn a predicate is not to learn which predicate it *is*, but which semantic properties it *expresses*. ... if I learn that the *predicate P* applies to x iff Qx, I learn a bit of thoroughly contingent information about the *linguistic form* 'P'. Predicates differ from concepts in that the conditions for individuating the former make reference to the syntax and vocabulary in which they are couched. Synonymous predicates are distinct although they express the same concept. Distinct predicates may, therefore, have identical semantic properties. But distinct concepts, presumably, cannot.

It is at least clear that 'predicate' is (usually, and fairly loosely) to do with items of the object language, and 'concept' is either an item of the internal language or an equivalence class of such. However, if the internal code is a language, and as such has a syntax, and a realization, it would seem natural that the conditions for individuating items of the language would make reference to the syntax and to realization-type (as it were phonological form) of those items, or if they are phrasal, to the vocabulary (of the internal language) in which they are couched. Hence my suggestion that the term 'concept' might be referring to equivalence classes of such items, if these properties are NOT relevant. The obvious choice for the equivalence class would be 'having identical semantic properties', thus rendering the last remark true by *fiat*. But it is not entirely clear what constitutes a 'semantic property'. It is something which both terms of the object language and terms of the metalanguage can have, and what is more it is to meet conditions like (1) above, so the properties can (and must) be shared. Is there any such thing?

Two candidates present themselves: extensions, or the inference rules of the logic. Fodor (p.66) in relation to 'understanding' a predicate suggests that if the predicate is in the NL, it is understood by virtue of having an (alternative) representation in the internal language, which is 'understood'. In the latter case in general, a predicate will be 'understood' because the computational processes which the device is constructed with are such that the uses of the predicate "comport with the conditions such a representation would specify." If this means anything, it suggests that what is still to be explained is how the inner language and its logic has a semantics in relation to the real world. And that as *I* understand it is a question of tying the external world to enough points to ensure that it (or something of it and its predictabilities) is *the* model (or part of the model) for the language and its logic. Further, we are in somewhat of a quandary about the meaning postulates since if they can be learned, they cannot be all built in.

It is apparent that Fodor conceives of it as being one of the main tasks of psycholinguistics to determine the stock of primitive concepts (p.124 footnote 18). Then there are certain rules of combination which enable complex concepts to be constructed. A complex concept is definable within the metalanguage, in the sense of there being two-way implications between some single item and some phrase: *bachelor* ⇔ *unmarried man*. A further task is to determine which concepts are internally represented as definitions (p.154). He suggests that such two way implications are relatively uncommon. In general, most of the analytic relations between natural language items are properly captured rather by the use of Meaning Postulates.

Again there is a confusion at least on my part. It is part of his argument that there is no decomposition at the stage of understanding a sentence of NL, and that with possibly some minor exceptions, the language of thought supplies a single word to correspond to each word of English or whatever. These are all going to have to be primitive, or most of them anyway. But it is absurd ... to suppose that these are CONCEPTS. Or if they are concepts, it is absurd to suppose they are

Theoretical Preliminaries

primitive. Consider for instance my understanding of the word *puce*. I comprehend sentences using this word of English, after a fashion. I know puce is a color, somewhere in the brown-purple-red area. Also I know that I do not properly know what color puce IS. What I have is partial information about the item; just the sort of situation where I can set up meaning postulates but not biconditionals. But what is it I am to attach these meaning postulates TO? Surely not a primitive concept. That is, it is not that I look for the primitive concept related by prior structuring in that particular way to *color*, and use that to be the translation of *puce*. There are two things wrong with that: first, if I learn more information about *puce*, I shall have to detach the translation from here and attach it to the new more structured concept; and second, I might have two distinct words of English (say 'maroon' too) both of which have identical partial information known now, except that I also know they do not mean the same.

The obvious solution to this problem is rather to set up some new 'blank' concept, designated as the translation of *puce* (and another, distinct, for *maroon*), and attach the meaning postulates to these. What we need then is an identifying name in the language of thought for each such 'blank' concept. We presumably have to construct these names from equivalence classes of whatever we are given as the realization of the language of thought (as words are constructed from letters, and letters are equivalence classes of marks on paper, say). The meaning postulates then serve to connect NEW concepts (new words) to old. These new concepts are primitive only in the sense of being available somehow (as distinguishable realizations), and of having no INTERNAL structure such that their semantic properties are predictable from this structure. But it is of the essence of this interpretation that the concepts came with no EXTERNAL structure: that has to be learned, and can be changed. And on this interpretation, the translation of *airplane* can be equally primitive, since all we require is another empty box onto which to stick a label and into which to put information.

In the chapters that follow, I intend to show that Fodor's pessimism with regard to the construction of new concepts is unjustified. That is, despite a relative paucity of contentful primitive concepts (*i.e.* those with a prior semantics, by virtue of associated inference rules or connections to the sensible world, for instance) we may still be able to construct novel and interesting new concepts. We might take mathematics itself as a proof that such creativity is possible. But in order to do this, we must allow that the devices for forming new concepts out of old are more complex than operations like conjunction and disjunction, which is all that Fodor seems to be prepared to countenance. We need variables, so that we can use implicit, not just explicit, definitions.

1.4 Model theoretic semantics

> This conception was not without grandeur; it was seductive, and many among us have not finally renounced it; ...
> Poincaré, *The Value of Science*

1.4.1 Models

It is sometimes supposed that model theoretic semantics is 'real' semantics. It is nothing of the sort. Model theoretic semantics as practiced by Montague and those who have followed is just what it says it is: it gives the semantics of a language and its logic in relation to a 'model'. In the usual case, the model is in fact some abstract mathematical structure. What it is NOT is some other language. Naturally, it must be described in some language; for this purpose we usually use a mixture of fairly formal English and ordinary mathematical or logical expressions. In fact Montague chose to give the semantics of his fragments of English by first translating into an intermediate specially designed language (Intensional Logic), and then giving a model theoretic semantics for IL; this indirectness has some exegetical advantages, but is of no theoretical significance in providing the semantics for the original fragment. A model theoretic semantics could only be 'real' if the model were itself 'real'; and I doubt if those who want real semantics consider that a mathematical structure is suitably real. The connection with reality is more indirect.

Suppose we start the other way. We have something, something not just amorphous but structured in some sense, that we wish to describe.[21] Then we can set up a language and a logic over that language to *model* that structure. The language is successful if it enables us to talk of the parts and relations of the structure, and if it enables us to use the logic to draw correct conclusions about the structure. Two things make this

Theoretical Preliminaries

non-trivial (a trivial language for instance would be one which simply gave a separate name to every true atomic proposition, where the number of such propositions was finite, and nothing else). One is that the structure is frequently not finite, or at least not small enough to be treated as finite. The other is that interesting structures have some sort of regularity, predictability or redundancy to them. The logic is a tool for exploiting statements of these patternings. The language and its logic would provide a perfect model for the structure if we have both soundness and completeness: we would neither be able to draw false conclusions nor fail to be able to draw true conclusions. Perfection is not in general attainable; soundness is presumably more important than completeness, though for survival, approximate or even probable truths may very well be more valuable than no decision.

Now suppose that the structure we intend to model with a language (the language of thought, say, or natural language for concreteness) is the real world. The mind boggles or at least it should do, and would do more than it does were we not provided with some language already. Perhaps we intend only to model parts—perhaps we lump things together that are really distinct, perhaps we circumscribe in all sorts of ways. In that case, rather than our language modeling the world, it will model little models (abstract, this time) which in turn model parts of the world in the way that a toy car may model a real one, perhaps, or in the way that billiard balls model the atom. The mini-models are constructed by experience and evolution, by physicists and philosophers. So if we construct a model for a fragment of natural language, it will at best be a model which might be isomorphic to one of these mini-models. We may speak of the intended model for a language; and we may if we want to emphasize that not all structures are abstract, talk of realizations of a model or structure.

Unfortunately, it is possible to construct non-isomorphic models for the same language, as well as to construct non-isomorphic languages to model the same structure. But the enterprise is not so easy as to be trivial, and there may not be many solutions in a particular case. For instance, all natural languages seem to have the equivalent of counterfactual conditionals, everyone seems to think there are necessary truths, and the 'possible worlds' model was the first remotely satisfactory model for a language and logic to include these. Here, the 'mini-model' seems to many to be quite unnaturally vast: if the intended model was the actual world, what is the rest of this stuff doing? This thesis will not be concerned with such problems, and I shall take a very simple view of what has to be modeled.

Model theoretic semantics supplies, roughly, a set of instructions which tells us how to describe—or, indeed, 'model'—the relation between a language and a structure. In this sense of model, we may find that the model is specified as an ordered set, which will include a function assigning denotations relating to the structure to the basic vocabulary of the language, and a set of possible truth-values, as well as something for the structure. The structure is given in two parts: a set (of entities) is specified; it is assumed that any mathematical construct relating to this is available—sets of elements, relations between elements, functions from elements to elements or from sets to functions or what you will. A complicated structure can have its entities sorted—say into points, lines and planes, if we are doing geometry, or into ordinary entities and points of time. The interesting part of the structure is imposed by adding a set of meaning postulates to this overabundance—to take a very simple example, one could stipulate with a meaning postulate that there were exactly one hundred basic entities in the model. The meaning postulates restrict the range of possible realizations of the model; and they are statements in the metalanguage. For any interesting language, the model must also include some function recursively assigning denotations to phrases of the object language—which presupposes a syntax for the object language.

Let us call the range of sorts of entity postulated in a model an ontology for the (fragment of) language modeled. Then one of the interesting questions is how such an ontology relates to internal or external reality, or what the world would be like if it did (partly or wholly) realize a structure with such an ontology. We may similarly ask questions about whether the natural world appears to realize the model when we consider the meaning postulates.[22] The linguist is more likely to be interested in what constraints we might be able to impose on possible denotations, both for basic items and in respect of the compositional assignment. If there is any sense in which the sorts of mappings required are psychologically real—and I shall argue that there is, although not in the direct sense that we have a realization of a mini-model in our heads—then the familiar questions of simplicity of theory, of universals and innateness, of learnability, arise, so that there is a possibility that the options may be narrowed down considerably and interestingly. There is also the possibility that the overall task is impossible: there is no model theoretic semantics compatible with our intuitions about our logic for natural language—I shall pretend I have not even considered this possibility.

The possibility that there is no model theoretic semantics for the language of thought is almost unthinkable, however. So it is tempting to see Intensional Logic as a suitable internal language, since it is at least capable of expressing the different readings that may be borne by some of the notorious ambiguous sentences of natural language. It does seem that the language of thought must be at least as expressive as IL. Given that its use is for inference as much as for representation, then we will expect it to have a transparent logic for inference. It seems natural that this would entail a simple compositional semantics, and very probably that its structures would facilitate the exploitation of Boolean algebras, since our model of the world seems to find these ubiquitously (see Keenan and Faltz 1985). Under this view of natural language semantics, the enterprise splits into two parts. On the one hand, we must investigate the lexicon, syntax, and semantics of the language of thought, and on the other we must investigate the relation between natural language utterances and their corresponding interpretations as sentences in the language of thought. This latter enterprise will be part translational semantics, and part pragmatics.

1.4.2 Functions, sets, and types

Here is a very simplified part of what a model theoretic semantics for a fragment of a natural language might look like. The intention is to revive intuitions, rather than to be formal. The level of syntactic representation offered for interpretation has a phrase-structure-rule syntax, in the sense that all its structures can be generated by PS rules (LF could be given a syntax in this way easily enough: it is generating ONLY the grammatical strings that is hard). The grammar given for this syntactic level is however normally a Categorial grammar (as in Montague 1974a and 1974b). In a categorial grammar, any head is given a syntactic category whose internal structure specifies the syntactic arguments the head is to take. A category A/B (where A and B may also be complex) is a category such that if given a complement B the whole will form a unit of category A. The grammar is usually arranged with binary branching throughout, in such a way that every pair of daughters consists of a functor category and its argument. With each syntactic category is associated in a systematic way a semantic type, which determines the kind of denotation in the model of an element of that category.

The model offers a set of entities A and a set of two truth values $\{T, F\}$; we are going to use first just entities, truth values, and functions from these, or functions to these, or functions ... etc. The function (often also named 'F'), mapping basic vocabulary onto things related to the model will map any proper noun onto an entity; it will map any intransitive verb onto a function from entities to truth-values. The compositional mapping will map a binary branching constituent onto that value in the model which is obtained by applying the value of the left-hand daughter as function to the value of the right-hand daughter as argument. Our grammar had better specify that VPs precede subjects. The value of [*John sleeps*] might be F, if the noun *John* happens to get mapped onto entity e_8 and the intransitive verb *sleeps* happens to be mapped onto some function from entities to truth values such that it maps e_8 onto F. Suppose we use the prime sign after a word or phrase to signify the value it is assigned by the function for basic terms, and '| |' to give the value assigned by either this or the compositional mapping. What we have just said amounts to: $|[John]| = John' = e_8$; $|[sleeps\ John]| = sleeps' * John' = sleeps'\ (e_8) = F$, where '*' is function–argument application, otherwise conventionally shown just with brackets.

When functions are more complex, it is convenient to give them a type-name. This is rather like a category name, but one that indicates the kind of argument it is expecting. The function for *sleeps'* would have type $<e,t>$, which indicates that it expects an argument of type $<e>$, the type for ordinary entities, and will return a value of type $<t>$, the type for truth-values. A transitive verb, then, will have type $<e,<e,t>>$; that is (assuming we have a VOS language), when offered its object entity of type $<e>$, it will return a function of the type $<e,t>$ (a function expecting an entity which will be the subject). When offered a subject of type $<e>$, the function will duly return a truth value of type $<t>$, as before. The advantage of this notation is that it is easy to keep

Theoretical Preliminaries

track of whether the functions are of the appropriate types. I shall be using it to record θ-role requirements, in chapters 2 and 4. There are of course elaborations possible, but if function argument application is the mode of composition, the type system will give us what we need however the types are interpreted. That is to say, if we want NPs to have a more complex structure, then we let our <e> stand as an abbreviation for the type of some other function; if the value of a sentence is to be a new sort of entity, then we simply consider <t> to be the type-name for this sort of entity (propositions, you might otherwise call them). We do not need to restrict the system to function–argument application, either, of course, but if more than one mode of composition is permitted, we need a record of which was used in order to use the type-system for checking well-formedness. It will be observed that I am assuming that a function must be offered the correct type of argument: if not, something was ill-formed. We can make various stipulations as to what is to be the value if the argument is the wrong type, but the issue is simply avoided if type-matching is a well-formedness condition on some representation; this is the way I shall be using the system.

Suppose for instance that we decided that the structure was to include sets, as well as or instead of functions. We might decide that the value of *sleeps* was a set, and that the normal mode of composition given by the function for the compositional values was set membership. We might therefore have |[*John sleeps*]| = T iff *John'* ∈ *sleeps'*, giving T or F according as to whether or not *John'* was in the set *sleeps'*; this is a fact about the structure. We could choose to use the type system exclusively for sets rather than functions, so that <e,t> would mean, a set of entities (interpreted as: if an entity is offered for membership, the result will be among the truth values). Alternatively, we could regard the notation in "*John'* ∈ *sleeps'*" as being a statement in another language (one which contains the set-membership sign, for instance), where this language has an interpretation relative to the structure ... an interpretation which is familiar. In this secondary language, we might after all use function composition, giving say '∈' the type <<e,t>,<e,t>>, so that (with the syntax suitably arranged) it would give a <t> value when offered first a function of type <e,t> *i.e. sleeps'* , and then an entity of type <e> *i.e. John'*. It is obvious enough that we can set up a one–one correspondence between a function and a set of the kind presupposed by my using *sleeps'* first for one kind of entity and then for the other. The function under such a correspondence is called the characteristic function of the set: it is that function which returns 'T' when offered as argument an entity in the set, and 'F' if offered an argument not in the set.

Whether we are dealing with functions or sets, it is useful to have to hand a systematic way of naming complex items, rather than just giving their type. A good name tells us as much as possible about the function or set: the name itself has a semantics. This is one way of looking at the lambda abstraction operator and the set-abstraction operator: they provide the means of naming complex functions and sets—a necessary thing to be able to do if the language is relatively impoverished in relation to the structure it is being used to describe. For this reason, it is not surprising that natural languages have closely related devices. Suppose for instance the language (our metalanguage, we may suppose) has a name for the function which returns 'T' iff a number is divisible by two: A; and suppose that B is the name for the function which returns 'T' iff the number is divisible by three. Then using the lambda operator, we can construct a new name $\lambda x(A(x) \& B(x))$ which is the name of the function which returns T iff x is divisible by two AND by three. That this is what the function does can be read off the name, since the definition of the lambda operator, the value of the function for any argument say n is given by the value of $(A(n) \& B(n))$. For any complex expression $F(x)$, the function whose name is $\lambda x(F(x))$ is defined to be that function which when offered any argument a returns $F(a)$. The equivalent set abstraction operator (written either with a circumflex or a colon) names a set: $\{x: (A(x) \& B(x))\}$ is the set containing just those entities which are divisible both by two and by three.[23] Whether these expressions should be regarded as names, or as functions (or sets), depends of course on whether in context the expressions are being mentioned or used.

Using the lambda operator like this, we can define conjunction over functions appropriate to categories other than sentences. For instance, if the A and B above were the functions *sings'* and *dances'*, then the expression $\lambda x(sings'(x) \& dances'(x))$ names a function which will, for instance, return the value 'T' for the argument *John'* just if John both sings and dances (assuming that the functions *sings'* and *dances'* have the appropriate values). Conjunction can be generalized to any type of function, by giving a recursive definition. There is more

Theoretical Preliminaries

than one way of doing this, and still more possibilities if intensionality is taken into account.[24] Mostly what matters for my purposes is that the appropriate functions are properly definable.

1.4.3 Quantifiers

In using the type-system mentioned above, we assume that variables over entities have the type of entities, and that variables over predicates (say) have the type of predicates, and so on. That means that an expression like $F(x)$, where F is a predicate and x a variable over entities, has the type $<t>$.[25] Its type corresponds to its syntactic category in a way that it would not if we treated $F(x)$ as an 'open sentence'. In the 'open sentence' interpretation, variables are regarded as placeholders, rather than as things in their own right, so that an expression with variables is not complete until values are given for the variables.[26] In fact, in our interpretation, the open sentence, or predicate, is rather what the lambda operator gives us: the operator binds the variable, and the resulting function $\lambda x(F(x))$ is of the type of a predicate, $<e,t>$. The lambda operator is distinct from a quantifier in this respect: a quantifier also binds the variable, as in $\forall x(F(x))$, but it returns a function of type $<t>$. If we consider the operator which binds a variable as a function, the lambda operator has type $<t,<e,t>>$, where a quantifier has type $<t,t>$.[27] If we see quantifiers as functions, then we do not need to talk about the binding of variables: the variable in an expression like '$\forall x(F(x))$' is sometimes referred to as a dummy variable, and it can be eliminated. So instead of writing '$\forall x(F(x))$' we could have a syntax and semantics allowing '$\forall : F$', with the same combined meaning—but we now have '$\forall$' of type $<<e,t>,t>$, applying to the predicate of type $<e,t>$ to give an output of type $<t>$. In natural language, surface structure suggests (at least at first glance) a variable-free notation like the latter, with NP VP corresponding to quantifier and predicate. But a Chomskian LF, with quantifier-raising gives us rather [QNP$_x$ [e_x VP]], which can rather naturally be construed as a quantifier-sentence structure, where we are making use of variables. I shall use both notations, and as above I shall sometimes use the same symbol for the two different kinds of quantifier. Whatever we think of natural language, there is no harm in having variables in our metalanguage, where we wish to describe certain functions; the linguist's metalanguage is not at issue.

If we consider NPs to correspond to quantifiers (in either of these senses), then we see that there are not just two, for '∀' and '∃'. We have *all cats* and *all holes*, *no problems* and *no hope*. Further, we have NPs like *most mice*, which demonstrably cannot be reduced to standard logical quantifiers. The theory of generalized quantifiers has been successfully applied to natural language, beginning with Barwise and Cooper (1981). If we take the notation with variables, a generalized quantifier may bind a variable, in the same way that a standard logical quantifier may. The meaning of the generalized quantifier is constructed from the determiner and the N' phrase. It is easiest to get a feel for the semantics of the determiner by switching temporarily to the interpretation of predicates (including N' denotations) as sets, and a variable-free notation. Consider *Two cats purr*. If the syntax were *Two [cats, purr]*, we could consider the *two* as a binary quantifier, which operates simultaneously on the pair of sets. It will correspond to a function which returns the value 'T' iff the intersection of the two sets, $cat' \cap purr'$, has two members. The standard syntax for such binary quantifiers is $Q : R ; S$. If we want a notation with dummy variables, we may construct the variant binary quantifier allowing '$Q(x) : R(x) ; S(x)$'. It is straightforward to see the determiner in its normal syntactic structure [*Two cats*] *purr* as corresponding to a function which mimics the effect of the binary quantifier just described, and we can use the lambda notation to specify this mimicking exactly.[28] This notion is sufficiently powerful to account for all natural language determiners, and for the corresponding NPs seen as generalized quantifiers.

The quantifiers considered above have been binders of just one variable, by type. It is possible to generalize the notion so that two or more variables are bound. This idea provides one solution to a subset of the problems posed by Geach's 'donkey' sentences; we meet similar constructions in definitions, and these will be discussed in chapter 3, section 3.4.2. The intuitive notion is quite simple. For instance, consider a quantifier corresponding more or less to the standard universal quantifier, but binding a pair of variables. A formula such as '$\forall (x,y) \ T(x,y)$' will be well-formed, and will assert that every pair $<x,y>$ satisfies the relation T. This of course is equivalent to '$\forall x \forall y \ T(x,y)$', but the use of pair-quantification permits an increase in the expressive power of the language, which is needed to accommodate a determiner such as *most*.[29]

1.4.4 *Wh*-elements

There are good reasons for supposing that at least in some constructions, *wh*-determiners and other *wh*-elements, and the empty operator, have semantic values closely related to the lambda operator. As we will see in later chapters, for relative clauses and for complement clauses headed by the empty operator, this gives the right results. For *wh*-complement clauses, not surprisingly, the move is over simple, since intensionality must be allowed for. Nevertheless, I shall assume that the simplistic values give a useful first approximation to what is needed, and will amend only when forced to.

A *wh*-determiner is a part of a generalized binder, and like an ordinary determiner in a generalized quantifier, it makes up the binder by taking as its first argument a 'restrictive phrase' (the N' meaning), corresponding to the R in the '$Q : R ; S$' formula. An empty operator on the other hand is a full NP, and as such we will expect it to correspond to the whole of a generalized binder (*i.e.* to both Q and R in the above, in some sense). Moving to a notation with variables, we can associate the empty operator directly with the ordinary lambda, so we have '$\lambda x\, Sx$' for '$O_x\, Sx$', where 'Sx' is some expression containing the variable e_x arising from movement. It turns out that we need the application of the *wh*-determiner on its arguments to produce '$\lambda x (Rx\, \&\, Sx)$'—so that we see that the binary equivalent of the lambda operator is generalized conjunction. The plain version can be obtained from this by setting R to be the universal set, or $R(x)$ to be true for all x. *Wh*-NPs like *who* or *what* will have a meaning equivalent to setting the set R to be the set of persons or things, respectively. So a relative clause like *who I saw* will be interpreted as a predicate, which we may give informally as '$\lambda x\, (person(x)\, \&\, I\, saw\, x)$. We may also need *wh*-binders which bind more than one variable, parallel to the multiple-variable binding quantifiers.

1.4.5 Type changing

The lambda operator enables us to make explicit relations between denotations. I want to give two more examples here, both connected with NPs. So far, I have contrasted NPs which are proper names or definite NPs, with denotations of type <e>, and QNPs, with denotations after QR of type <t,t>. Now, suppose that topicalization were QR at S-structure. But proper name NPs can be topicalized, so there has to be some QNP equivalent of a type <e> entity such as *j* (our e_8). A function with the required properties does indeed exist: it is given by $\lambda S((x=j) (S))$, where *S* will be an expression of type <t> containing a variable x. The '*(x=j)*' is a quantifier which binds the variable *x*, and the function just given has the proper type for QNPs, <t,t>.[30] The second example concerns small clauses. At least in English, a small clause can have an NP as predicate. How can this make sense? Consider

1 [I consider [John a fool]]

The predication has the sense of 'John is a fool' (ignoring the contribution of tense), and this is consistent with the parallelism in non-problematic predication cases: *I consider [John foolish]* means much the same as *I consider [John is foolish]*. If we assume that it is LF that needs interpretation relative to a model, and if QR applies to predicational NPs, then our problem reduces to accounting for a predicational e_x, in

2 [I consider [[a fool]$_y$ [John e_y]]]

One possible answer is plain: instead of giving e_y the denotation of *y*, as usual, it must have as denotation $\lambda x(y=x)$, which is a function of type <e,t> as required, and will give the effect of *is*.[31]

I have been implicitly assuming here that exactly what function a given phrase denotes in a particular structure is properly determined partly on the basis of that structure. If an NP must be functioning as a quantifier or as a predicate, rather than as an argument, then it may be assumed to denote a function of the appropriate type, subject to some constraints on how the correct function is determined. There has to be a certain amount of systematic type-variability, so that type may be determined not simply by category, but according at least to the quasi-semantic classification into head, argument, operator, predicate, adjunct and so on offered by the syntactic theory.

I take a head to be in some way equivalent to a logical predicate, so that on being offered a suitable number of suitable arguments, it returns a value of type <t>. The exact type will depend on the arguments, their order, and the assumed structure. A syntactic predicate, in contrast, is any function expecting one argument (normally of the type of an entity, and external). The two types <e> and <t> are taken as the fundamental types in a simple extensional model; they correspond naturally to entity and proposition, argued by Chomsky to be the only semantic types for arguments. However we should note that in what I have said above, I have largely ignored syntax, and have assumed where necessary that all arguments occur to the right of their heads. In natural language, there is often an asymmetry between internal and external arguments. In later chapters, I have used 'e*' to denote an argument that occurs externally, and <p> (predicate) for <e*,t>. Operators (in the strict mathematical sense) have type <k,k>, for some k that is, they return something of the same type as their argument. The lambda operator is NOT a semantic operator in the strict sense, then; but syntactically it is, since when it occurs at the front of a clause, we still have a clause. Adjuncts will be discussed in later chapters.

We may also note that in a multi-level categorial grammar, the types needed may change from one level to another. Suppose that we want a transitive verb to accept QNPs as arguments. At D-structure, these are in situ, so the types would have to accommodate this. But at LF, after QR, all QNP have become operators, leaving just traces of type <e> behind as argument to the verb.[32] An alternative is to permit the modes of combination to change from one level to another. For instance, we might consider the combination associated with subject and predicate to be set-membership where the subject is a singular, but it might be set-inclusion for plurals (as argued in Cormack 1984b). We might then go further, and allow identity, in order to account for the small clause cases like [*John a fool*] in (1) above. The correct combinator would be selected on the basis of the relation between the types of the subject and its predicate.

In an extended categorial grammar (combinatorial grammar) as proposed by Steedman, (see for instance Ades and Steedman 1982), we may use not only function–argument application to combine two types, but other modes of combination. Application requires types <a,b>, <a>, for some *a*, *b*; other combinators will take different types. Later, I shall use composition, which combines two functions, say *f* and *g*. It takes types <a,b> and <c,a>, to give <b,c>. Its semantics spelt out in terms of the lambda operator is $\lambda x(f(g(x)))$, where *f* is the function of type <a,b>, and *g* is the function of type <c,a>. Its syntactic effect is to permit the combination of two functions which would otherwise be the first two elements of a right branching structure:

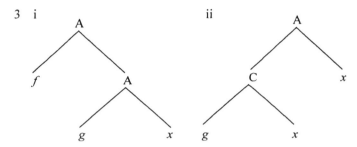

In the structure (i) in (3), the elements are combined by application (hence the constituent label 'A'), and the whole is well-formed. Exactly the same semantic total is obtained in (ii), where *f* and *g* are combined by composition ('C'). But a constituent with the ingredients of C may exist independently as well, so that for instance two categories of this type may be available for conjunction; and the item labeled '*x*' may be of arbitrary semantic type. We may thus obtain 'right node raising' effects. I shall use composition of functions in interpreting θ-theory.[33]

1.5 The formal interpretation of definitions

> It was not long before it was recognised that exactness cannot be established in the arguments unless it is first introduced into the definitions.
>
> Poincaré, *Science and method*

1.5.1 Setting constraints on meanings

Within a formal system such as an axiomatic construction of a subdomain of mathematics, the position and proper function of a definition can be specified. On the basis of this specification, criteria may be set up which will distinguish proper from improper definitions. The logician is concerned that the system he has set up is tractable, and hence requires that there is some finite identifiable basis for the system. In order to ensure this, the object language he devises is sharply divided into primitive and non-primitive terms, and it is required that the non-primitive terms are such that their use does not make any difference to the properties of the system as set up in terms of the primitives. The non-primitive terms can be seen as abbreviatory conveniences. The statements constraining the interpretation of non-primitive terms are usually called *definitions*, while those constraining the interpretation of primitive terms are called *axioms*. In addition, some subset of the primitive terms ('logical' terms) will have interpretations constrained by *inference rules*. Both the former are written in the same sort of format, being simply sentences of the object language with a special status. Both function by licensing inferences, through the inference rules which apply to the logical symbols which they contain. Inference rules are specified in the metalanguage, and refer to (mention, rather than use) items of the object language.

If the formal system is given a model-theoretic interpretation, then there are two further devices available for constraining interpretation. These are statements constraining the mapping from object language items onto elements of the model, and statements about the model itself. Both these of course must be stated wholly or partly in the metalanguage. The former are the clauses of the definition of the *assignment function*, while the latter are known as *meaning postulates*, in the terminology of Tarski, Carnap, Montague, and others. The model must be set up at least in such a way as to permit the axioms of the system and the definition statements to be true-with-respect-to-the-model, and to respect the inference rules stipulated.

All the five devices listed above might be called definitions, in a rather general sense. Every one of them serves to constrain what can be deduced from some object language statement, and hence directly or indirectly, constrains what it means. In as much as it turns out to be possible or interesting to treat natural language like a formal language, so it may turn out that those natural language forms usually classified as definitions are best seen as corresponding to any one of the five devices.

1.5.2 Definitions as object language statements

It is the first kind of meaning-constraint described above which is most usually seen as a definition, and so I shall consider this first as a candidate model for the definitions found in natural language. Suppes (1957), following the criteria laid down by Lesniewski, stipulates for these the property most commonly assumed to apply to definitions, which is that they should permit elimination of the defined term. To eliminability, Suppes adds non-creativity. A proposition is non-creative if it allows no more statements to be proved true than could be without it. It is important to bear in mind that this is a relative notion: creativity is relative to what is in the axioms and previous definitions.

It is not at all intuitively obvious that this is something we require of a natural language definition: in fact those who think that language acquisition can ever drive concept formation might well expect definitions to be in some sense at least creative. I will come back to this point; it should be borne in mind that it may turn out that the logicians' purposes make their formalizations inappropriate for the consideration of natural language (or language of thought) vocabulary. But in part the question is artificial: a statement of this sort which IS creative belongs with the axioms. So does any other statement which for some reason fails to conform to the criteria for definitions, but which is nevertheless deemed (as opposed to its being provable) to be true by virtue of the meanings of its terms.

Suppes proceeds to set out general schemata for definitions which will guarantee that they satisfy the two criteria of eliminability and non-creativity. These are couched in a metalanguage whose variables may range over the usual vocabulary of a logical calculus, naturally. It remains to be seen whether they can be adapted to or interpreted as schemata for definitions in natural language or the language of thought. The general form of definition is to be an equivalence, so that the definiendum (traditionally given on the left) and the definiens on the right are propositions. Unconditional eliminability dictates that the expression on the left be atomic—if other context is specified, then elimination is only possible when this specification is met. Variables appearing in the definiendum will appear free in the definiens,[34] and any other variables in the definiens must be bound in the definiens. It is also necessary (in order to avoid circularity, which would prevent

Theoretical Preliminaries

elimination) to restrict the definiens to containing just primitive symbols and previously defined symbols.

The variables of the definiendum are conventionally left unbound, but the convention gives universal quantification over the whole expression as the interpretation. It should be emphasized that apart from the convention just given, and the caveat about variables (given in footnote 34), the stipulations relating to the 'formats' or schemata described here are not just sufficient but provably necessary for the definition to satisfy the criteria (see Suppes 1957).

The format for a two-place relation term R will then be

1   $R(x,y) \Leftrightarrow S$

where S is a metalanguage variable over sentences of the object language, and where x and y occur in S and any other variables in S are bound in S.

For n-place relations, the same pattern is followed:

2   $R(x_1, x_2, \ldots x_n) \Leftrightarrow S$

where x_1 to x_n occur as the only unbound variables in S.

If we re-instate the universal quantifiers dropped by convention, we have

3   $\forall x \, \forall y \, (R(x,y) \Leftrightarrow S)$

Not every symbol is a relation symbol, of course, in formal languages or natural ones. In mathematics, there are as well operators and constants. These can always be defined using equivalences, but where possible they are normally defined using identities, or possibly conditional definitions. To use Suppes' example, in defining '2', we find that

$2 = 1 + 1$
seems more natural and elegant than the definition:
$2 = y$ if and only if $y = 1 + 1$

Note that here Suppes is using 'if and only if' as a term of the object language, which includes both logical and mathematical symbols. That is, it is not being used as a term of the metalanguage.

If we use identity, the format for a definition of an operator is

4   $O(x, y, \ldots) = t$

where the restrictions are as for 'S' in (1) above, except that 't' is a term rather than a sentence. If the same definition is to be cast in the form of an equivalence, it will become

5   $O(x, y, \ldots) = w \Leftrightarrow S$

where 'w' is a variable which will appear free in 'S'. In addition, in order for this form, (5) to be a proper definition it is necessary for it to be provable from the axioms and previous definitions that 'w' is uniquely characterized by S; otherwise mayhem will be let loose.[35]

A definition which has ONLY the definiendum on the left of the main connective is an explicit definition. The definition of '2' as equal to '1 + 1' is strictly explicit; the definition of an operator as in (4) is not, and is classified either as an implicit definition, or, because the extra on the left is minimal in some sense, as an explicit definition in the broader sense. I shall use the terms 'explicit' and 'implicit' for these two, respectively. A definition as in (5) is also an implicit definition, where the extra material is not minimal, but makes up a sentence. A definition which is not strictly explicit is close to what Russell and others call a 'definition in use'. The two kinds of implicit definition are distinguished by whether they make use of identity or equivalence.

At this point, it may well be asked whether natural language is sufficiently like the language of mathematics for these characterizations of satisfactory definitions to have any relevance to those natural language expressions usually identified as definitions. There are two questions here: one is whether the criteria are appropriate for natural language definitions, and the other is whether the formats given for simple first order languages by Suppes are close enough to natural language to be usable. The characterizations we have here are appropriate only if natural language text definitions should be construed as sentences which are entirely within the object language, and which are intended to function in the same way as formal definitions at least with respect to eliminability. This is obviously a possibility which has to be investigated: an *a priori* answer is not available. Even if such a construal is possible, it could turn out that

Theoretical Preliminaries 61

other construals are also possible, and that there is reason to reject this one.

It might also turn out that the formats discussed here were appropriate not for any level of natural language syntax, but for expressions over the language of thought. Chapter 3 will contain some investigation of these matters. In any case, if the object language is natural language rather than a first order predicate calculus, the forms a definition must take if the criteria are to be met must be somewhat varied from those given above. In particular, it would be natural to wish to associate say transitive verbs with two-place predicates, and NPs with arguments, but we cannot do this without introducing either restricted variables or generalized quantification. For the moment, all I shall do to show that the forms are plausibly relatable to a possible natural language definition is to give a possible definition with a pidgin-logic translation which roughly matches one of Suppes' formats.

Consider a definition which runs

6   A triangle is *isosceles* if and only if it has two equal sides

Let us construe this as a definition of a one-place relation *isosceles*. A pidgin-logic[36] translation of (6) might be

7   Isosceles($x: x \in$ triangle) $\Leftrightarrow$ Two-equal-sides(x)

This is close enough to what is indicated in (2) for us not to reject out of hand the possibility of using the formal language methods. Its existence does not entail that any translation into another language is actually required: it may be that (6) in itself satisfies the proper format, if the format is rewritten for the syntax of English instead of for the syntax of mathematics.

Similarly, we might wish to construe *king* as an operator. A definition on the lines of

8   Someone is the king of a country if and only if he is a male head of state of that country and the country is a monarchy

might have a pidgin-logic translation as

9   King($x: x$ a country) $= w$
    $\Leftrightarrow$ male(w) & head-of-state(w,x) & monarchy(x)

Again, this is sufficiently close to the format for operators given in (5) for the enterprise to be plausible, and maybe even revealing.

Suppes offers one more kind of definition, which does not strictly speaking satisfy the criterion of eliminability. This is a conditional definition, which essentially prefaces a standard definition with some condition. If the condition is not met, then the standard part of the definition cannot be used, so in such a case elimination is not possible. Of the example Suppes uses, he says that the conditional definition permits elimination 'in all "interesting" cases'. A conditional version of (9) above might be suggested by (10):

10 If a country is a monarchy, then someone is the king of that country if and only if he is the male head of state of that country

Translating this into pidgin-logic gives

11 Monarchy(x: country(x)) $\Rightarrow$
    [King(x) = w $\Leftrightarrow$ male(w) and head-of-state(w, x)]

The conditional definition of (11) or (10) tells us nothing about countries which are not monarchies, whereas (if we make certain assumptions) the definition of (9) or (8) tells us that no-one is the king when the country is not a monarchy. A conditional definition makes the mapping from expressions onto truth conditions a partial function.

A conditional definition gives a fairly natural version of (6), repeated here:

6 A triangle is *isosceles* if and only if it has two equal sides

12 If triangle(x) then [isosceles(x) $\Leftrightarrow$ has-two-equal-sides(x)]

Unlike the version in (7), this has no restricted quantification.

There is nothing to prevent further clauses being added to a conditional definition (though it should be considered as a change of definition, if this mattered). To (6) we could add a clause defining *isosceles* in relation to trapezia, for instance. The definition of the modulus of a number is usually given in two or three conditional statements:

13 If x is a real number, then
$$\text{if } x > 0, |x| = x$$
and   if $x < 0, |x| = -x$
and   if $x = 0, |x| = x$

It does seem that conditional definitions are used; since they fail to satisfy the criterion of eliminability, consideration must be given to what compensating advantages they have, especially with respect to natural language.

Two further patterns of definition should be mentioned here: definition by listing, and definition by 'abstraction'. These are appropriate for the definition of a predicate (or set). The commonest form of the former is the recursive definition, where the recursive statement ensures that in effect a countably infinite number of items are listed; what is being defined is the set to which these elements are assigned. The usual pattern for a definition by listing of a set P is simply:

14 i $a_1 \in P$
       $a_2 \in P$
       ......
       Nothing else is an element of P

The definition will be recursive if it contains any clause of the form

14 ii $\forall r \, (a_r \in P \text{ if } a_r = f(a_{r-1}, a_{r-2}, \ldots a_1))$

for some function f. Examples occur in the definition of a well-formed formula (wff) in logic, where we have for instance 'If S is a wff, then $\neg S$ is a wff.' Commonly, and conventionally, the last line (of 14i) is omitted, and so is the universal quantifier of (14ii). Ordinary natural language definitions do not seem to have this format, possibly for interesting reasons to do with our abilities in handling recursion. Peano's construction of the natural numbers is the paradigm instance of a recursive definition. Definition by abstraction is a special case; instead of allowing any function f, it uses some equivalence relation (see Carnap 1958, 137). Russell's construction of the natural numbers may be taken as the paradigm here. And young children's definitions may charitably be construed as of this kind—to the question, "What is a dog?" the reply "Pongo" can be taken to mean "that equivalence class under 'likeness for animals' which contains Pongo"—a perfectly good definition. A so-called ostensive definition must be construed in a similar way. However, clearly with these last two we have strayed outside the bounds of definitions to be construed as object language statements. Recursive listing and abstraction can be construed one way or the other, depending on whether the function f and the equivalence relation are taken to belong to object language or metalanguage.

There appears to be quite commonly a feeling that there is something unsatisfactory about implicit definitions.[37] Of course, if the only use of a definition is thought to be elimination, and the only method of elimination countenanced is substitution, an implicit definition is of no use; but these provisos are unnecessarily restrictive. In many cases, within a sufficiently rich language, they can in fact be eliminated in favor of explicit definitions (see for instance Carnap 1958, 133). What is needed is the lambda operator, and a starting point of a definition with identity. We simply abstract on all the 'free' variables of the definition. So for example, from a definition in the form of (4), given again here,

4   $O(x, y, ...) = t$

we can construct a strictly explicit definition of the form (13):

15   $O = \lambda(x, y ...)(t)$

With the usual definition of the lambda operator, only functors taking their arguments to the right can be defined in this way, but there are various ways of getting round this. The question of whether any natural language definitions should be construed as if they contained lambda operators will be considered in more detail later, but I will offer one possible example here.

Dictionary definitions by their very format are almost inevitably strictly explicit. Frequently, this causes no particular problems, but occasionally the lexicographer is constrained to include noun-phrases in the definiens, which appear to correspond to arguments of the definiendum. For instance, we can contrast the following definitions:

16   *destruction*   the action of destroying something   DEL

17   *destruction*   act of destroying

(This pair is discussed at length in section 2.5). Suppose we consider the noun *destruction* to be transitive, having a direct object which is case-marked by *of*. Then corresponding to the explicit definition of (17) we might expect a 'definition in use' of the form

18   destruction of something = act of destroying something

where the 'something' is acting as a variable; and corresponding in turn to this, a lambda version using 'something' as the name of a variable:

19   destruction = λ(something) (act of destroying something)

If a binder such as the lambda operator were available in natural language, we might expect that at surface, it, like QNPs among other LF-variable-binders, could appear directly in the place of the variable:[38]

20   destruction = act of destroying (λ-something)

So one way of construing (16) is to take the *something* as corresponding to a lambda-binding operator *in situ* at S-structure, rather than as a true quantifier or as a free variable.

Finally, should we consider ordinary definitions as possibly to be construed as axioms? At first sight, the answer is simply, no. For among the axioms we do not generally find statements such that they can be used to eliminate some term from any context in which it occurs. If this could be done safely, the term would be removed from the primitives and assigned to the defined terms. The proviso 'safely' relates to the non-creativity stipulation. It does follow that if what purports to be a definition IS creative, then it should be construed as an axiom. This may account for the uncomfortable feeling one sometimes has at being offered putative definitions incorporating definite descriptions: such propositions are creative unless an existence proof has been supplied. It may well be that the majority of expressions are primitive, and have their meanings constrained by axioms rather than by definitions. Axioms, like theories, frequently set up a web of relationships, with the several terms appearing in several propositions, no one of which would be eligible to be a definition. But it is possible that the same terms can be rearranged so that what was a primitive term before is a defined term after or vice versa. It is for this reason that in some cases it may not make much sense to ask whether such and such should be construed as an axiom or a definition. It is harmless to regard all definitions as axioms. However, I shall take it that what looks as if it is intended to be a definition should be construed as such if possible. The main difference which concerns us is that a definition will have a biconditional (or an equality), where an axiom need not. The issue of creativity is outside the concerns of this work.

1.5.3 Definitions as mappings from object language to metalanguage

We have a definition which for some reason we would like to take to consist of an object language word defined by means of metalanguage terms. We might be able to construe this whole as a translation-aid, merely, for translation into a postulated language of thought. Or we might construe it as part of a model-theoretic semantics for the object language, where the status of the model (as real or mental) is not at issue. It is this second possibility which will be discussed here. However, throughout the discussion, the possibility of construing the metalanguage as the language of thought, and hence of ascertaining some of its necessary or at least useful properties, will be borne in mind. For these purposes, it is advisable to assume that the postulated language of thought has at least one possible model (preferably non-trivial). That the language of thought is the metalanguage under either interpretation will follow from any theory other than one which takes NL (English, here) to be the requisite metalanguage.

Model theoretic semantics sometimes explicitly rejects any responsibility for the denotation of items of the object language beyond the specification of the semantic type available for the syntactic class to which they belong. (There are exciting exceptions to this, for instance in the theory of quantification). In general, this is because the theory being expounded is a recipe for semantics, including the semantics of some of the less obviously tractable fragments of (for instance) English, rather than an attempt to specify in full and uninteresting detail the semantics of the whole of English. In particular, we would be hampered by the absence of the requisite unambiguous metalanguage and by the dubious status of the world or worlds required in the model. Suppose however we did have a suitable metalanguage—what would this have to be like in order that a total semantics could be given? Idealizing as far as we can without eliminating all the interest, let us suppose that English' is not ambiguous either syntactically or lexically (which leaves the possibility of the composition rules introducing ambiguity). Let us

Theoretical Preliminaries

further suppose that the world which English' is set up to model is the single real world, *world'*, only, and that this consists of a countably infinite number of entities.[39] Of course, the English' we can even pretend to handle will be a very small part of our natural language English.

It is the lexicon which is our concern. The most convenient metalanguage would be one where the words of English' were in one-to-one correspondence with a subset of the words of the metalanguage, and the pairs set up by the correspondence had in common a denotation. The denotation we assume to be some mathematical construct over the entities in the world'. Then world' must be a subset of some world", where the latter provides the denotations for the items of the metalanguage.

In order to specify the denotations explicitly, we will also need in our metalanguage some expression capable of serving the function of *means* or *denotes*, so that we can formulate a complete sentence in the metalanguage roughly like

21   '*dog*' denotes what 'dog' denotes

The italicization is to show a word of English'. We do not know the vocabulary or syntax of the metalanguage: we have to construct some hypothetical fragment using minimal assumptions. Sentence (21) is relatively complex, as English. We can try for something simpler. It appears that we want to express a relationship between two things. The two things need to be namable within the language we are constructing, since the version of (21) is to be entirely within the metalanguage. We could suppose that for '*dog*' we have some proper name in the metalanguage, if this was supplied with a name for each word of English', eliminating the first pair of quotation marks. If supplied with a set of names for those words of the metalanguage corresponding to the (finite) list of the words of English', then we can avoid the other set of quotation marks. So we need to have the two sets of words among the entities in the world" (or among the other possible denotations of words of the metalanguage). If some word like 'denotes' is part of the metalanguage, and if relative clauses and the rest of the syntax is like English, then we would have no problem in stating what (21) is intended to state. We might suppose however that there should be a more direct statement of the relation between the word-names postulated: say equivalent to 'translates into'. This seems to be the minimal assumption, so I'll take it that there is a single metalanguage term here.

The rules of composition to give the denotations of phrases of English 'require that a syntactic specification of English' can be given in the metalanguage, and that at least some quantification over items in the various syntactic categories is available. This involves recourse to talk about numbers, or a generous fixed supply of variables in the metalanguage, unless the language of thought is like surface natural language in having QNPs *in situ*. Let us suppose that this is all possible within the metalanguage. In fact let us suppose that the specification looks like a simpler version of the translation patterns of Montague's PTQ, which uses a finite vocabulary (of symbols and English words) with a potentially infinite number of variables.

The question which I want to raise is this: what possibilities are there within this framework for the meaning-specification of English' lexical items OTHER than the one to one correspondence suggested above? The obvious relaxation is to give denotations as phrases in the metalanguage, rather than as words. This will add complications to the picture sketched above. The virtue of the move is to make the metalanguage vocabulary smaller, potentially, so that if it is to be the language of thought, we do not need to assume that it contains equivalents for every single item POSSIBLE in all the world's languages.

The first essential is that the phrases concerned have names. Now if each has its own arbitrary name, then we are no better off than before (in economizing). The natural move is to do what I did in (21), which is to construct a name out of the item in question by putting quotation marks round it; or some analogue of this. That forces the metalanguage to have 'words' decomposable into parts (*i.e.* the original phrase and the delimiter(s)). The denotation of this constructed name is to be the phrase in question, so this phrase must be an entity in the world". What does this mean? At worst it means that the world" contains as entities or otherwise, all strings of vocabulary items from the metalanguage (assuming that strings are the required structures for phrases).

To learn a new definition with the definiens phrasal in the metalanguage would be to add another pair of world" entities to the pairs falling under the 'translates into' relation. The denotation of 'translates into' with respect to world" would change, or would be more fully known. Another clause gets added to those already given for known vocabulary and for the recursive clauses. That is, we can understand that the clauses of the translation specification for English' are EXPLICITLY specified in the metalanguage, and that this specification provides an IMPLICIT definition of the extension of the metalanguage relation 'translates into'.[40]

That sounds possible, but there is something missing still. It is not sufficient to associate the English' word with the NAME of a phrase of the metalanguage. The idea of using quote marks is not just to save on new vocabulary. We need to make use of the fact that the name of a phrase or word is the name of something that has a denotation, a meaning. We cannot then just have a pairing associated with 'translates into'. Suppose for concreteness we have

22 '*Bachelor*' translates into 'unmarried man'

How do we actually get to use the information inside the second pair of quotation marks? One possible answer would be that we CANNOT use this information until we have amassed enough phrases inside the quotation marks to form a sentence (in the metalanguage); when we have this, then we can use a Tarskian sentence (which can be an axiom-scheme) of the form

23 'a' is *true* entails that a

where a is a variable over strings (which must be sentences) in the metalanguage, and 'a' is some appropriate structure-preserving name for that string.[41] Is there an equivalent of (23) where the variable can range over other syntactic categories, especially those smaller than that for a sentence? That is, is there a conceivable 'word' or relation 'R' in the metalanguage such that

24 'a' R a

is some use to us, where 'a' is not a sentence? The answer of course is that 'R' should mean roughly *denotes*. In English, that verb is such that its subject and object arguments must be noun-phrases; just this would not be any use. We would need it to have a syntactic category in the metalanguage which allowed it to have its second argument of varied category, or (trivially) to have a new item like R for each necessary syntactic category. (The other argument of course will still be by assumption a name (of the metalanguage phrase), so is not problematic). Let us use *m-denotes* for such a verb: and attempt to discover whether it can reasonably exist in the language. It must conform to syntactic rules. It must be capable of entering into suitable inference patterns, which can be explicitly stated (that is, it must have at least a partial implicit definition given by the inference rules).

The general form will be something like

25   '*a*' m-denotes *a*

We will have sentences in the metalanguage which might be like

26   '*a dog*' m-denotes a dog

27   '*dog*' m-denotes dog

28   '*barks loudly*' m-denotes barks loudly

(All this is supposedly in the metalanguage). Could these sentences be well-formed? If they were, what use would these statements be? It is hard to believe that a syntactically unambiguous language can be such that things like (28) are well-formed. The problem is that we want phrases as arguments, but we do not want any delimiters. It looks as if we must give the phrasal category, say

29   '[$_{VP}$ barks loudly]' VP-m-denotes [$_{VP}$ barks loudly]

As to what we can use these for: the content of such statements is fairly obviously trivial in some sense. They cannot actually be used for anything as they stand. What we could do is to use the predicate (I mean the collection of predicates *k*-m-denotes, for '*k*' ranging over the syntactic categories) to set up meaning postulates within the metalanguage. That is, m-denotes does not need to be defined solely by clauses derived from (25); additional clauses can be added:

30   '[$_{VP}$ barks loudly]' VP-m-denotes [$_{VP}$ yelps]

However, this seems to be an obscure way of stating the fact: it would seem more natural to have some sort of identity relation between items of the same type, or simply an axiomatic statement of some kind which stipulates that everything that yelps barks loudly, and *vice versa*. The other thing we could do would be to use the predicate in part of a recursive definition, so that from NP-m-denotes and VP-m-denotes we

Theoretical Preliminaries

could arrive at S-m-denotes, as it were, and so on. If the syntax is in part, S ⇒ NP VP, we would have

31   If [NP *a*] NP-m-denotes *u* and [VP *b*] VP-m-denotes *v*,
     then [s [NP *a*] [VP *b*]] S-m-denotes [s *u v*]

This is simply a statement within the metalanguage that its own semantics is compositional with respect to its syntax. And 'S-m-denotes' maybe could be subject to axioms such that it functioned as if it meant the same as the 'is *true* entails that' relation in (23), repeated here:

23   '*a*' is *true* entails that *a*

This is the sort of statement that we can presumably use: there is propositional content gained, and hence we can enter into inference chains. All we have achieved here is that we have gone around in a compositional circle to get to this point. But in fact I think we must reach this point: and the only question is, where is the compositionality permitting this? In the 'm-denotes' story, the compositionality is certainly in the metalanguage; and it has to be spelt out, as in (31), in order to be used. In the simple Tarskian story, we have to have *a* a sentence. So the answer to the question I posed earlier, what can we have OTHER than a word-for-word translation system, if it is not to reduce to the 'm-denotes' story, is that we must so arrange our initial definitions that the target is always wrapped up in a clausal definiendum, as in (1), (2) and (3) above. We could even use forms like (3) (given again below) but with no quantifiers outside to translate one idiom into another, with no obvious implications of compositionality anywhere.

3   $\forall x \, \forall y \, (R(x,y) \Leftrightarrow S \,)$

To the extent that smaller units appear, so must the metalanguage be compositional. In (3) as it stands, the implication of the quantified variables is that the contribution of '*R*' to say '*R(a,b)*' is systematic rather than idiomatic, so that the unit '*R(x,y)*' (which is a metalanguage description of a schematic sentence of English') is composed semantically as well as syntactically of three relevant sub-units. Is the same true of the variable occurrences in *S*?

If the metalanguage has a model-theoretic semantics, then 'compositional' above has the usual interpretation. But if what we have is rather a translation into a metalanguage, which might not have a consistent model, then what is implied above may be very much weaker. Suppose what we mean by 'compositional' in this case is 'the inference rules associated with the whole are derived from the inference rules associated with the parts'. If all quantification is taken as merely substitutional (*i.e.* it licenses various syntactic transformations) then for instance in the form (3) above, substitutions of say $x=a'$ and $y=b'$ might lead to a formula S', and substitutions of say $x=a''$ and $y=b''$ might lead to a formula S'', where S' and S'' could have ONLY entirely different and unconnected inference relations stipulated (or learned) $S' \Rightarrow A$; $S'' \Rightarrow B$, for arbitrary A, B. The 'only' above is necessary to ensure total lack of compositionality. Compositionality with respect to 'x' and 'y' is what is at issue. Then the arbitrary inferences suggested for substitutions for 'x' and 'y' would have to be repeated for EACH x and y; if any subset had a consistent interpretation, then we would in effect have compositionality with a finite list of exceptions. But this is a hypothesis rendering the putative language absurd. There would be no reason for S', S'' and so on to be composite syntactically (they would effectively be single words); and in any case there would have to be an infinitely large list or disjunction somewhere.

Let us take it, then, that a formula like (3) implies at least that the metalanguage is (largely) compositional with respect to the variables specified those given wide-scope universal quantification. Then what has been established (and perhaps is entirely obvious, now!) is that ANY definition of an isolated item (or phrase) carries with it the implication that there is some compositionality concerned in both the object language and the metalanguage. The compositionality relates just to whatever elements must be used to construct the minimal sentence incorporating that item, and hence also to the item itself in those minimal sentences on the left, and to some matrix within S on the right.

What is the implication of this for intensional effects? It might appear that I have simply ruled them out, so far, by the assumption that variables are variables (in the metalanguage) over entities or higher order objects in the extensional world. An exploration of the problems of intensionality is not part of the present undertaking, but it is worth noting that under the assumptions made so far, we have at least one way of producing some sorts of intensional effects. For we have in the ontology of the metalanguage names for the lexical items and phrases of the object language, and this being so, we may have variables over such objects.

Consider for instance *fake*. The discussion above has been of definitions seen as translations into metalanguage, with further discussion of the possibility of using the metalanguage part, which entails the construction of a full sentence in the metalanguage. We want to say that the *fake* in *fake diamond* and *fake jewel* are the same, and so on, so that there is clearly compositionality rather than idiomaticity involved. But it is not the case that we can usefully have as definiendum '*fake x*', for a variable over entities x, since in the case that x is a zircon, it could be a fake diamond without being a fake jewel, so that we cannot say it is a fake by virtue of its intrinsic properties. Somewhere, we need to refer to the description under which the object is a fake; we need to refer to the word. We need our definition to have '*fake N'*' as definiendum, where N' is a variable over N' expressions in English'. If *fake* is an operator, it is an operator not on sets of ordinary entities (which we are taking as N' denotations) but on WORDS or sets of words. There is no reason not to suppose that in one sense words are entities of the world—of any world—so this in itself does not explain the intensionality. What does explain it is the necessity to move from the word to its referent, or some such equivalent move, within the definition. Suppose we assume that there is a word just like *fake* in the metalanguage, FAKE. Then we might give a definition something like

32 $\quad \forall N' \ \forall x \ (F((fake \ N')(x)) = ((\text{FAKE ``}(F(N')\text{'' })(x))$

where N' is a variable over English' N' expressions, x is a variable over entities, and F is the translation function from English' to the metalanguage. The function of the quotation marks on the right hand side is to ensure that FAKE takes as its first argument a word or phrase of the metalanguage, mention as opposed to use. This addition to the expressive power of the metalanguage appears to be necessary. The expression in (32) follows the format of (3), and hence implies extensionality with respect to its variables. This is correct, but its variable N' ranges over WORDS. The intensionality is exhibited only if we try to apply to the words processes which properly apply only to their denotations: they will not be valid. Instead, there will be special inference rules—for instance in this case, there is presumably an inference rule which states that if (FAKE N')(x) is true then $N'(x)$ is false (N' here being a variable in the metalanguage over some suitable subset of metalanguage expressions). I take it that in those cases where the natural language sentence has no N' (as when I wave something at you shouting that 'it is a fake!'), you are expected to construct a pragmatically appropriate description to serve in the metalanguage interpretation.

What I am suggesting here is in a sense rather depressing. I have sketched a possible way of dealing with a particular problem word in English, which might otherwise be dealt with by assuming that the denotation of a word was a function from possible worlds to extensions.[42] I am suggesting that the fact that a model-theoretic semantics for NL appears to require intensionality does not mean that we can show that the language of thought has anything like the structure of IL, even though it cannot (presumably) be ambiguous in the way that NL is. We will need, not unexpectedly, to consider what explanatory power a particular hypothesis about the language of thought (including its description of a natural language) has with respect to the range of particular ambiguities shown in some natural language's constructions.

1.5.4 Definitions as supplying axioms or inference rules for the internal language

Within a model theoretic framework, meaning postulates are considered to be statements constraining the choice or properties of the model. However, they function as axioms in the metalanguage, allowing inferences to be made which otherwise would not be valid. Suppose an NL definition is simply translated into the internal metalanguage, and the translation treated as an axiom, which happens to be a biconditional. If the new axiom is non-creative, it may alternatively be taken as a definition. But suppose the target of the NL definition does not correspond to an existing word of the metalanguage? The translation is apparently blocked. Let us suppose that in this case, a new item is added to the metalanguage, to serve as the translation of just that item of NL. If the translation is then taken as a definition, this is natural: the NL definition is an instruction to add a new item of vocabulary to the internal language, and its meaning is specified. We

Theoretical Preliminaries

should also expect its syntax to be deducible, a point to which I will return. It is equally possible, however, to take the whole as an axiom: a new item has to be added to the PRIMITIVE vocabulary, at the same time as the axiom is added to the existing stock. Of course this may add to the expressive power of the language, and may change the models for the language—that is to be expected of learning. It seems to me that either of these two possibilities, where new items are added to the internal language, are very plausible interpretations of the function of an NL definition. They will be discussed further in chapter 5, after actual instances of natural language definitions have been examined in the next two chapters.

In those cases where a new item is added to the internal language, there will be restrictions imposed on the syntactic category of this item by the sentence in which it occurs, unless it is introduced in quotation. In the latter case, either the choice is fixed by the semantic type (*i.e.* we have a one to one correspondence between types and categories) or it could be less constrained (if the correspondence is one to many). But we have to regard the axiom not only as such, but as supplying the translation rule for the NL target item, since we have postulated that the new internal language item is the translation of this. Thus choices must be constrained by the composition rules. It is perfectly possible to imagine that the internal language has much the same syntax as some NL, however, so we cannot assume a one–one correspondence on these grounds.

Finally, we may consider whether an NL definition should be construed as an inference rule (or pair of such rules) for natural language. In this case, we would have, presumably, mention of the definiendum and definiens, since these would correspond to the input and output of the inference rule; the biconditional connective would be in the metalanguage. Something like this is probably the likely construal of a definition where the meanings of both the target and some item of the definiens are unknown; a situation which does occur. In these circumstances, introspection suggests that we are simply unwilling or incapable of adding two or more items to the internal inventory, items whose meanings are necessarily badly underdetermined. If an inference rule is added to the object language, it must be accommodated in the model. If we suppose, as before, that the metalanguage describes this model, then either the inference rule is already valid or it is not. If it is not, then we need to add to the axioms: most simply, if not most economically, by simultaneously treating the NL definition as to be translated into an axiom of the metalanguage, as discussed above. As far as any conclusions we may attempt to draw about the language of thought as metalanguage are concerned—there will be none distinct from what is required by the various other construals.

Notes

1. In some ways, it is deviance from functionality which is most interesting. The autonomy of syntax means that there may be arbitrary and non-functional constraints; and also means that there may be the possibility of the exploitation of structures for purposes for which they were not, so to speak, intended (Cormack 1987 explored one such possibility). Conversely, it might be that the exigencies of the grammar were sometimes counter-productive as far as the semantics required by the language of thought is concerned—for instance in demanding syntactic subjects where no semantic subject is wanted, and hence forcing the introduction of expletives. See Chomsky 1990 for discussion of dysfunctional properties of language.

2. If topicalization, for instance, as in *Bananas, I don't really like* is within S-structure, then clearly not all the movement is forced by the imposition of Case or *wh*-scope requirements. The motivation here is nothing to do with grammar, directly, but comes from pragmatically motivated choices. I shall assume that some optional movement is permitted, though I am not sure how to identify S-structure in this case; it would be easier to assume topicalization was a PF-movement rule. Exempt *wh*-phrases include those in echo-questions (which I take to be instances of mention rather than use) and the phrases left *in situ* in multiple questions (see also section 1.1.5). Exclamative phrases and a few others are also subject to S-structure *wh*-movement.

3. A syntactic variable excludes say bound variable pronouns, but might include resumptive pronouns. An alternative rather natural formulation would be that all NP arguments must be simple (*i.e.* not QNP) at LF (see May 1985). This however would require that the definition of 'argument' be changed at LF, with the notion of chain being dropped. Failing a logic defined over chains as units, and assuming that LF is very like the level over which the logic is run, this might indeed be correct. It could be that the notion of argument and type should be defined differently at each level; the differences would serve as part of the characterization of each level.

4. If what is visible to one module is contingent on the dispositions of another module, it appears that some sort of intrinsic ordering may be being imposed. Here we have θ-theory needing in some sense the prior application of Case-theory; or, looking the other way, here is theta-theory telling Case-theory how it should be behaving. In either case, it looks intuitively as though it would be highly unfortunate if the reverse dependency held as well; which puts constraints on the general set-up. In fact it does appear that Case IS dependent

on θ-role, at least to the extent that inherent Case cannot be assigned except to θ-marked elements. We would however need proof that parallel processing in a constraint satisfaction rather than a generative model would indeed object to such a situation. It might turn out that all we have is redundancy, with grammatical sentences.

5. Head-to-head movement for some bound morphemes together with the DP hypothesis offers a neat solution to the analysis of a phrase like [*nothing red*]. We may assume that it is derived from a D-structure [$_{DP}$ [$_{D'}$ *no-* [$_{NP}$ [$_{N'}$ [$_{N'}$ *-thing*] [$_{AP}$ *red*]]]]], and that at S-structure, the head [*-thing*] moves to the next head [*some-*].

6. The necessity for the "first branching node" addition is a consequence, I think, of the bar notation, and may be an artifact. Something more like the categorial grammar slash notation would allow say a verb to be entered as V if it is intransitive, but as V/N (leading to a branching node V) if it is transitive, avoiding at least some spurious branches. The notion of 'lexical' would still be needed, though, presumably as a feature rather than a category. There might still be problems with specifiers, but the only convincing ones, COMP and DET, are best treated as heads.

7. This is true of AP, PP and VP, on standard assumptions. Under the DP hypothesis, we may assume that the subject of N" is in Spec of DP. If we want the subject of VP to be under VP, then it must be generated in an adjoined position.

8. And for obvious reasons, the topmost node of any phrase standing alone is absolved from expecting an argument even if it is a possible predicate. C", typically, and any quoted phrase, or a 'short answer' to a question may have predicational status but no argument.

9. It is not clear what semantic interpretation would give substance to this distinction. Possibly the empty operator corresponds to a simple lambda operator, where a *wh*-NP corresponds to a 'generalized quantifier' version of this. This latter makes a *wh*-determiner equivalent to Curried generalized conjunction.

10. In later sections, I have for brevity and to avoid confusion referred to the output of the syntactic-semantic component as 'LR' (this being, I suggest, a translation from the syntactic level of LF into the Language of Thought), and to the explicature as 'UR' (for 'utterance interpretation'), also expressed in the Language of Thought.

11. Such effort may be with or without immediate justification. Some account needs to be taken of the undoubted fact that I may have an inkling that

Theoretical Preliminaries

something you said was important, and I'll work hard to try to understand you; but I know very well that it may be years before I discover just why it was important.

12. See Haack (1978).

13. One is not intended to infer "B)" or "$\neg$(A" from "($\neg$(A & B))." Without so many brackets, worse things would occur.

14. It would be what was needed if nouns behaved as expected; there are complications, as shown for instance by Bergmann (1982). But in a simple case for instance we may deduce "John is a lecturer" from "John is a lecturer and administrator," but not "No-one is a lecturer" from "No-one is a lecturer and administrator."

15. There are alternatives, one of which is to ensure that "*of a certain kind*" gets construed as *of the giraffe kind*. But this is tantamount to an introduction rule, and no use without the generalization of *and*-elimination to nouns, in effect, since we can only get rid of the *giraffe* subsequently by taking the N-PP as giving something like *animal and of the giraffe kind*. So this is hardly an advance. Keenan and Faltz (1985) suggests that the semantic structure of natural languages is in fact such that suitable environments for elimination rules of this kind are pervasive.

16. The parallel distributed processing models may register input entirely by change of state, and so in the sense I understand, would not be fully representational. It does not follow, however, that the sort of effects typically attributed to a representational model cannot be obtained. For instance, the effect of considering, in consequence of some input, one course of action, but after further thought deciding on another, could be an interpretation of a certain sort of patterning in the settling process of a network.

17. See Rumelhart and McClelland *et al.* 1986.

18. The realization of the internal language must presumably be chemical or physical or both. There is no reason why the representation should not be distributed, even if it is symbolic.

19. Learning the syntax of a particular Natural Language is supposed by Chomsky and others to consist in setting the parameters for that language. It seems unlikely that this would involve hypothesis formation: the usual metaphor is 'triggering'. See Chomsky 1990 for some comments on acquisition of a lexicon.

20. Actually 'P_y' in this version.

21. See Bridge 1977 for a rigorous treatment on these lines.

22. And why would one ever impose an inappropriate meaning postulate? Presumably because natural language reasoning appeared to require such, even though the way the world behaved did not fully support this kind of inference.

23. For a sufficiently detailed exposition, see for example Dowty *et al.* 1981.

24. See Sag *et al.* 1985, Keenan and Faltz 1985, and Partee and Rooth 1983.

25. It acquires this type not intrinsically, but only with respect to the function assigning values to variables introduced by Tarski, which I shall for simplicity take to be encoded in the '| |' function.

26. The seeming paradox of variables having values and yet being subsequently bindable is solved for instance by Tarski's ingenious device of relativizing values to infinite sequences which function as temporary assignments of values to variables. It all comes out in the wash—see Dowty *et al.* 1981.

27. Here I am taking '$\forall x$' and 'λx' to be the operators in question, rather than '$\forall$' and 'λ' within these.

28. Suppose we have in the metalanguage a binary quantifier Q, so that $Q : A \; ; \; B$ is well-formed for A, B sets. Then the corresponding determiner can have as denotation the function named by $\lambda U \, \lambda V \, (Q : U \, ; \, V)$.

For some N' like *cats*, the NP 'Q cats' will be the function given by $\lambda V (Q : \text{cats}' \, ; \, V)$. When variables are included, a mixed notation is often used, where the restrictive term is given with set-membership: we get expressions corresponding to '$[Q(x) \, : \, x \in \text{cats}'] \, [S(x)]$' where the first constituent is a generalized quantifier whose value as a function will be '$\lambda V (Q(x): x \in \text{cats}'; V)$'.

29. Pair quantification is explained in McCawley 1981; it has been exploited by linguists following Lewis 1975. See section 3.4.2.

30. This contrasts with the familiar type-lifting to '$\lambda P \, P(j)$' from extensional Montague semantics. This latter function is of course of type <<e,t>,t>, appropriate for a variable-free situation. That is, it is appropriate for a direct interpretation of an S-structure [NP VP], with the VP having a denotation of type <e,t>, and being the direct argument of the QNP subject.

31. Partee (1986) discusses the type shifting of noun phrases in detail. There are a number of alternative approaches here, some of which are discussed in chapter 4.

32. The semantic repercussions of the notion of 'argument' in a Chomskian grammar were discussed in Cormack 1986b.

Theoretical Preliminaries

33. Alternatively, type-lifting may be applied to the first element f, and then function–argument application used to give a structure like that in (3ii).

34. This is not a necessity, but can trivially be achieved. In natural language, the circumstances under which the possibility would arise would be few, if any. The possibility is that one might want to define a relation R, say "to shave oneself," by '$R(x,y) \Leftrightarrow P(x)$'.

35. See Suppes 1957, 154–9.

36. Pidgin-logic is a purely imaginary language—I make no claims about the possibility of even giving it a consistent interpretation. All that is required is that it makes the idea of some mediation between the formal requirements and natural language definitions plausible.

37. For example, Alston 1968.

38. Natural language does arguably have items approximating to the lambda operator: *wh*-elements and the empty operator. These are not generally *in situ* at S-structure. Carnap (1958, 135) introduces as an abbreviatory device something rather similar: "... the predicate expression '$(\lambda x)(Rxb)$' ... Let us introduce for this predicate expression the shorter form '$R(-,b)$'." Here Carnap's '–' is functioning like our '*something*'.

39. This idealization is hopelessly inadequate in general, but it will serve while we are talking of defined terms, if we assume that the definition is in any case only accepted as such if it does define a 'possible concept'.

40. The same relation will do for all languages if we assume that the naming device differentiates—as it must. So just quotation marks will not do, since we need to differentiate similar strings in different languages. The implicit definition will give the state of knowledge of whatever device holds these clauses at some moment. Plainly I am ignoring all sorts of things that it would be interesting to pursue concerning such questions as what sort of constraints could be placed on the set in order to ensure that additional clauses did not conflict with existing ones, or that conflicts could be resolved (if that is what we do), or anyway to ensure that the whole set functions adequately.

41. Tarski (1931) constructs antinomies based on such clauses, if the string substituted for the variable includes 'semantic' words such as *true*. This need not concern us even if it is insuperable (which it is not), since it is no part of this enterprise to demonstrate that the language of thought—if that is what the metalanguage is—is incapable of generating internal contradictions, or is capable of being given a consistent and non-trivial model. Besides, it is not the language that can generate problems of itself: it is the inference rules which would permit things to go wrong. I take it that Montague's 'English as a formal

language' is a demonstration that it is possible to include at least some 'semantic' terms in the object language without disaster; here, our left hand sentence names are names of sentences in the metalanguage, but they will for our purposes be a restricted subset, since they are going to be just those which translate sentences of English'. If this set is specified beforehand, then if the remainder of the metalanguage is of a higher order than this, then by Tarski's Thesis A, a 'formally correct and materially adequate definition of true sentence can be constructed in the metalanguage'.

42. See Higginbotham 1985 on *bogus* for a model-theoretic interpretation on similar lines (Higginbotham denies that he offers either translational or model theoretic semantics; but it looks to me like the latter where 'the real world' in some sense is the model).

CHAPTER TWO

Dictionary Definitions

> But I have delayed too long over generalities; it is time to enter into details.
>
> Poincaré, *Science and Method*

2.0 Introduction

In this chapter, I investigate some consequences of the assumption that dictionary definitions are put to use as such. Definitions of nouns, adjectives and verbs are looked at in turn. It emerges that the requirement that the definitions are interpretable in isolation has syntactic consequences. In order to account for the distribution of θ-roles, we introduce an extra empty category (2.1.2, 2.2.2; the ideas are taken up in more detail in chapter 4), and to allow V″ complements (2.2.2). These moves will be necessary whatever the function of a definition is taken to be. We find that dictionary definitions are compatible with a conventional view of the purpose and function of definitions, in particular with the view that they enable the definiendum to be eliminated in its every occurrence. Definitions of nouns (2.1) allow a conventional *genus et differentiae* interpretation, under the assumption that modifiers and N′ have type $<e,t>$. When we look at adjectives, we find that almost any category with type $<e,t>$ will serve as a definition (2.2.1–2.2.5; the absence of NP is discussed in 2.2.7). In consequence, elimination in NL could only be at LR (logical representation), a somewhat stripped down LF, with no category labels (section 2.3). There is evidence (2.4.2) that the definition of a non-intersective adjective, does not get assigned type $<e,t>$. Adjuncts to adjectives too must be treated as operators, having type $<p,p>$ (2.1.2), or $<t,t>$ (2.3.5). Some definitions of verbs are used to investigate questions about matching internal and external arguments in definiens and definiendum. The elimination environment seems to have the following properties: arguments are given structurally rather than by labeled roles (2.4.3); subjects are in some sense 'external' relative to internal arguments of the head (2.4.3.1); Case-marking is not a well-formedness condition (2.4.3.2). In addition, pragmatic or procedural effects ensure that there is opacity with respect to the definiens (2.3.2, 2.3.5). Various problems that the lexicographer meets in relation to complements are noted in 2.4.3.2 and 2.5.

A typical entry in a small dictionary juxtaposes the head word with an indication of its syntactic category and one or more words or phrases separated by commas and semicolons. There may be information about pronunciation too, but that will be ignored here. So for example from the Little Oxford Dictionary (1941) we have:

1   *effective, a.*   operative; striking; fit for service; existing

2   *egg, n.*   spheroidal body produced by female of birds, &c., containing germ of new individual

3   *egg, v.t.*   incite, urge on

The convention in many dictionaries is that commas separate alternative indications of the same meaning, and that semicolons separate distinct meanings associated with identical written forms belonging to the same syntactic category. The issues connected with such distinctions are not going to be discussed; they are clearly relevant to the storage and deployment of information related to written words, but they have no direct bearing on the questions concerning the syntax and semantics of natural language or the language of thought.

I shall be assuming that the definition is a piece of English, and as such has to have a syntax and semantics. At best, it will be a single constituent of a suitable kind at every level of syntax, and the LF will have the appropriate sort of interpretation. This requirement—that we can process the definition—is quite separate from the issue of what we do with it when we have got it. The possibility that the syntax might not provide a single constituent is discussed briefly below; there is good reason to suppose we must have coherence at SOME level, but this might be anything from D-structure to LF or LR (unadorned semantic representation in the Language of Thought), or UR (final utterance interpretation).

Since it is the definitions of simple nouns which most closely approximate to the classic *genus et differentiae* pattern, these will be considered first. I shall then consider some adjectives, before turning to verbs and more complicated nouns and adjectives.

2.1 Simple nouns

2.1.1 Typical definitions

In a very small dictionary, the simplest definitions offered will be a single word:

4 *dramatist n.* playwright. LOD

Simple synonymy is relatively rare, if it exists at all; in any case a dictionary which relied on this alone would simply be dividing the lexicon into unrelated equivalence classes. More commonly, we have a phrase containing a noun and one or more additional phrases:

5 *dude* foppish person
6 *spleen* abdominal organ acting on the blood
7 *souwester* waterproof hat with neck flap
8 *drawbridge* bridge hinged for drawing up or drawing aside
9 *bacon* pork which has been salted and dried
10 *backwoods* remote uncleared forest land

(These are all from LOD). In each case, we can see the head noun as supplying the *genus*, and the additional phrases as distinguishing the definiens from among the possible subdivisions of the genus.[1] The structure set up among the nouns appearing in definiens and definienda will be hierarchical, giving hyponymy or the subset relation: a dude is a certain kind of person, a spleen is a certain organ, a souwester is a hat, and so on. The other elements supply the distinguishing properties, with the mode of combination being essentially conjunction: a dude is a person *and* he is foppish; bacon is pork *and* it is salted and dried. If the structure of some part of the lexicon of nouns is genuinely hierarchical, and if the head noun selected in the definiens is always the closest above in the hierarchy, then the whole of that structure will be coded in the set of definitions, since each element will be related to its immediate superordinate.

The additional elements include adjectives, prepositional phrases, *-ing* phrases, *-ed* phrases, and *that*-relative clauses; in one case there is a noun (*forest* in 10). These are the usual repertoire; they may be used singly or in combination. The combination is cooccurrence—to left and right of the head noun as in (6) and (7), or to the left without commas, as in (10); or with conjunction or disjunction.² In a few dictionaries— including C20—definitions of nouns are given with an article, *the* or *a*.

2.1.2 Syntax and semantics

The meaning of the definiens can be understood apparently quite directly, which suggests that the whole forms a grammatical constituent. The modifying phrases are not complements or arguments of the head noun, so they must be attached above the lowest N'. Since no determiner is present, the whole should be an N' constituent (I leave open until chapter 5 the description under the DP hypothesis). The other phrases must be XPs adjoined to the left or the right of N':

11
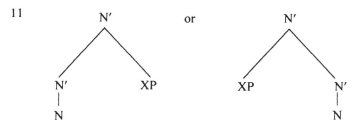

There are two possibilities for the structure where there is more than one modifier: multiple branching or successive adjunction. But if adjunction is the only building operation outside the X' structures, then successive adjunction will be licensed unless special stipulation is made; so we can assume that this is the only possibility.³ The projection principle is going to have nothing to say about the range of XPs; they must be otherwise licensed.

Chomsky (1986a) suggests that at LF every maximal projection must be licensed as an operator, an argument, or a predicate (p.101). Operators bind variables, and variables must be bound by operators; arguments are arguments of some predicate (*i.e.* internal arguments or external), and predicates must have arguments. I take it that 'operator' means 'binding operator', so that adjuncts, which may well be strictly speaking logical operators, are excluded. Let us set aside adjuncts for a moment. Suppose we take this principle to apply to every level, but stipulate that the criteria for identifying categories as belonging to these types may be distinct at different levels. In particular, at D-structure, the identification is canonic by category—lexical or other category-internal information is not available. Instead of lexical information, we have simply X-zero canonically as head. No NP can be licensed as an operator at D-structure, then, since it will not be possible to identify a variable for it to bind. In general, NPs are arguments and VPs are predicates.[4] The idea is to use this intuitively plausible principle to force clauses to have subject positions at D-structure, even when the clause is one where semantically and by θ-role assignment, no subject is required (as for example in *seems* constructions with expletives).[5]

It turns out, as will be shown later, that it is sufficient in all the cases within definitions of nouns to consider adjuncts to be predicates, which are licensed as 'secondary predicates' in some fashion. What this means is that they are not licensed by having their own sister-arguments, but by virtue of adjunction to some other predicate which is so licensed. The weaker position here would be that this is only true syntactically: we may pretend that the categories are predicates, where semantically they might be operators. The stronger position is that the correct semantics is such that the constituent is interpreted as a predicate, too (at least extensionally).

When what we are dealing with is sentences corresponding to propositions, these licensing principles will ensure that at LF, provided that a head has its correct internal arguments, the whole can be reduced to one (or perhaps more) elements of type <t>. If, as in dictionary definitions, we may be generating something other than a sentence, we clearly do not want the principle to apply to the topmost constituent, if this is maximal (nor do we want X' principles to force there to be a maximal projection).[6] The XP elements in (11) do not naturally fall under this principle. Simple-minded semantics suggests that as denoting properties corresponding to sets, they should be canonically predicates, but there is no obvious canonic argument to match. Even if the N' in (11) is maximal (under the DP story), it will not be a canonic argument, since that will now be DP. The XP elements in (11) are apparently distinct in this respect from the corresponding predicates like the AP in (12):

12   John left the room [$_{AP}$ angry]

Here, the Chomsky story (1986a, 97) is that the AP is a predicate licensed by taking as argument the NP *John*; the uniqueness condition on arguments and chains is not violated because there is only a single θ-position in the (one member) chain <John>, and this is all that is required. However, it is clear that we do not have two independent predications on the head NP, for two reasons. Consider

13   No-one left the room angry

This does not mean that no-one left the room and that no-one was angry: the two predications must be conjoined before the meaning is composed with that of the subject NP. Although this would happen if interpretation is made after QR has applied, it seems natural to require that it hold at S-structure too. It is also clear that there is some temporal constraint on the interpretation of [John angry] which corresponds to that given by the tense of the verb in (12), and hence to the content of INFL. If the adjunction is to VP rather than to I″, both these facts are naturally explained:

14   [[No-one] [$_{IP}$[$_I$ *past*][$_{VP}$[$_{VP}$ left the room][$_{AP}$ angry]]]

Let us tentatively assume (to cover our modifiers and the secondary predication in (12) and (13)) that any maximal projection which is syntactically a predicate is licensed as an adjunct if and only if it is adjoined to some independently licensed predicate. Let us further assume that this licensing is applied at all levels.

We need to confirm that all the modifying phrases which occur in our definitions can rationally be assigned to the class 'predicate' at D-structure and at LF.[7] There is no problem about AP and PP: this is their canonic status, so that *foppish* and *with neck flap* are typical. NP can sometimes be predicational, despite its canonic status as an argument (this does not arise here unless *forest* is an NP). Relative Clauses are predicates at LF, in an obvious way, if we interpret the WH element or empty operator as appropriately performing lambda abstraction on some variable. A question arises as to whether the predicational status is identifiable at D-structure. At D-structure, the projection principle requires that complements as specified in the lexicon (and visible at LF) are projected to other levels. If we take it that for a verb like *wonder* taking a [+WH] clause at LF, the clause has to be identifiable as [+WH] at D-structure, then we can similarly assume that Relative clauses are recognizable as [+WH], if features were visible. However, I do not see that this will be necessary: just 'clause', C″, as complement for *wonder* at D-structure (that is, no subcategorial features are visible at this level), with LF taking care of the [+WH] feature will surely suffice.[8] If this is so, then we will have to concede that at D-structure, any clause may in principle be a predicate. Full clauses (C″ [−WH]) are incapable of predicational status, I believe; these will be ruled out at LF.[9]

This leaves us with the *-ing* and *-ed* phrases. These must be either [+WH] clauses, or simple VPs, after we have excluded those *-ed* phrases which should be analyzed as adjectival passives anyway. Consider the phrases in (2) (repeated here):

2   spheroidal body [produced by female of birds], &c.,
    [containing germ of new individual]

The phrase [*produced by female of species*] is not an AP, since adjectival passives do not take *by* agent phrases (Chomsky 1981, 54). The projection principle requires an empty NP after *produced*; this must be properly licensed. The choice seems to lie between (15) and (16):

15   [$_{VP}$ O_i[$_{V?}$ produced e_i by female of birds]]

16   [$_{CP}$ O_i[$_{IP}$ e_i produced e_i by female of birds]]

If it is stipulated that at LF, WH elements (including O_i) must be in pre-IP position (Chomsky 1986b, 5), (15) will be ruled out. If the stipulation is merely the normal reflex of some semantic compositional principle, which seems likely, it might not apply where the VP does not have a containing IP. Adjunction by movement to VP is in general permitted (as argued in May 1985), so we could have 'V?' as VP. However, I shall suggest in chapter 4 that the relevant position in such a construction is in fact the base-generated specifier position, so that 'V?' is V′; for the present I shall show adjunction.

For the phrase *containing germ of new individual*, we could consider:

17   [$_{VP}$ containing germ of new individual]]

18   [$_{CP}$ O_i[$_{IP}$ e_i containing germ of new individual]]

19   [$_{CP}$ O_i [$_{IP}$ PRO$_i$ containing germ of new individual]]

But (19) has no possible D-structure origin.[10] In (18), the subject has a θ-role, and hence the chain in which it lies must have Case, for visibility. Conceivably (and *ad hoc*), Case could be passed from the N' to which the clause is adjoined via the operator O_i. But even if (18) is well-formed, there seems to be no reason to suppose that it will be constructed unless (17), the simpler structure, is ill-formed. If the predicate AP is licensed in (11), then VP would be too. The same argument would lead to the choice of (15) rather than (16).[11]

Similar problems appear to arise in (8), where we have

20   bridge [hinged [$_{XP}$ for drawing up or drawing aside]]

Possible analysis: *hinged* is AP, XP is an adjoined predicate. Alternative: *hinged* is A, XP is its complement clause. And possibly we have a passive participle, V not A. We need to consider what has happened to the object of *draw* (taking the other prepositions as particles; or to the complements of the prepositions *up* and *aside*, alternatively); and we need to consider whether *draw* must have a subject. It is not impossible for a head—*for*—to take a VP complement. However, VP seems unlikely, since the subject role of *draw* is not assigned to the bridge, and in any case we seem to want a PRO$_{arb}$ reading. By contrast, in (15), the subject role is suppressed by the passive morphology. So a PRO subject must be possible. We will then have a parallel with

21   The chicken is [ready O_i [$_{I''}$ PRO$_{arb}$ to eat e_i]]

and we may postulate a D-structure

22   bridge [hinged [for [[PRO$_{arb}$ drawing O up]]]

For (21), the standard account is that we have a complement clause, rather than adjunction. If what we have is a CP complement to an AP, where the CP is [+WH] at LF, in both these structures, the S-structures will be (23) and (24):

23   [$_{AP}$ [$_A$ ready] [$_{C''}$ O_i [$_{C'}$ [$_{I''}$ [PRO$_{arb}$ to eat e_i]]]]

24   [$_{AP}$ [$_A$ hinged] [$_{C''}$ O_i [$_{C'}$ [$_C$ for] [$_{I''}$ [PRO$_{arb}$ drawing e_i up]]]

The possibility that what we have for (22) is a complement clause is incompatible with the intuitive notions of s-selection, unless we argue that any man-made object (including a hinge) is inherently partially specified by its purpose—a knob for turning is just different from a knob for pulling, even though I do not usually bother to give a syntactic realization of this distinction. The possibility of a CP complement structure does not seem probable for (22).

Suppose instead we assume that we have an adjunct, for (22). An interpretation as conjunction will ensure that what is hinged is what is drawn up; in other words the empty operator is by virtue of the adjunction coindexed to whatever the AP on which it is parasitic is indexed to, and the AP and $C''[+\lambda]$ will assign their θ-roles to the same thing. Possibly the tenseless verbs within full clauses give an *irrealis* interpretation: there is a contrast between the potential of being eaten or drawn up, respectively, in (21) and (22), and the assertion of the production and the containing in (15) and (17) respectively. However, there are problems with this putative structure. We do not have any account of the "purpose" reading involved. And, we have a governed PRO.

The purpose reading for (21) came from the inherent meaning of *ready* in respect of its complement; but we have rejected that. Then we should expect to find the meaning in the *for* (unless it were derived entirely pragmatically). Suppose then *for* is a meaning-carrying preposition. Its complement is I think a CP not an NP:

25 [$_{AP}$ [$_{AP}$ hinged] [$_{P''}$ [$_{P'}$ for [$_{C''}$ O_i [$_{C'}$ [$_{I''}$ [PRO$_{arb}$ drawing e_i up]]

CP will provide a barrier to government of PRO by *for*. The "purpose" is carried by the *for*, and a conjunction interpretation of the PP-adjunction gives almost the correct semantics, if the empty operator acts as a role-transmitter. That is, we want to say that the purpose of the hinging is that one should be able to draw the bridge up. Simple conjunction would give us that the purpose of the BRIDGE was that it could be drawn up. So it appears that the adjunct here is an operator on the operand *hinged*, rather than a simple modifier. This is what we should expect of adjuncts to adjectives—otherwise they could simply be modifiers of N', parallel to the adjective. The semantics needed will be possible if *for* as a lexical property takes an XP of type $<e,t>$ (such as *hinged*) as its external 'argument' (operand).

In the examples shown, there are no other matters relating to the syntax that are peculiar to definitions, or on which these constructions can shed any particular light. In (7), we have *with neck flap*. The occurrence of NPs without determiners is of course a syntactically licensed option if determiners are in the SPEC slot; in any case, bare plurals are found frequently, and bare singulars occur, though less commonly outside abbreviated slogans, instructions and so on. It is rather the semantics of these phrases which is in need of explanation, though again there is nothing peculiar to definitions here, so I shall not take this up. The use of a noun as a modifier (*forest* in (10)) is common. If we have adjunction, then by hypothesis the N must be inside N″ or D″, but I shall not discuss the so-called noun–noun compounds or such structures here.

2.1.3 Semantic types for noun modifiers

The simplest extensional story goes as follows: the denotation of the head noun (together with its complements, had it any) is a set; all the other adjoined phrases have properties as their denotation, and these too correspond to sets.[12] Adjunction corresponds to set-intersection, or to generalized conjunction. I shall refer to all these adjuncts as 'modifiers'. In the case of (22), we have adjunction to AP or possibly A′. In either case (failing any use for SPEC in A″) we adjoin to an item of type <e,t>, so that conjunction is possible.

Do all the modifiers plausibly have a set as their denotation? In syntactic terms, any category with one θ-role still to assign should denote a set or property. If the θ-role is external, the category naturally corresponds to a set. This is ordinarily true of APs and PPs,[13] and of non-passive VPs with verbs assigning an external θ-role. If the θ-role still to be assigned is internal, this can only be because the θ-position is bound by an operator corresponding to the lambda operator: either an empty operator or a WH element.

We can assume that property-denoting adjectives intrinsically have type <e,t>, and that prepositions generally have type <e,<e,t>> at LF (if we assume QR) so that PPs have type <e,t>. The *-ing* phrases in (2) and (6) have been argued to be plain VPs, the *-ed* phrase in (2) is a VP with operator O_i, but only this operator and not the passive verb is looking for an argument, so again the whole should be of type <e,t>. The purpose clause in (8) was argued to have an argument subject PRO$_{arb}$, but to have an operator O_i in C″, thus giving it type <e,t>.

Because the adjunction argued for is semantically conjunction or something very similar, and because the theta-marking is in a sense joint, every noun-adjunct construction will yield something of type <e,t>—that is, suited to be a canonic N′. And because the pattern is always one of a head noun together with adjoined modifiers, the whole definition is going to be an N′, like the definiens.

In adjunction which is modification, then, we find that the adjunct is licensed at LF if it is a predicate adjoined under an already licensed predicate. By contrast, the adjunction structure of a small clause involves XP-argument adjunction to a predicate which is semantically licensed as a propositional argument: hence the XP and predicate must be in a predication relationship, yielding a type <t> category.

The articles which appear in some definitions, such as

26 *ivory*   the hard white substance composing the tusks of the elephant   C20

27 *J*   the tenth letter in our alphabet   C20

28 *isle*   an island   C20

will, if treated as binding determiners, render the whole of type <<e,t>,t>, which is not what we need. It seems that we need the articles to be treated as if they were heads of APs, or modifiers. This has been suggested by Higginbotham (1987). The interpretations would be perhaps "one," for *a*, and possibly the metalinguistic "which can be pragmatically identified," for *the*—leaving it totally without a type within our <e>, <t> system. Cormack 1984b discusses the conditions under which a determiner can have an adjectival congener. It is not obvious whether the same kind of explanation will do for (29):

29 *ism*   any distinctive doctrine   C20

There is a possibility that the construal of (29) must appeal to an object-language meta-language distinction: the 'any' is addressed to the user as a metalinguistic comment, rather than as part of the definition proper (and see also section 2.5 for related problems). This interpretation would be induced by the inappropriateness of the straightforward quantificational interpretation of *any*.

2.2 Simple adjectives

2.2.1 Examples

The definitions of adjectives given in a dictionary are much more varied than those of nouns. From a small dictionary, forms such as these are easily found:

1 *deaf*   inattentive
2 *decanal*   of a dean
3 *decided*   not vacillating
4 *dark*   with little or no light
5 *decent*   good enough
6 *decisive*   that decides an issue
7 *decadent*   showing decadence
8 *mortal*   subject to death
9 *mortal*   very great
10 *moribund* likely soon to perish
11 *mouldy*   covered with mould
12 *rickety*   like rickets

Of the dictionary entries given here (all taken from LOD, designated as adjectives, with parts omitted), only half the definitions can be categorized as headed by an adjective, and so as forming items of category A, A' or A". These include (1), (5), and (9), and (8) and (11). Most of the remainder, I shall argue, are categories of predicate phrases, like the noun-modifying phrases discussed in the last section. Prepositional phrases, as in (2) and (4) are frequently used, and *-ing* and *-ed* phrases are common. In (6), the definiens is a relative clause, so that most of the modifying categories are represented. The different syntactic categories will be discussed in turn.

2.2.2 A-projection definitions

Taking first the A-projection phrases, we find as we might expect, single adjectives, as in (1), and adjectives with pre- or post-modifying adverbs, as in (9) and (5), and perhaps (3). These adverbs clearly cannot be treated as having a meaning which is merely conjoined with the head adjective's meaning. In fact, given that the AP's meaning is conjoined with an N', this would be unlikely: such a meaning could just as well be expressed as an adjective. It has been suggested (e.g. Radford 1988) that because they intuitively indicate the quantity of the property ascribed by the adjective, they should be in specifier position like quantifiers for noun projections. Thus *very great* ascribes 'much greatness', *not vacillating* ascribes 'no vacillation' and so on.[14] We would however need to find either direct syntactic motivation for this move, or compositional semantic motivation—or preferably both in parallel. However, they function simply to make new A-meanings out of old ones, and in particular, the predicational status of the adjective is unchanged, so that no binding is involved. So it seems that they are simply adjuncts, but such that their semantic type makes conjunction with the A' impossible. They are essentially operators. On a simplified Montague style system, we could give them category A/A, and a type to match: <p,p>, on the simplest scheme.

In (10), the head adjective *likely* is accompanied by an infinitival phrase. Let us assume that this is the same *likely* as in (13) and (14):

13 It is [likely [that John will escape]]

14 John is [likely [to escape]]

The adjective of (13) is standardly subcategorized as taking a clausal complement, and as assigning no external θ-role. I shall assume that the θ-role may be transmitted compositionally across *be* as across a modal and hence by predication to the subject (small clause complementation for *be* will be discussed later). Since *it* is expletive, there must be no θ-role transmitted. If (13) and (14) have the same *likely*, then we must have (14) as a raising construction, so that the D-structure and S-structure have essentially the following forms:

15 *e* is [$_{AP}$ likely [John to escape]]

16 John$_k$ is [$_{AP}$ likely [e_k to escape]]

It would seem natural to expect the definition in (10) to correspond structurally to the AP constituent in (16). But there is a problem here. In isolation, the AP is not a well-formed LF phrase: it contains half a chain, or an unbound variable. Either the definiens does have a coherent LF, in which case it is not just like the AP in (16), or in fact it does not, but consists of say two LF phrases, whose juxtaposition can nevertheless be interpreted. Let us consider these two options.

Suppose [*likely soon to perish*] does indeed have a coherent LF. Since the whole is to assign an external θ-role, as the adjective *moribund* does, and since *likely* in itself does not do this (as is clear in (15)), we will expect an empty operator. The operator then can bind the variable in the lower subject position, perhaps via an intermediate trace:

17   O_i [likely [e_i soon to perish]]

We will assume that this structure arises through movement, and for the moment that the operator is adjoined to the AP. The question then arises as to whether this structure would be well-formed if it were embedded in a full sentence, and if so whether it is the only correct form then. That is, should we have not (16) with its A-chain at LF, but rather

18   John is [$_{AP}$ O_i [likely [$_{IP}$ e_i soon to perish]]]

with a normal predicational relation between *John* and the AP. If so, the notion that θ-roles must be assigned to A-chains is unnecessary, at least in this case.[15] It could be argued that the structure of (18) is more complex than that of (16), and so would not be constructed during any processing of (14), but that assumes that the assigning of θ-roles to chains is itself 'free' or at least not complex in the same way. It could also be argued that the structures in (17) and (18) are ill-formed because the operator is not outside IP. I shall argue in detail in chapter 4 that a θ-role (more or less equivalent to the empty operator) may land in a Specifier position of a major category. Until then, the reader may construe the structures offered as indications of what sort of effects we need to allow for.

Suppose, contrariwise, that we say that the definiens in (10) has no coherent LF. But it has a straightforward semantic interpretation: let us call this its SR. The SR is built from the two LF constituents we have: [*likely*] and [*soon to perish*]. Assuming that these have the semantic types appropriate for forms like (14) and (15), we have *likely* as a <t,t>, and *soon to perish* as an <e,t>. These can be combined by the rule of function composition, a rule which seems very natural.[16] Using '∘' to denote this operation, we obtain as SR,

19   [likely]∘[soon to perish]

This in turn is truth-conditionally (pretending simple extensional semantics is the right model) equivalent to (20):

20   λx [likely [x soon to perish]]

So we obtain something which corresponds to the supposed SR for (17), but without postulating that (17) as an LF exists. The same question can be asked as was asked for the first option, though: if this representation (as in (19)) is real, why is it not used directly in (16)? An Extended Categorial Grammar approach, like the 'extra operator' approach, will allow us to dispense with the NP chain. The effect of using function-composition on the two constituents is to pass the unassigned θ-role of the VP up to the AP constituent. Since compositional assignment of θ-roles is necessary in GB theory anyway (e.g. V' not V assigns subject role; and *easy to please* constructions), there seems no good reason not to use this mode of assignment here, within GB theory rather than Extended Categorial Grammar. So an alternative will be to have *likely* subcategorized to take a VP complement, but preserving its semantic type (which we may associate with its s-selection properties) as in the case where it has a clausal complement. The structure will be

21   John is [AP likely [VP soon to perish]]]]

The external θ-role of the lower VP passes to the AP and then to the upper VP, from which it is assigned to the sister NP *John*.

Another possible machinery is Williams' 'vertical binding', which he says is 'a kind of lambda abstraction', but which is shown just by coindexing (Williams 1987). The index for an external argument of some head gets carried up a particular projection, and may be passed to another projection; finally it may be passed across to a sister NP by predication.

It seems to me that we do not want to introduce distinct mechanisms unless we can see that distinct principles apply: if the behavior of the empty operator is distinct from that of binding operators (like ordinary quantifying NPs) and also distinct from the behavior of *wh*-NPs which have the same semantic type (and crucially, in a way that cannot be explained just by their being empty) then maybe we might usefully have a distinct notation. Williams' use of indices however implicitly indicates that the processes involved have something in common with other indexing devices (as does the use of indexing for various distinct processes in the GB format). In fact, the licensing of the eventual binding or θ-role discharging of an empty NP embedded in some phrase is governed by the usual restrictions on binding from outside the phrase. That is, we cannot for instance have

22   many men [hard to find the suit which fits *e*] use tailors

supposedly meaning 'many men who are such that it is hard to find a suit which fits them, use tailors'. The explanation is immediately available if we assume that the empty category must be licensed under the usual binding conditions. An appeal to 'vertical binding' as being 'rather like lambda abstraction' does not give us this, since

23   λx [hard to find the suit which fits x]

would be perfectly well-formed in the obvious logic. This same argument militates against the use of any device like composition of functions in a purely logical way: if it were used, it would have to be within the syntax as part of a properly constrained Combinatorial or Extended Categorial Grammar so that necessary effects of the binding principles were preserved. Within a standard GB framework, we obtain some of the required constraints on the transmission of θ-roles by assuming that there are A-chains. Another part is left to the 'compositional assignment' of a θ-role (Chomsky 1981, 148, note 110), which has not only not been much investigated, but where the θ-roles frequently do not even have any visible locus.

To make the question more concrete, take *John is likely to perish*. There are two possible syntactic structures, which are, with some simplification and a little ornamentation

24   John$_\theta$ θ_4 [$_{VP}$ is θ_3 [$_{AP}$ likely θ_1 [$_{VP}$ to *(θ)* perish]]]]

25   John$_\theta$ θ_4 [$_{VP}$ is θ_3 [$_{AP}$ likely θ_2 [$_{IP}$ e_θ θ_1 [$_{VP}$ to *(θ)* perish]]]]

We need to compare these with *John is mortal*:

26 John$_\theta$ θ_4[$_{VP}$ is θ_3[$_{AP}$ *(θ)*mortal]]]]

(In all these, I have shown θ-roles in adjoined positions for clarity). In each of these three, what needs to be explained is how the θ-role originating on an X-zero lexical item, (which I have shown by *(θ)* on that category) is assigned to the upper subject *John* (shown by subscript θ on *John*). The standard story for (26) is that the role at *(θ)* passes compositionally (I suppose) to θ_3 and then to θ_4, and from θ_4 by sister-to-sister predication to *John*$_\theta$. For (25), presumably we would have transmission of the sort just described within the lower clause, to get to the subject e_θ. From here, if the transmission is directly to *John*, the landing sites between are unneeded.[17] This last link forms an A-chain, and so is subject to Binding Theory Principle A. Movement, amounting to transmission of the role, is forced by failure of Case-assignment at e_θ. If we had rather (24), the role must pass from θ to θ_1, and then as before.

The problem with definitions of the kind we have for *moribund* is that substitution necessitates a θ-role assigner at the position θ_3, because this and what follows must be the LF structure of the definiens. For structure (25), I suggested that the transmission to the subject *e(θ)* is as usual; but suppose now that this subject is the trace of an empty operator which moves to θ_2, heading an A-bar chain. Subsequent links to θ_4 can be construed indifferently, it would appear, as compositional transmission or movement, if we regard the empty operator as, roughly, an external-θ-role assigner. The final link is as in (26), predication. In the alternative, (24), we need neither A-chains nor A-bar chains at any point. If my treatment of elimination is correct, one or other of these two analyses must be permitted by the grammar.

One way of side-stepping the need to make any decision about which of these moves is correct is to say that they are all notational variants. If the conditions on A-chains, A-bar-chains, and compositional transmission were all identical this would certainly hold. But one of two things might force a choice. One would be to show that there are actual syntactic or semantic consequences arising from the subject NP in (16) or (18) being part of a chain or the subject of predication. For instance, mixed conjunction might be barred; or VP anaphora might not be possible with chains—and the absence of any such evidence might be taken as showing that there should not be any difference in status. The other would be the unlikely arrival of evidence about what sort of notation the brain could handle—just suppose that the link needed between operator and variable in (17) could predict a limit to how much material could intervene in processing—and that the unlinked form in (19) would not predict any limit.

Conjunction of mixed cases is indeed fairly awkward. To show we do not have some sort of lazy ellipsis, we need quantified NPs:

27   No-one seemed to be running but really walked

VP anaphora is certainly possible with these phrases: *John is likely to come, and so is Bill*—but what conclusions should be drawn is hardly clear, since the representational level giving an appropriate value to the ellipsed VP is not adequately established.

For the present, I shall assume that both (18) and (21) (with structure as in (24) are legitimate alternatives to (16). The question will be taken up when further examples of adjectives followed by infinitives have been discussed, and in rather more precise claims will be made in chapter 4.

Definiens consisting of head adjective and infinitival phrase are common. Other examples are

28	*dainty*	hard to please	LOED
29	*deceptive*	apt to mislead	LOED
30	*disputable*	able to be disputed	

The adjective *hard* does not behave the same way as *likely*, although the two appear in some superficially similar sentences:

31   i   John is hard/likely to please

   ii   It is hard/*likely for us to please John

   iii   John is likely/*hard to please Mary

The standard S-structure analysis of *John is hard to please* is

32   [John$_i$ is hard O_k [PRO$_{arb}$ to please e_k]

where the empty object is a variable bound by the operator O_k. Of the relation between the operator and *John*, Chomsky (1986a, 109) says that the variable must be 'strongly bound', roughly, bound by an antecedent giving some set-content as well as quantificational content, and that the only available antecedent is *John*, which is "in a structurally appropriate position, as the subject of the predicate ..., for general reasons. ... It follows, then, that $i=k$." (Chomsky is considering the sentence *John is too stubborn to talk to*; the problem is why the empty operator is not like a subcategorized feature [+WH]. (I discuss the difference in chapter 4). It seems possible that Chomsky would have indicated that *hard* assigns a θ-role to [*John*]: in a footnote in Chomsky 1981, (p 148, note 110), he apologizes for referring to *easy* in similar sentences as dyadic, and says "Rather *easy* and *certain* assign a θ-role to their clausal complement and take part in the compositional assignment of θ-role to the matrix subject." Rothstein (1989) explores degree phrases with empty operators making similar but more detailed claims about the transmission of the θ-role. If we take it that *easy* assigns no external θ-role, then [*John*] is getting its θ-role only from the operator, but the possibility of expletive subjects is accounted for. If the final structure is just as in (32), we could give the phrase *hard to please* which is the definiens in (28) a coherent S-structure or LF:

33   [$_{AP}$ hard O_k [PRO$_{arb}$ to please e_k]]

But this has a θ-type obtainable only compositionally. Alternatively, we might suppose that the operator could move further, giving

34   [$_{AP}$ O_k [hard t_k[PRO$_{arb}$ to please e_k]]]

Here the effect of composition has been provided by the further movement. Provided *hard* is subcategorized to take a clausal complement, and to assign no external θ-role, the phrase in (34) will have the proper θ-role-assigning properties for a predicate through the empty operator which heads it: it will have type <e,t>. If (34) is well-formed, as it must be, then it seems likely that further leftward movement of the operator should be permitted, so that the θ-role is eventually transmitted by predication from the pre-VP position.[18] This renders the small clause story apparently redundant—but see chapter 4.

The constructions with *apt* and *able* by contrast can only have the embedded subject associated with the matrix subject.

35   John is apt/able [to snore]/[*to talk to]

There is an apparent object gap in (29), repeated here:

29   *deceptive*   apt to mislead

The intended reading is roughly "apt to mislead people"; the gap does not indicate that *deceptive* has an external θ-role to assign. Object gaps, whatever their syntactic status,[19] are common in circumstances where terse writing is desirable. The typical examples come from instructions:

36 Store *e* in a cool dry place

However, the interpretation in (36) is not indefinite, but specifically referring to the contents of the container on which the instruction is written. It is not clear whether this discrepancy has a lexical or pragmatic explanation; the relation of intransitive to transitive normally involves an apparent existential quantification of the transitive object, as we see with *eat*,[20] so we may have an intransitive of this sort.

The syntax of the defining phrases in (29) and (30) then might be expected to follow one or other of those given for *likely to perish* above, since they follow *likely* in (31). However, since for neither *apt* (in this sense, with an exception noted below) nor *able* is a construction with expletive *it* possible, these two would need to be subcategorized to take VP complements only. We could alternatively say that *apt* and *able* c-select for an external argument (*John*), and an internal VP argument,[21] or an external NP and an internal C" or I". These offer the correct move for *able*, I think, and I will return to them shortly. Under the first suggestion, although subcategorized for VP, the item may still semantically select for a proposition, in the same way as *likely*. The effect will be to force the transmission of the external θ-role of the complement VP through onto the matrix subject, which then cannot be expletive. There are three good reasons for accepting this alternative for *apt*. One is that intuitively, the meanings of *apt* and *likely* are extremely close; but *likely* must (for (13)) s-select a proposition, so that a solution which has *apt* s-selecting a proposition is to be preferred. The second is that there is a principle put forward by Higginbotham (1985) that no argument should be unsaturated. I am certainly suggesting that a VP complement may be c-selected (and it will normally have type <e,t>), but I am all the same under the *likely* version, stipulating that the adjectives s-select only for items of type <t>, propositions, or for <e>, entities, in relevant cases. The third is that the following are grammatical:

37 It is apt to rain on Sundays

38 It is apt to seem that John is a fool

If the *it* in (37) or in (38) is expletive, then it is clear that *apt* may have the type <t,t>. There is dispute about the subject for *weather* verbs, but none about *seems*. Since we do have an account consistent with the type <t,t> for the previous sentences, it would be wrong to postulate dual type, especially since the meaning is intuitively identical. It is just because there is no external θ-role assigned by the VP [*to seem that John is a fool*] that an expletive subject appears (untypically) with this meaning of *apt*.

Further, it seems right that the parsing process has to postulate as little structure as is compatible with the theory, so that VP is to be preferred over IP in any case where that is possible (as in the *likely* analysis). The cost in terms of the lexicon is that there is a discrepancy between s-selection and c-selection for these adjectives. The entries for internal arguments must be as follows:

39 | **item** | **s-selection** | **c-selection**
| --- | --- | --- |
| *likely* | <t> | C" [(*that*)] or V" [*to*] |
| *apt* | <t> | V"[*to*] |

We would like some explanation of the s- and c-selection possibilities.

Let us return to *able*. Replacing *apt* with *able* in (37) and (38) gives a dubious result in the first case and a thoroughly ungrammatical one in the second. The implication is that the adjective does not simply s-select for a proposition. Our intuitions too suggest that *able* is not a clause-operator—partly because agency seems essentially involved. If *John* is the underlying subject, then the internal argument is VP or clause. If arguments must be saturated at s-selection, then the former is apparently ruled out. How then do we account for the absence of any subject except PRO (controlled by [*John*]) in the embedded clause? If we consider something like *John is able for Mary to see him*, it appears that the answer lies in the meaning of *able* itself, in some further level of semantics. There is a sense in which *able* is a relation between a person (typically) and a predicate on that person, rather than a relation between a person and an independent proposition. In chapter 4 (section 4.1.2, in relation to $stupid_2$) I argue that it is possible to set up s-selection and c-selection choices to account for such constructions, and there is some discussion of how the range of possibilities for s- and c-selection in natural language might be constrained.

The definition in (30) can be compared interestingly with (40)

40   *debateable*   subject to dispute   LOD

I take it that *dispute* here is a noun (and NP), rather than a verb: it could be modified by an adjective like *acrimonious* for instance. But conceptually, it is clearly closely related to the verb, and the arguments of the verb, agent and subject of dispute, can be incorporated into an NP headed by the noun:

41   The judges disputed [the findings]/[about the findings]

42   There was little dispute ?of/about the findings by the judges

It appears that there is a similar process in action with the empty or implicit arguments of the noun *dispute* in (40) as there is with the overtly missing but syntactically present arguments of *eat* in (43):

43   The chicken is ready [e_1 to eat e_2]

That is, because there are two arguments, it is the subject which must get an 'arbitrary person' reading, and the object which must be associated with some external argument. The result is that we could approximately paraphrase (44) by (45):

44   The route is subject to dispute

45   Some persons dispute the route

but

46   John disputes some things

cannot be rendered by

47   John is subject to dispute

whereas

48   John is subject to grief

can be related closely to

49   John grieves

Dictionary Definitions

As we would expect, then, a sentence like *Chickens are subject to eating* has two readings (even if neither are very felicitous), as does *Chickens are capable of improvement*. I leave the syntactic description here entirely open—noting merely that it has been suggested (Chomsky 1982, 99) that a PRO-like element may be needed in the SPEC (subject) position for abstract nouns.

In example (8), we have *mortal* defined as '*subject to death*'. Here we have an adjective with a PP complement—where the *to* is a designated preposition which could be taken as a Case-marker of what is essentially a NP argument. The congeneric verb *subject* takes the same Case-marker:

50 They subjected him to a long inquisition

The other preposition which typically marks (and indeed Case-marks) an argument is of course *of*. We find, for example,

51 *dead*   devoid of force   LOD

52 *edacious* fond of eating   LOD

But both these fall under the 'designated preposition' noted above, most probably. The PP is not omissible (at least, not without change of meaning), and unlike the well-known cases of [*of* NP] complements to nouns such as *destruction*, there are no verb congeners. I have not (yet) found any adjectival parallel to such a noun. (See also the discussion of *like* as possibly assigning Case without a preposition, in 2.2.5 below).

2.2.3 Participles

The *-ing* and *-ed* phrases in (7) and (11) (repeated here)

7   *decadent* showing decadence

11 *mouldy*   covered with mould

can be analyzed as VPs in the same way as the comparable modifying phrases discussed above in the section on nouns. The structures will be

53 [$_{VP}$ showing decadence]

and

54 [$_{VP}$ O_i [covered t_i with mould]]

Note that the phrase in (54) will now combine in a full sentence with the copula *be* say just as an AP would, compositionally assigning the external θ-role derived from the operator to the subject. Then again we would have no need for the θ-role to be assigned to a chain, in a passive construction, as in the raising construction discussed above. If the whole is to function as a predicate even when it is (as in the earlier examples) functioning as an adjunct to an AP, there is no possibility of having a chain anyway: we must have something like the operator.[22] Williams' vertical binding or Higginbotham's θ-role discharging would have to be considerably adapted to deal with these cases where the extra role arises essentially from an internal variable.

It may be that *vacillating* in (3) (repeated here),

3 *decided* not vacillating

is a verb rather than an adjective, in which case we have an adverb–verb modification. There are however plenty of examples where the head is certainly an adjective, as for instance in

55 *light* not heavy (LOD)

2.2.4 Relative clauses

In example (6) (repeated here),

6 *decisive* that decides an issue

there is no doubt we have a full clause, not just a VP, but the semantic type is unproblematic. A relative clause always has either a WH element or an operator, either of which will have the required lambda operator interpretation, giving the type of a predicate to the clause. Another example is

56 *necessary* that must be done (LOD)

There do not seem to be examples with WH relatives.

2.2.5 Prepositional phrase

The definiens in (2) and (4) given as prepositional phrases are syntactically unproblematic at D- and S-structure: we simply have preposition followed by NP, as shown in (57) and (58):

57   *decanal*   [$_{PP}$ [$_P$ of] [$_{N''}$ a dean]]

58   *dark*   [$_{PP}$ [$_P$ with] [$_{N''}$ little or no light]]

If we take the *like* in (12) (repeated below),

12   *rickety*   like rickets

as a preposition, then here too we simply have a PP. If we were to take it as an adjective,[23] then we would have to explain why the apparent complement NP had no Case marker, since in general it seems that adjectives do not assign Case directly to their complements:

59 i   destroyed morale

    ii   destruction *of* morale

    iii destructive *of* morale

However, if adjectives can assign arbitrary Cases to their complements, which are realized in the form of prepositions, as I suggested for *subject* in (8), there seems no particular reason to suppose that all the Cases that adjectives can dispose must be realized by prepositions. The problem that would arise is the parallel between verbal and adjectival forms: it appears from (59) that at least sometimes, the direct object of the verb does need a preposition for the corresponding adjective. With *like*, there is no corresponding verb. There was however at one time an acceptable and possibly obligatory preposition *to* in the comparable use—the Oxford English Dictionary quotes Shelley: "sweet sleep, were death like to thee"; which suggests that an adjectival category is probable. It also asserts that the bare NP which follows is a dative, so there would be no conflict with the direct object's requiring an *of*.

Each of these prepositional phrases will have to have a well-formed LF, and this requires that any quantified NPs have been moved out of argument positions. It is just possible that both mass terms and bare plurals are effectively non-quantified, and are not subject to QR. It is possible that the PP in (2) is properly an NP with *of* as a Case-marker so that we do not expect QR from the inside of the PP to the outside. In the LOD, *of* is by far the commonest preposition heading adjective definitions, and even with the others, the following NPs are overwhelmingly determinerless, apart from the definite article marking inalienable possession. But there are definitions with real prepositions followed by plausible QNPs:

60 *binocular* with two eyes (C20)

61 *penniless* without a penny (C20)

If the NPs are QNPs, we must presumably have forms like

62 [$_{PP}$ [a penny]$_i$ [$_{PP}$ without t$_i$]]

There does not seem to be anywhere the QNP could move to other than adjoined to the PP. However, maybe both the indefinite article and the *two* are adjectival here, and QR is unnecessary. Certainly it is not possible to construct scope effects with these particular examples.

2.2.6 Noun phrases

The syntactic categories of the definiens given so far are not surprising in as much as they correspond to predicates. More surprising are a few definitions given in terms of incomplete noun phrases:

63 *most* the greatest number or quantity of

64 *much* a great amount of

In fact, although these are designated as adjectives by the LOD, and indeed in the OED and Chambers (1959) or Longman (1984), in the usage for which the definition is appropriate, there is good reason to believe the items are determiners. In particular, in a sentence like

65 Most birds can fly

where the *most* seems to correspond correctly to the definition offered in (63), the semantics needed is irreducibly determiner-like. That is, the semantics is that of a binary quantifier, and cannot be reduced to adjectival behavior.[24] There is an adjectival use of *most*, as we see in

66 I've got the most apples

Dictionary Definitions

but that use is not the one for which the definition offered in (63) is appropriate. The larger dictionaries do give definitions suited to this adjectival use as well as ones appropriate to the determiner use; for instance

67 *most*   greatest in quality or extent   LDEL

This comes from Longman (1984), and is given under the same head as the determiner version. The superlative of an adjective is still an adjective, so what we have here is a definiens with an adjective head *greatest*.

2.2.7 Why are definiens not necessarily APs?

It seems clear that what has been exploited for Adjective definiens is a large portion of the range of possible N' adjuncts. These are semantically characterized by having type <p> or <e,t>. Two questions suggest themselves: are the phrases of type <p> and the class of possible adjuncts to N' coextensive? and are all of either class exploited in definiens?

The answer to the first question is certainly 'no'. The most notable category whose elements are normally of type <p> is N itself. But N is excluded for the simple reason that modifiers must be XPs. The simplified type for an NP is <e>; a QNP *in situ* might need type <p,<p,t>>. However, as mentioned in section 1.4.5, it is possible for an NP to act as a predicate, as in

68 He left the room [a sadder and wiser man]

But all the same, we cannot use an NP with a determiner to modify a noun:

69 *Some [dogs [a/some/all spaniel(s)]] came bounding across

Parenthetical and attributive NPs function if anything as NP rather than noun or N' modifiers:

70 Some dogs, all spaniels, came bounding across

71 My uncle, a retired psychiatrist, is a Spaniard

72 The spaniel, a hunting dog, makes a good pet

It is clear that the NPs are at least not restrictive modifiers. There should be some explanation of this—it is not something one would wish just to stipulate, if possible. The explanation I think may lie in pragmatics. It appears that there are processes for which a differentiation between noun and adjective in a simple [AP N] construction is used. In my formulation of the semantics, this is going to disappear: for [small ball] we will simply get (ignoring the problems of 'relatively small for a ball' something effectively like 'x∈small & x∈ball'. But it is well-known that presuppositional effects exist: if something is asserted to be not a small ball, then we are likely to construe this as implying that although a ball, it is not small, rather than that although small, it is not a ball.[25] This differentiation must be triggered either by the head-modifier distinction, or by the noun–adjective distinction, or possibly by an X-zero versus X-maximal distinction. It is not triggered by surface order, since postmodifiers act like premodifiers in this respect.

What is interesting about this is not just the question as to how to characterize correctly the pragmatic processing done by the hearer of such a phrase, but the question of whether the requisite distinction is preserved in the language of thought itself (even by some different means, such as ordering). If, as seems more likely, the distinction rests on a head-modifier relation, then the problem of why NPs are not used as modifiers is unsolved. What is answered is rather why we have the head-modifier relation in the first place, rather than using conjunction directly and overtly all the time. We want to take advantage of the asymmetry;[26] though that still does not explain why it is the N' meaning which is generally preserved while the other is what is assumed to be denied. It is not likely that what we have is a convention of any kind. At least for English, the 'decision' as to whether to code some property as a noun or an adjective appears to depend in part on how changeable that property is with respect to an identifiable individual. Relatively stable properties tend to get coded as nouns; less stable ones as adjectives. But that description begs the question in a sense, because what I have assumed is the notion of an individual, and there seems something much more plausible about an individual 'apple' than an individual 'red'. Besides, it is more likely to be the stability of correlation of important but not directly identifiable properties with readily identifiable properties that is at issue. Edibility is not in itself

Dictionary Definitions

recognizable, but it has a more stable correlation with the properties of 'being an apple', than with 'being red'; hence the relegation of 'red' to the category of modifiers, while 'apple' is the head for any reference to or quantification over individuals. If this line of argument has any validity, we would expect this distinction to be preserved in the language of thought.

Under the DP hypothesis, what we should be asking is not why DPs do not turn up as adjective definiens, but why N″ does not. One possibility is that it does, in a 'noun-noun' structure; but here it is rarely the case that the semantic relation between the head and its 'modifier' is one of conjunction. That is, in compounds like *lawn mower*, *chair leg*, *garden party*, the set of items is a subset of mowers, but not of lawns; of legs, but not of chairs; of parties, but not of gardens, and so on. In many cases, we arguably do not have a modifier at all, but rather have an argument to the head noun in Specifier position. *Sheep dip* has plausibly an object fronted; and so does *lawn mower*; since we have *leg of a chair*, it looks as if *chair leg* falls under the same pattern. But it is not plausible that the location of a party is an inherent argument of *party*; if temporal and spatial adjuncts may anyway move to Specifier position, however, we may use the same suggestion. Certainly *Last year's destruction of the city* is grammatical, and we do similarly have both *The weekend's outing* and *Weekend outings*. In that case, it seems likely that *garden party* too is a Spec-head construction. The lack of possessive marking may be connected with the 'bare N' form (*i.e.* lack of determiner and plural potential). It seems to be a characteristic of 'relational' rather than 'verbal' types of nouns, so that the possessive marking only appears on fronted internal arguments of nouns which may assign a subject θ-role, suggesting an explanation along the lines of Burzio's generalization (Chomsky 1986a, 139). (We may have 'the city's destruction' or possibly coin 'city-destruction', but we cannot have 'lawn's mower', and 'John's mower' is merely an adjectival possessive).

The idea that 'adjunction gives conjunction' is simply the spelling out of the semantics of adjunction. It need not operate where there is a designated category of adjunct (*i.e.* we can and do have adjectives which are semantic operators on their head nouns, or adverbs which are semantic operators on their head adjectives). But for other categories pressed into use, conjunction will be the only interpretation available.

Then the strings above are plausibly XP-N, but cannot be adjunction structures, and must be SPEC-head constructions. The only exceptions will be fixed collocations (idioms)—see section 3.2. Apparent exceptions, like *prince-bishop*, or *washer-dryer*, possibly restricted to properties which correspond to some function of the entity, have to be taken as N–N combinations.

The explanation for the absence of N″ modifiers may lie in the fact that if we had simply an N or N′ dressed up as an N″ for purposes of satisfying X-bar restrictions, then there is no reason why simple conjunction of the head N′ and the putative modifier should not be used. It does appear to be generally the case that if two categories match sufficiently, conjunction rather than adjunction is to be used.[27]

73   John left the room angry / in a temper / torn with indecision

74   John is in a temper *in a hurry / *angry / *torn with indecision

75   John is in a temper and in a hurry / angry / torn with indecision

So in general, an N″ definiens will not do, because N″ does not function as a modifier.

The lack of noun-headed modifiers leads, anyway, to their absence as AP definiens. This results in some rather roundabout definitions in just those cases where an NP would be most appropriate:

76 *precatory*   of the nature of a request   C20

77 *crystalline* having the structure of a crystal   C20

78 *cubical*   cube-shaped   LOD

79 *canine*   of the nature or qualities of a dog

If something has the nature of a request, it is a request; if it has the structure of a crystal, it is a crystal; if it is cube-shaped, it is a cube, and if it has the nature or qualities of a dog (at least, if it has all of them and was not a construct of Putnam's imagination) then indeed it is a dog. It is true that most of such definitions at least in the larger dictionaries either give only, or go on to add, the possibility of likeness rather than identity:

80 *feline*   pertaining to the cat or the cat kind: *like a cat*   C20

Dictionary Definitions 113

(The first part of the definition here is not relevant). But I do not see that we need to understand the first set of definitions that way; in fact it is not part of the dictionary's business to allow for non-literal use, and I fail to see why it should do so for adjectival uses any more than for noun uses. The fact that adjectives if used non-literally may be felt to be less metaphorical than nouns used non-literally presumably has a pragmatic explanation, connected with the differences between noun and modifier which was needed above.

In the compositional semantics suggested for [$_{N'}$ [N' AP], which is simply conjunction at N' level, no provision has been made for there to be such a thing as a 'non-restrictive modifier', despite the fact that it has been argued that say preposed adjectives may be restrictive or non-restrictive (*the lazy Greeks*), and that relative clauses and perhaps other post-modifying phrases may be used non-restrictively. The reason is that in definitions, practically all modification is restrictive, contributing to the *genus et differentiae* pattern. Non-restrictive modification provides extra information, which must then be encyclopedic, and which may well be considered irrelevant to a proper definition. The question of the eliminability of an adjective from a non-restrictive position might still arise, however, if there were anything distinctive about that position in relation to either syntax or semantics.

2.3 Elimination of simple nouns and adjectives

2.3.1 Necessity for elimination

For every noun defined, we found that the definiens was a constituent of category N'. Since a simple noun is just one where N' does not branch, the lexical item is effectively under N'. This means that wherever the definiendum goes in some well-formed expression at any level of the grammar, so would the definiens equally fit.[28] This will be true even of a level at which semantic types are checked. As it happened, all the definitions were of the *genus et differentiae* type, where the head noun was simple anyway: the N' level was reached on account of the modifying adjuncts. The same substitutability preserving well-formedness does not apply to the adjective definitions. There are for a start at least three distinct environments in which APs occur: as noun modifiers, as predicates after the copula, and as predicates in small clauses. The same set do not occur equally in all these positions. The noun modifiers may also be placed either before or after the head noun, or may even be discontinuous. And as we have seen, adjectives may be defined by PPs, VPs or relative clauses, and these do not have the same distribution as APs.

It seems plausible, then, that dictionary definitions are put to use as 'word–word' constructs. I shall consider this possibility in some detail below. Much of what is said is just as relevant to construal as 'word–meaning' definitions, but discussion of this kind of interpretation will mostly be postponed until chapter 5.

If a word–word definition is to be put to any use, it must permit the elimination of the definiendum from any environment in which it occurs, with the definiens entering instead, in such a way that the whole is still a well-formed formula. It seems clear that such an elimination must be attainable at least at some level of semantic representation: either SR or UR (semantic representation of the sentence or phrase; utterance interpretation). If SR is close in form to LF, then we might expect eliminability at LF; and indeed we might expect elimination at any and every level to be possible. Alternatively, it might be that elimination at say D-structure would lead to well-formed associated LF, SR and UR, without direct elimination being possible at any of the latter levels. What, then, happens to adjective definiens? I shall discuss first the elimination of adjectives in attributive position, since for various reasons this is often considered to be the canonic position.

2.3.2   Elimination of adjectives from attributive position

If we consider attributive adjectives, it is at once obvious that there can be no direct elimination at the surface string (PF). To take one example, *a dark room* is not grammatically equivalent to *a with little or no light room*. It appears that substitution must be at a level at which either left and right adjunction are equivalent—just adjunct status—or a level at which the adjuncts are all on the same side of the head. Neither S-structure nor LF have these properties.

Could elimination be at D-structure? Let us suppose for the moment that all these modifiers are base generated to the right of the N' when used attributively. This is a natural assumption.[29] Then of the

Dictionary Definitions

phrases offered as definiens in (1), (5), (9) and (28) of section 2.2, repeated here

1 *deaf*   inattentive
2 *decent*   good enough
3 *mortal*   very great
4 *dainty*   hard to please

we would need to explain the following changes at surface:

5 a [boy [inattentive]]   ⇒   an [[inattentive] boy]
6 a [meal [good enough]]   ⇒   a [[good enough] meal]
7 a [terror [very great]]   ⇒   a [[very great] terror]
8 a [girl [hard to please]]   ⇒   a [[hard] girl [to please]]

Note that some adjectives, like *apt* and *able* (as in (29) and (30) of (2.2)) do not behave like *hard* from (4): the phrase remains continuous, as in

9 Any fact able to be disputed should be disputed

These contrasts are discussed in chapter 4. We can combine the adverb *very* with the *hard* in (8), giving

10 a girl very hard to please ⇒ a very hard girl to please

In this case, the movement is optional. If we assume that *very* is an adjunct and that the clause [*to please*] is a complement, then *very hard* is not a constituent. This suggests double movement: first of the whole modifier [*very hard to please*] to the pre-head position, and then a movement of the complement [*to please*] to the right of the head (or N′) again. Then after this movement, the traces will be bound by their antecedents in such a fashion as to permit proper interpretation from an S-structure or LF derived in this way. We must assume that [very hard to please] has a structure allowing the empty operator at its head, as argued in section 2.2 (see example (33) there).

11 $[O_k$ [very hard $[t_k$ [PRO$_{arb}$ to please e_k]]]]

Then for the right hand of (10), we would have

12   $[[O_3[\text{very hard } t_2]_1 [\text{girl } [t_1]]] [t_3 [\text{PRO}_{arb} \text{ to please } e_3]_2]]$

Suppose then the task is to interpret or draw conclusions from a sentence containing an unknown adjective in pre-nominal position, on the basis of a definition. From the original sentence, a D-structure must be constructed, despite the offending adjective. The adjective (now in post-nominal position) is eliminated and the definiens (11) substituted. The new structure, call it S, must serve as source for an LF. The structure S does not conform to the constraints on D-structures, since it will if I am correct in my arguments, contain operators for instance already bound to their traces, and D-structure does not contain argument-chains. This alone makes the D-structure hypothesis probably untenable. However, we may suppose that move α will produce a suitable LF from the structure S, involving whatever movement to prenominal position is dictated by the items in the definiens, and hence that an interpretation can be obtained. But given that D-structure information about initial positions of elements is preserved at other levels, this suggestion amounts to asserting that the elimination IS at a later level. The hypothesis may be abandoned, then.

The other syntactic level that might suggest itself for the elimination of the unknown adjective is LF. Although in an LF derived from a licit D-structure via S-structure, the modifiers are not uniformly arranged with respect to the noun, maybe it is not a necessary property of an LF that it be associable with an S-structure. Let us investigate the possibility of elimination at LF. It is not directly obvious what this should mean under the assumption that simple adjectives have moved, since we could apparently replace either the head of the chain or the 'whole' chain of antecedent and trace, say in

13   a $[\text{deaf}_i [\text{dog } t_i]]$

Suppose that it is *deaf* that we need to eliminate, and that the definiens for *deaf* is *inattentive*. Then there is no problem in substituting just the head of the chain. Suppose instead the definiens is the PP *without hearing*: only a substitution of the whole chain at its t_i position will give an LF corresponding to a possible S-structure. But such a move will in principle allow not only the movement needed to get a licit S-structure, but further instances of QR, if the definiens contains suitable NPs, and spurious readings may be generated. If we substitute at the position of the head of the chain, and allow no more movement, we can avoid generating the spurious readings. On the other hand, we will be left with a non-standard LF, in that there is no well-formed S-structure to which it corresponds. If we drop the assumption that all modifiers are base-generated to the right of the noun, we will still obtain an LF corresponding to no licit D-structure. That in itself might not matter: it is interpretation which we need. But can we even assume that the putative LF is well formed? This appears to depend on whether the limited QR postulated is sufficient. We can always move QNPs out of their A-positions, by adjoining them to the constituent as a whole (PP in our example above). Provided the structures resulting from the elimination have an interpretation, perhaps the non-standard LF is admissible. In as much as LF is normally derived from a well-formed D-structure, the conditions which would be imposed on it in isolation have not been stated. If we had a formal compositional semantics for LF, the well-formedness conditions would be given as part of the description. I will take up the question of constraining QR below.

Let us pursue this idea of elimination at LF in relation to the discontinuous adjunct of (10), shown in (14):

14 a *very hard* girl *to please*

which appeared at LF as (11) given again below

11 $[[O_3[\text{very hard } t_2]_1 \text{ [girl } [t_1]]] [t_3 [\text{PRO}_{arb} \text{ to please } e_3]_2]]$

We may suppose that in this, at LF, the whole set of parts relating to *hard to please* are seen as a 'generalized representation' of the adjunct in the same way that chains may be seen as generalized representations of arguments. It is simply the initial adjunct structure now seen at $[_{N'} [_{N'} \text{ girl } [t_1]]]$ which identifies the whole as an adjunct. Interpretation refers just to the adjunct (in effect as if it was packed down onto its traces again, as is true for A-chains).

Now suppose we were using *very hard to please* to eliminate some adjective at LF. There are three possible conditions: the two suggested for (13) above, and another if the adjective had been base generated to the left. So we might obtain

15 $[O_k [\text{very hard } [t_k [\text{PRO}_{arb} \text{ to please } e_k]]]]_j \text{ [girl } t_j]$

16   [girl [O_k [very hard [t_k [PRO$_{arb}$ to please e_k]]]]]

17   [[O_k [very hard [t_k [PRO$_{arb}$ to please e_k]]]] girl]

Given the interpretation of adjuncts as conjunction, and seeing the set of elements related to traces as a generalized representation of an adjunct, there will be no problem with any of these. In fact they are simpler than (11).

What we have in (11) is an operator-headed nested set of constituents; (11) is considerably more complex than (15), (16) and (17) above, but it is needed on account of the S-structure of (14). We may assume that the infinitival clause must move before or at PF because it is too heavy for processing in its pre-N' position. The operator must move by LF. The only question is (if all this is correct) whether the processes must be accomplished at S-structure rather than later, and what the correct formulation of the rules is.

For the operator movement, the simplest statement seems to be that we must have the correct types at LF, and that only a restricted set of compositional rules is permitted to operate. Suppose the rules are just application and conjunction, with operators acquiring their binding type at S-structure by virtue of movement to an A-bar operator position (Cormack 1986b). Then the empty operator must somehow come to the front of the structure, because it will not be able to combine giving the correct type otherwise. Stated in more conventional terms, we will need to stipulate that a [+WH] or [+λ] element must be raised to the front of its 'licensing' maximal projection. What we require of this 'licensing' projection is that for ordinary purposes it is CP, but for these adjuncts, it is the adjunct itself, or rather the extended set of related adjuncts such as we have in (11). These can be regarded as the abstract representation of the D-structure adjunct in rather the same way as a chain can be regarded as the abstract representation of a D-structure argument. The required set of adjuncts can be identified by the fact that the outer ones are coindexed to some empty element in the next inner one, successively. The interpretation is as it were at the inner trace t_i.

The other suggestion I made was that we looked for a level at which adjunction of modifiers is not characterized as being linearly ordered with respect to the noun or N'. Clearly LF does not satisfy this requirement, but nor, given the semantics of conjunction I have suggested, is the linear order of the adjuncts either with respect to the noun or with respect to each other significant in itself. We might imagine, then, some successor to LF which was stripped of anything not relevant to interpretation: a rather drastic version of the principle of Full Interpretation. In this LR (logical representation) we have sets of relations, such as "adjunct to X," "internal argument of X," with no intermediate structure or linear order. Under these circumstances, substitution of one adjunct to N' by another would raise no problem of linear order. Then at LR, we might imagine that the adjunct was repacked at the inner trace position, and that even this was neither to the right nor to the left of its head adjoinee—it could be above it in a two dimensional representation. It is not clear whether this is anything but a notational variant of a representation which does have intermediate traces and left right ordering; certainly it could be regarded as a way of seeing such a representation. So let us take LR to be LF stripped of what is not needed for interpretation, leaving it open as to exactly how this is defined.

It seems from what we have so far that substitution at LR, a stripped LF, is possible. Note that I am equivocating in using 'LR'; if this is still a level of the grammar, it should be rather LF'; if it is not, we might suppose that translation into the language of thought should have taken place.

The question remains as to whether this will necessarily be the correct interpretation. In many cases, the answer would be affirmative, but it is possible that the procedure outlined would lead to incorrect interpretations. This may happen if the definiens contains any scope-inducing operators, and the matrix contains scope-sensitive elements in positions such that the two can jointly produce alternant scope interpretations. As Fodor and Fodor (1980) point out,

18 Everyone ate

does not have the two readings associated with

19 Everyone ate something

so that if say intransitive eat_0 is defined in terms of transitive eat_1, and substitution is carried out before scope interpretation is fixed, we will get a spurious meaning for (18). Even if this did not occur for noun-modifiers, because of constraints on QR for instance, the procedure will not be reliable in general. Obviously, if we were in some way to isolate the definiens in the structure S we could avoid this problem, but it is undesirable to introduce *ad hoc* constraints on what are otherwise regular grammatical processes. But a pragmatic explanation, if forthcoming, would be legitimate.

There are a number of possibilities. One is the possibility of invoking something like 'semiquotation'. What would justify this, and how would it work? For definitions, the rationale would be something like this: the speaker has produced an utterance containing a particular linguistic unit; the hearer has had recourse to a definition which is linguistically complex. But the speaker was intending the hearer to construct the correct utterance interpretation (UR) on the basis of the items he supplied, not the items the hearer has unearthed. So processing, including scope disambiguation via QR, should be done without separating the items in the definiens from each other. The hearer then must ensure that they are in 'semiquotation'; that is, kept as a unit, but accessible for interpretation.

This explanation relies on the Principle of Relevance: the speaker is assumed to have produced the most relevant utterance. Even if the dictionary information is part of what every hearer is suppose to know, if a part of it were to be used in a marked way (*i.e.* with wide scope over earlier material), then it should be appropriately salient in the utterance. That is not to say that encyclopedic information cannot be accessed in processing, but it would have to be required (as in bridging cross reference), not optional as scope switch always is. This is why the Fodor and Fodor example (18) cannot mean (19), whether the relation between transitive *eat* and that in (18) is lexical, mediated via a meaning postulate, or syntactic, relying on an empty object

An alternative to this is to suppose that the definition is taken as a 'word–meaning' definition, in that part of its function is to require the user to construct a new unit of the language of thought. Then the speaker's utterance can be processed with this unanalyzable unit, so preventing unwanted scope effects. The definition is called into use further in giving a meaning postulate concerning the new item. This will have exactly the same effect as semiquotation.

2.3.3 Elimination from canonic predicate position

Predicate position for adjectives. is by convention the position after *be*. It has been argued recently (Burzio 1986) that the predicate is in fact the small clause predicate of a raised subject, so that

20 John is sad

derives from the underlying structure

21 – is [$_{SC}$ John sad] SC = AP

If this is so, and if *John seems sad* is derived in the same way, then we might expect that any of our AP definiens, which I have argued have at least the θ-role properties of predicates, should fit in any of the structures

22 i – is [NP PRED]

leading to

22 ii NP is [*t* PRED]

23 i – seems [NP PRED]

leading to

23 ii NP seems [*t* PRED]

24i/ii I consider [NP PRED]

Only if the subcategorization of the verb restricts the range of SCs will we expect deviance.

There is not going to be any problem here with adjectives whose definiens are APs, in general. Apart from objections one might have as to the equivalence of meaning, substitution even at surface will often suffice for PPs and participial phrases. Examples of syntactically acceptable elimination of items from 2.2.1, from *be* SCs are:

25	Philology is	*moribund*	
		likely soon to perish	LOD
		at the point of death	LOD
26	The cloth is	*moist*	
		slightly wet	LOD

27	Stilton is	*mouldy*	
		covered with mould	LOD
28	Orff's music is	*decadent*	
		showing decadence	LOD

However, although the first three here will equally follow *seems*, and can be put in a small clause in for example "I believe [NP PRED]" in these cases, the *-ing* phrase gives ungrammatical results.

29 *Orff's music seems showing decadence

30 *I believe Orff's music showing decadence

If we force a passive VP (by adding a *by*-phrase) in contrast to a possible adjectival passive in examples like (27), the results are acceptable:

31 John seems overcome by boredom

32 I believe John overwhelmed by inertia

Chomsky (1981) gives a number of examples of ungrammatical effects with past participles (from page 54, his (17)):

33 John seems *taught by Bill / *believed to be a fool / *killed

These are very bad, certainly; worse than my examples are good. It may be that mine then need another explanation, and in fact *seems* permits neither kind of participial in its SC. This necessitates subcategorization of the head for particular types of small clause. Provided the predicate inside the small clause is its head, this is technically unproblematic. Since 'SC' is not an ordinary category, this is indeed what we should expect, within the limits set by CSR of s-selection. We need to use the s-selection information that the complement is to be propositional to force the small clause structure.

On the face of it, infinitival phrases fit perfectly well, so that there is an apparent SC analysis available for

34 The cheese seems   [$_{SC}$ *e* [to be covered with mould]]

The relation between the interpretations of (35i) and (35ii) is however much closer than that between the interpretations of (36i) and (36ii):

35	i	The cheese seems	[e	mouldy]
	ii	The cheese seems	[e to be	mouldy]
36	i	The cheese is	[e	mouldy]
	ii	The cheese is	[e to be	mouldy]

If what we have is a small clause structure in each of the four cases, the discrepancy of interpretation in (36ii) is hard to locate. If however there is no SC in (35ii) and (36ii), we can postulate that this peculiar interpretation for *be* is to be associated with an I″ predicate to *be*. Since I″ contains a subject position, we would not be able to force an I″-headed small clause (*i.e.* with an adjoined NP). We might also hope that if any [+V] SC is forbidden after *seems*, then they all are.

Maybe what we should be saying is the opposite: a small clause is by definition a clause without any verb (head), not just one without tense. So *seems* and *be* both take as complements the normal range of clauses (which I have characterized as permitted to be realized as C″, I″, and V″), and in addition, small clauses. These latter may have AP, NP, or PP predicates in them. The former may be tensed or infinitival. Participial VPs are semantically predicates, but fall between two stools here: they cannot count as SC predicates because of being headed by a verb, and they do not count as clausal because they are inherently incapable of having subjects (as opposed to external arguments). So the participials and the infinitival phrases are only superficially like each other (just when the subject of the infinitival is apparently bound from elsewhere, either because it is controlled PRO or because it is bound by the empty operator). The apparent *be* SCs with VPs would be misanalysis: these should be not main verb *be* but auxiliary *be*. That is, the 'subcategorization' is for a VP predicate, not a VP headed clause (and the auxiliary should be regarded as an operator with an operand, not a head with an argument). So the apparent surface substitution in (27) and (28) is illusory.

The fact (if it is one) that *seem* and *be* refuse some types of predicate in a SC complement does however mean that elimination cannot always be carried out properly at surface. At what level then could elimination take place? Or is there no possible linguistic level? The only likely candidate level is LF; and here we would have to assume that the Projection Principle was indifferent to subcategorization requirements. This is not an unnatural idea: it seems superfluous to have these somewhat erratic deviancies from the canonical s-selection facts recorded at the level which is input to interpretation. If only θ-types must be correctly taken from the lexicon, the elimination will be possible. If it is provable that we need subcategorization at LF, then one would simply have to postulate that the next level, LR, had no such filter, and use this. Gross subcategorization can be met at D-structure or S-structure; the finer detail given by features such as [+WH] can only be stipulated at D-structure—but they can be checked at S-structure.

2.3.4   Elimination from other predicate positions

As we have noted before, adjectives and other predicates turn up as VP adjuncts in sentences like *John left the room [angry]*. In this position we can certainly have most of the categories of definiens for adjectives: complex APs, PPs, and participial phrases of both kinds. The same is true of the adjective position in sentences like

37   John likes his cheese [mouldy]

or

38   John leaves his room [untidy]

where I assume the verbs have small clause complements. This is what we should expect if the phrases are predicational.

It should be noted that in structures apparently like (37), and (38), we can also have infinitives:

39   John likes his cheese to be mouldy all through

40   John left his room to get in a worse muddle

41   John left Mary to get the supper

(on the reading where Mary gets the supper). As argued above, these will be I″ complements. In any case, there are no adjective definiens of the shape of *to be mouldy all through*, because a definition in this infinitival form is preempted for the definitions of verbs. Infinitival phrases can also be used attributively, in NPs like *the man to mend the sink* and *the man to see about the sink*. These modifiers can be treated as V″ or I″ phrases in the same way as the participial phrases discussed earlier—the NPs will be parallel then to *the man mending the sink* and *the man asked to see about the sink*.

2.3.5 Problems with adverbial modification

With APs, there is a problem of elimination where there is adverbial modification with *not*:

42	i		The room is	very *dark*
	ii	*		very not light

In any case, adverbs in the initial string cause problems with meaning that cannot be attributed to the inadequacy of the definition:

43	i		The room is	*dark* enough
	ii	?		not light enough
	iii		(The room is	not too light)
44	i		The room seems	*dark*
	ii	*		not light
	iii	?		does not seem light
	iv		(The room seems not to be light)	

The queries mark inappropriate meanings. The problem appears to arise from the fact that *not* in English does not seem to combine freely with every category, even when it can sometimes combine with that category. We can get a *not* in front of NPs with complex APs:

45		I think that	not too blunt a knife to cut the meat
46		I think James	not a proper man for you to know

where the *not* is possibly an operator on the AP, whereas we cannot have

47	*	I think James	not a fool / not stupid

But we can have

48		I think James	not the best man to do the job

49 I think James   not unintelligent

What we do have for constituent negation of adjectives of course is a bound morpheme—*un-*, *in-*, for instance, which can be fairly freely used, and a large number of lexical opposites. But what are we going to say about the definiens *not dark*? Does it have a coherent grammatical structure? It seems unlikely that it is understood so readily if it does not, so let us suppose that it does. Then suppose *not* is classified as an adverb, and that adverbs may from the syntactic point of view function as modifiers of (or rather operators on) adjectives in APs. Suppose further that the item has a suitable meaning (which will be discussed below). We will then get a perfectly good reading for our definiens, but are left with having to account for the failure of constituent-negation to turn up as a possible reading in phrases like (43ii).

We might try imposing a surface syntactic ordering on the adverbs in (42ii); this could also account for (43ii), if ordering is taken to apply not to string-order, but to the nesting of bracketings. The *seems* case of (44ii) perhaps can be explained as a violation of the preferred placing of the adverb *not*; unless processing is hard, it should be after the auxiliary verb, which is as far to the front of the sentence as it is permitted to be.[30] And only if confusion might result (from more than one negation in the sentence, as in *not unhappy* or from scope interactions with other adjective modifiers, should it be transferred to the relevant constituent.

The argument so far has been motivated by the fact that if this constituent negation use of *not* WERE freely permitted, then the direct substitutions in (43) and (44) would be both grammatical and (reasonably) appropriate in meaning. There is another possibility, and that is to invoke a non-truth-conditional use of *not*. There is a whole pattern of use with *not* where it can apparently occur with almost any constituent, including adjectives:

50 John, but not anyone else, listens to opera

51 I am coming not when you expected me, but later

52 I'd like black coffee, not white

53 I'd like not white coffee, but black

54 Gentlemen seem to prefer redheads nowadays, not blondes

55 Bill likes rooms somewhat dark, not light (as I do)

It can be seen that the uses in (50) to (55) are not what we need directly for (43ii) and (44ii): in (50) to (55), the scope of the negation is not just the immediately following constituent, but at least some reconstructed matter; and indeed this is in all probability not truth-conditional negation at all, but rather some sort of denial. The phrase after the *not*, at least, is to be construed as what Sperber and Wilson call 'interpretive' use. The *not* is a rejection of the supposed suggestion that the item in its scope was to fill the slot in the sentence occupied either by the *not*-phrase or by the matching positive phrase. But the fact that there is interpretive use does not exonerate us from supplying a syntax for the whole; and unless a normal semantics can be supplied, an abnormal one must be, since pragmatic procedures rely on the construction of representations derived somehow from the syntax. It does appear that what we have at least in (51) to (55) is a metalinguistic *not*. That it is metalinguistic is verified by its total lack of syntactic discretion: it will even mark out a morpheme, as in

56 She has not hyper- but hypo-glycemia

or worse still part of a phrase

57 She's suffering not from hyper- but from hypo-glycemia

Such syntactic promiscuity is typical of a metalanguage item, since the metalanguage item is not required to enter into compositional meaning relations with the object-language items. This *not* functions very much like a "search and replace" instruction in a word processor; it has not been executed, and deleted from the text, because the speaker is gaining effect from leaving it visible. Because it is "search and replace," we must always have the two parts, so that (51) and (53) are ill-formed with the *but* phrases deleted unless some other non-standard interpretation is invoked. This use of *not*, then, is not what we need.

There is another non-standard use of *not*. These two, (51) and (53) without their *but* phrases, and (44ii), can be rescued by isolating the *not*-phrase as some sort of 'semiquotation'. For instance, if I ask you what you would like, holding out a cup of milky coffee, you could reply with

58 I'd like ... not white coffee

This however does not necessarily suggest that you would like black coffee. The scope of the *not* is at least probably the whole of *white coffee*. On the other hand, the scope does not naturally extend over *I'd like...*, so that some alternative is probably being solicited. It appears here that what interpretive use (semiquotation) does is simply to license the use of *not* with a non-standard scope, leaving all the rest of the compositional semantics intact. Since the reply in (58) above could in fact be followed by

59   ... not black coffee, ... in fact not anything

we do have to allow that the scope of the *not* may or does in fact extend over the whole sentence. QR will neatly achieve this, while preserving the intuition that the *not* has scope over just the NP:

60   [not white coffee]$_k$ [I'd like e_k]

61   [not anything]$_k$ [I'd like e_k]

It is clear enough intuitively what the semantics of the *not* has to be here; and that it will give exactly the same truth-conditional effect in (60) as the standard sentence-negation *not* in

62   [not] [[white coffee]$_k$ [I'd like e_k]]

(Whether (60) would have to be converted to (62) by some process of 'neg-raising' is a question to which I will return.) What is achieved of course is a matter of focus. But it seems to me to be fairly clear that this is achieved by assuming that constituent negation is possible, in syntax. Both those remarks need some support.

This is not the place to embark on a study of focus. Within the framework assumed, the natural line to pursue would be one that started with the premise that constituent negation (whether achieved by lexical 'semiquotation' or ordinary compositional means), was a device for constraining the operation of inference rules or the selection of context. Roughly, it seems to require the entertainment of alternatives just at the constituent negated, along with the rejection of the proposition with the constituent unnegated. This line would suggest that 'neg-raising' in these circumstances would be counter-productive: it would destroy the shape which is to suggest the proper way of processing the sentence.

Constituent negation in syntax raises syntactic issues. Is there more than one item to be entered in the lexicon? Or is there a partially-specified item, capable of masquerading as this or that? Suppose we allocate it to the syntactic class of Adverbs, as is traditional. And suppose adverbs are more or less by definition capable of being adjoined to a variety of categories: let us not worry which, now. The structure building principles will need to accommodate this. I suspect that we need provision for items which are operators in a semantic sense (operators on operands, not binding operators), but at D-structure we might get away with pretending they were adjuncts (predicates by nature but not by function), with the two-place operators as heads of CP and DP. What of θ-types? The logician's *not* is of type <t,t>, an operator on propositions. It would be highly desirable to be able to keep this type, if we can still account for its distribution. We would be looking for an account rather like the one I gave for *likely*: a single θ-type but different complement possibilities. The tool used there was a θ-role chain, essentially equivalent to composition of functions over the types being combined.

We can use this idea directly to obtain constituent negation of a predicate. These will have type <e,t>, and so will combine by simple composition. The semantics will be, for a predicate with meaning 'P':

63   $not \circ P \Rightarrow \lambda x\,(\neg\, P(x))$

This produces the set of all things which do not have the property of being P, whatever P is. If P is *dark*, it will produce things not dark. Apart from problems of inapplicability (we will get *courage* in that set, if *courage* were an entity) this is the correct effect.[31] That is, so-called 'semiquotation' in this context amounts to no more than fixing a mildly non-standard operand for *not* in the syntax; θ-type stays constant.[32]

And our definiens can be treated in the same way: we can use constituent negation, provided we keep them isolated on elimination, keep them in 'semiquotation'. Why should this be so? The answer is as it was for quantifier scope: the speaker did not provide these separate items (*not* and *light* for (42ii)) to be played with in finding the correct UR (utterance interpretation), and so the two words should not be separated in processing.

Examples like that of (43ii), repeated here,

43 ii   ? not light enough

where there is an unwanted parsing as (*not* (*light enough*)), can be dealt with similarly by assuming that the definiens is kept as a 'semiquoted' unit—giving us ((*not light*) *enough*) as required. As before, the same effect can be obtained by supposing that we eliminate AFTER translating *not light* into some non-complex item in the language of thought. The discussion above has shown that semiquotation is used in ordinary language processing, so that it is not invoked just for definitions. And the cross-categorial negation needed is also needed for other sentences, and here indeed needs no special semantics.

Elimination at LF or at LR then is possible, with the now familiar proviso that filters referring to categorial distribution are not to operate, and that semiquotation (or prior translation) in effect provides a pair of brackets which must be respected.

2.4 Dictionary definitions—elimination and complements

2.4.1 The problem

Dictionaries contain words, catchwords, the definienda, and phrases which purport to supply meanings for these. The possible relations between the two are roughly indicated by "word–word," "word–meaning" or "meaning–meaning" pairings of definiendum and definiens. I shall argue in this section that either of the second two places interesting constraints on the semantics of the language of thought.

The problem that is to be addressed is the one of valency, or the number and distribution of θ-roles associated with an item in natural language or the language of thought. I shall continue to use the type notation of formal semantics for these roles.

If an item is polyvalent, and there is no internal/external distinction in the language of thought, then there is going to be a problem matching up the arguments in definiendum and definiens IF the latter is conceptually or language of thought based rather than linguistically based. If the definiens is to be taken as linguistic (word–word) elimination, then we can assume that the arguments are identified in the linguistic ways, if necessary simply by well-formedness conditions imposed on the substitution-form.

Dictionary Definitions

Consider first monovalent NL items. These may have an internal or an external θ-role (for instance *seems* has an internal role to allocate: a clause; *sleeps* has an external argument, an entity). Suppose that the definiens for *seems* is *phrase*₁ and for *sleep*, *phrase*₂. Now if we construe the definition as being 'word–word', what we are expecting is that there is some level of NL SYNTAX at which elimination or substitution can take place. It is clear enough that such a substitution will not be possible unless the θ-roles of definiendum and definiens match not only in number but in whether they are internal or external. Subcategorization must match, but possibly minor features might be ignored, unless we have a stripped down LF. For full grammaticality, it will also have to be true that Case assigning properties match, though conceivably semantic processing could ignore this. In many instances, there would be no problem with subcategorization or Case-assigning potential, because there are canonic correspondences between these and θ-role assigning properties, given the syntactic category of the definiendum. So for example, if we know that *destruction* is a noun, then we know that in the unmarked case it Case-marks its internal argument with *of*.[33] Possible problems with verbs are discussed in section 2.4.3 below.

I am working on the assumption that the language of thought if it is a language, must have categories of some kind, and that one should impute to it no more complexity than is forced on one. If it has at least the expressive power of NL, then we may assume that arguments may be propositions or entities. The simplest assumption would seem to be that its categories were in one to one correspondence with the semantic types, and that all arguments are internal. It could also be supposed to have a simple categorial grammar, with nothing but function–argument application, matching in syntax and semantics. This would mean that the language of thought equivalents of *seem* and *sleep* would have category/types <t,t> and <e,t> respectively, unless we can prove that there is an internal/external distinction in the language of thought, whereas their NL types will be <t,t> and <*e,t> respectively. Simplicity here is relative to assumed logical operations involved in inference and pragmatic processing; since I have not been attempting to spell these out, guesses may well be wrong. For instance, suppose that for NL (following Kayne 1981), we can explain away all apparent double object constructions, leaving just binary branching (with external arguments). Then it might well be that a logic for the language of thought over such representations was simpler in some sense than one over representations with two (or more) internal arguments.

2.4.2 One-place predicates

It would appear that there should be little problem with one-place predicates in a word–meaning or meaning–meaning mapping, if the hypothesis about no internal/external distinction in the language of thought is correct. There would be no need for such distinctions to be consistent from definiendum to definiens. (Though of course if the NL distinction is not preserved in the definiens, the entry will be of little use to someone who wants to know about the NL syntax of the definiendum). There are many adjective definitions which superficially appear not to preserve parity of this kind: a subset of those that I have characterized as incorporating the empty operator in their syntactic form. An example is

    1   *dainty* hard to please   LOED

Minimally, the syntax of the definiens, by the projection principle, must have an argument e which is the internal argument of *please*. But it is not the θ-role associated with this argument directly which becomes the external θ-role for *dainty*: there is a complex which incorporates *hard*. The empty operator postulated for this definition ensures that the phrase forms a coherent syntactic whole; this is essential to allow compositional semantics. The operator can be construed as turning PRO_{arb} *to please* of type $<e,t>$ into $O_k[\text{PRO}_{arb}$ *to please* $e_k]$ of type $<*e,t>$: it turns a missing internal argument into a missing external argument, which can then be appropriately combined with *hard* to give a whole phrase requiring an external argument.

This is not particularly interesting in as much as the analysis of a sentence containing the phrase *hard to please* (as a surface phrase) has to postulate the empty operator anyway. Rather more interesting is the example of *putative*:

    2   *putative*   commonly supposed to be   C20

I shall just ignore *commonly*. Consider *supposed to be*. The phrase is not peculiar to abbreviated definitions: we could have for instance

3   John is less stupid / of a fool / awed by authority than he is commonly supposed to be

(I will return to this example). The θ-type for *suppose* is <t,p>, since *John supposed that Mary had gone home* is well-formed. The passive then will effectively have type <t,t> since the external θ-role is suppressed. Since we can also have *John supposed her to have gone home*, *suppose* is capable of c-selecting for an IP complement. On the evidence of *It is not that John is a fool* or *It is a fact / obvious that John is late* we may assign the θ-type <t,t> to *be*, and hence consistently derive *John is a fool / late* from a small clause (SC) complement. That raising is obligatory in the small clause construction indicates that *be* does not assign Case (the NP *a fool* is a predicate, not an argument, and as such neither it nor any chain it is in needs to have Case).[34] Then the D-structure corresponding to

4   i   John is supposed to be a fool

will be

4   ii   [– is supposed [$_{IP}$ – to be [$_{SC}$ John a fool]]]

The S-structure will be (assuming raising):

4 iii   [John$_k$ is supposed [$_{IP}$ e_k to be [$_{SC}$ t_k a fool]]]

Now if we wanted *supposed to be a fool* as a well-formed phrase, we would as usual have to bind the leftmost e_k by an operator at the front of the phrase. This operator will be the usual O, which is, or denotes, a spare external θ-role, which can be transmitted to a subject NP via the inert passive *be*.[35] We then have (5i) and (5ii):

5   i   supposed to be a fool

   ii O_k [supposed [$_{IP}$ e_k to be [$_{SC}$ t_k a fool]]]

The next move is to have an empty category at the position of *a fool*. This NP is functioning as a predicate, and hence somehow (as discussed before) acquires type <p>. Let us use p as a variable (as it will turn out) over elements of the category of predicates. I shall assume that even if it is a variable, it does not need to be properly governed because when realized as an NP it does not need Case; and it might so to speak have been an A″ or P″, not an N″. We might suppose that there is a generalized sense of 'proper government' which means something like 'predictable from context'; in this sense, the predicate is predicted as the essential part of any clause, where the presence of the clause ('SC' here; actually NP) which is determined as complement of *be*. Either way, an empty element will be licensed, provided it is bound within the proper domain. Let its binder be *P*. Let us suppose our empty predicate binder P_j hops from clause to clause, by adjunction. We will then obtain (6ii) for (6i)

6 i supposed to be

ii $P_j O_k$ [supposed p_j [$_{IP}$ e_k to be p_j [$_{SC}$ $t_k p_j$]]]

The θ-type of this expression will be <p,<e*,t>> (*i.e.* <p,p>), on the assumption that the only proper interpretation of an empty operator is as a lambda abstractor, or a θ-role assigner. Suppose (as seems to be the case) that our usual *O* always assigns an external role. Then necessarily, any other operator assigns an internal role.[36] In any case (assuming something like function–argument application), the outer operator would always have to assign an internal role, since the internal category will be met first. Suppose we had tried to construct the representation of *supposed to be* the other way round, by abstracting over the position of *a fool* first? This would reverse the operators, and hence confuse the roles. I shall argue in Chapter 4 that the subject-operator (O_k here) is constrained to move from SPEC to SPEC, and is finally in SPEC of VP. Other operators cannot move to this position, unless they first move to SPEC of CP, and so in the absence of a CP must be adjoined to the VP. Hence the order of the two operators cannot get reversed.[37]

After all this, we have a phrase with a non-standard θ-type. I have so far assumed that for θ-role semantics, adjectives are of type <*e,t>, adjoined to the head N′ in an NP, and construed as conjunction, or functioning as predicates. But we know very well that for adjectives like *putative* this is quite wrong. Conjunction is totally inappropriate: a putative solution to the problem may not be a solution at all. Nor can these 'non-intersective' adjectives function as predicates,[38] so it is helpful if they do not have type <p>. On a standard Montague-style analysis, extensionalized, they would of course have type <p,p>; it was because non-intersective adjectives exist that Montague uniformly gave all adjectives the type of a function from (in effect) N' to N' denotations.

So far, I have simply evaded the issue of these adjectives, but the definition here forces us into recognition of the problem. That is in itself interesting, because it means that at least if we take these definiens seriously, NL is not capable of sustaining a myth that ALL adjectives are of type <p>. If the myth is perpetuated at D-structure, ("any AP is a predicate") then we will get the proper positioning of the adjective in attributive position, but might also have it turn up in predicate positions. If we do have <p,p> rather than just <p> for the operator adjectives, then these latter structures would be ruled out as soon as the 'real' type was visible.[39] In order for grammaticality to obtain, it is only necessary that the complex type is visible at SOME level at which type-checking takes place. It should be noted that the type does not take a saturated argument. This means that the restriction on θ-types for lexical items must apply only to logical predicates, and not to operators licensed only by the 'operator–operand' relation. I shall continue to refer to operands as arguments, often.

The type supplied is, however, just what we need for elimination. It is a type which states that it is expecting an internal argument which is a predicate. Suppose we are eliminating in the phrase

7   [$_{N'}$ putative [$_{N'}$ solution]]

Then *solution* is of the right type, and we will get

8   $P_j O_k$[supposed p_j [$_{IP}$ e_k to be p_j [$_{SC}$ $t_k p_j$]]]

followed by [$_{N'}$ solution]. Since we have not yet established any mechanism for showing how a θ-role is passed from a phrase to an internal argument (in general, we suppose that internal roles are passed only from X-zero items to their internal arguments), we may invent one *ad hoc*. Let us use the same as for external arguments, but put the operator on the right, so that we have (adjoining to the right):

9   [[[O_k[supposed [[$_{IP}$ e_k to be [[$_{SC}$ t_k p_j] p_j]] p_j]]] P_j] [$_X$ solution]$_k$]

The only thing wrong with this is that in THIS structure, we might expect the 'X' to be NP, and as it came from (7), it was N'. But recollect that we have an adjunction structure in (7), not a phrase–argument structure.

All we have done is to substitute a VP for an AP. We may suppose that elimination takes place at LF, and at LF, subcategorization and indeed any categorization is not relevant to interpretation and hence is deleted in the interests of the Principle of Full Interpretation. The important thing is the preservation of the correct θ-type, and the X' structure; and this is ensured.[40] It is true that for (9) to surface, we would need a full DP: we would have to have 'supposed to be a solution'. But note that here we would most usually take the structure as predicate-argument; and if we decided to analyze it in the manner of (9), we could do so (given that in any case we would have to take *a solution* to have the θ-type <p>).

What is needed is a formulation of the licensing of θ-role discharging which will allow the operator P_j of type <p,p> to be discharged appropriately in the operator-operand structure, since the conjunction assumed earlier is not appropriate. Function–argument application to the types is appropriate for operator-operand combination. But we might question the syntactic category of the operator. In (9), there is no evidence as to what it should be, since many SC heads are permitted. Then perhaps it needs no specified category, but can be left at 'X', where X must fall within what is subcategorized for by *be*, and of course it must have the type <p>.

As with the discussion in section 2.3.2, we are faced with questions about the well-formedness of LF (or LR) when the form in question has not arisen by the usual generative devices. There seem to be viable options which will keep the level of elimination at or near LF, rather than at some level of representation in the language of thought. If we assume that word–meaning translation is intended, then it follows that the language of thought translation of the definiens can only determine the proper distribution of internal or external roles to the definiendum (or rather, its translation) if there is a compositional way of transmitting θ-roles like the ones I have suggested here, which is fully determinate as to which is which. In the case of NL and word–word interpretation, with substitution, we have seen that there will not be problems with role confusion (but it remains an open question how many syntactic constraints there are on the transmissions). The language of thought however will want a properly specified entry in its syntactic lexicon, so either there is no internal/external role distinction, or the means exist for determining it. It is hard to see that anything other than correspondence with NL could determine such a distinction in general for a 'new' item of the language of thought; and our definitions here are supplying suitable information.

I promised to return to example (3), repeated here:

3   John is less stupid / of a fool / awed by authority than he is commonly supposed to be

Intuitively, there is a discontinuous constituent *less than he is commonly supposed to be*, which indicates John's degree of stupidity. This whole, like *very*, should be a predicate-operator, of type <p,p>. Suppose it does acquire this type, in somewhat the same manner as *supposed to be* as just discussed, so that the whole is expecting an INTERNAL predicate argument (operand). The alternative arguments offered in (3) are an AP, a participial VP, and an NP with *of*. What is interesting is the source of the *of*—and the necessity for it.[41] It is intuitively clear that it is just the Case-marking or empty *of*. It turns up in phrases like 'He is something/somewhat/no end of a fool'. It appears on the basis of this evidence that when the predicate is an NP, it has to have Case. This is anomalous, until we consider that its relational status is as operand to an operator, rather than directly as predicate to an argument. In the phrases noted above, there is the same relational status: in fact the phrases *something*, *somewhat* and *no end* are functioning as quantifiers, which are also operators, and here too an *of* is inserted.[42] Because *a fool* is not the argument of an X-zero item, there is no normal Case-assigner. It appears that the Case-assigner must be *less* (the head of the operator), which is string-adjacent (or possibly the whole discontinuous operator). It presumably assigns Case also in *Give John less of that*. Let us suppose that *less* is an adverb taking a [*than* X] argument for some X (to say it is an adverb is to say little— possibly just that it is an operator with a predicate as operand, but the question is not important here). The interpretation will be as indicated in the structure (10),

10   John is [[less than λv [he is supposed to be [v e]] [$_{Pr}$ a fool]]

where v is a variable over values or measures bound by an operator which I have shown as 'λ'. This latter is probably to be construed as something more like the set abstraction operator, returning the set of values. e is an empty category of the type <p>, and is, I assume, to be interpreted as ellipsis for just [$_{Pr}$ a fool]. The implication is that John can belong to the set of fools to a greater or lesser degree, or something like this, so that at the least, the set of fools has to have a partial ordering on it. It will still be a set, however. In (11),

11 John is less than honest / a genius

it appears that the absence of the comparison class is construed as indicating simply a two-state grading (a threshold), so effectively forcing John out of the set of honest persons, or geniuses.

2.4.3 Polyadic predicates

2.4.3.1 Verbs with direct objects

It might be supposed that the normal form of definition for a transitive verb would have a definiens consisting of another transitive verb, modified if necessary by some adverbial phrase. Such definitions do occur:[43]

| 12 | *modify* | qualify | LOD |
| 13 | *necessitate* | involve as condition or result | LOD |

For each of these, there is a simple object gap in the definiens. There are other definitions where the verb of the definiens has at least at some level of representation two arguments, one of which is marked by a preposition. The gap may still be the direct object:

14	*graze*	to feed with grass	C20
15	*guard*	to protect from danger	C20
16	*hatch*	to mark with fine lines	C20
17	*grind*	to reduce to powder	C20

The prepositional phrases here are not VP adjuncts, since their argument is in no case the subject of the main verb. In fact, if it was clear that the PP did have an argument, then the argument of the PP in each case would be the omitted object: it is what gets fed that gets to have the grass, or the lines, and gets not to be in danger. But we cannot directly say that the cows are *with grass*, or the soldiers are *from danger*; these are not independent, predicational PPs, but rather the preposition is a marker of one of the participants in a relation set up by the verb.[44] *Feed* relates the food and the recipient of it, as internal arguments. And as Fillmore (1968) noted, we often have alternants with the same phonological form of verb:

18 fed grass to the cows / fed the cows with grass

19 mark lines on the page / mark the page with lines

In other cases, a reversal of the arguments needs a different verb:

20 reduce the grain to flour / produce flour from the grain

We may note that further specification of the conceptual argument is still permitted with the definienda, possibly with a distinct preposition. We have *grind to a fine powder, guard against attack*. This suggests that there is an inherent redundancy in all the verbs, with respect to the content of the PP, and that it may be this which permits the omission of the PP in most cases. That is, if the argument PP is omitted, we assume some general item of the appropriate kind, as we do for the direct object of *eat*.

There is equally the possibility of having the gap at the second participant, after the designated preposition:

21 *renew* to substitute new for   C20

This is despite the fact that there is an alternant using *with*, so that instead of (21) we might have had

22 to substitute with new

In the definition of *repose* (*v, t*), both positions are offered:

23 *repose* to lay at rest: to give rest to

There are some verbs which appear to have just a single internal argument, but all the same mark this with a preposition:

24 *lament* to mourn for   C20

At least in my dialect, *mourn* may be used with a direct object, (as well as 'intransitively' as here); the preposition in (24) has to be a designated one for the object, unless it is taken that the mourning benefits the object of mourning. The use of the preposition emphasizes the object gap.

Other verbs have a single internal participant role (if we restrict the notion of role so that the only bearers are propositions and entities, clauses and NPs or PPs), but some further state must also be given. So we find missing objects in verb-particle constructions, as in

25	*egg*	urge on	LOD
26	*modify*	tone down	LOD
27	*muffle*	deaden sound by wrapping up	LOD

and in complexes like

| 28 | *monetize* | put into circulation as money | LOD |
| 29 | *necessitate* | render necessary | LOD |

Possibly these last are small clause constructions, which I will discuss in a moment; but at least all the others discussed so far have the property that the missing NP, which corresponds to the direct object of the definiendum, is plausibly assigned its θ-role directly by the verb of the definiens, as it is by the verb of the definiendum. However, it is easy to find examples where this correspondence does not hold. There are several kinds of example. Frequently, the role is assigned by a noun, as in (30), (31) and (32):

30	*modify*	change form of	LOD
31	*monopolize*	secure monopoly of	LOD
32	*move*	change position, posture, place or abode	LOD

(In this last, the definition was for both the transitive and intransitive meanings, so that for the latter, the nouns are taken as not having objects, and for the former they should. The dictionary maker has not thought it necessary to insert the default preposition *of* for the transitive reading). Less commonly, the θ-role is given by a locative preposition:

| 33 | *leap* | to bound over | C20 |
| 34 | *lap* | to flow against | C20 |

In these, the PP can be construed as genuinely predicational (on the subject), so the PP is adverbial in nature, being adjoined to the VP.

Dictionary Definitions

It is possible for the definiens to have its missing object in an clausally embedded position, as in

| 35 i | *seek* | try to get | LOD |
| 36 i | *imitate* | be like | LOD |

These might have S-structures

35 ii   [$_{V''}$ try [$_{I''}$ PRO to get e_k]]

36 ii   [$_{V''}$ be [$_{SC}$ e_j [like e_k]]]

In both these representations, there is an external θ-role to be assigned: in (35ii) it is assigned obligatorily by *try*, and in (36ii) it arises from the empty NP e_j. The other empty NP then must pass its θ-role on internally, which is what is required by the definiendum. The question again is what ensures that the roles of the two empty NPs do not get muddled up, particularly in (36ii). It is possible to envisage an answer in syntactic terms: there is a wealth of conditions we could appeal to. What is important—and I am assuming that the relevant syntactic principles can be given a proper explicit formulation—is that such conditions are entirely plausible AS SYNTAX. But any appeal to "kinds" of θ-role, allowing an unordered set of arguments in the language of thought, seems doomed.

It is true that in (35i), the subject and object roles in both definiens and definiendum are plausibly canonically associated with those positions (percipient rather than agent, for subject, patient for object of both *seek* and *find*). But in (36i), the two arguments involved are essentially those deemed to be alike: it is hardly plausible to assert that there is some intrinsic asymmetry between the two roles here (although there should be if the definition adequately reflected the properties of the definiendum).

It is not even the case that there is any intrinsic differentiation between roles suited to be internal and external arguments. There are definitions where the internal role of the definiendum apparently corresponds to an external role in the definiens:

37	*leave*	to allow to remain	C20
38	*lean*	to cause to lean	C20
39	*launch*	to cause to slide into water	C20

In each of these, the definiendum object must correspond to the subject of the embedded clause: to *leave Bill* is to *allow [Bill to remain]* and so on. Thus we cannot use the fact that there is an NL internal and external role in (36i) to help us label these differently for the language of thought. We see this again with respect to subject and object in cases like "Ruin faced John" compared with "John faced ruin." The conclusion, I think, must be that the language of thought does not differentiate its arguments one from the other by labels, but at least in the case of roles assigned to external argument and direct object in natural language, by means of structure.[45] If this is so, then we may legitimately and harmlessly refer to the external role of NL as the external one in the language of thought, though it will not follow that the realization of this notion is the same.

Of an example somewhat like these ("cause to die"), Fodor said it was immediately recognizable as dictionaryese (Fodor 1975, 127, footnote 20). The implication is that they are ungrammatical. But this may be a premature judgment; and in any case it does not explain why they are used and how they are understood.

Interestingly, the property which (37) to (39) share with the object-gaps in the earlier examples of this section is the Case-marking: the matrix verbs are all 'Exceptional Case Marking' verbs, so that they assign objective Case to the embedded subjects. We might ask whether it would be possible to have a subject gap with non-objective Case. Suppose the clause is tensed—could we have a definition like:

40   to believe [$_{CP}$ [$_{IP}$ *e* exist(s)]]

where we could certainly have (parallel to (37) to (39))

41   to believe [$_{IP}$ *e* to exist]

Intuition says the answer is negative. This correlates with the impossibility of heavy-NP-shift from the same position:

42   *I believe exists more than one solution to the problem

This can be rescued by *there*, but it is doubtful whether (43) improves much on (40):

43   to believe there exist(s)

The fact that the inner verb if tensed will have to agree in number with our putative missing NP is of course a bit awkward.[46] The *there*-insertion is perhaps a redherring—we could try:

44   to believe [*e* catches mice]

It seems as if this is irredeemably ungrammatical. If so—and again there is correlation with the impossibility of heavy NP shift—there is presumably some binding violation. Movement from this position is possible when the movement is to the left, where what is moved is a *wh*-element: we can have

45   Who$_k$ do you believe [$_{CP}$ e_k [$_{IP}$ t_k catches mice]?

So either the empty operator, or movement which is properly rightward, is to blame for the unacceptability of (40) and (44). Since at least phonologically null *wh*-elements can occur in the parallel relative clause (*the cat (that) I believe catches mice*) it looks as if it is rightward movement that is special. One obvious possibility is that it is the fact that the SPEC node is available only on the left that makes the difference. The movement in (45) would result in an ECP violation if the second landing site were not the CP SPEC, since INFL is not a proper governor, whereas in (41) and (37) to (39), the matrix verb properly governs the trace. But if movement is rightward in (40) and (44), there will be an ECP violation. We then have syntactic motivation for what was when I introduced it in section 2.4.2 largely a mnemonic convenience: we do want the empty operator for internal roles to be on the right, and we require that the traces of its movement are subject to the ECP. Assuming for a moment elimination at surface or LF, the operator will now be adjacent to the NP to which it assign a role. We may assume the role is allocated by something like predication—that is, requiring adjacency and sisterhood.

This line of argument raises the question of whether elimination or any other use MUST be at a level where we have objects to the right. Clearly, LF' will satisfy this requirement anyway, for English. But if we move to LR, then we pass through some translation procedure. Even supposing that the language of thought has a syntax with structures of the familiar kinds, conforming to X' theory, little can be deduced. For there is nothing to stop the translation procedures turning external to internal arguments, choosing different parameters for X', and so on.

What IS crucial is the adequacy and generality of the incoming information. Because for translation from English, internal arguments can be recognized as expected to the right of the head, it is necessary that the item offered for translation has this property. Hence (44) for instance, which will permit only leftward operator movement, will not do as a definiendum.

But only a system with SPEC and internal argument on opposite sides of the head will allow the ECP satisfaction to be preserved after translation. Would we expect such a property to hold of the language of thought? I will pursue this question further in chapter 5.

A minor consequence of the impossibility of definitions like (40) and (44) will be that the gap in the definiens corresponding to the missing object of the definiendum does always receive objective Case in English. In a language like German, word-for-word translations of some of the definitions like those above could lead to mismatches of Case assigning properties in definiens and definiendum. The dictionary maker must take steps to match up Cases, ignore the problem, or stipulate Case separately.

If we suppose that the definitions are to be taken under a meaning–meaning interpretation, so that to every (or at least, this) new lexical item of English, a new concept is constructed, then we have a complex concept. That is, it was not one of the primitive ones, but is constructed out of such (or out of previously known complex concepts). However, it is constructed by interesting means, not just by conjunction, which is often apparently supposed to be the only available mechanism. If an empty operator corresponding to lambda abstraction is available, then clearly the range of possible defined concepts is qualitatively greater than just with elementary logical operators. There are interesting questions about what restrictions (if any) there are on such processes— for instance, for ruling out the trivial, or by constraining the type of variable which can exist.

2.4.3.2 Other polyadic predicates

Dictionaries traditionally designate verbs as transitive or intransitive, or both. The majority of transitive verbs take a direct object; the corresponding definitions were discussed in the last section. But verbs may take clausal complements, or may subcategorize for prepositional features on an NP argument. Adjectives and nouns may have arguments. Dictionaries of the ordinary kind are surprisingly unhelpful about these other arguments.

If the definition is used only for elimination, then arguably it is not necessary to provide any characterization of the syntactic categories of possible complements, but it is certainly necessary to indicate the semantic role of those that may appear. Such indication is not always supplied, or if supplied it may be in an unhelpful form.

It is hard to know what conclusions to draw from the forms of definition here, on account of these apparent inadequacies. On the one hand, one could attribute these to the exigencies of the dictionary format, and to the lack of a suitable theoretical foundation for the implicit analysis. On the other hand, one might deduce from the presumed utility of the dictionary that the distinctions which are not made, or which are blurred, are in fact inessential in some interesting way. One possibility if dictionaries are treated as supplying word–meaning pairings is that the meaning indicated may only approximate to an existing concept, but that if this is in some way sufficiently close, it will be assumed under normal pragmatic processing assumptions that this concept was in fact being indicated: all the definiens has to do is to point in more or less the right direction. It is likely to be the case that a combination of these approaches will be required, and that in consequence any conclusions drawn must be fairly tentative.

There are three main interconnected questions which arise in relation to the discussion of earlier sections. These are: How does the dictionary indicate the argument structure of the definiendum? How is the lack of necessary correspondence between s-selection and c-selection handled? and, What provision is made for arguments introduced by designated prepositions?

The obvious way to indicate the argument structure of the definiendum is to make sure that the definiens has a matching structure. This is the process which has been discussed in relation to the items of previous sections. For example, we have

46   *impute*   to ascribe   C20

The three obligatory arguments of *impute* correspond in all respects to those of *ascribe*: we have 'NP [V NP [to NP]]', with a correspondence at the level of interpretation too. If only elimination is required, the failure of an obligatory argument of the definiendum to be obligatory in the definiens is not serious, so long as a corresponding phrase is at least optional. The example of *lean* (transitive) from section 2.4.3.1 illustrates this:

47   *lean*   to cause to lean   C20

The transitive verb *lean* has three obligatory arguments, the third being introduced by a preposition. The preposition I think must be *on* or *against*, but any preposition with a suitable meaning would do—it has to denote the relation of the object NP to some support. It is possible to calculate that the *lean* in the definiens must have an 'intransitive' agentless interpretation, as we saw in the last section. But it is not possible to calculate whether or not this verb is one which has a prepositional phrase argument: is it the verb that occurs in (48i), (ii), or (iii), or are these all the same verb anyway?

48   i   The chimney is leaning (badly)

     ii   The plants are leaning away from the house

     iii The broom is leaning against the wall

Of these three, only the last has a congener with the causative *lean* (I believe). It is only this one which might be analyzed as having a PP which was a simple V" modifier, predicating *against the wall* of the broom: the plants in (ii) may be planted close up to the house. However, it seems most likely that all three should be taken to contain occurrences of the same verb, with a PP argument (or suitable Adverbial such as *outward*) which is optional. If this is so, then occurrences of the transitive *lean* of the definiendum will be comprehensible when they have an accompanying PP of the required kind. What cannot be deduced is the fact that not every PP which is suited to the definiens will do, nor the fact that the PP is obligatory as argument to the definiens.

It is commonplace for an item which does not immediately strike one as ambiguous to have multiple syntactic subcategorization possibilities. In some cases these are predictable, as when there is s-selection for a proposition, which will typically be realized as a CP clause, but may surface as an NP—with or without a designated preposition. It is reasonable in these cases that the definition is phrased

Dictionary Definitions 147

so as to incorporate both possibilities, or that the user may have to infer the one from the other. Examples of both these strategies occur:

49	*eager*	ardent to do or obtain	C20
50	*believe*	to regard as true	C20
51	*entail*	to bring on as an inevitable consequence	C20

The entries for neither of *believe* nor *entail* offer anything where a complement *that* clause could be eliminated at surface.

We may take it that for *eager*, the alternatives offered are for the alternative elimination contexts of say *eager to escape* and *eager for justice*. Possibly we have to interpret the *to do* in (49) as a kind of dummy, conventionally present as a place-holder (see 2.5 below for discussion). Alternatively, and perhaps more interestingly, the elimination environment does not distinguish clauses from suitable nominalizations. That is, *eager to escape* can produce after elimination *ardent to do escape/escaping*. This is consistent with the lack of categorial labeling already suggested, and with common s-selection lexical entries for such related items. The verb *obtain* is expecting a direct object, whereas the argument of the NP-complement *eager* must have a preposition (*for*): it seems to be assumed that the presence of such a preposition in the elimination context would cause no problem.

For *believe*, we need first to know what the subcategorization for *regard* is. I think we have a proposition, of type <t>, headed by *true*. (The *as* is, I take it, an operator on *true*, adding some dimension of 'let's pretend' to it. *As* may take as its complement AP, NP, at least). With ordinary AP, we will need a small clause kind of construction, to get the propositional type. With APs assigning no external argument, we must at surface have an external expletive argument *it* (for reasons which are considered in chapter 4). Since this latter is not present, the definiens apparently offers only a possible NP gap. So a phrase like [*believe what Mary said*] will be unproblematic, but no surface elimination is available for [*believe that mermaids sing*]. Elimination at LF will produce something like

52 [regard [as [true e_k]]] O_k [that mermaids sing]

But if LF does not refer to syntactic categories, then we can take the chain <e, O> to be capable of transmitting its θ-role to a proposition which happens to be realized as a clause, as required. The expletive referred to above is forced by the Case filter (see 4.2.5). It follows that the Case filter does not apply to the level at which we eliminate. That a propositional content is required is indicated by the status of the predication *true*: it is predicated of propositions, realized by clauses or special NPs. If we record this fact by giving such an adjective a θ-type which reflects this—not <p>, equivalent to <e,t>, but <t,t>, then the expression in (52) will have consistent θ-types. It would follow that some NPs (such as [*what Mary said*]) would have to have type <t>, at least in some environments; this is not implausible.

The definition offered for *entail* is suited to elimination at surface in phrases with NPs, such as *This will* [*entail* [*our early departure*]], but not *This will* [*entail* [*that we depart early*]]. Again, intuition about s-selection suggests that the type <t> is appropriate for both arguments of *entail*. There is an added complication that *bring on* undoubtedly may have an inappropriate type <e> argument. It is perhaps a trifle perverse of the dictionary maker to have chosen to give just an NP-suitable definiens, if a clause-suitable one could have been produced instead.

In the definition for *eager*, we noted that the user would need to ignore the designated preposition of an NP argument to the verb. There seems to be an assumption that suitable prepositions can be added, ignored or substituted. This tends to reinforce the view that these prepositions are rather like Case-assigners in a highly inflected language: they serve merely to distinguish one argument from another, in many instances, and in others, are apparently present only because the head is incapable of assigning objective Case. A noun like *inside* for instance is relational—it must have an internal argument, but cannot assign that NP objective Case. The *of* is the normal Case-preposition.

53   *inside* the side, space, or part within   C20

The definiens, unlike the definiendum, permits the argument to appear directly, but this should cause no problem. If Case is not a relevant constraint on the level at which the definitions are processed, and if these prepositions are indeed Case markers, the failure of the lexicographer to account for them is largely justified.

Suppose then that the preposition *of* should be eliminated at LF/LR. However, the existence two or more internal arguments on an equal footing would lead to problems in the representation, since in general arguments DO have to be distinguished one from another. If we have rejected labels, including role and Case labels, then we are left with structure and ordering as the sole means of discrimination.

If multiple arguments do not need to be distinguished, they can, but need not, be amalgamated into a single plural NP. So we find:

54   *separate*   to divide: ... to disunite   C20

All of *to separate A and B*, *to separate the As*, and *to separate A from B* are grammatical; but *divide* cannot be used with *and* in the relevant sense (?*divide the sheep and the goats*), nor can *disunite* any longer be used with *from* to introduce a second argument (?*disunite nation from nation*). The various definiens offered could of course be taken as alternatives, to be selected in part by their fitness to eliminate when particular arguments are present. But it seems equally possible that *separate* s-selects for a set of entities, and that a listing, a plural, or a pair of arguments where one has a designated preposition, are all equally good realizations of such a set. Elimination at a level which recognized just the set, and ignored the categorial variation, would allow all the definitions to be used for any case. Predicates taking set-arguments are a somewhat separate issue, which will not be discussed here.[47]

Sometimes, the existence of a designated preposition with the definiendum is recognized, and a comment is added. Among many offerings for *apt* is

55   *apt* open to impressions, ready to learn (often with *at*)   C20

Without the parenthetical, and given that definitions separated by commas usually relate to the same interpretation, we would expect the item defined to be intransitive. But *learn* may be transitive, and it is the argument which may be the object of *learn* that is introduced by *apt* with the preposition *at*, as in *John is apt at crossword puzzles*. Apart from this helpful piece of information, the entries for *apt* are simply listed, with nothing to mark what sort of complements are possible. They are grouped to run 'intransitive', 'clause-taking', and 'intransitive or transitive', followed by an American usage:

56 *apt* fitting: fit: suitable: apposite: tending:
liable: ready or prone: open to impressions,
ready to learn (often with *at*): (US) likely

The grouping follows what in a larger dictionary would be a separation under distinct headings. The OED (approximately) puts the groups each under a separate numbered section, with subdivisions within these. This corresponds to my understanding of *apt*: there are (ignoring the US usage) three distinct meanings—the word is ambiguous. But when it comes to *believe*, there are in the OED again separate headings for the NP and clausal complement cases:

57 6.   ... to accept (a statement) as true
    7.   With clause or equivalent inf. phrase: To hold it as true *that*

In this case, there is no ambiguity; the distinct definiens are required simply to accommodate the syntactic categories permitted as argument when a head s-selects for a proposition. However, the headings are adjacent, and the separation according to complement category is probably helpful to the user.

The cases just discussed have indicated that s-selection rather than c-selection was of importance in distinguishing distinct meanings, both with respect to the syntactic category of the argument (at least, clause and NP), and with respect to any designated prepositions. The argument may be carried further, so that a common lexical entry may be made for verbs and derived nominals, and possibly for adjectives too. This suggests that we might attempt to derive from a common source the selection requirements (and, implicitly, the meaning) of other sets of related items. But it is clear that the strategy of simply assuming identical argument structure is not appropriate for all cases, at least given the standard treatment of adverbs and determiners. Elsewhere[48] I have explored the possibilities in relation to the various lexical items *two*: noun, adjective and determiner; systematic type-changing is needed. There are plenty of other inviting items, such as *opposite*, which Chambers's gives as adjective, adverb, preposition and noun. This item indicates yet again that we need a systematic treatment of operators.

2.5 Problem definitions

The problem of indicating argument structure is worse with nouns and adjectives, since the complements are more often optional. For example, nominalizations are frequently defined using phrases such as "the act of," followed by the congeneric verb, as in (1) and (2):

1 *destruction*   the action of destroying something   DEL

2 *destruction*   act of destroying   C20

Of these, the first suggests that there can be no object NP for *destruction*, since the appropriate place in the definiens is filled by *something*. The second, contrariwise, suggests that an object NP is obligatory, since there is an object gap in the definiens, and the verb is always transitive. The problem of *something* is taken up below; let us suppose (as we need to) that it can indicate an object gap. Then it is expected that the dictionary user will know that arguments of nouns may in general be omitted, with a fixed semantics (existential). Nouns like *destruction* have subjects as well as objects. The possible subject argument as seen in

3 the enemy's destruction of the city

will fit into the subject slot of the head of the definiens in (2), since this gives just an N' constituent. But in (1), the definiens is an NP with determiner, apparently precluding this possibility. The incompatibility of the definite article and the subject possessive may well be due to constraints which fail to apply to LF/LR. Given the frequent lack of determiners where they would usually be expected, we may take it that some determiners, and in particular perhaps *the*, are indeed not represented in UR (the final utterance representation) at least. If the definite article is essentially metalinguistic,[49] it will not ordinarily contribute to well-formedness conditions, and so is possibly not visible at LF. Whether there are any syntactic as opposed to pragmatic conditions actually requiring it in certain environments at S-structure, I am not sure. There could be, even if the semantic content is metalinguistic, since the item has a syntactic category and a phonological realization, and is constrained to occur only where those features allow.

In the definiens in (1) and (2), there is an agent role unfilled: the gerund *destroying* is itself capable of accommodating a possessive NP as agent; for (2) we will need, presumably, (4):[50]

4   [[the enemy's]$_k$ act] of [PRO$_k$ destroying the city]

It is necessary to consider what representation will permit elimination to produce the equivalents of (4) when the elimination context does contain subject and object associated with *destruction*, and what happens when these arguments are absent. Assuming that there is a common s-selection lexical entry for *destruction* and for *destroying* (possibly non-distinct from the entry for *destroy*), will entail that this provides the maximum number of argument places.

We may assume that objects of nouns will succumb to the same procedures as objects of verbs—we assume operator movement to the right. It is unlikely that subjects of nouns follow subjects of verbs, since the SPEC position of DP seems not to have the same 'escape-hatch' properties as the SPEC of CP. If an operator binding an empty subject cannot go there, and if adjunction to argument DPs is forbidden (Chomsky 1986b), the only alternative to admitting that sheer substitution is at work is to use PRO. So we may postulate that the representation for (2) is

5   [[PRO$_k$ act [of PRO$_k$ destroying t_j]] O_j]

The two PROs must be coindexed whatever interpretation they receive. It seems likely that if (5) were substituted for *destruction* in (3), that ordinary rules of control for PRO would ensure that it was referentially dependent on *the enemy*, as required.

The question that arises when the elimination environment does not contain overt arguments is the proper representation of the 'optionality' of the arguments. Semantically, roles cannot be optional: if the conceptual or pseudo-semantic notion has a given number of arguments, then no propositional form will be attained if these arguments are not filled. Of course, we may invoke ambiguity, postulating two related items with different numbers of arguments.[51] And we may postulate regular devices which construct new items with increased valency from old ones, rather than following the easier course of constructing items with fewer apparent argument slots out of old ones. There is also the device of using empty categories with designated meaning, like PRO$_{arb}$.

Let us consider first the lexical representation for *destruction*. There are good grounds for supposing that it has two arguments—see for example Chomsky (1986a, 192 ff., and 168). If it has two arguments, we would give it semantic type <e,<e*,k>>, for some k,[52] where the star marks the external argument. If it occurs without either of its arguments, then it should apparently have type <k>. However, we may ask with respect to the interpretation of the type <e,<e*,k>> predicate what values have apparently been supplied for the missing arguments, in the reduction to type <k>. There are three possibilities: a value found from context; an existential quantification; or a 'PRO$_{arb}$' kind of universal quantification. For objects, see Cole 1987. For subjects, the first of these might be obtained by means of a controlled PRO interpretation, if the value is linguistically available within the required domain, as suggested above. The second kind of interpretation could use a designated empty category, but there is not such a one for subjects in English, it seems. However, passive (implicit) subjects ARE usually given an existential interpretation in the absence of a *by* phrase, so that if we take nouns like *destruction* as optionally passive, we may obtain this reading (from an implicit PRO in (5)). We should also determine to what extent unassigned roles can function like implicit arguments in other constructions. It would be reasonable to find that which (if any) of these options are available depends on the syntactic category or Case-marking properties of the head, on the external versus internal nature of the θ-role applicable, or on structural matters. I will leave this for now, coming back to some of the questions in chapter 4.

The existence of definitions such as (1) repeated below may raise doubts as to the plausibility of the mechanisms for using definitions on which I have been relying. It might be suggested that there are special conventions for definitions, and that these have little to do with ordinary processing.

1   *destruction*   the action of destroying something   DEL

It looks as if what we have is a place-holder of some sort for the argument of the definiendum. Such place-holders seem to be used particularly when there need be no overt complement at surface, so that they do usefully provide the correct semantics for such an empty argument. If in processing definitions we can search for these and replace them by the actual argument from the elimination context, then is all the assumed construction of representations with empty operators unnecessary? The output constructed as in this suggestion can be incorporated in a more orthodox elimination process after all the internal arguments have been dealt with. That is, we would substitute not the definiens as an X term but rather a completed X'. This sounds possible, but in fact the procedure outlined would not be viable where the argument of the definiendum in the context is an NP which has been subject to movement: there is no saturated X' unit any more. It is clear that what is needed to make movement possible is a detachment of the chain from the initial site of θ-role assignment, and this can be supplied in the notation I have been constructing (see further in chapter 4). In section 1.5.2, I suggested that we could treat such items as empty operators *in situ*, which has the same effect.

Other items which perhaps occur for reasons other than providing the proper definiens are the *to* of verb definitions, and the stray determiners of noun definitions. The former is probably semantically null and I treat it as morphologically part of the verb; among the latter, the definite article has been discussed above, and the indefinite articles may perhaps be treated as effectively adjectival (see 2.1.3). But there are determiners less easily explained, as in (6) ((29) of 2.1):

6 *ism* any distinctive doctrine C20

7 *isobare* either of two atoms of different chemical elements but of identical atomic mass C20

These are probably best explained as having a metalinguistic function: by which I mean that we need to introduce quotation in the explanation of their use.

There are a number of dictionary definitions offered which include other phrases unsuited for use in elimination. An example is:

8 *egret* a white heron of several species C20

(A shorter definition might offer just 'a heron'). It cannot be the case that if for instance I saw an egret, I saw a white heron of several species. If the definition had run "... heron of one of several species" all would be well. It is also true that there are several species such that a white heron of that species is an egret—interestingly, this suggests that

Dictionary Definitions

if we perform QR of [*several species*] to interpret the definiens, then we can use this as telling us when we may use the definiendum. This is reversing the usual assumptions about dictionary use. Normally, we assume that it is to be used for interpreting an existing sentence, rather than for licensing production.

A failure to recognize encyclopedic information would lead to some bizarre effects. Consider (from the 1983 edition of Chambers's)

9 *Juggernaut*   an incarnation of Vishnu, beneath the car of whose idol at Puri devotees were supposed by Europeans to immolate themselves

Dictionary definitions have problems, not unnaturally, with relational terms or other items where reference to context is natural. Anaphoric terms can be distinctly odd, as in

10 *neuter*   neither one thing nor the other   C20

In other cases, failure to provide for anaphoric or other argument links leads to sheer error, as in

11 *factor*   a number that divides another number   SMP

The definition given in (7) above is implausible: I assume that this too is properly a relational term—the atoms are isobares of each other. Relational nouns—those with NP arguments, or possibly, as suggested in 1.5.2, properly operators on NP operands—seem to force reference in the definiens to what should also appear as the complement of the definiendum. Since the complement is perforce absent in the definiendum, error results. It is the surface optionality of these complements (particularly if the relation is symmetric), together with the need to stipulate what they range over, that forces their mention. Implicit definitions avoid these particular problems with defining such terms, but are not without their own (see 3.3.1, example 31).

Notes

1. A possible counterexample is a unicorn, defined say as an imaginary or fabulous animal. I shall take it, however, that unicorns ARE animals, and that pragmatic processes determine that in more ordinary cases, speakers and hearers conspire to exclude animals of such kinds, according to the requirements of relevance.
2. The interpretation of the conjunctions and disjunctions is not always simple, or even consistent, but I am not going to discuss the problems now.
3. This rules out flat structures. If these are needed for a particular language, it would be necessary either to invoke some parametrizing of possibilities at the structure building level, or to parametrize whatever structural relation depends on the flat structure. The notions of domination and command associated with adjunction structures can be designed to treat these just as if they were flat (see 1.1.2).
4. NPs can be predicates too. The bracketed NP in *John left the room [a sadder and wiser man]* is clearly not an argument, and needs to be licensed (see below). Because NPs cannot be seen as operators, *wh*-NPs will be *in situ* at D-structure. I do not exclude the possibility of VP as a non-canonic argument (complement), either. We have to require that it is V" that is canonically a predicate if we want to keep to maximal projections here: otherwise, it is I' which has the subject NP as a sister. If subjects are adjoined to VP (Koopman and Sportiche 1985, Manzini 1989), the problem vanishes. Otherwise, we need to stipulate as well that since I is canonically an operator, it is not a head for the purposes of licensing an argument V".
5. Rothstein (1984) relates the two clauses of the EPP on the basis of regarding the requirement that clauses have subjects as a special case of the requirement that all lexical and syntactic functions must be saturated. VP is a syntactic function (*i.e.* predicate). I am indebted to Alessandra Giorgi for discussion. The matter of expletives will be taken up in Chapter 4.
6. It will become obvious that not every item defined could be a maximal projection. Many are of X-zero level. It is not particularly obvious with NP, since on the DP analysis we might regularly have no N-max specifier position.
7. There is more than one way of setting up the requirements on S-structure. The simplest is to assume that they match those for LF; this should always be the unmarked assumption.

8. See Chomsky 1986b, p. 26–27, on Specifier-Head agreement, and the possible treatment of the complement of *wonder* as a selection relation satisfied at LF.

9. It is not entirely clear that even this is true at a syntactic level. Chomsky (1982, 32) discusses an example attributed to Howard Lasnik: 'the coach is too incompetent [for the team to win any games]' where the infinitival clause more usually has another gap—a connecting pronoun is also possible, though gaps are the norm. Possibly the explanation is pragmatic, but possibly there needs to be a type-changing mechanism such as the one I constructed to explain how NPs could be predicational in semantic status. Another mechanism is that proposed for Russian in Rappaport (1987). Alternatively, what we have here is not a predicate.

10. I am rejecting '$PRO_k[e_k ...]$' on the grounds that the semantic type is wrong—there is no lambda operator, so we would not have a predicate.

11. Participial phrases like this are discussed in Williams (1987). He considers the 'small clause' story about *-ed* phrases, but does not consider semantic objections, nor does the idea of using an operator instead of PRO seem to have occurred to him. The Russian relative clauses without gaps (Rappaport 1987) seem in the end to have postulated for their explanation a deleted COMP element which semantically is as it were a phrase containing the variable to be bound by the operator. Note also that in (3), which will be discussed in section 2.4.3.1, we will expect the whole to be a projection of V, probably V', and the missing object in *urge on* will have to be bound by an empty operator (of a non-standard kind) giving $[[\text{urge } e_i \text{ on}] O_i]$ perhaps.

12. Something more has to be said about the intensional adjectives like *former*: what Montague said of course was that all adjectives should be treated as functions taking the N' as argument. It is I think correct to assume that only designated categories may have logical operator rather than conjunction reading: only AP can provide what are essentially operators on N'.

13. There may be other things to be said about locative PPs. Giorgi's hypothesis about locative PPs denies this connection between predicational and θ-role assigning properties of a category (Giorgi 1988).

14. In fact, *not* is an adverb not free in its combination with an adjective—unlike the morpheme *non-*, for instance. See section 2.3.3 for discussion.

15. For more argument, see Williams 1987.

16. See Ades and Steedman 1982 for argument, especially concerning left to right processing of standardly right-branching structures.

17. The θ-role may otherwise be described as being allocated to the whole chain <*John, e*>, which is described as an abstract representation of *John* in the structure (Chomsky 1986a 96).

18. Note that the θ-criterion as relating to types cannot be met in the normal fashion at D-structure, since [John] would have no θ-role assigner. It would be possible with the type-theory to remedy this: we could use non-standard ways of composing the functions.

19. For some discussion of object gaps see Cole (1987), Brody and Manzini (1988).

20. Given that quantification is usually binary in NL, to say simply 'existential' is a bit odd. And in intransitive *eat*, what is eaten must be suited for eating: not just eatable but edible. The binary version of the existential quantifier does in fact have a nice gap just waiting for this sort of thing—where we may suppose the content is to be supplied pragmatically. We may construct a generalized quantifier with meaning '$\lambda P\ (\exists : Q\ ;\ P)$' where Q is what I am talking about. In the case of *mislead*, we seem to want Q to be 'people', despite the fact that one can mislead an animal.

21. The GPSG solution would be like this, and *likely* would belong to two ID rules, one for each of the structures (13) and (14). It will quite often be the case that the c-selections I posit are close to those required in a monostratal grammar.

22. Unless we introduce the whole I″ expansion, and have the operator outside that, as in (25) of section 2.2.2. We'd then need an explanation of the absence of tensed versions. In fact, Enç's hypothesis (Enç 1986) for semantics suggests that tense sensitivity is rarely if ever needed in adjectives, and indeed only needs to be allowed for in nouns (or perhaps more probably higher under D″) and verbs (we might suppose under I). This suggests that I″ with its I node would be inappropriate for an adjective definiens.

23. It was suggested to me that this was implausible. Consider however: (i) *small-minded* and *like-minded* (ii) *This hat is like that*; *the hats are alike* and *this line is parallel to that*; *the lines are parallel*. Maling (1983) however argues that *like* is now a preposition.

24. See Barwise and Cooper for discussion.

25. I seem to have taken this processing procedure rather too strongly as a child: on reading "Untouched by human hand" on the cornflakes packet, I hazarded the suggestion that Mr. Kellogg might be a monkey.

26. There is of course some asymmetry even in ordinary conjunction, since there is linear ordering at least in the NL representation. This is indeed

Dictionary Definitions

exploited, but normally exactly to mirror relations which are essentially ordering relations: for example temporal ordering, and causal or inferential orderings, as in '*Do that again and I'll smack you.*'

27. The facts here need some explanation, since the structures I have proposed for (73) and (75) are rather similar, and have similar interpretations. Consider

i John left the room angry / *and angry

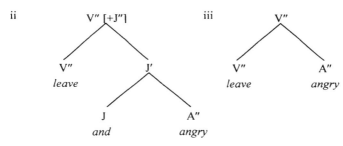

But (ii) is ungrammatical, although some VP predicates can be conjoined with non-matching categories—*a man [greedy and attracted by riches]*. It seems that it is the tense under I that makes (ii) ungrammatical; presumably some feature (say to give coindexing of the trace when the verb moves to I) is assigned to the top V". In a conjunction structure, the feature passes to both conjuncts and hence to A"; in (iii) it passes only to the head, via the lower V".

28. The only possible complication would be that the modifiers in the matrix phrase and in the definiens were improperly ordered after elimination of the definiendum. If modifiers of the type under discussion are semantically conjuncts, any effects of the variation of order could only be stylistic or pragmatic. There is indeed a preferred ordering on adjectives, but as far as I know there is no non-redundant semantic content to this.

29. There are a number of reasons for assuming that APs are always generated on the right. (a) other modifying XP phrases appear invariably on the right; (b) Even "small" APs may be on the right if they are conjoined to another normally-right phrase: "a man [sick and suffering from fever]"; (c) Rightward movement of the whole AP would violate the spirit at least of the ECP, since the trace would precede its antecedent for proper government, so that the predictability would be lost in left to right processing; (d) leftward

movement of a whole AP could be connected with the operator status of some adjectives.

30. There are sentences like *Not that I ever thought he would arrive on time*; possibly this may involve 'semiquotation', as discussed below, or perhaps there is omission of an initial "It is ..."

31. Blakemore 1989.

32. See Keenan and Faltz 1985. It is not clear to me whether it is possible to induce all the required cross-categorial negation uses from one of type <t,t> using just the combinators we need for θ-theory within syntax. If not, then a genuine cross-categorial semantics must be set up in the lexicon, so there will not be just the type <t,t> there.

33. There are other possibilities for the preposition: it may be *to, with* or *from*, at least. If the suggestions of section 2.2.7 are correct, the pairing of *secretary to the director* and *director's secretary* indicates that there is an internal argument *director* marked by *to*, for instance.

34. There is in fact another *be*, equative *be*, which has, I think, an external and an internal argument, and is a Case-assigner. I suggest in chapter 4 that small clause *be* can account for *there* existentials.

35. In 2.3.3, there was some indication that there is a separate auxiliary *be*, which is an operator taking a V" operand, and hence transmitting the θ-role. I am assuming that this is what we have for passive-*be*.

36. In general, no word or phrase ever assigns two external roles, unless it is an adjunction structure, where the two have to be jointly assigned to the same entity. Certain nouns, typically nominalizations, are exceptions to this— see discussion of example (4) in section 4.2.1.

37. The same effect shows with *wh*-movement:

i   I do not know [how clever]$_j$ [John]$_k$ is supposed to be t_k t_j

ii   * I do not know [who]$_k$ [cleverest]$_j$ is supposed to be t_k t_j

38. But see Keenan and Faltz 1985, 319 ff., with *seems phony*.

39. Because Montague had all his APs of type <p,p>, firstly he could not use the distinction between these and simple <p> predicates to tell whether an AP would go in predicate position; and secondly he had to postulate in effect an empty N' for every predicate AP. There are argued to be certain advantages to doing this:

John is small $\Rightarrow$ John is (a) small MAN/OBJECT/ANIMAL

Dictionary Definitions

etc. We obtain a locus for the ambiguity. But this is only useful if *Bimbo is a small elephant* can only mean 'small for an elephant', and not, for instance, 'small for a two-year-old-elephant'; which latter, surely it could. So I suppose the comparison class to be pragmatically determined, and not to be syntactically present.

40. As formulated in Chomsky 1981, the Projection Principle requires that both kinds of argument structure information from the lexicon are projected from LF to the other levels. In other places, we seem merely to have a requirement that subcategorization (and presumably θ-role information) is projected from the lexicon uniformly to all levels. In Chomsky 1981, the justification given is that "Clearly, subcategorization properties of lexical items must be satisfied at LF. This is true by definition ...." With the distinction between s-selection and c-selection made in Chomsky 1986a, it seems to me that what is true 'by definition' at LF is that *s-selection* properties must be properly realized, if LF is the input to interpretation, and if s-selection bears a systematic relation to a simple categorial language of thought. We can then drop the c-selection requirement on LF, though of course in general in an ordinary derivation, if these are met at one level, they will be met at the next. The problem with this under the interpretation as I have it at present, where θ-roles are taken to be s-selection features, is the optionality of subjects in NPs. But that is hardly insuperable: we could make every higher-type N optionally 'active' and 'passive' with no morphological change, for instance, and/or postulate a PRO-like element in the subject position.

41. Actually, the preposition is not always necessary, at least for some speakers—in for instance one of the related constructions: *John is less a fool than lazy*. We might have quotation here, so that we should not expect Case-marking.

42. See Cormack 1987.

43. Most dictionaries except the smallest give an infinitival form. I take it that this represents either a citation form or a morphological default of some sort. That is, the presence of *to* does not indicate that we have an I″ or C″.

44. It is tempting to generalize the ordinary predication relation to cover these, so that they may be brought under the small clause analysis (as suggested by Kayne 1981). I will resist the temptation now.

45. On alternative analyses of the verbs involved, this argument is not valid. Suppose we have *leave* c-selecting for a [+locative] small clause, where the PP is empty in (37), and suppose intransitive *lean* in (38) is locative in Burzio's (1986) sense. We might then construct a strict mapping between

putative θ-roles and syntactic positions. But this trivializes the question: this would immediately permit a meaning postulate to be stated referring to the s-selected internal <e> argument, obviating the need for roles as an intermediary. What we need to know is whether there are any meaning postulates depending on θ-roles as such, rather than on the lexical heads: and I doubt it. More interestingly, the suggestions above indicate that there may be a tighter relation between syntactic positions in definiens and definiendum than I have supposed: we could take the embedded external argument in the definiens in (37) to determine that *leave* must have a SC rather than an NP c-selection.

46. A dictionary for a language where object features get marked on the verb presumably would have a standard solution to this problem. Note also the comparable absence of AGR in verb definitions.

47. See Cormack 1984b.

48. Cormack 1986a.

49. See Kempson 1986 for proposals relating to the pragmatic treatment of definites.

50. Unless the subject of *act* is raised from a position as subject of *destroying*; this will not be correct if *act* assigns a θ-role to a subject. Consider the parallel (i) *John acted to destroy the vermin*. There seems to be no possibility of a full clause after *act*, which might suggest raising, but nor is an expletive subject possible. It would be in line with arguments in the next two chapters if the complement is subjectless (VP in (i) here; N″ in (4)). This will eliminate the problem of the governed PRO in (4), and achieve the effect of the coindexing required for (5).

51. See Dowty 1987.

52. If we are just considering a simplified semantics, then $k=p$, the proper type for nouns. If we want to step up to a more elaborated type system which takes into consideration the essentially proposition-like rather than entity-like nature of an NP containing *destruction*, then we will have $k=t$. The comment under example (49) in 2.4.3.2 suggests that the latter is correct.

CHAPTER THREE

Text Definitions

> The reader may set his mind at rest. In order to understand the considerations that will follow, he does not require to know what a transfinite ordinal number is.
>
> Poincaré, *Science and Method*

3.0 Introduction

Definitions given in running text or isolated within expository works are very different from dictionary definitions. In a dictionary definition, we have two separate linguistic entities, the definiendum and the definiens. In a typical text definition, there is a single linguistic unit, a sentence, which incorporates parts corresponding to these two. Because there is a single unit, there are possibilities such as the use of anaphora between elements connected with definiendum and definiens which are out of the question in standard dictionary definitions.[1] And if what we have is running text, there are requirements to do with normal processing which affect the form of a definition; the consequence is that such definitions are in most respects not distinct from a sentence used for some other purpose. An isolated definition has a conventional format, and would not sit happily as a definition in running text, although it is usually well-formed as a sentence of English.

Most of the examples I shall give are drawn from mathematics textbooks of a fairly discursive nature, addressed to eleven-year-olds. Bold face, underlining, or italic print in the books is shown here with italics. The definitions are similar to those in textbooks for other subjects for older students: I have taken some examples from logic and linguistics student texts.

1 A triangle with all three sides equal is called *equilateral*   SMP

2 A *convex* deltahedron is one in which all the vertices point outwards   SMP

(For the effect of the *one* in (2), see examples (46) and (47) in 3.2.2). The first example is what I shall call an 'introductory definition': it introduces in running text what should be the first occurrence of the new word—*equilateral*, here. Characteristically, but not invariably, the definiens precedes the definiendum, which appears at or near the end of the definition. The second is an isolated definition, with the definiendum at or near the beginning, and certainly preceding the definiens; and I shall refer to a definition such as this as a 'formal definition'. Among the introductory definitions, there are sub-species. There are what I shall call 'phoric' definitions. An example from the mathematics text books is (3):

3   This special isosceles triangle is called an *equilateral* triangle   A

The referent of *This special isosceles triangle* has to be found from the preceding text,of course, as in normal processing of the sentence. In some examples of phoric definitions, what has occurred previously is simply an instance of what is to be defined, so that what we have is what is traditionally known as an ostensive definition. My introductory definitions of 'introductory definition' and 'formal definition' above were merely ostensive. Also, in texts, definitions may be parasitic on some previous statement; they are introduced by apposition.

4   ... context, they have a probability of 1 and their information content is 0: they are *totally redundant*.   (Lyons 1968)

The definitions given so far have contained definiens and definiendum within a single clause (aside from the phoric and appositional definitions). 'Complex' definitions, where definiens and definiendum occur in separate clauses are quite common:

5   When two lines are a quarter of a turn apart, we say they are at right angles to one another   SMP

6   Two lines are said to be parallel if they are always the same distance apart   SMP

It is immediately apparent that the analysis of text definitions has to be very different from that of dictionary definitions. The main reason for this is that text definitions are almost always couched as implicit rather than explicit definitions. That is, the definiendum and definiens are not isolated. In consequence, there is no suggestion that elimination from some linguistic context is simply a matter of taking out the definiendum and plugging in the definiens. It does not follow that elimination does not take place, but it is clear that some further processing is involved. This processing is presumably at least largely normal processing, starting from the usual syntactic and semantic analysis of the sentence comprising the definition, but with the possibility that the interpretation or use is partially driven by the recognition that this IS a definition. There is also a sense in which an implicit definition is a more powerful device than an explicit definition, given the resources of English, which may lead to more elaborate or subtle semantic information.

I shall approach the interesting issues which arise here gradually, by starting with text definitions which are nearest to dictionary definitions in their properties, and progressing to those whose properties and functions seem reasonably clear, before turning to those where alternative analyses have to be considered. In the next two sections, any issues arising from the properties of complex definitions will be ignored.

3.1 Characteristics of text definitions

3.1.1 Identification of a definition

Since a definition in a text is in general an ordinary sentence, the question arises as to how the sentence is recognized as a definition—if indeed it is, or needs to be. In practice, in a text book, there is not usually any doubt. The plainest indication is some overtly metalinguistic terminology, such as the word *define* itself, or a reference to a *word* or *term*, so that we must recognize 'mention' as well as or instead of 'use'; quotation marks may have the same effect. In the following, I have italicized such metalinguistic terms:

7   By a system *is understood* a set ...

8   "Downgrading" is the *term* I attach to the assignment ...

9   A designative *is defined as* either ...

(The three examples above were from Leech 1969)

10   By the angles of a triangle we *mean* ...   SMP

These were from formal definitions. With those, there is also the possibility of setting the definition off in the text, and maybe even announcing it: "Definition: ...." Or the previous sentence may give warning:

11 ... the *term* "formator" has the following *interpretation*. Formators are those ... (Leech, ibid.)

In an introductory definition, the metalinguistic terms are most commonly the verbs *say* and *call*:

12 Any number that can be shown as a rectangular pattern of dots is *called* a rectangle number A

13 We *call* this field the 'Universe of Discourse' MME

14 Two straight lines that cross at right angles are *said* to be perpendicular to each other

Interestingly, each of these definitions involves, either explicitly, or implicitly as the suppressed agent of a passive verb, an agent. That is, the fact that attaching meanings to words is a human activity is frequently reflected in the form of a definition. The agent may be given as *we*, and further indication of the agent-directedness of the activity is quite often introduced by the addition of a modal such as *may* or *shall*:

15 A sentence may be said to be *analytic*, ... (Smith and Wilson)

16 We shall call the set of entailments obtained from surface structure in this way the *grammatically specified entailments* of a sentence (ibid.)

The agent is more likely to be explicitly mentioned when the definition is temporary, or idiosyncratic to the text.

It need not be the case that any agent is implied—definitions may use simply the copular *be*, or (less commonly) the word *occur*:

17 A polygon is convex if ...

18 Formators are those ... (see (11) above)

19 Ambiguity of cross reference occurs when a word ... (Hodges)

(We could paraphrase (17) with "A polygon is *said to be* convex ...," or (19) with "Ambiguity of cross reference is said to occur ..."). The verbs *be*, *call*, *say*, *understand*, and phrases containing them, serve to connect the definiendum with its supporting matrix to the definiens in its matrix, roughly. There is a lot more to be said than this; the matter will be taken up below. It is also possible in principle to have nothing to connect the two parts—consider (20)

20   An *equilateral* triangle has all its angles equal to 60°   SMP

A dictionary definition of *equilateral* might be *having all its angles equal*. If (20) were a definition, the word *triangle* would be part of the supporting matrix of *equilateral*, so that there would be nothing between this matrix and the definiens. Similarly,

21   A mammal suckles its young

could be construed as a definition, where *mammal* has the definiens *suckles its young*, again with no intervening connective. I have no clear examples of such definitions, however—the SMP quotation is part of a summary, and in other cases it may be that what we have is not intended even as a conditional definition. The example given in (22) below I do not identify as a definition, although it is probably correct to regard it as deliberately providing a context from which a meaning appropriate for immediate use can be deduced.

The other identifying feature of a definition is the indication of the target, the definiendum. In continuous text, and in a text book, the target is normally italicized; other typographical devices (such as the use of capital letters) may be used. It is not in practice safe to take just any italicized or underlined word as part of a definition, even when the item is new and apparently so recognized by the author. The author may be marking new terms without giving a definition (a habit that can be annoying).

22   By virtue of its potentiality of occurrence in a certain context, a linguistic unit enters into relations of two different kinds. It enters into *paradigmatic* relations with all the units which can also occur in the same context (...), and it enters into *syntagmatic* relations with the other units of the same level with which it occurs and which constitute its context.   (Lyons 1968)

What is confusing in such uses is whether or not we are being given information: we are entitled to expect information other than about meanings (*i.e.* relevance) from a piece of text which is NOT explicitly a definition.

As I mentioned above, quotation marks may be used. These usually identify the definiendum, as in (8), (11) and (13) above. Sometimes both definiendum and definiens may be so marked:

23   By 'natural' here we mean 'in accordance with the principle of relevance'   (Sperber and Wilson 1983)

It is necessary that SOMETHING serve to identify definitions, because the linguistic forms utilized have other (and in some sense prior) uses. In particular, if the simple copula is used, rather than one of the metalinguistic terms, we can have an interpretation as either a particular or a general statement, rather than as a definition. In a mathematics text, at least, we can frequently find statements of the form

24   A triangle has two of its sides equal

25   A number is divisible by eleven

where in context it is clear that this means "a certain hypothetical triangle," "A certain number." In ordinary discourse, where things have a more concrete existence, we would be more likely to find not

26   A cow is piebald / has a white patch

but

27   There is a piebald cow / a cow with a white patch

Generalizations however are frequently made using the copula and an indefinite:

28   A cow is a mammal

29   An equilateral triangle is isosceles

Occasionally, definitions include some indication at least of non-specificity. The *any* in (30) fulfills this function.

30   Any number that can be shown as a rectangular pattern of dots is called a *rectangle number*   SMP

The question of how the syntax and semantics of copular and other sentences of these three kinds (particular statements, generalizations, and definitions) contribute to the proper interpretation will be discussed in section 3.2.2. The point for the moment is simply that definitions are in general recognizable as such independently of their construal as such, and in particular independently of their context of use.

3.1.2 Targets

In a dictionary, we expect to find definitions of words. We look up a catchword (a string of letters), and under this we search for the meaning of the particular word (a linguistic entity) we have in mind. Sometimes, we find our word as part of a phrase, listed below the other meanings. A dictionary of the size of Chambers's 1960 has relatively few phrasal entries—taking a page at random, beginning with *photoelectricity*, I find just one (for *pica*), and on the following page phrases for just *Phrygian* and *physical*, if hyphened forms are ignored.[2] But in text books, targets identified by underlining very commonly include more than one word.

The commonest cases consist of an adjective-noun pair,[3] for instance *rectangular number, logical positivist, leptokurtic distribution, Cartesian coordinates*. It would be misleading to say that all these phrases were idioms, although it is true that the meaning of the whole is not fully predictable from the meaning of the parts. The noun head in each does have its usual meaning, and the contribution of the adjective is intersective: a logical positivist is a positivist, but is not necessarily logical. The adjective is one that could be applied to other entities,[4] and is such that once you know the meaning of the whole, and the meaning of the noun, the contribution of the adjective becomes apparent. It was Descartes who invented the coordinate system; the numbers are such that that number of objects is capable of being arranged in a rectangle; the graph of the distribution is pointed ... the positivists?

There are two kinds of explanation for the occurrence of these pairs as targets. Both require that the learning involved in making use of a definition is seen in a wider context of language use. We may try to explain, first, why there ARE such pairs at all: why are not the adjectives consistent in meaning; or why, given that the combination has a unique meaning not fully predictable from the parts, is the whole not lexicalized as a single noun? The answer lies I think simply in economy. By using a noun which has a fixed meaning, many of the inferences connected with the whole are predictable; by re-using an adjective with other uses, at least something is gained in the way of familiarity, and it will serve at worst as a mnemonic for its contribution to the whole. Further, the way is at least open for this adjective in this interpretation to be re-used—a potential obviously non-existent if a new lexical item for the undecomposed whole had been introduced. So for instance the 'Cartesian' of *Cartesian coordinates* is exploited in the phrase *Cartesian product*, and children go on to consider the properties of *triangular numbers*. Given, then, that there are pairs with partially unpredictable meaning, it is reasonable that the target cover not just the adjective but as much else as is necessary to determine the meaning. It is not however necessary, especially if the adjective in fact will not occur in any other sense in the surrounding text. It would be not unexpected if the *leptokurtic* on its own were the target; it would be otherwise with *logical*. But even dictionaries often give the range of application of an adjective (for instance), as in the classic example

31   *addle* a.   (of egg) rotten, producing no chicken   LOD

We might regard the inclusion of the noun as a warning, both in the dictionary and the text definition, that the adjective cannot be freely combined in the inferred meaning with other classes or entities.[5] In some cases, it may even be impossible to use the adjective predicatively in the relevant sense—but this may be determined by whether there is a 'noun-neutral' sense. Compare

32   The positivists were logical

33   The coordinates I gave you were Cartesian

The existence of an ordinary use of *logical* interferes with the special interpretation required (but unobtainable) in (32); where (33), though fairly odd, will be correctly construed just because *Cartesian* is inherently vague or variable, or more precisely, underdetermined in its contribution as an adjective—or alternatively because close relation to the man or to his philosophy can be ruled out.

I spoke above of the 'inferred meaning' of the adjective in the combination. It is not necessarily the case that there is such a thing. It is possible, for a start, that the reader who is offered the definition does not yet know the meaning of the head noun. It is fairly unlikely (though not impossible) that the child introduced to Cartesian coordinates has grasped the notion of coordinate systems as such. In formal logic, it is usual to give a recursive definition of the technical use of *formula* which begins by defining *atomic formula*. In both these cases, the complex adjective-noun pair has initially a non-decomposed interpretation. Any inferences which can be made can only be attributed to the whole, not to the parts. The situation that arises when the head noun IS known is rather more complicated; the interpretation of the whole may be as a conditional definition (see discussion in section 3.2.2). But it may be noted here that the adjective–noun combination is fairly regularly replaced by a noun related just to the modifier: 'prime numbers' become 'primes', 'semi-detached houses' become 'semis'.

Noun-noun targets are common, which is not surprising since the contribution of the non-head noun is notoriously variable, and it would be confusing to target this word, since its use as a head noun is probably both known and only partially helpful. A mathematics text produces examples like *flow diagram*, *rectangle number*, *product register*, *shift number*. The modifying or argument noun—the non-head—cannot be treated as an adjective, and is never capable of being used predicatively. Further, in contrast to the adjective-noun pairs, we seem to have a genuine collocational relationship. That is, we cannot have anything except the designated head noun, not even another noun referring to the right class of objects. There is a contrast between (34) and (35), despite their very close connections (both *rectangular number* and *rectangle number* are used in elementary books for *composite number*):

34   That number is a rectangular one

35   *That number is a rectangle one

Similarly, although figures and diagrams are as far as I know just the same, we cannot speak of a *flow figure*, only of *flow diagrams* or *flowcharts*. One can (counterfactually) talk of *rectangular primes* but not of *rectangle primes*.

Adverb-adjective targets can also be found: examples are *tautologically equivalent* (Suppes), *totally redundant* (Lyons), *distributionally equivalent* (Lyons), *linearly dependent*. If the equivalent adjective-noun pair is in use, then probably this would be subject to definition, usually—it would not be considered necessary to define *partially ordered* as well as *partial ordering*, for instance.

What constraints are there on phrasal targets? If the discussion of the adjective-noun pairs is on the right lines, we are looking for any minimal phrase which may have non-compositional semantics. (By 'minimal' here is intended 'minimal with respect to non-compositionality'). True idioms are unlikely to be used as technical terms in text books, or elsewhere. Apart from the reasons for non-compositionality discussed above, it also rather trivially occurs when items are fairly arbitrarily chosen for syntactic reasons—typically in English and many other languages, these items will be prepositions. So we may expect PPs as targets—*in free variation* (Lyons), for instance, and could also expect that the preposition initiating the complement might be included—*in free variation with*. Occasionally (and these conventions are after all *ad hoc* rather than explicitly advised by anyone) we have a non-minimal target, as in *powers of the number* (Sk).[6] It could be that the target is to be a syntactic constituent of the definition, so that *in free variation with* would be disallowed, and the inclusion of the arbitrary (even if unmarked) preposition *of* accounts for the extent of the target in *powers of a number*, or in *a family of parallel lines* (Sh)). Inclusion of the article in the target is rare, so it does not appear that a maximal syntactic constituent is required.

Targets consist very largely of nouns, or noun–adjective pairs. That seems to be what occurs to our authors as in need of definition. Adjectives, or adverb–adjective pairs form the next most frequent category. Verbs, or adverb-verb pairs, occur less commonly (examples are given in (40) and (45) in section 3.1.3). This roughly parallels the frequency of items in a dictionary, and these three are the major 'open class' categories. It appears that non-compositionality is confined to pre-modification.

3.1.3 Matrix of the target

Once the target is selected, a definition can be constructed. If the definition as a whole is to be a sentence of English, then it may not be possible simply to link the target to a definiens by embedding both within the appropriate metalanguage. (Even if it is possible, it may not be desirable, for reasons which will be discussed in section 3.2.2). Direct linking will in general be possible only if both target and definiens are in quotation. Let '+++' be some target, and '***' some definiens; then the definitions schematized in (35) will be well-formed as definitions:

36 i   '+++' means '∗∗∗'
    ii '∗∗∗' means '+++'
    iii By '+++', we mean '∗∗∗'

There are some variants of these, using different metalanguage links. The quoted items presumably count syntactically as NPs, whatever their internal content, so that the schemata in (36) will do equally for noun, verb, adjective, or even for non-linguistic symbols.

In general, we will need to embed the target in some other material, its 'matrix', before it can be part of a definition-sentence. Without quotation, the target in its matrix must be suited to be for instance a complement or subject of the metalanguage verb; it is necessary that these form an XP category. Suppose for instance we have an introductory definition using the passive of *call*. Then we require that the target and matrix produce an NP (or possibly an AP). If the target is a noun or N', then it must have a determiner if it is (as usual) singular; if the target is an adjective, there will have to be a supporting noun; if the intention is to define a verb, then the gerund can be chosen. Complements may have to be added (for other reasons).

37   ... is called an *angle bisector*

38   ... is called the *associative property* of natural numbers

39   ... are called *supplementary* angles

40   ... is called *factorizing*

41   A triangle with two equal sides is called *isosceles*   A

(I am doubtful about this last: I'd prefer the adjective to be quoted, or *called* replaced by *said to be*).

Similarly the use of *say* in the passive will determine the form of the matrix needed. If the link is taken to be *said to be*, then the complement of *be* will be an NP, PP, AP or participial VP. (Alternatively, the *be* may be taken to be a further part of the matrix— this will be discussed below). Instead of *be*, a verb like *form* can occur:

42   ... are said to be 'complementary'   A

> 43   ... is said to form a 'rigid' framework   A

We can have an infinitival phrase directly—this is suited to a definition of a verb:

> 44   When the sets have some members in common, they are said to *intersect*

This is a complex definition. There should be simple examples, on the lines of

> 45   Two sets that have some members in common are said to *intersect*

Examples where *call* is used in the active are:

> 46   We usually call the full name of a point its '*coordinates*'   A
>
> 47   We call this field the 'Universe of Discourse'   MME

In both these cases, the real content of the definition is in the preceding text: the idea of the 'full name' of a point has been introduced; 'this field' is overtly anaphoric. So even here, the metalanguage link separates most of the content of the definition from the target.

Formal definitions put even tighter constraints on what is needed as matrix to the target. In simple definitions, the target in its matrix must form an NP. The link is usually just *be* in some form, or perhaps such phrases as *is defined as / to be*.

> 48   An *acute* angle is an angle less than a right angle   A
>
> 49   A *designative* is defined as either ...   (Leech)

Because this format is so restrictive, for verbs, a formal definition (with definiendum preceding definiens) will need to be complex unless the gerund is the form defined. But formal definitions of verbs seem to be rare—I do not have an example.

3.2   Interpretation of simple definitions

3.2.1   Definitions with 'call'

By a simple definition, I mean one in which the definiens and definiendum are in the same clause. Of these, those that are most like dictionary definitions use the metalanguage item *call* to connect the two.

Text definitions with both definiendum and definiens quoted are essentially no different from dictionary definitions in their interpretation, and I shall have nothing to say about them. The forms next most closely related to dictionary definitions are those using *call*, where the two internal arguments of *call* are (as they usually are), NPs. Suppose the definition is

1 Solid figures which have plane faces are called *polyhedra*   A

There is a direct correspondence between this and a possible dictionary definition of *polyhedra*:[7]

2 *polyhedra* solid figures which have plane faces

The question of whether a definition may be construed as a word : word, word : meaning or meaning : meaning statement has been discussed in section 1.5. In (1), there is no doubt that the whole of *Solid figures which have plane faces* is to be construed as use, not mention, with respect to the level of *are called*. Evidence for this is provided by the existence of phoric definitions, where the whole of the phrase in question could be replaced by *These*, say. The word *polyhedra* on the other hand is there AS a word. If we replaced it with *Vielflach* (German), then the whole would still be a good definition (of a different word); but replacing one of the words in the definiens with a German word would render the whole linguistically ill-formed. There is also a sense in which the MEANING of the term *polyhedron* does not contribute to the comprehension of the whole; another indication that it is being mentioned rather than used. There is of course a contribution to the truth of the whole. The relation of the term to the whole is just as it is in a statement like "Those solid figures which have plane faces are labeled 'polyhedra'." The use to which such information can be put is much the same too. If those objects are labeled 'polyhedra', then I shall assume, (in the right circumstances), that that is because they ARE polyhedra. That is, even if I had been ignorant of the word before, I can assume that if the labeler is sufficiently authoritative, the term 'polyhedra' is correctly used by him, and may in consequence be used by me, of objects such as the ones so labeled.

This analysis strongly suggests that the utilization of a definition such as (1) involves the representation of the meaning of the definiens *Solid figures which have plane faces* (by hypothesis, in the language of thought), and the connection of this representation with the lexical item *polyhedra*. The whole of *Solid figures which have plane faces are called* is in metalanguage just with respect to the object-language item *polyhedra*, and this division corresponds to the inappropriateness of representing *polyhedra* as a piece of the language of thought in the normal way. It has to be kept as a piece of alien English.

The question naturally arises as to whether this analysis has implications for the correct treatment of dictionary definitions, since 'translation' (into the language of thought), and 'elimination' (from some level of syntactic representation) are distinct enterprises. Furthermore, the discussion above did not license us to say that we had in fact what would be called "a translation" of the target word into the language of thought: we only obtained a one-way relation, where the word could properly be used of those things covered by the language of thought description. The elimination requirement (for suitable environments) is just the opposite: we require that the items falling under the meaning of the English word are properly described by the language of thought expression.[8] The question will be taken up again below.

If the target of the definition is being cited rather than used, we might expect that it could be of any syntactic category. But even the adjective which did occur ((41) in 3.1.3) strikes me as unfortunate, and certainly we cannot have a proper definition with say a verb as target. But the reason is that the first internal argument of *call* must also be an NP, so that mismatches occur. We might try

3 Lifting oneself off the ground on one leg is called '*(to) hop*'

Is this ill-formed, or is it simply erroneous? I am inclined to think it is ill-formed. If so, then it would appear that we should take it that the second internal argument of *call* must syntactically be an NP, and that the use-mention distinction is not sufficient to license just any category. This suggests that the mention be imposed at some other level. For instance during the translation of the whole into the language of thought, it will be necessary eventually to isolate the English word in quotation marks or some equivalent; this could be derived as part of the translation of *call* and its arguments, or perhaps via some meaning postulate. The fact that we can say things like "He is called the same as his grandfather" suggests that the latter may be the right approach. On the other hand, if QR is within syntax proper, we have to make the distinction earlier, since cited items should not be subject to QR: To call a friend an idiot is, (in this case non-generically) for there to exist a friend such that you called him an idiot; NOT, for there to exist a friend x and an idiot y such that you called x, y. We probably have here 'semiquotation': that is, the item must be available both as use and as mention within the same level—LF.

In the frequent cases where the target is embedded in a matrix, it must be the case that the syntactic category of the target is involved in the grammaticality of the whole. Consider

4   This special isosceles triangle is called an *equilateral* triangle   A

We cannot assume here that the target is in full quotation, otherwise it would count as an NP. Suppose that we try to preserve as much of the analysis given to the previous definition as we can. Where does the metalanguage stop and the object-language take over? It seems that for consistency, we need to assume that the complement of *call* (the second internal argument) consists entirely of object language. (That does not prevent its being translated during the complete processing of the definition.) If we turned the target to French, we would indeed have to turn the rest of the matrix to French too. Then, following what we suggested for the last example, the whole definition enables an expression in the language of thought to be attached to the English string *an equilateral triangle*. From the text, we find that *special* in (4) can be identified as 'having the third side equal to one of the two given as equal by virtue of the triangle's being isosceles' (property 'L' in the language of thought). The situation is (using pidgin-semantics for the language of thought): [9]

5   i $Lx \& lx \& Tx$ then $(F(\text{'equilateral triangle'}))\, x$

where F is the translation function from English to the language of thought.[10] (I have ignored the effects of the determiners, too.)

However, within this string, the target is just *equilateral*; the fact that only this is identified allows us to deduce that the meaning (translation) of the phrase is fully compositional. Suppose that that means that translation of an indefinite NP with modifiers is simply the conjunction of the translations of the N' and its modifiers. (That is, we assume a *genus et differentiae* pattern.) Provided that the adjective is recognized as such, then this will give:

6   F 'equilateral triangle' $= F(\text{'equilateral'})$ & T

Using this on the information in (5i) gives

5 ii Lx & lx & Tx then $(F(\text{'equilateral'}))x$ & Tx

which given what we mean by 'fully compositional' entails

5iii Lx & lx then $(F(\text{'equilateral'}))x$

What this is supposed to mean is "If something has the properties 'L' and 'I' (as given by the language of thought), then it may properly be called 'equilateral', and so has whatever property corresponds to the translation of 'equilateral'. Suppose this property is 'E'—what (5iii) gives us is

7   L & I $\Rightarrow$ E

(where '$\Rightarrow$' is a generalized implication or inclusion relation). The chain of inferences sketched simplistically (but I think not implausibly) above is to allow the phrase *an equilateral triangle* to function first as object language and then as something subject to translation. In consequence, the matrix of the target can in effect be stripped off, leaving just the translation of the target on the right in (5iii) and (7). If we postulate something slightly weaker than full compositionality (allowing for collocational restrictions) then we need to reformulate (5ii) as the equivalent conditional version:

8   Tx $\Rightarrow$ $(Lx$ & lx then $(F(\text{'equilateral'})x)$

This can be interpreted as giving the same as (7) just if we are talking of triangles.

    I have gone through the steps in some detail to show that even under the assumption of one-way implication, the inferences can be made. For more complex cases, the inferences might not be valid, or if valid, might not plausibly be deducible, unless we have not one-way but two-way equivalence.[11] If we did have two-way equivalence, then our procedures would enable us to produce the language of thought translation of the English item 'equilateral' in isolation (for (7), or if we speak of triangles (for (8), so that it could be eliminated (by translation) from contexts like

9   That triangle is equilateral

In earlier sections, I argued that eliminability was criterial to a definition. In this section, I have taken it that *call* in its ordinary interpretation gave us an implication in the wrong direction for elimination from the simplest contexts such as (9). But it has also been shown that definitions are readily identifiable in a text, so that it must be from this fact, since it is not from the ordinary meaning of the terms used, that the two-way implication arises. In the case which has just been discussed, it would be not implausible to postulate that the assumption of a two-way implication was introduced only at the stage of (7), where it looks as if (in simple contexts) the information is sufficient to allow the language learner to use the term, but not sufficient to allow him to translate others' use of the term. In this situation, if he assumes that others' information is the same as his then he can infer that they will be using the term just when he would. That is, the occurrence of the term will be evidence for the condition 'L & I' from (5iii), provided that the context is, and is known to be, positive (monotone decreasing, or downward entailing).[12] So we very nearly obtain 'L & I ⇔ E', by this reasoning. The case of negative (monotone increasing, or upward entailing) contexts can be dealt with in a similar way, if we can reason about them at all. Suppose someone else uses the term *equilateral* in a negative context. Then the direction of the implication in (7) will permit elimination (more or less by definition of 'negative context'). The problematic situation is when the learner can use the term, if the context is negative. But if he reasons that the hearer will eliminate just in the circumstances when he himself would do so, then he can introduce the term exactly when that is appropriate—that is, he can take 'L & I' as sufficient for the introduction of *equilateral* in negative contexts. This is equivalent to the assumption of 'L & I ⇐ E', so that in negative contexts too we obtain equivalence. If the context is not monotonic, then there is possibly no point in elimination anyway, since having got 'L & I' into the expression, there would be no way of using it. The obvious way of using it is indeed to have it in a positive environment, since this will enable either 'L' or 'I' to be dropped, perhaps leading to otherwise inaccessible information. If the whole of 'L & I' must stay as a unit, then it might as well remain as a unit F('equilateral') anyway, or as a new unit in the language of thought to correspond to that.

This last suggests that we might want to construe a definition as a 'meaning–meaning' pairing, where essentially what we give is an implicational meaning postulate for a new concept constructed to match the English (object-language) word. However, it seems clear that JUST this cannot be what has to be retained as a representation of the information given in a definition, since we would lose the licence to go through the processes I have suggested above for the environments where the meaning postulate did not in fact license the inferences directly, that licence having arisen from the recognition of a sentence AS a definition. Either we would have to construct a two-way implication, an equivalence, rather than a simple meaning postulate, or we should annotate the meaning postulate in some way to indicate that it does give licence for extended use.

The exercise above was based on the assumption that it was proper to assume compositionality. I shall be discussing conditional definitions further in 3.2.2; their derivation may indicate revision of what has been suggested here. In particular, we might want to retain variables and quantification as in (8), and (5iii). It has also been assumed that the stripping off of the matrix from the target (and from the other half of the definition) was at least desirable. The limits to this process need to be discussed, along with the question of whether this turning of an implicit definition into an explicit one is in fact necessary, and if it is necessary, whether it amounts to a claim of decomposition of meaning. These more general issues will be discussed in chapter 5.

3.2.2 Definitions with 'say'

In this section, the origin of the biconditional interpretation of definitions is pursued again. I shall explore various possible ways of locating a helpful ambiguity. It turns out that the contribution of the indefinite NPs which usually occur is crucial.

Simple definitions with *say* as the metalanguage operator are not necessarily like those with *call*, because the complement of *say* is a clause, whereas the complement of *call* (I have assumed) is generally a

Text Definitions

sequence of two NPs, each of which has a distinct role, the named and the name. With *say*, a sentence used as a simple definition is schematically as in (i) or (ii),

10 i   We say [NP_1 is NP_2]

    ii NP_1 is said [to be NP_2]

Why should the target appear in NP_2 rather than NP_1? For the passive, the answer is clear: it is inappropriate to take as topic of the sentence something not only 'new' in the discourse sense, but actually new as a lexical item. The same explanation lies behind the use of (11) as a definition or meaning-explanation:

11   NP_1 is NP_2

Here again, in an introductory definition, we cannot have the unknown as NP_1. In a formal definition, we can have just this—as in (2) of 3.0 for instance) above. It looks as if the implied thing that is said in (10i) must conform to what it would have to conform to if it WERE said alone as (11). This is not unreasonable, if we assume that there is some topic-comment structure or some such thing to the embedded clause: we still need to be talking about something, and something intelligible, within the clause. Although it is not possible to embed a formal definition under *say*,

12   # We say that a *triangle* is a figure with three sides

(where the '#' marks the unavailability of the reading in question), we can report such definitions:

13   They say that a polygon is a PLANE figure with straight sides

This is a consequence of the special status of formal definitions: they are not pieces of normal text. The report however is assuming that the hearer is already acquainted with the term 'polygon'. The use of definitions with *say* does not necessarily follow that of those with *call*, even when what we have is essentially an embedding of a pair of NPs. With *call*, there is a metalanguage assertion about words, about naming. With *say*, there is simply an embedded proposition, perhaps with special status of the subject, and with identification of the target in any case. The neutral assumption is that the embedded sentence is taken to represent a true proposition, and that its utility comes at least in part from that interpretation. The embedded proposition will function as an axiom, or meaning postulate, at least temporarily. We need to examine the consequences of this, to see whether, all the same, the identification of the definition as such forces an interpretation with the equivalent somewhere of a two-way implication, and whether it is necessary for the implicit definition to be made explicit at some level if it is to function properly.

Let us consider two definitions with *say*, one with *be* and one without.

14   A triangle with all its sides equal is said to be *equilateral*

15   Two sets that have some members in common are said to *intersect*

(I have had to invent both these; complex definitions with *say* are much more frequent than simple ones, and many apparently simple ones are phoric). The surface structure will be derived by move-α from an S-structure carrying the argument structure shown directly in the respective D-structures, approximately as in

14 i   – say [a triangle with all its sides equal is equilateral]

15 i   – say [two sets that have some members in common intersect]

(I have given the verbs in the most convenient rather than the correct forms here). The content of the *say* embedding is to indicate the status of the embedded clause, to indicate presumably that there is some sort of stipulation involved, as is necessarily the case when what is at issue is the meaning of a word. In (14i), then, by stipulation, a triangle with all its sides equal has whatever property corresponds to the term *equilateral*, this word being by hypothesis new. That is, we are in the position (given as (14ii)) rather like that given informally in (5i), repeated here

5 i Lx & Ix & Tx then   (F 'equilateral triangle')x

14 ii Tx & Sx then   (F 'equilateral')x

(where 'S' is for the property of having three sides equal). However, there is no overt occurrence of *triangle* in the consequent in (14ii). In any case, the assertion that (14ii) represents in any sense what is derived from (14i) is not supported by any semantics as yet. Taking these problems one at a time, suppose first that we DO have the triangle mentioned in the complement of *be* in (14), as (16):

16   – say [a triangle with ... equal is an equilateral triangle]

The standard (extensional) Montague semantics for this would use as translation of *be* something relying on the identity of individuals, and hence would derive a truth condition paraphrasable as "There is a triangle with all its sides equal which is identical to a triangle which is equilateral." That is, we do not have even a one-way implication (or set inclusion), we merely have possible coincidence—set intersection. That is on the assumption of the *be* of identity. If we take predicational *be*, we unfortunately obtain the identical assertion, that some triangle with all its sides equal has the property of being an equilateral triangle, if (as before) argument indefinites are taken as existentially quantified. What we need is something like a generic or universal interpretation, to obtain the one-way implication, if we are to proceed as before with a pragmatic account of the two-way use. How is this to be obtained? The obvious moves are (i) to postulate ambiguity or (ii) to construct a pragmatic account. Even if we assume (as we have to) that pragmatic processes will account for the selection of the correct interpretation, we have to provide some way of representing the choice, or at least of representing what is chosen.

A semantic ambiguity account on conventional lines might locate the ambiguity at *be*, or at the NP [*a triangle* ...], and if here, then most probably at the determiner. Less conventionally, one might attempt to locate the ambiguity in the composition rules rather than in the lexical items, say by type-lifting. But if we have, as postulated, a further syntactic representation in the language of thought, including representation at a meta-level, then we might attempt to locate the ambiguity in alternative instructions on processing a constant form. These various possibilities will be explored in turn.

If we just consider simple 'NP is NP' clauses, there are five kinds to be accounted for:

17	i	John is the treasurer	identity
	ii	John is a man	set-membership
	iii	A rabbit is an animal	set-inclusion
	iv	An oculist is an eye-doctor	set-identity
	v	An idea of mine is a mistake	set-membership

To these we may usefully add:

	vi	To live is to love	set-inclusion? / identity?
	vii	John is handsome	set membership

I have given the natural readings for these, from which we can determine which *be* can supply the reading. Small-clause (single argument) *be* is predicational, with a normal subject argument. This will cover (i), (ii), (v), (vii), provided indefinite and definite NPs can act as predicates, and provided (which I think is correct) that the subcategorization permits NP small clauses. Equational *be* has two arguments, which should normally entail that only NP and CP are to be expected. Categories otherwise representing propositions IP and VP, might be permitted. If in (vi) we have IP with PRO_{arb}, then PRO_{arb} will have to refer to an arbitrary object in the sense of Fine 1985, in order that there is identity of the PROs in each IP. This *be* can account for (i), (ii),[13] and (vi) if there is identity. Given the implicational reading of (vi), and (iii) and (iv), there is clearly something missing.

We could try to amend the meaning of one or other *be*, perhaps by appealing to a type-driven semantics, but there are principled objections to doing this here (it is the argument NPs we would need to change the types of). More importantly, no interpretation of *be* appears to have any connection with the required interpretation of (15)—(15i) is repeated below:

15 i   – say [two sets that have some members in common intersect]

The embedded clause could, with a bit of effort to contextualize it suitably, be read as about a pair of individual sets. The natural reading is general, however. But there is no verb *be* here. So if any verbal element is to be ambiguous, it will have to be a systematic ambiguity across many verbs. This of course would be satisfactory in that a purely lexical story for *be* may (and does) explain various syntactic facts, but it lacks motivation; and similar ambiguity is exhibited across other languages. A systematic ambiguity might be associated with the supposed 'timeless' quality of generalizations and definitions. But this timelessness is only relative: as we have seen, even definitions may be personal, temporary, and confined to a local environment.

Locating the ambiguity at the verbal element makes the strong prediction that clauses either do or do not have a general reading. Locating the ambiguity at an NP would on the contrary apparently permit every suitable NP to take its value independently—at least, if no mixed occurrences appear, something would be amiss. Clearly we can have non-generic NPs in sentences with generic interpretations—as Smith (1975) points out, proper names can be substituted for any of the NPs in

18   The aristocrat prefers the amateur to the professional

leaving the possibility of a general interpretation for what is left. But the question is whether we can give (18) a mixed interpretation. It seems to me easy enough to suppose that the first NP is being used referentially, with the other two general; and not much harder to construe other combinations. However, this is not sufficient evidence for mixed interpretations, I think, because it might be held that the referential use was identical to the general, with the difference arising merely from pragmatic control of the extent of the class of persons both accessible and answering to the description.

It might be argued that matters will be just the same with indefinites, if these are taken to have a possible specific, referential reading, as a special case of an 'arbitrary object' reading (Fine 1985). However, I think this is incorrect (and still agree with most of the arguments to that effect put forward in Cormack and Kempson 1991). At least, it seems to me that there certainly is an 'existential' reading. So what readings can we get from the indefinite equivalent of (18)?

19   An aristocrat prefers an amateur to a professional

Uniformity of interpretation is preferred, certainly, but that is what one would expect, in the null context. Let us manipulate contexts.

20   A solution to a binomial equation may be found by the N-R method

I have no difficulty here in supposing that this means "for any binomial equation, there is a solution which may be found by the N-R method." There is a dependency of an existential on a universal quantification, roughly. Of course this is mediated by what we know about solutions belonging to equations, rather than having independent existence, but I think it proves the point, particularly since the all-generic reading exists. This supports Smith's claim that there are only generic NPs, then, rather than generic sentences or generic-inducing verbs.[14]

Before abandoning the notion of a helpfully ambiguous *be* entirely, we might note the parallel possibility that there is a systematic fluctuation or progression through from one sort of interpretation to another within the language of thought representations, where we might have something a bit like *be* in every case including that of (15i) if conversion to explicit form has taken place. This would be one way of carrying out the final suggestion among the alternatives put forward above.[15]

Suppose then that we locate the ambiguity at the NP. Consider again the embedded clause in (15i), repeated here:

15 i – say [two sets that have some members in common intersect]

Clauses like this should have, it seems, four possible interpretations: with individual, generic or universal quantification over the two sets, or with the definitional interpretation, if we are giving an explicit representation. Whatever 'generic' quantification is, it is going to have the sort of properties that *most* has. So we need a notation as powerful as that of generalized quantification. Also, the *two* will need to be treated as an adjective rather than as a determiner, at least for all except the first reading. Let us suppose (following recent work on plurals (Reinhart 1987, Cormack 1984b) that we have various properties predicated of a set (a set, as it happens, of two sets), in (21):

21   Two sets that have some members in common intersect

(I am keeping to the plural case because singulars tend to involve one of the other two issues: adjectival predicates or *be*). The quantification needed in the four cases will be given mnemonically; the two predications should be uncontroversial; I've used abbreviatory notation:

22	EXIST(X)	: two(X) & set(X) & com(X)	; intersect(X)
23	GENERIC(X)	: two(X) & set(X) & com(X)	; intersect(X)
24	EVERY(X)	: two(X) & set(X) & com(X)	; intersect(X)
25	EQU(X)	: two(X) & set(X) & com(X)	; intersect(X)
26	QUANT(X)	: two(X) & set(X) & com(X)	; intersect(X)

In general, for a form like (26), the truth-condition[16] is some condition on the two (higher order) sets A and B, where
$A = \lambda X (\text{two}(X) \& \text{set}(X) \& \text{com}(X))$
$B = \lambda X (\text{intersect}(X))$
The conditions are, respectively,

27   *EXIST* $A \cap B \neq \varnothing$
       GENERIC $|A \cap B| \approx |A|$ (approximately equal)
       EVERY $A \subseteq B$
       EQU $A = B$

To give as alternative translations for the indefinite NP and its VP one of the four expressions in (22) to (25), with semantics as in (27), is possible. But the set of conditions in (27) does not look much like a natural class.[17] Another possible complaint is that we should not postulate in the language of thought quantifiers with no NL congeners. The idea that there are language of thought items which never surface in any NL, although other items with very similar properties do, is indeed highly suspect. However, we seem to be in just that position inevitably, if most NLs have the indefinite article (when it exists) interpretable as at least EXIST or EVERY; because EVERY matches *every*, but there is by hypothesis nothing for EXISTS, since the likeliest candidate would be *a*. In fact the existence of apparent systematic cross-linguistic non-syntactic ambiguity in NLs is to my mind a very strong argument for something amounting to systematic ambiguity in the language of thought—a line which I cannot pursue here.[18] I shall use the forms under (27) where the inferences are clearer, but will discuss later the supposition that it is the forms in (22) to (25) (or something more like a Chomskian LF on these lines) together with a set of inference rules which determines the use to which these sentences could be put.

In the last section, I argued that we could use pragmatic processes to derive the definitional properties from something in effect giving only one-way implication. Above, I have suggested four distinct interpretations for an indefinite. But a similar argument can be produced for the sentences here to show that pragmatic procedures can derive what is needed for the definitional interpretation from something weaker. In what follows it can be taken that the use of EQU may be unnecessary, with in every case a pragmatic construction of the implied facts from a form with EVERY.

Suppose for the moment that the analysis depending on ambiguity of indefinites is accepted. Is it going to be adequate for all definitions embedded under *say*? The structure of the clause is (simplifying) [NP – VP]. The target is in the VP, and may be of any category. Is it sufficient that the subject NP is given an 'EQU' quantification? The effect will be to equate the subject N' and VP meanings; this will at least give something of the format of the logician's definition, with the main connective an identity relation. This identity connective is induced independently of the main verb of the VP, so that we will no longer expect this to be *be*. Taking (21), the translation of the zero article of the indefinite NP as some function of EQU (whose exact nature is not important now) can induce a logical representation equivalent to

28   $\lambda X(\text{two}(X) \,\&\, \text{set}(X) \,\&\, \text{com}(X)) = \lambda X(\text{intersect}(X))$

The way I have things set up, we can only have equality here, equality of sets or functions; there is no way of construing our quantifiers as giving equivalence of propositions.[19] Nor can we suppose we are in any 'mixed' representation of object language and metalanguage. This will all be metalanguage. Of course, it follows from (28) that

29   $\forall X ((\text{two}(X) \,\&\, \text{set}(X) \,\&\, \text{com}(X)) \Leftrightarrow (\text{intersect}(X))$

and from the form with EVERY instead of EQU we would similarly derive

30   $\forall X ((\text{two}(X) \,\&\, \text{set}(X) \,\&\, \text{com}(X)) \Rightarrow (\text{intersect}(X))$

so that we do get in these two cases the effect of wide-scope universal quantification, and of propositional connectives. But (28) is the sort of representation which will serve as an eliminative definition.[20] In fact, it is tantamount to an explicit definition, since

31     $\lambda X(\text{intersect}(X)) = \text{intersect}$

The question as to whether it will actually function as an eliminative definition depends on the details of the translation, including the compositional component of this, and on exactly what substitution and simplification or inference patterns are postulated to be available. Let us simply assume for the moment that there are suitable operations available, and continue by looking at the rest of what may appear in such a definition.

There may be other NPs in the definition. What will we expect of these? On the translation procedure assumed above, every NP is likely to introduce its own variable. Various devices exist in natural language for identifying with each other the variables introduced by a pair of noun phrases (for example anaphora). One of the necessary properties of a logician's definition is that no variables other than those occurring in the definiendum (target plus matrix) should occur free in the definiens. We need a variable for every argument place of a relation or operator which is being defined, and good style will require that the same variables occur unbound in the definiens. These unbound variables are in fact interpreted as universally quantified over the whole identity, standardly.

If we consider the demands of the format of a definition with *say*, we can see that the association of one NP with another anaphorically is highly restricted. The subject NP forms the whole of the definiens, and the embedded VP is the definiendum.

32   we say [[NP *definiens*] [VP *definiendum*]]

One variable which occurs is that associated by predication with this NP and VP; and it is this which we are assuming may be bound by the determiner EQU to give the identity discussed above. Any other variable in the definiendum must be inside the subject NP, say in a relative clause, and will hence not be available as an ordinary anaphoric antecedent for an NP in the verb phrase (the c-command requirement will not be met). However, anaphora of Geach's 'donkey sentence' kind will be available.

33   Every man who owns a donkey beats it

Here, it is clear that there is a reading where *it* is anaphorically dependent on *a donkey*. I shall follow Heim 1982, in assuming that this is only possible when the indefinite *a donkey* is taken to be dependent on the quantification induced by the determiner of *man, every*, here, and does not have independent quantification. Following Heim 1982, Kamp 1981, Cormack 1984b, Reinhart 1987, I shall take the head determiner to operate on and bind two variables. For (33) we can construct a logical representation[21] on the lines of

34   EVERY $<x,y>$: $x \in$ man & $y \in$ donkey & x owns y ; x beats y

This will have truth-conditions to parallel those in (27), so we have

35   $\lambda<x,y> (x \in$ man & $y \in$ donkey & x owns $y) \subseteq \lambda<x,y>$ (x beats y)

which in turn is equivalent to

36   $\forall<x,y> ((x \in$ man & $y \in$ donkey & x owns $y) \Rightarrow (x$ beats $y))$

as required. Then if instead of *every* we had the indefinite, and if the translation chosen were EQU, but in a two-variable-binding version, we could construct similar forms for definitions. Suppose we had a definition for the transitive verb *intersect*

37   A set which has some members in common with another set is said to *intersect* it

This can have a representation

38   EQU$<x,y>$: $x \in$ set & $y \in$ set & $\exists z(z \in x$ & $z \in y)$; x intersects y

The intended interpretation of this is

39   $\lambda<x,y> (x \in$ set & $y \in$ set & $\exists z(z \in x$ & $z \in y))$
    = $\lambda<x,y>$ (x intersects y)

equivalent to

40   $\forall<x,y> ((x \in$ set & $y \in$ set & $\exists z(z \in x$ & $z \in y)) \Leftrightarrow (x$ intersects $y))$

Thus if the subject NP is given either EQU or EVERY quantification, any anaphoric dependency of an NP in the VP on the subject NP will in fact inevitably induce in effect wide-scope universal quantification of the associated variable. Any number of NPs can be made dependent in this manner.[22]

It will naturally be the case that definitions or generalizations which are simple sentences without any *say* matrix can be treated in the same way as those with *say*. It must also be the case that 'donkey anaphora' is licensed in definitions or generalizations with *call*, because we may have definitions of the forms

41   A line which bisects an angle is called its *bisector*

42   We call a line which bisects an angle its *bisector*

As with the example in (33), the antecedent of *it* is in a relative clause, and so does not c-command the pronoun. But the relative clause itself is within an NP which does c-command the pronoun, which is what we need for donkey-anaphora to be licensed (see Heim 1982, chapter 2; Reinhart 1987).

Given this approach to indefinites, can we now account for the readings in (17)? (The examples are repeated here).

17	i	John is the treasurer	identity
	ii	John is a man	set-membership
	iii	A rabbit is an animal	set-inclusion
	iv	An oculist is an eye-doctor	set-identity
	v	An idea of mine was a mistake	set-membership
	vi	To live is to love	set-inclusion? / identity?
	vii	John is handsome	set membership

We have a direct account of (iii) and (iv), using EVERY and EQU, respectively. If the latter is induced pragmatically, we just need EVERY. For (vi) (if it is not entirely unaccountable) we perhaps would need to appeal to some event variable. That this does not appear with an explicit indefinite article is not significant, since I do not necessarily suppose that the article itself is ambiguous. It may rather be that the indefinite does just permit an unbound variable, and the binding is determined elsewhere, as has been proposed for such indefinites by Kamp (1981) and Heim (1982); (see also discussion of (33) in section 3.3.1).

There is however still something to be accounted for in the intuition that we have at least a conditional definition (relating to triangles) here, and similarly for (15), one relating to sets. A suggestion as to how this may be derived is given below.

In summary, it has been argued that an ambiguous *be* alone cannot account for the range of meanings of sentences like those in (17); that a variety of quantificational readings of the head NP can do so. It has also been argued that the quantification may be such that it binds multiple variables, including other variables associated with indefinites, and concomitantly can induce bound-variable readings of pronouns within the VP. The question of whether GENERIC and EQU are genuinely independent available quantificational options has been left open, though it is fairly clearly preferable that their apparent existence should be given a pragmatic rather than semantic account.

We obtain by using this apparatus representations of definitions which are such that the definiens appeared in the VP. In all our examples, the target was either a verb, or it was a noun or adjective where the main verb of the VP was *be*. The normal consequence of this (ignoring possibilities of type-lifting) will be that the target together with its internal arguments must form a constituent of type $<e,t>$—as suited to the open class items of verb, noun and adjective.

Two related matters need further exploration. If EQU is not a semantic option, exactly how does the interpretation as a definition arise and become represented? And, is there some way of ensuring that we obtain a conditional rather than an absolute definition, if this is needed? These matters are related because both depend on knowledge of what is being defined, and on expectations about definitions, as well as on the representation of the literal meaning of the sentence given as a definition. I think that neither depend on whether the definition itself is construed as 'meaning–meaning' or 'word–meaning' in the sense that the whole must be given a metalanguage translation, so that the difference between the two construals depends just on whether say "intersects" as a language of thought item is being defined, or whether it is rather "*F* 'intersect'" that appears instead.

The approximate form of the explanation for both is the same, I think. Suppose we treat the one-way implications as part of an implicit definition. One of the standard forms for a definition of a set is by listing: "*a* is an X, *b* is an X, ... and nothing else is an X." Suppose the logical entry for an item X lists such initial clauses as they are discovered, and by convention or maybe explicitly, the final clause is just given; then in the expression of a definition no two-way implication is needed. Two things will make this usable: the fact that the initial clauses are filed under 'X', so to speak, and the fact (which depends on this) that the final clause can be taken as given. It is the storage along with the final clause that makes a statement function as a definition. Thus (43i) is equivalent to (43ii)

43 i   (i) $A \subseteq X$
       (iii)   nothing else is in X

   ii $A = X$

(Note that I am assuming that the items of X are given not one by one, but in bunches, in sets). The addition of another line, say

         (ii) $C \subseteq X$

will lead to a viable extension of the coverage of X: it will now be defined as '$(A \vee C)$'.

What distinguishes a conditional definition from an ordinary one is that one or more ranges of application are demarcated. The final clause must refer to the range:

44   (i)   if $y \in R$, then $A(y)$ & $B(y) \Rightarrow X(y)$
        (iii)   nothing else which is in R is in X

Extensions to the meaning of 'X' here will be potentially of two kinds. Either an independent clause can be added, as suggested for (43i), or the range R can be extended leaving the rest of its clause intact. This is what we might expect for instance of a definition of 'equilateral' if initially defined for triangles: a suitable description of the condition will permit the definition to be extended to polygons in general, or to successively named varieties. How do we get the final clause, though? Either we have to assume that it is specially written as the result of processing something as a conditional definition (and there do seem to be cases where the linguistic evidence points this way), or it has to arise naturally from the postulated filing system. The latter suggestion might work something like this: the definition for 'equilateral' if perceived to be pertaining to triangles, is in fact filed under the node for triangles. Under this node, we have a subsidiary node for 'equilateral', with the implicit definition just as in (43i) (not conditional). However, by convention, the unbound variable appearing in the definition is restricted to triangles (bound variables must not be so restricted—we need for instance to be able to have variables over sides, in our definition of 'equilateral'). Thus we cannot get access, so to speak, to the 'equilateral' node without accessing the 'triangle' node.

If this last story can be made viable, it is clearly better than the first suggestion. It also permits us to suppose that this filing under a subsidiary node might be triggered either by the particular form of the definition being processed—because it has the appropriate form—or because we were as it were working entirely on one subject (say triangles) so that it is natural to file the definition where we are.[23] This would suggest that the representation for (14) does not have 'T' for triangle on the right (compare (14ii) with (5i) above), but rather has an implicit restriction of the variable to triangles, by virtue of the filing system. We may make the same assumption about the definition leading to (5ii), giving:

45 $(x \in T)$ (Lx & Ix & Tx then $F($'equilateral'$)x$ & Tx)

The 'Tx' is now redundant, and if dropped will give us the translation of *equilateral* as 'I & L'. Similarly from (14ii) we obtain (conditionally) a translation as 'S'. Of these two, it is just the second (where 'S' is the property of having all sides equal) that will turn up in a generalization of the definition outside the context of triangles. But the definitions themselves give no clue as to this. And this sort of generalization, whether guided by further information given, or by an act of the imagination, is not within the domain of language processing as such. To take another example, the definition of (37) is about sets, and indeed the two variables representing the arguments to the predicate 'intersect' must range over sets. There is no natural way (or even an unnatural one that I can formulate) of using for instance QR to give us a conditional definition reflecting this fact, but it is logically possible to consider the variables as restricted to sets, and to file the whole under the node for sets.

There is a good deal more to be found out about how the various postulated processes are set in motion. Consider (46) versus (47):

46 An equilateral triangle is isosceles

47 An equilateral triangle is one/a triangle that is isosceles

The former can be individual (with an effort) or general, where the latter can only be a definition (incorrect, as it happens). The difference is that after *one* has been processed, it is equivalent—probably through retrieval of ellipsis—to *one triangle*; it looks as if the reiteration of reference to triangles first forces EQU rather than EXIST and then forces the whole to be filed in a special place in relation to triangles. (The general statement is equally pertinent, I think, to the nodes for 'equilateral', 'triangle' and 'isosceles'). The only special place, perhaps, is in the section designated for definitions.

The idea of having a definition consisting of an implicational clause followed by an "and nothing else" clause is similar in its effects to my earlier suggestion of assuming a one way implicational clause together with a "the other participant in the conversation knows the same as me" meta-statement, which is what I used earlier to derive definitional effects from a weaker interpretation of a given "definition," but it is more plausible partly because it does not need recourse to meta-statements, and partly because it solves the problem of filing the information which was given by a definition in such a way as to legitimize later use of the extra clause (or meta-statement).

3.3 Complex definitions with 'if' or 'when'

3.3.1 Definitions of the form 'A if B'

In running text, we frequently find complex definitions consisting of two clauses, with the subordinate clause introduced by *if* or *when*. Examples are

1 Two lines are said to be *parallel* if they are always the same distance apart   SMP

2 When a polygon has all its sides equal *and* all its angles equal, it is called regular   SMP

In all such definitions, the definiendum and definiens are in separate clauses: the definiens is the antecedent clause, and the target in the consequent clause (using this terminology for *when* as for *if*). The main matters of interest in these definitions are the way in which Natural Language produces the equivalent of the logician's variables, which have to be common to both clauses, and the usual questions about conditional and biconditional interpretation.

In (1), the item *parallel* is the target: this is an adjective whose external argument must be an NP designating a pair of two lines. The item is semantically a one-place relation, having type <E,t>, where <E> is the type for a set of entities. The logician's definition for such a relation 'R' would have the form (3i) or (3ii):

3   i $R(X) \Leftrightarrow S$,

    ii $C \Rightarrow [R(X) \Leftrightarrow S]$

for variable X over sets of entities, and with X appearing unbound in S. In the conditional definition, we expect X to occur in C, too. If instead of (1) we take

4   Two lines are *parallel* if they are always the same distance apart

then the construction of an LF similar to (3ii) is plausible. The NP *two lines* must be taken as an indefinite with EVERY quantification (with *two* an adjective not a determiner). Let us suppose for the moment that it is subject to QR, leaving an empty category with index 'X'. Then this empty NP functions like a bound variable X, and will be shown as such in a moment. The pronoun *they* is intuitively anaphorically dependent on the first NP, and also functions, and will be shown as, a bound variable. So we would have

5   EVERY(X): two(X) & lines(X) ;
    (X are parallel) if (X are the same distance apart)

Given the interpretation of EVERY, this is logically equivalent to a conditional definition where C is 'two(X) & lines(X)', if only we had *if* equivalent to $\Leftrightarrow$. Ignoring this latter proviso for the moment, the interpretation as a conditional definition does seem to be the correct one. We can certainly without any feeling of having been misled, follow (4) with say a similar definition starting 'and two planes are parallel if ...'. What we have then is a sentence as in (4) arranged so that the main N' contains the condition, its VP contains the target, and the *if*-clause forms the definiens. Because the unknown target word is not the initial NP, or within it, the whole may (and does) function as an introductory definition. A similar interpretation is correct for (1), so we need an account of four things: the exact operation of QR to give (5), or something similar; the syntactic and semantic function of *are said* in (1), the syntactic structure permitting the interpretation of *they* as a bound pronoun, and the ultimate interpretation apparently needing *if* to become '$\Leftrightarrow$'. I shall consider the syntax first.

In (5), I have assumed not only QR, but 'OR', (operator raising, Reinhart 1987), to give the raising of the DET, if this is supposed to have originated as the phonologically empty specifier of the initial NP. There are alternative explanations, as noted before, but it is convenient for reading the interpretation to have a variable-indexed determiner. Nothing hinges on this at present, so I intend to use the notation without implying any commitment to a syntactic rule of OR. Since a determiner D is inherently a binary operator, there is no particular problem in defining its logical scope to include material within the logical scope of DP, as noted in section 1.5. That there is ordinary quantifier-binding of the pronoun from the subject position is demonstrated by comparable sentences with true quantifiers in the NP:[24]

6 Every girl laughs if she is tickled

7 No cat purrs if it is angry

It is intuitively clear that in each of these, the pronoun is functioning as a bound variable, and hence must be within the scope of the quantified NP at LF.

The subject position in the main clause is the only one from which a quantified NP can give bound-variable effects from one clause to another. We cannot get anaphoric dependency of the pronoun on the quantified NP in any of the following:

8 #John feeds every donkey if he meets it

9 #If John sees every donkey, he feeds it

10 #If every girl is tickled, she laughs

(The '#' marks unobtainability of the relevant reading). In (9) and (10), we might suppose that the ECP would prevent QR from taking the QNP to an appropriate position, if C″ is a barrier to government;[25] the possible structure will be discussed below. What is more surprising is that (8) does not permit anaphora, given that (6) and (7) do. The asymmetry is only naturally accounted for on the hypothesis that true bound-variable anaphora can only be obtained if the antecedent c-commands the anaphor at S-structure, not just at LF: any form of QR at LF would leave the quantified NP in (8) as well as (6) capable of c-commanding the pronominal NP position. This is the position argued for by Reinhart (1983 and 1987); the definition of c-command required is not the simplest one, as we shall see shortly.

We might suppose that the natural way to achieve the required configurational relations would be to have the subordinate clause within VP.[26] Certainly there seem to be cases suggesting such an analysis for predicates in VPs:

11   Tigers are [dangerous if sick / provoked by humans]

However, as we should expect, the two phrases to be semantically put together have the same semantic type—all of *dangerous*, *sick*, and *provoked by humans* will have the simple type <e,t>. In the case of (6) or (7), the constituent introduced by *if* is a full clause, however, and so there will be no way of putting it together with a VP.[27]

There are other possibilities, which take the *if*-clause to be attached at clause level. Two assume that *if* is in COMP; the other assumes that *if* is like *and* in providing only a quasi-projection. I shall first discuss the adjunction possibility. Suppose that at S-structure (and D-structure), the *if*-clause is adjoined to I". The adjunction structure will be schematically as in (12):

12

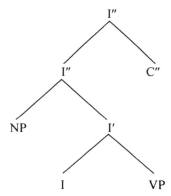

It is clear that the original simple definition of c-command in terms of branching nodes does NOT give NP c-commanding C". Reinhart 1983 and 1987 offer replacement definitions which give the right results for (12). The first allowed for two matching categories (like the two I"

nodes); the second made special provision for specifiers (like NP here). But we should also consider versions that involve two *if* clauses:

13 John will bring his car if he is asked to, if he remembers
14 No-one would eat a bun if he had just stepped on it, unless he was starving

Assuming that what we have is successive adjunction to I″, we will need a structure like (15):

15

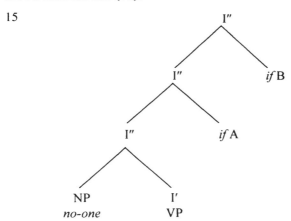

The lower N″ must c-command (in the relevant sense) both A and B. It appears that we need to generalize Reinhart's earlier version to cover arbitrary adjunction structures. This is most easily done using the 'exclusion' notion of Chomsky 1986b (p. 9), where exclusion is defined as in (16)

16 α excludes β if no segment of α dominates β

Let us reformulate Reinhart's c-command condition to read:

17 α c-commands β iff α does not dominate β and there is no γ that dominates α which excludes β

So in (12), since at S-structure there is no categorial evidence of the origin of the two I″ nodes, they will be treated as segments of the same category, in the same way as if they had arisen by adjunction arising from move-α, rather than (as I am assuming) from a base-generated adjunction structure.[28]

Adjunction to I″ as suggested above then can give an explanation for the right bound-variable reading if c-command is suitably defined. Further, since the topmost I″ can be embedded under C″, we will (correctly) expect to be able to preface the whole with *that*, as in

  18 I know that [John will go if Mary comes]

The second possibility is adjunction to CP. In the face of (18), this seems unlikely, and it will not give the c-command facts we require. However, it does seem to be needed for other constructions which are not relevant here.[29]

The third possibility is that *if* is entered in the lexicon as belonging to a defective category, so that the ordinary tree would be

19
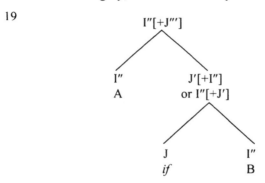

The facts about c-command will be the same here as they are in (12), provided that there is not a continuous segment I″ from B to the topmost I″ (so we need J′[+I″]). The fact that *if* has an internal and an external argument is given explicit recognition here. The suggestion may well be correct, but since there is almost no theory available for such projections, I will use the familiar ones of (12).

To return to our original problem: the S-structure configuration based on (12) will meet the requirements for the interpretation of a pronoun as a bound variable, with the adjunction extension to the c-command condition. The LF c-command restrictions must be met too.

At LF, the quantified NP must be subject to QR, which might be supposed to yield (20):

Text Definitions

20

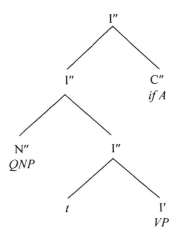

In this configuration, we must assume, I think, that the three instances of I″ are segments of the same category. *QNP* does still c-command all the other material in the tree. But what we need is for the material to be within the logical scope of the *QNP*, if LF is the input to interpretation. On standard assumptions, with brackets corresponding to tree structures, *if A* is not within the logical scope of *QNP*. The tree must be different at some level of interpretation, if we want to use a representation with the familiar scope device of brackets.[30] Since I am assuming a level of representation suited to inference, a direct semantic interpretation using an extension of 'c-commands' to determine 'may have in its logical scope' is not in itself sufficient.[31] Note also that we cannot use semantic types to determine logical scope, since there is nothing about QNP which requires that it have more than an I″ in its scope, if it is given type $<t,t>$, with I″ as type $<t>$. (This contrasts with the situation for determiners noted in considering OR, above). The obvious move is to make *QNP* higher by letting the QR take it from its position in (12) to one where it is adjoined to the higher I″, as in (21) below. This move should be permitted if the two I″ nodes are in some sense one: our pretheoretic interpretation of the *if*-clause as being subordinate to the main clause suggests just this. Possibly the adjunction shown in (20) is not even possible, and move-α can adjoin only to the topmost segment of a category.

21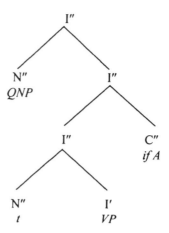

We also require that the trace of NP is properly governed, so the two I″ projections must not form a barrier to government. Since it is actually possible to have *wh*-movement to the specifier of a higher C″ node, movement of *QNP* out of the trace position must be permitted:

22 Who would worry if he were late for work?

Note that in (21), the *if* clause has in its scope the clause *t VP*, which is as required for standard interpretation.

There are well-known problems involving the interpretation of *if* as material implication, one of which appears with (7). A simple-minded translation of (7) into a restricted-variable predicate calculus notation with *if* as material implication will yield

23 $\neg \exists x\colon x \in \text{cat}\ ;\ [\text{purrs}(x) \Leftarrow \text{angry}(x)]$

Unfortunately, (23) is trivially falsified by finding a cat which is not angry, which does not seem to be the purport of (7). The undesirable implication is removed if we have any sort of universal quantifier immediately (and non-trivially) binding the clauses of the conditional. In this case, a plausible candidate is some temporal or event variable, so that we might have

24 $\neg \exists x\,(\text{cat}(x)\ \&\ \forall t[\text{purrs}(x)\text{ at }t \Leftarrow \text{angry}(x)\text{ at }t])$

One suggestion, argued for by Kamp, Heim, and others, following suggestions of Lewis (1975) is that it is *if* itself that induces universal

Text Definitions

wide-scope binding of all free variables: there is 'unselective' quantification. I will come back to this below. For now, let us assume that some universally quantified variable renders such interpretations non-trivial, where the universal quantification may be applied to the head NP. (And that any other problems are dealt with either by introducing a finer-grained semantics with intensions, or by pragmatic processes which can determine that the proposition retrieved as a result of processing the literal meaning is not identical to the literal meaning of the utterance, or can make use of the propositions in ways not directly compatible with standard logic).

Suppose then that the LF for (4) (repeated here) is (25):

4   Two lines are *parallel* if they are always the same distance apart

25 [two lines]$_X$ [[e_X are parallel] [if [they$_Y$ are ...]]]

This structure will permit the interpretation as for (5), (repeated below), since we may have $Y=X$.

5   EVERY(X): two(X) & lines(X) ;
    (X are parallel) if (X are the same distance apart)

The overall logical structure of the definition (4) is (schematically)

26 lines(X) $\Rightarrow$ [(same ... (X)) $\Rightarrow$ (parallel(X))]

(I have swapped round antecedent and consequent for ease of interpretation). The logical structure needed is

27 lines(X) $\Rightarrow$ [same ... (X) $\Leftrightarrow$ parallel(X)]

That is, we need 'iff' for the 'if', but not '$\Leftrightarrow$' for every '$\Rightarrow$'. That means that to substitute EQU for EVERY in (5) is never required—and it would lead to an LF which can never be the interpretation of such a sentence, in fact.[32] This strongly suggests that EQU as a determiner meaning is a myth. It is of course frequent that more formal texts will actually write '*if and only if*' in the *if* position, and '*iff*' is used readily. In Horrocks 1987 we find both forms (and both are functioning as definitions):

28 X is a *descendant* of Y if X is dominated by Y

29 X is a *constituent* of Y iff X is dominated by Y

A simple explanation is that *if* is ambiguous.[33] Note that it would be the English word that had to be ambiguous, rather than the translation-symbol, since we want different effects in (26) for the two occurrences of '⇒'. Hence for instance in comparable definitions with *when*, we would also have to postulate lexical ambiguity, and even with the possible exclamative definitions with no overt connective, as

30 Remember: it has two parallel sides, it is a trapezium!

Furthermore, the logical connective '⇔' has similar bizarre properties to 'exclusive *or*'.[34] Suppose then that there is no such connective in the language of thought, and that ambiguity is ruled out. A pragmatic explanation must be sought. In the particular case of definitions, an explanation along the lines suggested at the end of the last section (3.2.2) seems plausible.

In examples (28) and (29), Horrocks used letters as variables, rather than introducing them via NPs. Natural language has various kinds of anaphoric device available, but especially when two NPs with the same N' are needed, the results can be clumsy.

31 ... we say that one node *precedes* another if it occurs to the left of the other node on the printed page   (Horrocks)

Here, the target *precede* is a two-place relation, where both arguments are to be nodes. The definiens is phrased as *one node precedes another* rather than as *a node precedes a node*; the latter would be barely acceptable. In the definiens, there are two anaphors, *it* and *the other node*, which are interpreted as bound variables, one for each of the NPs of the definiendum. The order matches (so that there is crossed dependency), but the assumption of parallelism in the two clauses seems to be strong (although not inevitable). The selection of antecedent is assisted by the use of *other*, which has an implicit argument. Since in *another*, it is understood to mean 'other than the node just mentioned', and is most naturally interpreted as keeping the same implicit argument in *the other node*, the pairing will be correctly made. The logical from if QR applies to both NPs should be something like

32 [one node]$_x$ [another –]$_y$ [[e_x precedes E_y]
    [if [[it]$_x$ occurs to the left of [the other node]$_y$ on ...]]]

Interpretation must take the two NPs of the definiens just as bound variables, possibly with the addition of some clause like '& $x \in$ node & $x \neq y$' deriving from the content of the definite NP *the other node* (see Kempson 1986 for discussion of definites as anaphors). It also seems likely that at LF, or at some later level that we can assume has similar structure, the missing N' in the NP *another* is retrieved, so that the condition is specified as being that both arguments are to be nodes.

Since the argument above showed that we could not have bound pronouns dependent on any quantified NP except the subject NP of the main clause, an explanation is due of the dependency on *another* occurring in (31). The fact that the dependent NP is in (31) a definite NP *the other node* rather than a pronoun is not relevant—it is easy enough to construct natural examples with pronouns. What IS required is that the antecedent NP is indefinite. Heim (1982) refers to indefinites in such constructions as 'genuine generic indefinites' (p.47), her example being

33 John beats a donkey if it kicks him

However, it seems clear that the indefinite (together with the bound pronoun as dependent variable) have all the readings one could expect for an indefinite: that is, the whole can be construed as existential, generic, general, or definitional. The existential is clearest in sentences like

34 John always beats a certain donkey if it kicks him

I take it that this can be paraphrased approximately as "there is a donkey x, whose identity is certain (to the speaker), such that for all t, John beats x at t if x kicks John at t." The indefinite *a certain donkey* is indefinite in the usual way, except that the speaker is asserting that he has direct rather than circumstantial evidence that there is such a donkey.[35] A generic interpretation for (33) is likely—one favored donkey who does not get beaten will not 'falsify' (33). In formal discourse, the most likely reading of sentences of this form is as an exceptionless generalization:

35 Two divides into a number exactly if [it]/[the number] ends in a zero

Given that a normal 'quantifier and bound variable' account is not available, there are two kinds of explanation potentially available for the indefinite and its dependent anaphor: pair-quantification and unselective binding. Pair-quantification was used in section 3.2.2 for the 'single clause' definitions, and is invoked for the solution of the quantification in the sentence

36 Every man who owns a donkey beats it

$EVERY{<}x,y{>} : x\in man\ \&\ y\in donkey\ \&\ x\ owns\ y\ ;\ x\ beats\ y$

Unselective binding in some form or other is advocated by Heim, Kamp, Reinhart and others for

37 If a man owns a donkey he beats it

Simplifying, this amounts to supplying wide-scope universal quantification for ALL the indefinites in the sentence. Something like this is needed for definitions like (2) above, which are discussed in section 3.3.2 below.

In view of examples like (33) and (34) where the head NP is a proper name, the first solution seems unlikely.[36] The cases where (as in example (31) or (37)), the initial NP is undoubtedly an indefinite are perhaps more useful. The pair quantification approach predicts that in every such sentence with two indefinites, both must have the same interpretation. So the whole must be existential, or a generalization without exceptions, or (if this is a kind of quantification) a generic. But unselective binding too predicts that all free variables must be bound by the SAME binder, so any evidence of divergent readings will reject both solutions. It is of course likely that such readings would be hard or impossible to obtain, if the surface form is not giving any indication that two separate choices must be made. A choice of existential reading can be forced by using *a certain..* (though it may be possible with some effort to obtain the reading by imposing the uniqueness given by the certainty on a universal quantification); we can put *every* or some other true quantifier in the first position:

38 i ? Every man offers a certain donkey sugar if he meets it

   ii ? A certain donkey always kicks a man if it distrusts him

   iii ? Any donkey would kick a certain man if he comes near it

iv   No sensible person would eat a bun if he had just stepped on it

v   ? No sensible person would mount a certain donkey if he'd kicked it

vi   If a certain man meets a donkey he beats it

(We are only interested in readings where there is anaphoric dependency of both the pronouns in the second clause on NPs in the first clause). The fact that (iv) is fine, but (i), (ii), (iii) and (v) are dubious suggests that only pair quantification is available for sentences like (i) to (iv), where the quantification is that given or imposed on the head NP. This is consonant with the observations about *wh*-movement, in as much as it is the case that only the head NP can move to a position outside both clauses. Unselective existential binding of all indefinites, without any restrictions, would give a reading to (i) with a wide-scope 'a certain'; I think this cannot be obtained.[37] There is perhaps a narrow scope reading, which is obtained by pair-quantification on *every*, with the paraphrase "For every man and donkey pair such that the speaker identifies the donkey (in relation to the man), the man offers the donkey sugar if he meets it." With (iii), I do not think either reading is available. The contrast between (ii) and (v) is clear, I think. In (ii) there can be no reading where the subject NP is (as forced by the 'certain') existential but with the object NP universally quantified, but in (vi), this is perfectly possible. (It may however be possible to interpret (ii) by using universal quantification and then imposing the uniqueness of 'a certain'). Moreover, in (vi), we must have an indefinite as the head noun, suggesting that some kind of special binding for indefinites is in use, and that this is dependent on the structure in some way that precludes its operation in the cases like (i) to (iv). Tentatively, we may suppose that a QNP in the QR position blocks unselective binding of items within the scope of the QNP. Cases like (vi) will be discussed in the next section.

The conclusion reached is that in cases of 'A if B', any anaphoric dependencies other than on the head NP must be pair-quantification mediated by the quantification of the head NP.[38] (It must be remembered that independent binding is available for indefinites in simple clauses, as discussed in section 3.2.2).

In example (31) above, then, the form given above as (32)

32 [one node]$_x$ [another –]$_y$ [[e_x precedes E_y]
    [if [[it]$_x$ occurs to the left of [the other node]$_y$ on ...]]]

should rather appear as (39)

39 EVERY<x,y> [one node]$_x$ [another –]$_y$ [[e_x precedes e_y]
    [if [[it]$_x$ occurs to the left of [the other node]$_y$ on ...]]]

Given the remarks above, because the head NP is indefinite, we can take this as either unselective binding by EVERY, or pair-quantification depending on the determiner of the indefinite head NP, this itself given EVERY interpretation. In this latter case, we do not actually need to raise the determiner; the licensing of the binding would follow from a suitable definition of scope for binary operators.

In accounting for the definitions with *if* so far, I have simply omitted the phrases *we say*, *is said to*, and so on. In section 3.2.2, discussing simple definitions, I took these phrases as indicating the stipulative nature of the clause that *say* takes as its complement. In complex definitions, we should expect the same to hold. That is, the *say* is to be understood as making a stipulation about the truth or propriety of a proposition expressed in the language of thought, and not (as might seem possible) about what word we say as an English translation for such and such an expression in the language of thought. This latter *say* takes *that* (and *whether*) clauses as complement, as well as quoted phrases, so it is not immediately obvious which account is right for our cases.

Consider (1), repeated here:

1   Two lines are said to be *parallel* if they are always the same
    distance apart   SMP

One question is the scope of *say* here: does it extend over the condition or not? If it does not, then we have a reading with the whole of the kind of definition we have been discussing above embedded under *say*, so that nothing more than the remarks above are needed. However, suppose the scope of *say* is just [*e* to be parallel]. Then the whole (using (26)) will have a translation something like

40 lines(X) $\Rightarrow$ [(same ... (X)) $\Rightarrow$ say ('X parallel')]

where the quote marks are for English. Is this feasible? And what would its use be?

To take the second question first, we would presumably be taking (1) to be a 'word–meaning' definition, so that the whole would be, let us say, filed under the lexical item of English *parallel*, rather than under the matching concept. We could then take it that a definition was to give exhaustively the conditions under which it was proper to use the word, with a similar arrangement as the one postulated for the previous meaning-meaning definitions. That is, we could expect a place to store lists of permitted uses, with an implicit or explicit "and these are all the cases where anyone (else) says 'parallel'" as the final clause. Such an arrangement would enable (40) to function as a definition.

It is the first question whose answer is I think doubtful. In (40), we have

41   say ('X parallel')

which was a shorthand for

42   say ['e_X to be [t_X parallel]']

When I was discussing the possibilities before, I rejected mixtures of English and the language of thought. If we just had (41), we might argue (as in 1.5) that we may use variables common to both languages, which implies that there is some kind of matching of syntactic categories in the two languages at least for the category of the variable and for its status as argument. Similarly, we might not object to the empty categories in (42). However, we have '*to be*' as well. If we had a VERY close relationship between a subset of the language of thought and English, (we are bilinguals, after all), we might not mind this: we could so to speak move the quote marks along to the right, translating '*to be*' into ... *to be*:

43   say [e_X to be [t_X 'parallel']]

This looks somewhat more useful, in that we now know when to use the English word in isolation. Alternatively, suppose we can only have in effect '*to be parallel*' defined. This too is probably useable, even if more limited (we will not know how to use or understand the adjective attributively). I cannot see any very convincing argument against these suggestions, but they do seem unnecessarily complicated in comparison with the other explanation of the purpose of *say*. It is also clear that alone they would be inadequate, since in section 3.2.2 we had examples without any passivization, on the lines of "We say that a triangle with all three sides equal is *equilateral*." No amount of moving the quote marks along (translating as we go) will produce what we want here. Somewhat reluctantly, I leave the matter open, noting only that it is in fact quite independent of the conditional definitions.

Anaphora may be introduced in a more indirect way. Consider

44 A language is *recursive* if both the set of sentences and the set of non-sentences are enumerable in a finite time by some formal device,   (Horrocks)

The target is a one-place relation, *recursive*. Following the usual strategy, we suppose that *a language* is subject to QR and supplies EVERY quantification of its associated variable (say, x). But variables unbound in the definiendum, which will now be [x is recursive], should occur in the definiens. The only exceptions would occur for a somewhat bizarre relation which was so to speak syntactically transitive but logically independent of any value for its complement argument. Certainly that does not hold here. And the presence of the definite article in *the set of sentences* and *the set of non-sentences* indicates that these NPs may have dependent rather than independent reference. 'The sentences' must be the sentences of the language, and the non-sentences must be non-sentences with respect to the language (the non-sentences of the language?). The logic of the definition requires that we consider *sentence* to have an implicit argument—quite correctly—so that its logical status is that of an operator (it is an operator rather than a relation because the output of offering to it a suitable argument does not produce a proposition—it produces rather a set, something of the type of an N′ denotation). The presence of the definite article indicates that the NP is contextually determinate—which will be fulfilled if the implicit argument is identified. In this case, the argument must be identified with the 'x' of the definiendum, rather than say contextually identified.[39]

The post-disambiguation logical form must be roughly

45 [a language]$_x$ [[e_x is recursive] [if [[both the set of [sentences of e_x] and the set of [non-sentences of e_x]] are enumerable ...]]]

This satisfies the requirements of a logical definition, if it is taken as one clause of an implicit definition, following the suggestions of 3.2.2 to obtain the 'bottom line'. The interesting question is whether we can find syntactic justification for inserting an empty category as argument to *sentence*, or whether this appears only on translation from say LF to the language of thought. We can force the production of the empty categories at LF easily enough by assigning just the syntactic type <e,t> to the lexical item *sentence*, so that the conceptual selection matches s-selection. The argument might be syntactically either explicit or implicit.[40] Or we might suppose that this added complexity was not initially present in either conceptual or linguistic lexicons, but was learned later as an option. Even if obligatory conceptually, there is no impossibility in supposing that there is an option in the syntax (provided that general principles do not forbid such options).

These definitions with *if* and two clauses are more suited to complex definitions than are the 'single-clause' definitions discussed in the previous sections. For instance, the last definition (44) could be restated as (46) or (47)

46 A language of which both the sentences and the non-sentences are enumerable in a finite time by some formal device is said to be *recursive*

47 A *recursive* language is one all of whose sentences and all of whose non-sentences can be enumerated in a finite time by some formal device

Neither of these are either stylistically pleasing or easy to process. If the target is a two-place relation, as in (31), re-phrasing may not be possible at all. When it is possible, and not too appalling stylistically, it is usually because one of the two arguments can be PRO. So if the target were the transitive *precede* of people in processions to the dinner table, we could have something like

48 Walking in front of someone in a line is *preceding* him

However, it is not acceptable to force PRO to range over non-animate entities, so we cannot have

49 *For a node, to *precede* another node is to occur to the left of it

Most of this section has been concerned with the treatment of indefinites, either as corresponding to QNPs which must be subject to QR and need to license bound variables, or as species of variables which are subject to quantification by other NPs, where the former have determiners acting as pair-quantifiers. Problems of interpretation have also been considered. Most of the questions raised must be asked again with respect to definitions where the conditional clause comes first, rather than second, at surface; this is the matter of the next section.

3.3.2 Definitions with 'when'

For some reason, definitions with *if* are usually of the shape of the examples in the last section. That is, the main clause precedes the *if*-clause. It is perfectly possible for the opposite arrangement to be used. For say (28) or (29) above, the clauses can simply be changed round, but in general, the anaphor and antecedent NPs will preferably be rearranged. So for instance, (1) (repeated here) could alternatively have been given as either (50), or, better, (51):

1   Two lines are said to be *parallel* if they are always the same distance apart

50 If they are always the same distance apart, two lines are said to be *parallel*

51 If two lines are always the same distance apart, they are said to be *parallel*

If the relation or operation being defined requires two arguments, then the anaphora-antecedent relation in a form like (51), with the antecedents in the *if* clause, will have to be mediated by unselective binding as in the parallel *donkey* sentences:

52 If a man owns a donkey, he beats it

Since I do not have definitions like this for *if*, the anaphoric relationships will be discussed below along with definitions with *when*—on the assumption that the syntactic structures are identical, or near identical, for the two.

In contrast, all the definitions I have collected with *when* start with the *when* clause, like the definition of (2), repeated here:

2   When a polygon has all its sides equal *and* all its angles equal, it is called regular.

Superficially, the *when* has just the same properties as an *if*, in these definitions, the difference apparently being that *if* is used in formal definitions and *when* in introductory definitions. Just occasionally, the temporal nature of the connective surfaces, as in (53):

53   It often happens that two sets have no members in common, so their intersection will have no members. When this happens, the sets are said to be *disjoint*.   SMP

The fact of a pair of sets having no members in common is seen as an event, which happens, and happens often. If it happens often, it happens at particular times, by implication, so that the *when* can be taken to refer to such a time. One can rationalize this by ascribing the recognition of an event entirely to the human observer, who imposes his own temporal span of attention on the essentially timeless mathematical entities and relations. Usually, the use of *when* is as time-neutral as the use of *if*—and as the use of the *then* which may accompany it. Even in (53), the actual definition, when the phoric *this* has been identified as referring to 'that two sets have no members in common', there is no sense that disjointness somehow vanishes when the right sort of sets are not being attended to. (Contrast this with something like "When this happens, the lecture is boring").

The anaphoric possibilities in a structure like (2), with the antecedent in the subordinate clause, requires different treatment from cases like (1) in the last section, where the antecedent is in the main clause. As we saw above, true quantificational binding of a pronoun in the other clause is not available from this antecedent position. Given the semantic type of the operator *if*, and the apparently identical functioning of *when*, we might expect that the syntactic configuration for (2) would be as in (54), with X being C":

54

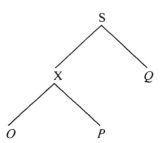

Since the whole of a conditional like (2) can be embedded under *that*, say, the topmost node should be I".[41] If this is so, then the only possible structure must have X (*i.e.* C") adjoined on the left of I":

55

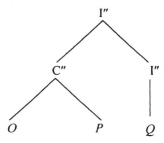

This structure could be base-generated, or obtained from a right-adjunction structure by movement from the structure (12), given again here:

12

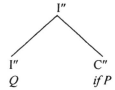

If base-generated adjunction of modifiers is ordinarily to the right, as suggested in section 2.3.2 (for (13)), then obviously the movement option must be correct. Note that in (55) (and indeed in structures like (12)), it would be possible for the operator to appear either under C, if an X-zero item, or in the specifier position if it were a maximal projection. It seems likely that *when* like other *wh*-words should be in the specifier position, being an instance of an adverbial phrase (P″).

The same could be true of *if*, since it is often in free variation with *whether* which again looks like a *wh*-item.[42] Also, it used to be possible for a complementizer to appear in addition to *if*:

56 If that Palomon was wounded sore Arcite was hurt as mooche as he or more
    (Chaucer *Knight's Tale* 267, (*c*.1386); from OED)

But it may be that we should take this as evidence for a 'defective category' operator analysis, with CP as operand; I shall not pursue this here.

On the face of it, from a structure like that of (12), we could obtain S-structures like those needed here by leftwards movement of the subordinate clause or rightward movement of the main clause. Leftward movement in the case where the whole is embedded under *that* has no landing place provided or licensed by D-structure, if the base-generated adjunction is to the right. In general, leftwards S-structure movement, but not LF movement, is to existing or D-structure-licensed slots, under the C″, I″ scheme. However, certain adjuncts typically can be to left or right of their adjoinee at S-structure—consider adverbs, so this may not be a sufficient argument. We might suppose the optional *then* of *if then* structures moved from a post-adjoined position too, so that the structure could be as in (57).

57

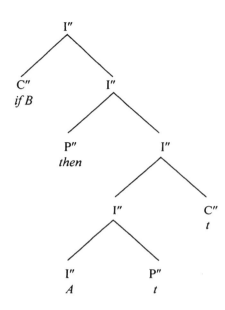

In this structure, it looks as if there should be no difficulty in having bound variable pronouns within *B* licensed from the subject position of *A*, under the suggested c-command extensions. LF movement is permitted, since *wh*-movement is possible from this position:

58 Which cat, if no-one is looking, *e* jumps onto the table?

Then only the backward pronominalization accounts for the unwieldiness of (50) above.

The alternative might be as in (59):

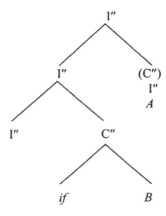

The movement (extraposition) of the main clause I" from the initial position to a right-adjoined position is either direct, or it might be supposed that it is under C". This would be the case if we suppose that all S-structure landing sites must be D-structure licensed, and what is licensed is in fact only a C" adjunction to I" (or C"). We might expect this given the canonic nature of CP as an instantiation of a type <t> item: IP appears at D-structure only if c-selected.

That this is indeed the only permitted adjunction is supported by the examples like

60 i   John sees a donkey—he feeds it!

   ii * Every boy sees a donkey—he feeds it!

That is, if we replace [$_{C''}$ if B] by [$_{I''}B$] for (60i), we would expect true quantifier binding of the pronouns to be possible; but it is not—so it seems that the C" node is obligatory in (60i).[43] I assume that rightward extraposition at S-structure need not be to existing D-structure positions. The purpose of this maneuver is to provide a possible landing site in the specifier of this C" for a *then* which we may suppose originated right-adjoined to the I" above *A* (as in (57)). If it could move simply by adjunction to the left of I", our story would be inconsistent.

Under this extraposition story, there can be no true quantifier binding form the subject of *A*, in the configuration (59). Thus we predict that (61) (i) and (ii) are ungrammatical, but (61iii), like (50), may have a reading (with unselective binding):

61 i   * If he is hungry, every boy may have a second helping

   ii   ? Even if he is hungry, no boy may have a second helping

   iii   If he is hungry, a boy may have a second helping

The prediction seems to be correct. It has no account under the leftward movement postulated in (57), however. This in turn suggests that S-structure leftward adjunction-movement of adjuncts is in general subject to restrictions (with possible exceptions for topicalization). I shall assume that the extraposition account is correct, tentatively.

Definitions like our original (2) will be unproblematic, with unselective binding (by EVERY) of [*a polygon*] and its dependent pronoun [*it*]. But the construction of any logical representation with the right distribution of variables in cases like that of (53) is clearly not as straightforward as in previous examples.

53   It often happens that two sets have no members in common, so their intersection will have no members. When this happens, the sets are said to be *disjoint*   SMP

Before, we have been able to manage with relatively small deviations from a postulated syntactic LF, granted some syntactic representation of implicit arguments, and recovery of an ellipsed element (as required for (44) and (31) of 3.3.1). Here, even if (as I have asserted above) there is an actual linguistic phrase which is the antecedent for *this*, matters are not straightforward.

The problem is the need for [*two sets*] and [*the sets*] to act as variables bound jointly by EVERY. Intuitively, we need to substitute the antecedent in place of the *this*, and then process as if we had a syntactic surface structure, from which we could derive an LF and hence an interpretation. But this is hardly a plausible syntactic procedure. What CAN we do? One obvious move is to suppose that the anaphoric dependency of [*the sets*] on [*two sets*] is licensed as discourse anaphora, and is given by coindexing. Then the unselective binding of the indefinite [*two sets*] by EVERY is to be such that it may extend over more than one sentence. We might suppose, for instance, that the very existence of the anaphoric relation licensed this. We will need a

Text Definitions

parallel EVERY binding of the 'event' [*two sets have no members in common*] and its anaphoric dependent [*this*], however, which takes us outside NP anaphora, and indeed outside the simple semantic model I have been using so far. I envisage that it should be possible to justify the construction of a representation which corresponds approximately to this:

62   EVERY X EVERY e (unselective binding)
    $X \in$ [two sets], $e \in$ [X have no members in common]
    [many t (e happens at t)
    & every t (e happens at t ; X are disjoint at t)]

Note that the restrictions on the variables are not independent of each other: they are scope-ordered rather like quantifiers. Furthermore, although I have written "$e \in$ ..." to match "$X \in$ ...," the 'set' of events of the "X have no members in common" is a one-member set. What is most obviously totally incorrect about (62) is the occurrence of time. Time is what most naturally should be introduced, on the basis of *often* and *when*, but it is clearly not finally actual time that is wanted here. However, if we suppose as I suggested above that the time is the pupils' imagined attention to what is essentially timeless, things are not too disastrous. For if I know that the properties of sets do not change over time, then, concentrating on the definitional part, and deleting reference to time, I shall have

63   EVERY X EVERY e (unselective binding)
    $X \in$ [two sets], $e \in$ [X have no members in common]
    (e is true ; X are disjoint)]

A certain amount of sleight of hand has been used, but possibly it could be justified. However, we cannot patch up the "it often happens ..." translation in this way; it is just wrong. What we need is more like

64   many X (e happens)

but we have already quantified over X. It seems that we want the restrictions on X and e to fall outside, rather than inside, the quantification:

65   $X \in$ [two sets], $e \in$ [X have no members in common]
    [many $<X,e>$ (e happens) & EVERY $<X,e>$
    (e happens $\Rightarrow$ X are disjoint)]

This time, I have assumed that the *when* may be translated as '⇒', as if it were *if*, or indeed *whenever*. A generalization is probably being missed (and any number of other issues glossed over), since there is a parallel 'at' interpretation corresponding to EXIST quantification and conjunction, at least with temporal interpretations. However, the interesting thing is the status of the representation in (65) with regard to the order of the restriction and the quantification. If the representation has a semantics (which intuitively it has), and it is more or less correct, and if some such representation can and must be derived at least in the language of thought as a translation of (53), there may be interesting consequences. If LF is as close to some subset of the language of thought as possible, we may suppose that (65) is close to the LF for the pair of sentences in (53). The first line of (65) might plausibly be derived by QR of some sort, where not only NPs but complement clauses are subject to QR. Furthermore, the NP which is subject to this 'QR' is not a binding-quantifier at all, since this line gives the range over which the variables vary, and binding, however it arises, is given subsequently. Furthermore the NP in question is indefinite; one of the questions is whether (and why) purely restricting NPs of this type should be subject to QR (see footnote 21). But before jumping to the conclusion that we need just such a form as (65), it might be considered whether the top line of (65) might rather be derived by post-NL-syntactic procedures. For instance, it might arise implicitly or explicitly from pragmatic procedures, rather as I suggested at the end of section 3.2.1 for the interpretation of conditional definitions; we would then, as there, sometimes have duplication of information on restrictions on variables, as in (66):

66   $X \in$ [two sets], $e \in [X$ have no members in common]
     [many $X : X \in$ [two sets], $e \in [X$ have no members in common]
     (*e* happens) & EVERY <X,e> (*e* happens $\Rightarrow$ X are disjoint)]

There are various possibilities here, but exploration needs consideration of a wider range of data,[44] as well as syntactic investigation of the possibilities of reversing the restrictive clause and quantification as in (65). The minimum assumption seems to be that the syntax (LF) provides something like

67   [many X: $X \in$ [two sets], $e \in [X$ have no members in common]
     (*e* happens) & EVERY <Y,f> (*f* happens $\Rightarrow$ Y are disjoint)]

Text Definitions

and either syntactic or pragmatic processes, triggered by anaphoric dependency between Y and X, f and e, derive either (65) or (66). If syntax ends at the sentence, then anything further than (67) must presumably be outside natural language syntax. However, it could be within the proper domain of the syntax of the language of thought—that is, some process like QR might be capable of applying to some representation which in fact arose from two English sentences to give say (65). Alternatively, it is more general pragmatic processing which sets up something like (66).

This last example, (53), has been treated largely as an example of a phoric definition involving variables. I have for simplicity ignored the contribution of '*are said to*'. Its significance has been partly that it provides an example of the new problem of phoric definitions, but mostly that it tends to reinforce the suggestion that the restrictions on variables which arise in the ordinary case from QR should at some stage be treated as quantifier-less indicators of what we are talking about—genuine restrictions on the ranges of the variables—rather than as the first clause bound by binary quantifier.

It may have been observed that it has turned out that definitions with conditional clauses correspond to conditional definitions by virtue of QR or possibly other processes, but not by virtue of the conditional clause. The conditional (*if* or *when*) in fact corresponds to the main connective of the definition. The complexity in these definitions arises from the necessity to have a common binding of variables in the clauses on either side of this main connective. For definitions with the main clause first, this usually involved QR and pair-quantification; for the others, it involved (at some level of representation), unselective binding by EVERY.

Notes

1 Some dictionaries, for instance LDEL, incorporate explanatory sentences which may amount to text definitions.

2. Larger and more recent dictionaries may supply far more. Longman (LDEL) lists many of the targets I discuss as separate entries.

3. Strictly speaking, 'AP N' pairs. Most of my examples consist of two words, but more complexity is possible, as in (16) above where we have *grammatically specified entailment*.

4. *leptokurtic* is not used other than of frequency distributions or their graphs, but in as much as it indicates a shape, it could be.

5. Such restrictions are frequently referred to as collocational restrictions. This is misleading: the term collocation should be used only as a relation between lexical items. So for instance *fro* collocates with *to and*. But *addled* does not necessarily collocate with *eggs*; there is nothing wrong with a sentence like *These are all addled*, where the referent of *these* is indeed eggs.

6. I designate this as non-minimal on the assumption that *power* is simply ambiguous. Even if it is so, the *of a number* might be included because this complement is in fact obligatory (unlike many N complements).

7. There is a sensible convention under which this definition is not proper. It should be the singular *polyhedron* which is defined; plurals are to be used only where they are essential, as in defining set-taking predicates. So we might properly have 'Polyhedra which are exactly the same shape and size are called *congruent* polyhedra'.

8. I have simplified here. Elimination can only be successful even in all (non-opaque) environments if we have identity, not just a one-way implication (inclusion) between the respective referents of the English word and the language of thought description. One-way implications may lead to valid elimination or translation in logically suitable environments, depending on the monotonicity.

9. Of course $L \Rightarrow I$, and $I \Rightarrow T$, but that complication is not relevant now.

10. And note that we need the F to be available in the vocabulary of the language of thought.

11. For instance, suppose the matrix corresponds to some function taking the target as argument. If $g(s) \Rightarrow g(t)$, we cannot deduce that (taking a generalized form of inclusion or implication), $s \Rightarrow t$. It just might be that definitions would eschew any such complex format, I suppose, or that if used, the use in itself carries the guarantee that the stripping is possible.

12. In the next section, I suggest an alternative derivation of the equivalence relation, for some types. But the question of whether during language processing we can determine in general or in particular whether or not an environment is upward or downward entailing needs to be addressed.

13. Montague subsumed (i) and (ii) under identity of individuals, and argued for a distinct *be* for (vi), reducible to the former one. This is Montague 'English as a formal language' (1974b); he in fact introduces the equational *be* as a transitive verb and the other syncategorematically.

14. I do not mean to exclude the possibility that there are other constituents of some level of representation which also fluctuate between generic and other interpretations—something like this is very probably needed for temporal phrases, for instance.

15. Cormack 1986a is an exercise along these lines.

16. The truth conditions are to give the reader an adequate characterization of what is intended. Processing requires rather some inference rules, which should more or less correspond to these conditions (I say 'more or less' on account of the generic). It would of course be possible that the actual translation mechanism from English to the language of thought gave rise to expressions incorporating what I have given as 'truth-conditions'. In any case, we are to understand that the internal representations postulated function as if the main logical connective is as given in the truth-condition '=' in the case of EQU, and so on.

17. The answer to this might be: that is an artifact of the notation. Or it might be: we do not expect the notation itself to give us any natural classes: rather what we should be looking for is some similarity in the possible inference rules or meaning postulates permitted for indefinites. In any case, the generic may very well be spurious, in that pragmatic interpretation principles do not necessarily require literal truth of an assertion. If the proposition offered by a speaker is such that the implicatures are in the circumstances a fair match to those required, that may be the best that can be achieved. In effect a *ceteris paribus* clause may always be taken to apply. It is just that in a subject like mathematics, there are few exceptional cases (and where there are exceptions, the usual strategy is to treat them as 'degenerate cases'; which is the equivalent of interpreting 'dogs have four legs' not as having a few exceptions, but as universally true under the understanding that on occasion a dog has a leg of length zero).

18. Obviously FORMAL languages, like predicate calculus, are perfectly capable of making this distinction unequivocally. So it will be something to do

with the normal processing procedures that has the effect we see. We would not wish to suppose that there was an arbitrary built in ambivalence in the language of thought. (See Cormack 1985 and 1986a).

19. The implicit idea is that we must give a coherent set of alternative readings for the quantifiers. So I cannot just set up as truth-conditions for EQU

i EQU(X) : A(X); B(X) iff $(\forall X)(A(X) \Leftrightarrow B(X))$

when all the other determiners receive translations where the 'X' of 'EQU(X)' is used in forming a set-abstraction operator. We know that a form like that in (i) is inadequate for determiners like *most*. So anything on these lines would be justified only if we want to treat indefinites quite differently from other quantifiers. And even if this difference is accepted (which in the end I think it must be), we still need a justification of some sort for the particular variety of readings apparent for the indefinites. In this, we have to account not only for the sorts of readings I have been discussing just now, but of course for scope dependence and for binding as in 'donkey' sentences like (82) discussed below. What does seem amply clear is that a simple translation as an existential will not suffice, and that something developed from Heim's account is likely to be correct.

20. It does not supply a very plausible translation of the supposed NL definition, though. A conditional definition allowing extension to other situations is more likely. This will be taken up below.

21. As May points out, we need to constrain the introduction of this pair-quantification so that it does not (incorrectly) operate in say

i *Every man saw a donkey*

since we would then get a reading under which every man saw every donkey. May derives an appropriate restriction from the LF configuration after QR has operated on both the NPs:

ii $[_{S'}[_S[_{NP}$ a donkey$_2$ $[_{NP}$ every owner of $e_2]]_3[_S\, e_3$ beats it$_2]]]$

As I understand it, this representation is only coherent if we take it that the phrase [a donkey]$_2$ stipulates the range of the variable e_2. That this may be the correct interpretation of quantified NPs and of variables is suggested by (45) below, and by my treatment of example (53) in section 3.3.2.

22. It is easy to demonstrate that giving the indefinite of the relative clause (the 'donkey' NP) universal wide-scope quantification directly will in general

give inadequate results. Thus *Few men who own a donkey beat it* does not get the intended interpretation from a logical form interpretable as equivalent to

i ($\forall x: x \in$ donkey) (few men who own x beat it)

Hence we do need the pair-quantifiers *every*<x,y>, *few*<x,y> etc., for the general case. The actual semantics of these forms is not entirely straightforward, however: I have argued (Cormack 1985) that in generalizing from the single-variable form to the double-variable form, there are alternative routes leading to different inferential possibilities— *most*<x,y> is ambiguous, in explicable ways. Note also that we do need forms like (i) in addition: in particular, both the individual, the general and the generic readings are available for suitably chosen examples. The generic is the plausible reading, for instance, for *a rattlesnake* in

ii Few animals which disturb a rattlesnake are attacked by it

23. Note that this makes sense, since items may be defined by listing their kinds, and then following with the usual "and nothing else is a ..." clause. For instance, we might define equilateral, isosceles and scalene triangles, under the heading 'triangle', and then have the clause stating that nothing else was a triangle. This will amount to stating that no other kinds of triangle exist. We need never define triangle as such.

24. There are more natural examples, such as:

  i No-one would go there if he could help it

  ii No-one likes it if he is teased about his accent

Interestingly, these have clausal antecedents for *it*, once from main to subordinate clause, and once the other way. I take it that the obligatory occurrence of expletive *it* when the verbs *help* and *like* have *that*-CP complements (like my *take* here) is not a factor in these constructions.

25. It does not seem to be the presence of a phonological COMP that is the block, since with indefinites but not with QNPs, the conditional reading is available in:

  i John sees a donkey, he feeds it!

  ii #John sees every donkey, he feeds it!

26. For argument to the effect that there are in fact several kinds of *if*-clause, with distinct properties, see Takami 1988.

27. This is not strictly true: it is possible to give a semantics to *if* such that it will take a clausal argument and yet act as an operator on a VP—or any other specified type. For the VP we would need

    i $\lambda S \lambda P \lambda x (P(x) \Leftarrow S))$

where S, P, and x are variables over propositions, predicates, and entities, respectively. I do not like this; it is quite a different matter from postulating a cross-categorial *if* which might account for what I take to be dislocated elements in for instance

    ii   He is surly, if not downright rude

    iii   I get few letters, if any

28. There is evidence provided by the existence of indices on moved elements; I assume this may not be used. One class of cases accounted for in Reinhart's Specifier version, possessive NPs in prenominal position, may fall under the adjunction version. Suppose that a possessive DP is generated as an N'-adjunct, like an adjective, but must move to the specifier position of a DP (presumably to get Case). Then we will have fortuitously something that looks at this point like an adjunction structure:

    i

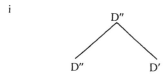

If the lower D" does in fact behave as if it were at the upper position, then it will c-command what the upper one would c-command, thus accounting for examples like

    ii   Everyone's mother loves him

True subjects may also take scope over pronouns in the VP from this position:

    iii   No-one's attempts to bribe the jury will do them any good

29. We will also expect that questions may be formed which require movement of a *wh*-NP into the specifier of C", as in (i) and (ii):

    i   Which child will cry if he loses the race?

    ii   Who will John talk to if Mary does not come?

Text Definitions

(i) is unproblematic with the *wh*-element having wide scope. But if we assume that the C″ referred to is outside the whole in (ii), then there will be a semantic anomaly, since the conditional is tensed and will after movement be adjoined to a tenseless constituent:

iii   Who will [John talk to if Mary does not come]?

The same anomaly appears in

iv   Seldom does [John appear if Mary is not expected]

Note also that the two clauses can be reversed in (ii), but not in (i); this suggests that there is a conditional question in the former, but a questioning of a conditional in the latter. If the movement is to be internal to the consequent clause, in (ii), in order to avoid the anomaly, we must adjoin the *if*-clause to C″ rather than to I″, giving (v) at D-structure, instead of (12):

v

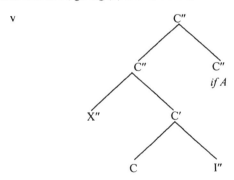

There can now be movement out of I″, of N″ to X″ and of I+V into C. Note that the subject NP of I″ here would no longer c-command *if A*, but neither can we any longer get bound variable pronoun interpretation with a true quantified NP as antecedent, across the clauses. Nor can we have a complementizer in front of the whole:

vi   #Seldom does every boy appear if he is not expected

vii   *I know that seldom does John appear if Mary is not expected

where the latter contrasts with

viii   I know that John rarely appears if Mary is not expected

It appears then that adjunction to CP is also possible.

30. The use of brackets to indicate scope is not enough: we need also to know which is operator and which operand. Assuming that this is given either by left right order, or by semantic type, then brackets are enough. The brackets include the maximal c-command domain of the operator, where c-command is dependent on the former notion of dominance referring just to nodes, not to any category—and hence without any special effects in adjunction structures.

31. It could be sufficient if the inference rules were written to allow for the non-standard determination of scope. Then at least the status 'adjunct' would have to be recognized; possibly the whole set of syntactic categories would have to be preserved. This is a possibility I cannot investigate now.

32. The effect would be to assert that the property of being a pair of lines was identical to the property of being parallel if always the same distance apart. This does make sense. (It is false: consider a pair of planes).

33. On Heim's account, the *if* itself is not interpreted, but the conditional effect is due to the EVERY binding of the free variables. This simplifies the account for such sentences as

    i   Mostly, if a man owns a donkey, he beats it

34. See McCawley 1981 (p.77ff). The problem is that both these connectives are associative, but a multiple use of the binary connective gives a curious result: the truth value depends on whether the number of True or False propositions is odd or even.

35. It would be strange, for instance, to say: "A certain postman came to the door; I know because he put a letter through the box."

36. It is of course quite possible to treat proper names as QNPs, at some level of representation. Most simply, we can take say *John* to correspond to $\forall x : x = John$ (with the usual assumptions about the pragmatic identification of the relevant John). Then equally well we could take the pair-quantifier version to give EVERY$<x,y> : x = John$ ... This would produce readings for sentences like (13) and (15) which were exceptionless generalizations. The generic would have to appear as some pragmatic weakening of this, (an assertion, we might suppose, of something having more of less the right implications), since we can hardly suppose that there is any generic quantification equivalent for *John*. It is less implausible to suppose that there is an existential version: $\exists x : x = John$, with a pair-quantifier mate leading to EXIST$<x,y>: x = John$; $-$. This seems somewhat obscure, but it would give correct readings.

37. The pair-quantification reading is probably obtainable here too (he gives sugar to his favorite).

38. The term 'pair quantification' is inaccurate in that it suggests that just two variables could be so bound—in fact, it could be any number.

39. It appears, on the basis of this single example, that the implicit argument of an operator must be identified. The question arises as to how much work is being done by the definite article in our case. Suppose someone said "Pablo wrote a sentence on the blackboard." Is there a reading with just existential quantification, amounting to 'There is some language such that he wrote a sentence of it on the blackboard'? Or is the assertion only felicitous if the language in question can be contextually identified? It is hard to be certain, unfortunately. What IS clear is that existential quantification is not wanted in the case in (44).

40. For some discussion of implicit arguments, see Cole 1987, Roeper 1987, Brody and Manzini 1988. The type for *sentence* will be <e,p>, rather than just <p>.

41. If the whole is free-standing, we could have the topmost node C", with X in the specifier position. Such a structure might apparently be base-generated, or arise from movement of an adjoined higher C" (as in (v) of footnote 29 above) into an empty specifier position. The latter possibility will be ruled out only if the binding domain postulated as appropriate for determining bound-variable possibilities is not identical to the domain for the binding of traces. Base-generation seems a natural possibility, and I cannot see what would rule it out if the content of a specifier position is freely determined. But the fact that the whole must at least sometimes be an I" renders this account at least unnecessary.

42. This is not true for most speakers now, since we have

    i   I am not sure about how/when/whether/*if he will mend the mower

(Adapted from Radford 1981).

43. Unless rather QR of the relevant QNP is blocked—but since *wh*-movement out of a right branch seems to be acceptable in (58), I assume this is not so. I take it that in such constructions, the whole is a single CP, just as if there were an overt *if*.

44. We should obviously consider the parallel kinds of example with existential import, like

    i   Mary saw a rabbit, and Billy saw it too

These are discussed by Heim (1982), Kamp (1981) and others.

CHAPTER FOUR

Syntax: Conclusions, Problems, and Speculations

> The only facts worthy of our attention are those which introduce order into this complexity and so make it accessible to us.
>
> Poincaré, *Science and Method*

4.0 Introduction: argument structure in syntax and semantics

> And why? Because if we had known how to predict it in the one case, we should know how to predict it in another.
>
> Poincaré, *Science and Method*

In order to draw together the various speculations made concerning the workings of the θ-types and subcategorization assumptions which I have made use of, I am going to consider a range of structures involving adjectives. The various possibilities need to be syntactically distinguished, and the postulated lexicon needs to be learnable. The next section attempts to substantiate the viability of my claims; this one collects the theoretical assumptions made. The final section offers an alternative formulation of the mechanisms proposed.

I have argued that we need several levels of representation with sometimes non-isomorphic constraints on argument structure. By argument structure here, I mean the set of internal and external constituents which are related to a head (via the lexicon) or a constituent (via some principles of transmission). The constituency itself remains constant from level to level provided that 'abstract representations' of constituents are accepted, like the representation of an NP as a chain.[1]

I have also suggested that we may need to consider different levels of representation as identifying X as an instance of Y in different ways. For example, the projection principle suggests that θ-theory should apply at D-structure. If the principle projects information from the lexicon at each level, then in order to check internal NP arguments, we must accept QNP *in situ*. One way of doing this would be to allow a complex relation between the head and its arguments, so that say a verb of type <e,t> could combine with an argument of type <<e,t>,t>. Alternatively, if the projection principle is a constraint on the relationships between different levels, projecting structures relating to subcategorization from LF to D-structure, we can see the θ-criterion as functioning somewhat differently. I suggested that we could suppose that at D-structure, only categories are visible, and that every A-position NP, even if QNP, has semantic type <e>, including expletives. VP is canonically a predicate, and D-structure simply sees any VP as having type <p> or <e*,t>. If the θ-criterion involves type-checking over these categories, then we will get the effect of the EPP, that clauses have subjects.

Type-checking as I have used it so far is essentially a well-formedness condition: it is not constructive in the sense that c-selection is. The reason for this is that I have assumed more than one possible mode of combination of sister-types, even given the head-argument relation, so that essentially, the requirement is non-local: saturation does not have to be immediate or total. In contrast, under X-bar theory (the categorial well-formedness conditions) a head and its complements must be related in the one given way (*i.e.* the c-selection requirement must be met immediately and totally).

I am arguing that the possibilities and constraints set up by my use of the θ-type notation should replace alternative constraints as currently expressed in GB theory, otherwise there will be a huge redundancy. Of course it may turn out that the things really do come apart. If they do then the area of redundancy is just the area of canonic correspondence between the levels of representation, like the canonic correspondence between c-selection and s-selection suggested by Chomsky.

The lexicon is supposed to give at least (for the purposes of syntax) θ-role assigning properties (the theta-grid) and non-canonic subcategorization properties. I shall continue to use the semantic type notation for the theta grid, but will mark the external θ-role. The advantage of the notation is that it straightforwardly gives compositional effects, at least partly because it records the end result of saturating the item with its internal and external arguments.[2]

Syntax

The notation gives in a pair of angle brackets first the argument required and second the result. Most of the time, we find just one internal argument, which must be a proposition or an entity, and at most one external argument, usually an entity. Entities and propositions are the 'quasi-referential' things, in Chomsky's terminology; they are 'saturated' in some intuitive sense, and are basic in the type system in that they are given primitive non-complex types.[3]

The description should not be taken literally: it is just that this very simple model is easy to grasp and apparently suitable. Propositions have type <t> (for truth-value-bearing), and entities type <e>. A predicate assigning an external θ-role would be of type <e*,t>: you give me an external entity and I will return a proposition. To simplify the coding, I shall use <p> for all such predicates. Thus a normal transitive verb will be given a type <e,p> rather than <e,<e*,t>>. In the latter notation, the 'e' and 'e*' are the two θ-grid equivalents.

		θ-type (s-selection)	c-selection
a	*hit*	<e,p>	NP
b	*believe*	<t,p>	CP
c	*seem*	<t,t>	CP

The types, I shall assume for the moment, give the s-selection information. If c-selection is canonic, we will have *hit* subcategorized for an NP (the canonic category for entities, and if we are in LF and all QNPs have been raised, the only NP argument type); *believe* and *seem* will be subcategorized for CP, the clause type which is the canonic realization of a proposition. After being combined with their internal arguments, their complements, the first two will be of type <p>, that is, still expecting an external <e> (NP) argument. The third, *seem* will not, so that there is no further θ-role to assign, and any subject NP will have to be expletive or part of a chain.

In addition to s-selection and c-selection, an item in the lexicon may have idiosyncratic Case assignment properties. As with the relation of c-selection to s-selection, there should be canonic correspondences, or predictable uniformities between Case and c-selection.

I have suggested that there are possible deviations from the canonic c-selections. For instance, sometimes, when a clause may be selected, then an NP with suitable semantic content may be selected:

1 John believes that Mary is here

2 John believes what Mary said / a lie / that

Discrepancies between s-selection and c-selection of this kind will be discussed in the next chapter, along with discrepancies between s-selection and the selection associated with the corresponding language of thought item.

I have also argued (in section 2.2.2) that an item of type $\langle t,t \rangle$ may c-select for V″, or for an operator-bound clause. It should be borne in mind that in some or all instances, the same effect might be achievable by keeping canonic c-selection and invoking different Case assignment properties. In a way, it does not at this minute make much difference which option is chosen, because I shall be immediately concerned to see what patterns must be distinguished, and whether there are the means to make the distinctions in the lexicon. If subjects are optional, then there is some sense in which C″, I″ and V″ should indeed be the same kind of thing. They belong to the same generalized projection, in the same way that D″ and N″ do (with possibly P″ in addition).[4] More pertinently, all three CAN have type $\langle t \rangle$—a VP if it has no external argument, and I″ and C″ in the usual way; one may speculate that the potential is sufficient to justify their inclusion as possible $\langle t \rangle$ correlates; and out of this arises the possibility of c-selection of V″, without the possibility of stipulation as to type of that V″ itself. The 'incorrect' type can be accepted provided that the deficiency is made up elsewhere in the construction in a permitted manner—essentially, by transmission and predication.

The basic premise on which we are working is that learning of the lexicon must be minimized. There are no lexicon-triggered transformations, so any improper instances of move-α which appear to be lexically differentiated must depend on the various permitted lexical properties. These are s-selection (assumed for the moment to be identical to θ-role type selection); c-selection (perhaps with feature selection); Case assigning properties. Of these properties, the most fundamental is s-selection. That is, if an item has two s-selection frames, we will be positing an ambiguity. What we would like to do, then, given the varied distribution of the adjectives, is to postulate an s-selection type for each from which its total behavior can be predicted. But the distributional facts taken at face value would then suggest

Syntax

multiple ambiguity, which in itself would increase the learning task. If postulating distinctions of c-selection or Case assignment will preserve s-selection, and the distinctions postulated are learnable on positive evidence, then such non-canonic entries will be preferred to the ambiguity alternative.

It is almost certainly going to be that s-selection is not directly related to conceptual argument structure (essentially because the language of thought has a poorer syntax than NL). This would mean some learning of s-selection too (along with syntactic category), and so it will be advantageous for learning (other things being equal—which means, work out whether that is true when I have a theory), that we should postulate a restricted set of s-selection possibilities. It is easier to select from a smaller set. As far as adjective types are concerned, the best candidates would seem to be: <p> for simple predicates; <*t,t> for an adjective which was predicated of an external propositional subject, or <e,t> or <t,t> if the argument is internal; <t,p>, <t,<*t,t>>, (like the first two but with internal propositional arguments). Other possibilities are <e,p>, and <p,p>. Examples of the first would be adjectives like *parallel* in *The first line is parallel to the second*, if we take the *to* as a designated Case marker. The second will be ruled out if we stipulate that all arguments must be saturated. It seems that this is true of s-selection of the logical-predicates as given in the lexicon, though (I argue) not necessarily elsewhere; and it is not even true in the lexicon of operator categories (e.g. DET and some Adjectives). Below, I shall be considering logical predicates, rather than operators; the assumption that arguments must be saturated (in our pretend-types) would be consonant with a view that constraints on different levels were the same but what counted as this or that might change from one level to another. So I shall keep to the assumption unless forced to abandon it.

With just the restrictions we have indicated so far, we may not have sufficient to make all the decisions we must make. But let us try.

4.1 Distinctions between adjectives: c-selection and learnability

> We must distinguish.   Poincaré, *Science and Hypothesis*

4.1.1 Some data

The adjectives which will be discussed are a subset of those that have clausal or propositional complements, and others which superficially appear to do so. I have omitted exclamative complements (see Grimshaw 1979). Table 1, below, shows the main constructions for diagnosis. It is immediately apparent that there is a good deal of variety in what is permitted for a given adjective, so that the analysis and learning problems are not trivial. At least the following adjectives differ syntactically from each other: *easy, eager, likely, apt, able, ready, stupid, probable, necessary, unlikely*.

4.1.2 Complements with fully lexical CP, PRO, or Raising

Let us first consider the frames in (1) to (10) of the table, and the obvious necessary s-selection options. The frames can be divided into those with a complete embedded clause, (1) to (4) and (9) and (10), and those where there is not a lexical realization for all the θ-positions of the embedded clause: (5) to (9). If the post-adjectival clause is complete, then the surface external argument is present at D-structure, and so is that given by s-selection. The *it* subjects given are all expletive (as can be ascertained by attempting to replace them with a full NP). The status of the clause is less immediately clear, since in principle it could be an obscure sort of modifier (obscure in that its type would be wrong). If this possibility is rejected, these clauses will be internal arguments, so that the s-selections for many adjectives are fixed as soon as one or other of these constructions is heard (provided that the completeness of the clause is recognized). From (1) to (4) and (9) and (10), we obtain the following:

17 type $\langle t,p \rangle$ *eager, ready, certain$_2$, uncertain$_2$*

18 type $\langle t,t \rangle$ *necessary, likely, probable, certain$_1$, uncertain$_1$, easy, apt$_2$, stupid, unlikely*

Table 1

1	John is	eager ready$_1$	[*PRO$_{arb}$ / for us to go]
2	John is	eager	[that Mary come(s)] * without *that*
3 a b	John is John is not	certain$_2$ certain$_2$	[that Mary came] [whether Mary came][5]
4	John is		uncertain$_2$ [whether Mary came]
5	John is	easy ready$_2$	[PRO$_{arb}$ / for us to see e]
6	John is	likely unlikely apt$_1$ certain$_1$ stupid$_2$ able	[[e / *for us] to go]
7	John is	eager ready$_1$	[e to go]
8	John is		uncertain$_2$ [whether [e / *for us] to come]
9 a	It is	easy stupid$_1$ necessary	[PRO$_{arb}$ / for us to please John]
b	It is	stupid$_2$	[of us to please John]
c	It is	unlikely	[*PRO$_{arb}$ / ?for us to please John]
10 a	It is	(un)likely probable certain$_1$ uncertain$_1$ stupid$_1$	[that Mary won't come]
b	It is	necessary	[that Mary come(s)]
c	It is	uncertain$_1$	[whether Mary will come]
d	It is	apt$_2$	[that Mary came]

Continued on next page

Table 1—*Continued*

11	John is a(n)	...	man [PRO$_{arb}$ / for us to beat him] (compare the *too* possibilities)
12 a	John is a(n)	easy likely stupid$_1$	man [PRO$_{arb}$ / for us to beat e]
b	That was a	silly	train [PRO$_{arb}$ / for us to catch e]
13	John is a man	easy	[PRO$_{arb}$ / for us to ignore e]
14	John is a man	ready$_1$ likely eager apt$_1$ certain$_1$ able	[(PRO$_i$) to go far]
15	John is	stupid able	
16	It is	easy stupid	[PRO$_{arb}$ / ? for us believing John]

(The two *apt*s are quite distinct in meaning: *apt*$_1$ means, roughly, 'likely', where *apt*$_2$ means roughly 'appropriate'). It appears that *certain* and *uncertain* are ambiguous, but the meanings are clearly closely related, so something more needs to be said.[6]

Given this much, and the usual principles of the grammar, we can make various predictions about what else should occur. If <t> is canonically realized as ANY kind of clause, we should expect all the type <t,p> items to occur in all the first four frames, and all the type <t,t> to occur in both of (9) and (10). Consider first the <t,p> types. We need to say (somehow) that *certain* with expletive subject refuses a *to* clause. Some speakers reject (2), so that for those, *eager* is to refuse C″[*that*]. The tense difference between (2) and (3a) is presumably something to do with the kind of semantics which is not amenable to description with syntactic features, and so is the alternation with *whether* in (3) and (4). We may note that all four items characterize propositional attitudes, so that their status as <t,p> is in some sense canonic with respect to the associated concepts.

The differentiation with respect to possible complements may be accomplished by adding features which are realized on the specifier or head of the complement. I am taking *to* to be a feature on V which may be assigned directly or via an I[+*to*]. If only positive evidence is used, the learner will need to assume that NONE of the c-selection possibilities is possible unless it has been observed. The form of the differentiating property will be left open for the moment.

Next we observe that if an overt subject with *for* is available in the clause, and the clause is untensed, we expect that PRO will also be available. This will be so, because the *for* subject ensures that a θ-role is available, and the *for* itself (on the standard story) that the position is not governed since it necessitates a C" constituent. This prediction is borne out by the readings for (9a), with PRO$_{arb}$ interpretation. If PRO and *for*-subjects always go together, then in (6), we should suppose that *e* is not PRO. In any case, PRO will not be possible for *likely, certain*$_1$ or *stupid* if these are of category <t,t>, because the *e* must somehow pass its θ-role to the matrix subject. This suggests that *apt*$_1$ too is of type <t,t> (further arguments were given in section 2.2.2). However, the child cannot use the evidence of the absence of the *for*-subject to ascertain the type for *apt*; all we can say is that if it is indeed <t,t>, the occurrence of *apt*$_1$ in (6) is consistent.

We may take it that the empty category in (7) which matches (1) except for the absence of an overt subject of the embedded clause has a PRO subject, with control being dictated by the availability of a possible controller.

Because of the occurrence of *stupid* in both (9a) and (9b), and in both (6) and (9a) (raising and non-raising), the possibility that there are two related items *stupid* suggests itself. In fact, there is a difference in sense: in (9a) and (10a), the stupidity is not directly imputed to anyone, so that

19   It is stupid for the cards not to fit in the envelopes

like (20) is fine,

20   It is stupid that the card won't fit in the envelope

whereas stupidity is imputed to the cards in

21 ?The card is stupid not to fit in the envelope

22 ?It is stupid of the card not to fit in the envelope

and both are bad for the same (pragmatic) reason. Using a non-referential subject distinguishes even more sharply:

23 i   It was stupid that no-one finished the cake

    ii   It was stupid for no-one to finish the cake

    iii No-one was stupid to finish the cake

    iv   It was stupid of no-one to finish the cake

The first two entail that no-one finished the cake; the second two can only be understood as entailing that stupidity is not to be imputed to anyone who DID finish the cake (or, so as not to prejudge the issue here, stupidity in finishing the cake is not to be imputed to anyone). Let us distinguish *stupid*$_1$ (for (9a) and (10a), and *stupid*$_2$ (for (9b) and (6)). We will come back to *stupid*.

Able, like *apt*, fails to occur with expletive *it*, but as we saw in 2.2.2, the two do not pattern in the same way, and it seems that *able* should have an external argument. Because of this, I shall leave *able* aside until section 4.1.3.

The entries of (6) (repeated here as (24)) with t_k for e represent the classic Raising construction. Why does not every one of the items of type <t,t> fit this frame? On my θ-transmission alternative, a similar question arises.

24 John$_k$ is   likely   [t_k to go]

               apt$_1$

               stupid

               certain$_1$

The items *necessary*, *probable*, and *easy* do not fit, and we get *apt*$_1$ not *apt*$_2$. First, we need the adjective to subcategorize for a non-tensed clause.[7] How is this subcategorization information learned? The occurrence of the adjective in (9) should help, but this is clearly neither a necessary nor a sufficient condition. Ungrammaticality as opposed to semantic infelicity seems to be the judgment on

25 We are easy [*e* to please John]

so there must be some syntactic information in the lexicon to prevent the unwanted movement.[8] The obvious tool to use is government, since traces must be properly governed, by the ECP.[9] Thus there must be a barrier for *easy* and *necessary* which is not present for *likely*.

For Raising verbs, the current standard story is to add I″ to C″ as possible subcategorization realizations of the <t> required, just for the Raising items; where I″ is not a barrier for its specifier. In addition, there is no Case-marking of the specifier (*i.e.* no exceptional Case-marking), so that movement is forced. I have argued (in section 2.2.2), that for some Raising adjectives, the requirements of eliminability for defined words suggest rather that we add V″, while keeping the θ-types unchanged. With V″ as complement, there is no empty subject category, but θ-transmission of the role otherwise assigned to that subject. Assume that the copula is transparent, for the moment. Then a raising adjective like *likely* takes both C″ and V″ complements:

A *likely* <t,t> C″[*that*], V″[*to*]

I have shown selection features too; I will return to this. If an I″ complement were chosen, this would force a subject because the V″ will no longer be an argument, at DS, and hence as predicate must have an argument. (Arguments at D-structure must be sisters to their predicating category). Since the construction parallel to (9)

26 *It is not likely [$_{XP}$ PRO$_{arb}$/for Bill to come]

is ungrammatical, we may assume that XP = I″[*to*] is not permitted for *likely* (where the I″ is the complement, as I shall suggest, or where it is inside C″, so the c-selection not permitted is C″[*for*]). This will be learnable on the assumption that no complement is assumed unless positive evidence requires it.

In the standard treatment, where we have I″ selection (what used to be S′ deletion), (26) with PRO is blocked if XP = I″ and (24) is permitted, because *likely* governs the PRO in (26); but PRO must be ungoverned. The *for Bill* version will not occur if *for* is treated as a feature, requiring not only C″ but that particular feature [+*for*] on C″ is specified—and again we are assuming that no complement specification is assumed without positive evidence.[10]

On either story, then, the Raising items are distinguished by c-selection, and the addition of V″ or I″ is learnable.[11] However, the stories for raising structures and for the presence or absence of tense in full complement clauses must be consistent. The standard story needs C″[*that*], C″[*for*], and I″ (and the presence or absence of Case assigning by a head); my θ-transmission story needs V″ as an option, and along with C″[*that*] either C″[*for*] or I″[*to*]. I shall use I″[*to*] to designate that choice of subcategorization which leads to an I″[*to*] whether or not we suppose it to be enclosed in a C″ constituent. Then we can postulate:

A	*(un)likely*	<t,t>	C″[*that*], V″[*to*]
B	*apt*$_1$	<t,t>	V″[*to*]
C	*apt*$_2$ *probable*	<t,t>	C″[*that*]
D	*necessary* *stupid*$_1$	<t,t>	C″[*that*] I″[*to*]

The 'I″[*to*]' entry is intended to carry with it Case-marking by *for*, at least if we do not have PRO. Suppose alternatively we take *for* as a Case-marker, where the Case is assigned by the head adjective. If we change the status of PRO, and suggest that it is in fact governed and Case-marked, with a *for* that is phonologically null, PRO falls in with overt NPs. We need to stipulate that PRO may only be Case-marked with 'weak' Case, *i.e. for* (and possibly genitive in the subject position in NPs),[12] but cannot carry nominative or accusative Case. We will obtain the most obvious facts about the distribution of PRO, and account for the otherwise curious property of its apparently having 'inherent' Case (with respect to visibility for θ-role assignment). There is a naturalness to this taking of *for* as a Case-marker if all and only C″ specifications are tensed, since otherwise the subject of the embedded clause will not be Case-marked. I will return to the realization of I″[+*for*, +*to*] as a CP, below.

The other main type of clause-taking adjectives is like *eager*. Here we have an external θ-role assigned to the subject, so that the θ-type is <t,p>.

Syntax

E   *eager*   <t,p>   C″[*that*] I″[*to*]

An empty subject (as in (7)) is controlled PRO.

We have now discussed the occurrence or non-occurrence of at least some of the items in all the frames up to (10) except (5) and (8). Consider next (8). It is clear enough on the standard story that the complement must be C″, but since *uncertain* has both types <t,p> and <t,t>, this is not particularly helpful. The reading for this sentence however certainly imputes doubt to John (as in (4)), rather than to fate in general as in (10c); we need to know why this is so. It is not, then, a congener to (6) with *certain*$_1$. That the only item for this particular frame is *uncertain* is unsurprising, since we have a [+WH] complement. However, we should at the same time consider the alternatives in (28).

27 i   John$_k$ is uncertain$_2$ [$_{XP}$ whether [*e* / *for us to come]]

27 ii   John is   uncertain$_2$ [$_{XP}$ how [*e* to do it] / [who *e* to see]]

28 i   * John$_k$ is certain$_2$ [$_{YP}$ that [*e* / for us to come]]

  ii   * John is   not certain$_2$ [$_{YP}$ if [*e* to come]]

Note that the complementizers *that* and *if* are acceptable at least after *not certain* in both <t,p> and <t,t> constructions. I shall treat *certain* and *uncertain* as having identical properties, since the differences will not serve to explain anything here (both occurrences of *uncertain* can be replaced by *not certain* and *vice versa* without changing the grammaticality). It is clear enough that the difference between the (27) and (28) examples must depend on one of three things: the category or status of XP as opposed to YP; the C″ internal position of the *wh*-items (including *whether* with *how* and *who*) as opposed to the complementizers *that* and *if*; or some difference in category or status between the *wh*-words and the complementizers.

Consider the status of *e*. We need to ensure that it can be PRO$_k$, and not t_k or PRO$_{arb}$, in (27). There is no possibility of letting *e* be a trace bound by the empty operator in (27), because this would produce an argument for the adjective of type <p>, with no proper transmission of the 'spare' θ-role possible on account of *wh*-island effects.[13] If it were a trace, the empty NP would have to have a proper governor. If C″ is a barrier to government, and XP = C″, it cannot have one. But if the position is ungoverned, PRO is an option. I shall simply assume that control can be accounted for. Since certainly YP = C", this offers no account of the ungrammaticality of (28). A simple answer is to suppose that both *if* and *that* are subcategorized to take I"[+tense], ruling out the infinitive. If neither *for* nor *whether* are true lexical complementizers, one can assert that all complementizers have this property.[14] Let us assume that *for* is a Case-realizing preposition (like *of*), with the privilege of occurrence under C (there are a number of alternatives here—it is not clear how the decision should be made).

Pursuing this, one might speculate that the subcategorization for *uncertain*$_2$ in (27) is I"[+WH]; then all complements lacking true complementizers would be c-selected as I". A subcategorization feature must be realized on a SPEC or Head. A [+WH] element must be in an A-bar operator position. Let us assume that this induces the CP projection, which has such an operator position available (SPEC of IP is an A-position; adjunction to IP is an alternative, but may be generally impossible).[15] Equivalently, the CP is always there when IP is present, but is not visible for gross c-selection or as a barrier for government, unless it is c-selected explicitly. The absence of the '*for* NP' alternant in (27) and (8) is due simply to the analogue of the 'doubly filled COMP' filter.

If we suppose that the occurrence of PRO and *for NP* is in fact evidence of a 'weak' Case assigned by the adjective, then c-selection for IP or CP, with visible CP a barrier to Case assignment will account for the data here. Note that if we delete the *that* in (28i), we obtain a grammatical sentence just with *e*, but having the other meaning of *certain*. This means that an occurrence of *that* which is c-selected but phonologically null must have syntactic properties: it will itself still c-select for I"[+tense] and block Case assignment.

Let us add a feature [+WH]—which very probably should be the reflex of a <q,t> s-selection option—to the entries. It may be rather that a semantic generalization of a sort not given by the simple s-selection types will account for [WH] choices. We now have (continuing to record the option of having at least I"[*to*]—whether or not there is an enclosing C"—by I"[*to*]):

| F | *certain*$_1$ | <t,t> | C"[*that*/WH] V"[*to*] |
| G | *uncertain*$_1$ | <t,t> | C"[*that*/WH] |

(where the [+WH] on a C″ entry is for a WH complementizer *i.e. if* as the head of C″, or for a *wh*-item in the specifier of C″)

| H | certain₂ | <t,p> | C″[*that*/WH] |
| I | uncertain₂ | <t,p> | C″[WH] I″[*to*, WH] |

The subcategorization information supplied in A to I already makes some predictions about the data in the second half of the table. We may assume that in (13), the sentences with *likely, apt* and *certain* are the result of adjoining an AP to the right of the N′ [*man*]. In each case the AP is capable of assigning an external θ-role, and hence of being licensed as a predicate in this position, because the adjective although having type <t,t> is followed by a V‴[*to*] complement, which forces θ-role transmission (of the subject role): the adjective-complement complex has type <p> by composition. Thus we predict (correctly) that we have *certain*₁ and *apt*₁ here. There are of course equivalent versions with *that* and [+WH] complements, such as

29 i   John is a man uncertain whether to leave

  ii   John is a man certain that the day will be a disaster

We also predict that an adjective of type <t,p> with its correct complement should form a licensed predicate in this position—hence the entry with *eager* (and, as we shall posit similarly) *ready*. However, the possibility of having 'controlled' PRO is in need of explanation:

30   No [man [eager [PRO to help]]] should keep getting in the way

The problem is what PRO is controlled by. It looks as if provision must be made for PRO to be coindexed with the external argument of *eager*—a possibility if this were represented, as suggested in chapter 2 and explored further in section 4.2.7 below; and reflexives could be similarly coindexed. Note that PRO can also be controlled by syntactically suppressed θ-role bearers such as agents of passives (Chomsky 1986a, 124). Then in examples like (31) (from (7) above),

31   John is [eager [PRO to go]]

the PRO is not directly controlled by *John* at all, and similar remarks will apply, presumably, to similar cases of PRO-complements after verbs.

Note however that this will not apply in (32) (from (5)):

32   John is easy [PRO to see e]

Here (even if *John* qualifies as an external argument, by virtue of predication by the empty operator) we cannot have PRO and e coindexed, since there would be a Binding theory violation, so that PRO must be PRO_{arb}.[16]

4.1.3   Complements with the empty operator, and doubling of θ-roles

It is time to face the problems posed by *easy* and the other adjectives which occur in constructions with the empty operator. In chapter 2, I assumed with little discussion that the embedded clause in (5) was indeed a complement clause. In view of examples like those of (9a), where the clause is complete, it is perverse to doubt this, so that we expect to assign to *easy* the s-selection type <t,t>. The c-selection required by (9a) is I″[*to*]. One must presume that the c-selection allowing the empty operator is also given, since this is not a case of simple θ-transmission: in relation to types, the empty operator turns an internal argument into an external one. If the operator is a maximal projection, and an operator, then it must move into the specifier position of C″. Let us for the moment give the c-selection as I″[*O*], paralleling I″[WH] in c-selection option 'I' above, since all the examples are infinitival, with the C″[*O*] being derivative.

Several questions immediately arise. One is, why it is apparently only adjectives which have this c-selection available. Possibly the answer to this (if in fact it is true)[17] is that adjectives are canonically of type <p>, so that devices which make the type <t> APs concerned into type <p> are to be expected. Another question is why, although semantically the operator appears to be almost identical to a *wh*-item (as witness the alternations in relative clauses), we do not have [+WH] items instead of the empty operator in these constructions. A very partial answer to this appears to be that a C″[WH] is at least capable of representing an embedded question (or indeed a direct one), whereas C″[*O*] is not. If I had, as I suggested earlier, used <q> for the type(s) of questions, then this amounts to saying that C″[*O*] never has type <q>. It has, rather, the function of producing always an external θ-role which is

Syntax

to be deployed somewhere in the construction; where by contrast, <q> counts as being saturated. All the central 'propositional attitude' adjectives (like *certain*) then will have [+WH] if they have either. This means that the [+WH] feature is not necessary, and so in particular, it does not have to be given for my 'I″[WH]' suggestion for *uncertain*$_2$. If <q> is selected, we may take it that the realization must either have type <k,t> for some k by virtue of a [+WH] item (the empty operator being excluded) or by virtue of the occurrence of the [+WH] operator *if*.[18] In giving the subcategorization in table II below, I shall omit these entirely predictable choices. Similarly, any C″ without specified or <q>-induced features is to be C″[*that*], with or without phonological realization.[19] It will then be not unexpected that constructions with the empty operator turn up in adjunction structures like purpose clauses, or in parasitic gap constructions, for instance. What now needs explaining is why certain C″[WH] and C″[*that*] clauses turn up as relative clauses—but that is outside what I can discuss here.

The rhetorical purpose of the empty operator construction with *easy* appears to be to enable a non-subject participant in the embedded proposition to be focused, by moving it (in effect) to matrix subject position (the corresponding effect for a subject can be achieved in principle either by movement or by the allocation of a V″ complement). The logic behind this, if I have it right, is that it is this matrix subject which is typically seen as causally responsible for the state of affairs. I assume that there should be a default meaning postulate to this effect associated with the structure, so that there will be economy of representation. The intuitive distinction between adjectives like *easy* and those like *stupid*, (which are similar in fitting (9a) and (12) above, but differ on (5) and (13), and (6) and (9b)), can be seen in the primary environment like that of (9a), repeated here,

9 a   i   It is   easy   [PRO$_{arb}$ / for us to please John]

  ii   stupid

In (i) we may wish to pick out as being causally involved in the ease the non-subject (*John*) of the embedded clause; where in (ii) it is the subject of the clause (*us*), if anything, which is causally involved in the stupidity.[20] So we can add:

J   *easy*   <t,t>   I″[*O*], I″[*to*]

This will predict the occurrence of the AP as an adjunct, as under (13), as well. We find too that the head can occur in the normal adjective position in front of the N', as in (12a). This seems a privilege of $C''[O]$ heads, so that we cannot have for instance

33 i * John is an eager man [PRO to go out this evening]

   ii * John is an eager man that justice be done

This fact (if it is one; which it had better be) is in need of explanation. It will be considered further in the discussion about *stupid* below.[21]

Another adjective which appears, like *easy*, to be of type <t,t> and to allow an operator-bound c-selection option is *worth*. This apparently takes a gerundive (nominal) complement of type <t>, and has no external argument role to assign:

34   It is worth [your/PRO looking at that jug]

Somewhat surprisingly, the same complement can be bound by the empty operator, so as to produce an <e,t> predicational AP by compositional transmission:

35   That jug is worth O_i[PRO looking at e_i]

On the assumption that the normal gerundive complement is an NP, there is a question to be resolved as to how the c-selection option is to be stated in the operator case, and the correct structural description of the positions and categories of the elements O_i and *your*/PRO in the NP. It seems incorrect to have both O_i and *your*/PRO in the specifier of NP. But we must, I take it, assume that the O_i is in the specifier position rather than adjoined; the DP analysis will permit the O_i to be in the DP specifier and the *your*/PRO in the N'' specifier, which is a partially satisfactory answer (further suggestions about the structure of DP are made in section 4.2.1). We may then give *worth* subcategorization which includes a type <t,t>, and c-selection for D'' and $D''[O]$, where in addition we need to ensure that the N'' is a gerund.

There do occur *-ing* forms after *easy*, as shown in (16) of the table, but these are participial (clausal) complements. Furthermore, one can have

36   Believing John is easy (for you)

Intuitively, it is just the same *easy* in all the occurrences; the syntax I do not wish to elaborate. The *for you* in (36) is the "extra" beneficiary which can indeed appear simultaneously with the clausal subject in infinitival clauses:[22]

37 It is easier for the boys for the girls to make the beds

That leaves us with just *ready* and *stupid*. There is no problem with *stupid*$_1$, which has type <t,t>, and falls under pattern D along with *necessary*. However, it does not have a I"[O] complement licensing it under (5), so we should not expect it under (12a). Since we have already postulated a *stupid*$_2$, for (6) and (9c), and we should hope that the same s-selection can account for the plain adjective as in (15), and for the occurrences in (12a). A natural analysis is to suppose that in (9c), what we actually have is

38 It is stupid [of John$_i$] [PRO$_i$ to go]

If we assume that the *of* is the manifestation of the Case-marking of the post-adjectival NP position, then we might suppose that (6) could be analyzed as lacking the Case marking, and hence as

39 John$_i$ is stupid [t_i] [PRO$_i$ to go]

We would be postulating K$_1$:

K$_1$ stupid$_2$ <{e,t},t>   {N", I"}

where the braces are to indicate the types and categories of a set of (internal) arguments.[23] Case theory will take care of their ordering. We also would need an optional assignment of Case, which is a dubious notion (but there is an alternative interpretation of this, discussed below). However, we still need an account of the unavailability of anything except PRO as subject of the clause. Mere association of the two NPs with the same person (via some semantic postulate) will not do, since we might then expect an alternative with a pronoun:

40 i ? It was stupid of Joe$_j$ [for him$_j$ to do that]

  ii * It was stupid of Joe$_j$ [for the toast to have been burnt by him$_j$]

Since the PRO is in the specifier position of the I" assumed, it would be technically possible to subcategorize for the item. However, this seems to be a regrettable step. 'Avoid pronoun' (Chomsky 1981, for instance) might be invoked, although the pragmatic motivation is missing (see Smith 1989). Chomsky declares that the principle is 'grammaticalized', however.

An alternative analysis for (9c) is of a clause with exceptional Case-marking: we superimpose the NP onto the clause, obliterating the PRO, as it were:

41   It is stupid [*of* John to go]

The selection frame will be just like that for *stupid*$_1$, given in D above, but there will have to be explicit provision for the Case-marking. We could postulate the selection

K$_2$ *stupid*$_2$ <t,p>   I"[+*of* Case, *to*]

We might take the *of* Case as indicating that the subject NP of the embedded clause is selected as a 'second' (conceptually-selected) argument by the adjective. We seem to have to assume that the exceptional marking of the NP is sufficient to trigger the assumption of the 'meaning postulate' concerning the referent of the NP; for the rest, *stupid*$_2$ is just like *stupid*$_1$ (*i.e.* with respect to the attitude expressed to the proposition as a whole). Again, the (6) sentence can be obtained by movement if we assume that the Case marking is optional (and that *for*-Case is not supplied)—and of course we need to assume that the same 'meaning postulate' applies. The problem of the lack of overt alternative embedded subjects has been eliminated. Against this story is the fact that the *of* Case is inherent Case, and this is supposed to be assigned only when a θ-role is assigned (Chomsky 1986a, 193). A further argument against ECM for adjectives is given below.

Consider now the plain adjective (as in (15): *John is stupid*). If this is to be assimilated, we must suppose that the predicational part can be null. If we take K$_1$, with an independent N", the whole clause I" will be null; if we take K$_2$, we need to delete I'. I assume that this latter is not permitted. There must be systematic reasons for this, but they seem to be at least partly semantic rather than syntactic. Suppose we regard 'short answers' as elliptical; then to respond, "John," in answer to "Who shaves himself?" is perhaps to have supplied a clause with a null I'. But in this case the I' has a semantic value (at least) which is to be reconstructed precisely from the context, in contrast to what we have

Syntax

with *stupid*. If such a specificity IS required with *stupid*, we use a proform for the proposition, which is (as usual) an NP:

42 It/that was stupid of John

Since the propositional NP must receive Case, of course it must be moved into the matrix subject position.[24] However, note that we can move the predicational part of the 'clause':

43 To go out just then was stupid of John

which is not possible with a *for* infinitive

44 *To annoy John was stupid for Mary

This is further evidence for the independence of the NP. But there are problems with K_1, which can only be solved by eliminating PRO. Suppose that the clause is in fact just a V‴. This can be accomplished with little extra apparatus if we assume first that John's role in relation to the usual propositional argument of *stupid* is initially coded as an external argument (as in (6)), and that when the proposition is realized just as a V‴, the external role of the V‴ is transmitted to this external argument. The external argument will now bear two θ-roles—a possibility discussed further below, but certainly not semantically anomalous nor syntactically unique. This will account for the non-occurrence of alternative subjects. In order to account for the occurrence of the external argument in an *of*-PP, we would, I think, have to permit it to be coded as optionally implicit or 'explicit'—and maybe the *of* Case is one used when this is so. Verbs of course have alternately explicit and implicit arguments, but with change of morphology; nouns appear to have an option similar to that postulated for $stupid_2$.[25] This third suggestion gives us:

K_3 <t,(p)>   V‴[*to*], where '(p)' is to mean, 'p or t'

The postulation of a possibly implicit external argument predicts that

45 It would be stupid to go out now

has one analysis with $stupid_1$ and PRO_{arb}, and another with the external role of [$_{V''}$ to go out now] identified with the implicit argument of $stupid_2$, and hence having an existential interpretation. That there is a possibility of identifying the subject has been noted before, for example in relation to PRO in Bresnan 1982. The possibility seems to depend on the existence of optional PPs: our *stupid$_2$ of*, and *foolish of, risky for* and *unclear to* from Bresnan.

I assume that the optionality or ellipsis of the V" argument can be predicted on general grounds, and does not have to be listed in any way. This assumption is made not on the basis of any direct evidence, but on the assumption that if idiosyncratic, it would add vastly to the learning task.[26] This still does not answer the question as to where such an optionality would arise, though. There are three possibilities: prior to the establishment of the information in K_1 above, so that the s-selection differs; after s-selection but before c-selection; after c-selection (*i.e.* at lexical entry or by ellipsis). The middle one of these is in fact impossible, since it would wreak havoc with the type-checking of θ-theory. Given the Recoverability of Deletion hypothesis and the vagueness of the missing predicate, the last suggestion might be implemented through a designated empty category with an 'existential' reading—there is some behavior of John's which led us to impute stupidity to him. The first suggestion would make the new option K':

K'   stupid$_3$ <p>   –

This would have the advantage of predicting the contrast between (46) and (47):

46   It was stupid of John

47   John was stupid

We cannot take (46) as a simple variant of (47). In (46), there is either ellipsis of a fairly drastic surface kind of the clause after *John*, or, more naturally, the *it* is not an expletive at all, but the proform for a clause corresponding to that in the subject position in (43)—being an NP, of course, the proform could not remain *in situ*.[27] It is possible that canonic structures are preferred, and (47) is the canonic one for adjectives generally: the alternative exists partly to permit the external argument bearer for the V" to be near to it. So the contrast between the two sentences is not sufficient evidence. Parsimony would of course dictate that if the third suggestion were independently shown to be correct, then the first should not be invoked, but that again is not convincing, unless something prevents the first option from being considered. It seems to me that there must be such principles, guiding the correlation of conceptual and s-selection choices. Humans both learn and invent natural language which has conceptual meaning, and it is perfectly clear that a one–one correspondence between conceptual and s-selection would be desirable in some rather vague sense (as reiterated by Chomsky 1990). Deviations from this must be predictable, or at least explicable.

Let us take it that the task is to choose between K_1, K_2 and K_3. We want to reject K_2 (since its acceptance would force unnecessary ambiguity, with K' required). Suppose then it is simply not licit to superimpose one role on another, where either of these is an internal argument, or contained within such. In our case, we have the 'contained within' disjunct. This is a particular consequence of the fact that internal arguments must be realized: they must be realized as independent units, not overlapping with something else. Can we rule out either of the others in principle? Let us assume that the NP which may be in subject position is indeed an external argument of the adjective, in both cases, so that for each the s-selection is <t,(p)>. I think the answer is negative for K_3. The distribution of θ-roles to arguments is a combination of two permitted moves: the holding of two external θ-roles by one NP, and the transmission of θ-role to a higher subject position. Of course a rule could be formulated, but it has no naturalness. K_1 is possible if 'avoid pronoun' is a syntactic rule. However, K_3 is a grammaticalization of the same principle in the lexicon, since the internal argument is just V''', instead of I'''. If it could be shown that this was the proper locus of the principle, we would have a decision procedure. The effect would be to ban obligatorily controlled PRO of certain kinds (see Farkas 1988). Alternatively, perhaps for complements, minimal structure is always postulated, so that V''' will be assumed unless *for*–NP occurs as well. (An exception to this is (8), where *for*–NP could never occur; but there is independent evidence for more than V'''). Thirdly, and perhaps most interestingly, the choice might be made according to the requirements of the meaning postulate concerning the subject: the choice might be canonic in some natural way with respect to the expression of the postulate.[28] However this decision is made, we may then obtain the correct predictions for (40) above.

We are left with the interesting case of sentences like the one in (12a), or the rather more plausible

48   That was a stupid thing [to do *e*]

Note that here, the external NP is missing, but that it is supplied as part of the pragmatic processing as referring to someone contextually accessible—not a PRO$_{arb}$ reading. But we have only to change the tense for the opposite to hold:

49   That is a stupid thing [PRO to do *e*]

These facts suggest that in fact both *stupid*₁ and *stupid*₂ are available here, with the reading being selected pragmatically. Further, a little more effort produces other examples which are acceptable on the lines of (12b), where the examples like (12a) are marginal or odd. So:

50   i   That was not a necessary thing (for you) to do *e*

  ii That is an unlikely plant to find *e* in a bog

  iii That is a very probable place to find your glasses *e*

What is quite clear in all these constructions is that the adjective is not a modifier of the noun directly. In every case, the adjective normally takes an infinitival clausal complement to give something of type <t>, and the modification is mediated just by the existence of a gap bound by the empty operator. But the operator is not, in these cases, c-selected. It arises, apparently, rather as part of a somewhat deviant case of relative clause formation. So for (12b), for instance, there is a paraphrase:

51   That was a train [which [It was silly PRO$_{arb}$ / for us to catch *e*]

The structure [*silly for us to catch e*] is not a clause, but like a clause, it has type <t>. Suppose this is sufficient to license the use of the construction as a "relative" at some level; and that this in turn is sufficient to license the movement to the SPEC of the AP of the empty operator (originating at the position of *e*), so that we obtain a predicate of type <e,t> as required. Suppose that this AP is preposed, and the complement subsequently postposed. The motivation for this maneuvering appears to be that the final string has the innocent appearance of a simple 'AP-noun-Relative clause' construction, where there are two independently adjoined modifiers. If it is obligatory (as seems to me to be the case) it is presumably because there is some level which objects to postposed "relatives" which are not actually clauses, but which will accept as an N' adjunct a clause which just has the trace of the empty operator in COMP. The restriction to empty operators (or trace of this) in COMP for the postposed clause will explain the ungrammaticality of (33) (i) and (ii) mentioned above. The other examples we have had with such maneuvering concerned 'a very hard girl to please' (see section 2.3.2 for discussion), and here too we had an empty operator construction, this time with a complement clause.[29] It is not clear how easy it may be to implement these suggestions. However, if they are correct, we know why only *easy* falls under (13), with the complement adjacent to the head adjective: the whole is not a "relative" headed by the empty operator, but an ordinary AP headed by an adjective which takes I"[O] as its complement.[30] It is also fairly clear why we may not have the *of us* explicit:

52   * That was a silly train of us to catch

The nearest that can be attained to the meaning of (52) has *for us*, which, if I am right about the difference between the two versions of such adjectives, does not directly entail that the silliness is our fault (though this could well be the reason for the silliness of our catching that train).

Next, let us consider *ready*. The problem with *ready* is that it patterns with *eager*, as in (1), (7) and (14), and with *easy* in (5) but not in (9a), or (12). A partial answer is that the item is ambiguous, with two closely related meanings. If the complement is a full clause, the readiness is a readiness of mind in relation to the event described in the clause; if the complement is operator-bound, the readiness is physical. Thus we can produce anomalous sentences like

53   ? The carpet is ready for you to sweep it

and mild garden-path effects as in

54   The chickens are ready for you to feed *e*

The full-clause complement *ready* is straightforward: it has an external argument and an internal propositional one, where the latter must be infinitival, giving type <t,p> with c-selection I"[*to*]. In addition, the same meaning (indicating readiness of mind) occurs in (7). Here we may postulate controlled PRO, which needs no special provision if it alternates with '*for* NP'.[31] So we have:

L   *ready*₁   <t,p>   I″[*to*]

It is regularly acceptable for the complement clause to be omitted, if its content can be contextually retrieved, as in

55   Billy is ready

The occurrence of *ready* with *easy* in (5) however is accidental. The second *ready*, like the first, (and unlike *easy*) has conceptually an entity as one argument; its second is some proposition concerning that entity. Thus we have a case akin to that of *stupid*₂ (*stupid of* N″), except that the involvement is not as agent, typically, but as patient. We see this in the classic

56   The chicken is ready PRO$_{arb}$ to eat *e*

Given that the empty operator must bind the gap, what do we say about the structure? We might suppose that the conceptual selection was as I have indicated above, which does not have a canonic realization in terms of s-selection (because of the overlap of the 'arguments'); let the s-selection be <t,t> (giving priority to the propositional part), but let the c-selection be just I″[O] (forcing some non-subject element out of the proposition into an empty matrix subject position, in effect). This combination adequately mimics the conceptual selection requirements. We would have the pattern M₁:

M₁   *ready*₂   <t,t>   I″[O]

The problem here will be semantic, I think, since the <t,t> classification is misleading. An alternative approach keeps two separate arguments at s-selection. Suppose the type were <<e,t>,p>. We now expect an external N″ argument, and it is possible to give the internal argument as I″[O], to give the predicational type. We would be postulating a pattern

M₂   *ready*₂   <<e,t>,p>   I″[O]

There are two disadvantages here: firstly the internal argument is not saturated, which we have taken to be a principle for s-selection; and secondly, the relation between the external argument and the internal one is not carried by the types, so there is a gap between conceptual- and s-selection which is still undesirably wide. We know how to remove both these disadvantages: we need the internal argument to be of type <t>, so that it has a spare role to transmit to the subject. This suggestion amounts to

M_3 $ready_2$ <t,p> $I''[O]$

This has the further advantage of identical s-selection to that for $ready_1$; the difference being just in the association of the external role with some non-subject role of the proposition in the case of $ready_2$, forced by the c-selection of $I''[O]$ instead of full I''. The disadvantage of this is that in the structure

57 The chicken is [ready O_i[PRO$_{arb}$ to eat e_i]]

the matrix subject *the chicken* will have two θ-roles, one the external argument of *ready* and one transmitted by O_i (which then would have moved to the front of the AP). There is no reason to suppose that the theta-criterion cannot be formulated to permit this: the configuration is not one provided for except in as much as transmission has been suggested before. Because of small clause constructions

58 I thought [the chicken O_j[ready to eat e_j]]

we see that we need to assume that the joint assignment of the two θ-roles counts as constructing an item of type <e,t>, which suggests that the operator somehow gets amalgamated directly with the external θ-role of the adjective (a process which should be seen in relation to parasitic gap constructions, and to the control of PRO noted in relation to example (30) with *eager* above).

If instead the operator bound clause were an adjunct to the adjective, the joint assignment of θ-roles to the matrix subject would be just what would be expected, but this would give a conjunction as the interpretation:

59 "the chicken is ready and the chicken is for someone to eat"

A pragmatic construal of this is not implausible, but the difficulty is the licensing of the adjunct for just the right set of adjectives. To rely on the conceptual argument structure seems too weak. Adjunction of such clauses does seem to be needed for ordinary predicational adjectives. So for instance

60   That chair is hard to sit on

is ambiguous. The *easy* reading (as it were; $hard_2$) has been accounted for; the other ($hard_1$) can be accounted for if we suppose that the *to sit on e* clause is an adjunct, so that the reading is constructed from something like 61 "Consider that chair for sitting on; it is hard." Note that this argument precludes any explanation of *easy* on adjunction lines, since we would then lose the account of the ambiguity of (60). A substitution of *ready* for *hard* in (60) and (61) is not difficult; the difference between the two adjectives would be a conceptual one—when something is ready, it must be ready for some use; hardness is less relative, and does not usually require explication in this manner. If this is the correct explanation, then the pattern for $ready_2$ is M_4:

M_4 $ready_2$ <p>

For this explanation to work, we must make our construal after QR, so that *No chair is hard to sit on* is construed as something like: "There is no chair x such that, considering x for sitting on, it is hard." Against this set of selection options is not just its lack of correspondence with the conceptual selection. There is, I think, a difference in interpretation for subject-present clauses.

62   i   That chair is $hard_1$/soft for children to sit on *e*

  ii That chair is ready for children to sit on *e*

It seems that the adjunct in (62i) can now only be a purpose clause (an adjunct under VP, I assume); whereas in (62ii) there is no change in status as compared to the subjectless version.

I have come down in favor of M_3, in the end. How can the child come to such a decision? We have seen that M_2 should not be an option. Probably the use of the adjective without the clausal complement helps to establish the external argument, ruling out M_1.[32] The rest of the answer has to be that the child expects a correspondence between conceptual and s-selection structures which is strong enough to rule out M_1 and M_4—though not so strong that it rules out M_3. In effect, this means that if he postulates the wrong s-selection (and c-selection to match), it can only be that he has postulated the wrong meaning; and

Syntax

that either there is a regular way of mapping the overlapping type of conceptual selections onto s-selections, or that the language of thought itself has had to compromise in the same way. Again, a proper formulation of the relevant inference rules or meaning postulates is needed before any more can be said. However, at least we have come to the same decision as for *stupid$_2$*, in as much as we require that the subject bear two θ-roles.

Finally, I come to *able*. It looks as if *able* is very similar to *stupid$_2$*. If we compare

63 John was stupid (*for him) to swim in the pond with

64 John was able (*for him) to swim in the pond

we see that the two have in common the inability to take *for*–NP infinitivals. Both allow the omission the complement, as in (15) of Table I in 4.1.1, giving an assertion of stupidity or ability in general. And there is an intuition of an external role. We cannot however have any *of*-NP version, like (42) and (43) above. This suggests that the pattern should be simply

N *able* <t,p> V″

However, the two behave differently when the complement clause is passive. Compare (65) and (66):

65 John was stupid to be caught (by the police)

66 John was able to be seen (by the police)

It is quite clear that in (65), the stupidity is John's, whereas in (66), the ability resides with the police. I shall argue in section 4.2.8 that the facts in (66) are just what one would expect if *able* has a 'passive' (which is morphologically identical to its 'active'). The obsolete *easy* behaves in the same way. It is the behavior of *stupid* in (65) which is surprising, then. We must regard the *of*-NP as still related to the 'active'. The alternation of external argument and *of*-NP, shown in pattern 'K' by the '(p)', perhaps should be seen as an alternation between external and internal argument, with the internal one acquiring *of* Case either structurally or inherently. If this is so, then we can accept the pattern 'N' above for *able*.

The results of the discussion above are summarized in table 2 below. In addition to omitting [that] and [WH] as predictable, I have omitted the infinitival [*to*] for I" and V", since this is also predictable.

Table 2

A	*(un)likely*	<t,t>	C"		V"
B	*apt*$_1$	<t,t>			V"
C	*apt*$_2$ *probable*	<t,t>	C"		
D	*necessary stupid*$_1$	<t,t>	C"	I"	
E	*eager*	<t,p>	C"	I"	
F	*certain*$_1$	<t/q,t>	C"		V"
G	*uncertain*$_1$	<t/q,t>	C"		
H	*certain*$_2$	<t/q,p>	C"		
I	*uncertain*$_2$	<q,p>	C"	I"	
J	*easy*	<t,t>		I"[O], I"	(V" obsolete)
K	*stupid*$_2$	<t,(p)>			V"
L	*ready*$_1$	<t,p>		I"	
M	*ready*$_2$	<t,p>		I"[O]	
N	*able*	<t,p>			V"

There is no completeness in the table: in particular, I have failed to discuss fully or to collect further examples where the adjective has a version with a secondary person that can be offered as an apparent internal argument. An example is *obvious (to us)*. The only other *to us* so far is *necessary*; but the recipient is of something else: with *seems* and *obvious*, it is the vision (as I said in footnote 6); with *necessary* it is the receiving of the event or the consequences of the event of the *that* clause which is indicated (as desirable). In footnote 20 and above in relation to *stupid*$_2$ I suggested that at least some of these may be like passive *by* phrases, PPs linked to an implicit external argument. In either case, I would suppose them to be generated to the right of the clausal complement, with extraposition of the clauses. The exclamatives are also missing. The entries for *ready*$_2$ and *able* fill gaps in the paradigm: we now find that each of the four c-selections given (C″, I″, I″[O], V″) occurs with both <t,t> and <t,p> heads.

One final point: why do adjectives not subcategorize for small clauses? By definition, a small clause requires an adjoined NP as external subject. This NP is an argument, and has Case (see further in the next section for expletives). The adjective can only assign prepositional case, with (normally) *of*. Suppose this is given like other subcategorization facts as a feature, to be realized on an appropriate Head or Specifier. Then the construction will allow the preposition to be realized on the SPEC, NP. Suppose the head of the SC is AP:

67 i ... [$_{AP}$ [$_{NP}$]$_{of}$ AP]

ii ... [$_{AP}$ [$_{PP}$ of NP] AP]

If such constructions are impossible, the reason must lie in the structure, rather than in the Case assignment conditions, since accusative Case can be assigned by an ECM verb in conditions comparable to (67i). It seems that it must be the head AP whose requirements are not met. We may suppose that for this AP, the PP category is visible (since the AP has so to speak no knowledge of why it arrived); and external arguments must indeed be canonic—NP or CP. Similar reasoning will explain the absence of 'ECM' adjectives, as hypothesized for the c-selection 'K$_2$' above.

4.2 Syntactic mechanisms for θ-roles

> I know very well that it is easy to save oneself and that, if the facts do not verify, it will be easily explained by saying that the exterior objects have moved.
>
> Poincaré, *The Value of Science*

4.2.1 Specifier positions and subjects

> if it does not succeed, we hie to exterior objects which we accuse of having moved; in other words, if it does not succeed, it is given a fillip.
>
> Poincaré, *The Value of Science*

Consider those syntactic heads which are ordinarily logical predicates: A, V, P and N. AP, VP and PP are ordinarily syntactic predicates. If we take the DP analysis, we can add N" to this list; I shall assume this. The canonic argument categories are then CP and DP, which essentially include V" and N" respectively. Only CP and DP include a designated slot for subjects (of V" and N" respectively). The parallelism goes further: C and D are the only categories capable of holding what are essentially two-constituent operators—items like *if* and *every*, which semantically relate a pair of propositions, and a pair of predicates, respectively.

Suppose we take it that the parallelism between V" and N" extends to the relative positions both of the operators just mentioned and the subject position. Traditionally, for the N projection, these are both placed in the SPEC position of NP. Under the DP hypothesis, we might expect quantifiers in the head of DP, and subjects in the SPEC of N", or possibly of D". More structure is needed to parallel the V" structure, with its subject external under I". So let us suppose that a further layer intervenes between N" and D", which I shall call E", and that the subject of N' must appear external to N" under E". Under this analysis, there is apparently never any item in the specifier slot of A", V", P" or N". One reaction is to eliminate this position. Another is to use it as a location for the external θ-role as such, but link this by indexing to some other position when the θ-role is 'assigned'. Thus for a DP (NP)

Syntax

or DP-chain to receive an external θ-role is for it to be linked by coindexing to a non-empty θ-role.

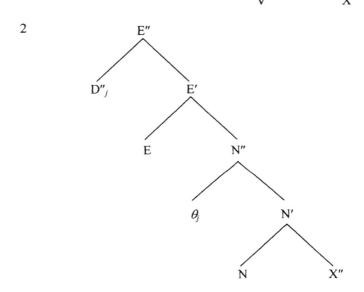

In all these structures, the item in SPEC of a major projection is an NP (DP), but I shall usually omit the category brackets for clarity. Where the DP has a quantifier, we may consider it to bind the open variable of the predicate supplied by the N″. Suppose then we place an appropriate symbol, θ, in the specifier of N″ to indicate the existence of such a logical variable. Then in (3), the Det binds (or discharges, in Higginbotham's terminology) the external θ-role arising from the predicate N′.

3

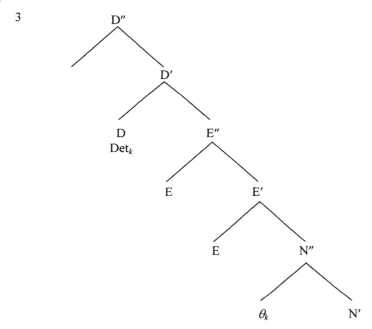

The format of (2) for NPs will allow for those languages where determiners and subjects can be simultaneously present in a prenominal position, with the determiner outermost. In English, this does not normally happen, but there is no conceptual or syntactic ban on having both quantifying determiners and subjects of N realized in some way or other simultaneously, as in

4 i [Every attempt by the enemy to cross the river] will fail

  ii [The enemy's every attempt] will fail

iii   [All [the enemy's attempts] will fail

There is a sense in which such abstract nouns have two external θ-roles. In (4), it is clear that in contradistinction to the usual case, the determiner (*every* or *all*) is not binding a free external role variable of N', since there is none (all the ordinary arguments of N are filled); roughly, it is binding times or events of the 'enemy crossing the river' kind. With respect to the verb and its projections, such properties are coded in INFL; we may suppose that E″ is the nominal parallel to I″.[33] Let us then suppose that it is only when E contains or otherwise disposes an event variable (which must be free for binding by the determiner) that such nominals may be inserted in the tree. We may also suppose that *fail* may be intrinsically predicated of events, so that a variable of the same type (or a predicate of the same type) is available to be the second predicate of our determiner. This may be achieved by a similar mechanism, I take it: event-taking verbs may only be inserted into the tree if INFL contains a free variable.[34] It is still necessary to account for the restrictions in English on the occurrence of pre-nominal subject and determiner, but I shall not discuss that here.

4.2.2.   External θ-roles as empty categories

> These fillips are legitimate; I do not refuse to admit them ...
> Poincaré, *The Value of Science*

We are now in a position to produce a geometric construal of the mechanisms of θ-role assignment, rather than the algebraic one I have been using. The advantage is that the relevant constraints can be stated in the same sort of terms as those applying to other sorts of movement or coindexing, and we may expect to see apparently complex phenomena reduced to interactions between the constraints of different modules. I have been working mostly with X' theory and type theory; the notions introduced above allow θ-theory and binding theory to apply to DPs in the new role-positions. Much of what I am doing in this chapter can be thought of as an attempt to account for the sorts of effects which Chomsky ascribes to "compositional s-selection" (1986a, 92).

To persist in the algebraic mode would be to move perhaps towards a full Combinatory Categorial Grammar (see for example Steedman

1988); but I do not exclude the possibility that the algebraic system I have discussed above is in fact needed in whole or in part alongside the geometric interpretation I shall offer below. It is very likely to be the case that in relatively simple constructions, there is apparent redundancy in the mechanisms offered, and it is only when more complex constructions are brought in that the independence of the principles can be seen. What I intend to do in this section is to indicate how I think the introduction of these new θ-role positions into the grammar can be exploited, and suggest various preliminary formulations of some of the relevant conditions concerning them.

First, the notion above allows of a simple characterization of a predicate (where this is to be understood as a predicate of type <e,t>). Any category having a θ-role in its specifier position is of the type of a predicate, and must function as such in a structure. Most adjectives, prepositions, nouns and verbs assign an external role, and hence their projections are typically predicates.

5   $[_{AP}\theta$ [fragile]]; $[_{PP}\theta$ [at home]]; $[_{N''}\theta$ [cat]]; $[_{VP}\theta$ [likes pitta]]

6   $[_{AP}$ − [possible that all is lost]]; $[_{VP}$ − [seems that she is right]]

So far, we have tried to ensure that an unambiguous lexical item had a single s-selection type. More than one c-selection may be offered. The canonic one will allow function–argument application; a non-canonic one will need generalized composition of functions.[35] These possibilities are simply instantiated with the θ-roles postulated:

7   $[_{AP}$ − [unlikely $[_{CP}$ that John will go]]]

8   $[_{AP}\ \theta_k$ [unlikely $[_{VP}\ t_k$ to go]]]

From (7), we read off that the whole needs no external argument, but in (8) we see that movement of the θ-role from the VP results in the whole having the status of a predicate. The introduction of an external θ-role which may be moved allows us to formulate movement rules which will effectively mimic the actual modes of combination of the types.

4.2.3 Predicates and Small Clause subjects

> If we had wished to verify other laws, we could have succeeded also, by giving other analogous fillips.
>
> Poincaré, *The Value of Science*

With the adjectives, there cannot be small clause constructions, so the proper c-selection for these has not been discussed. A verb like *consider* takes type <t> complements, and may take an AP small clause:

9   John considers [$_{AP}$ [Mary]$_i$ [$_{AP}$ θ_i [beautiful]]]

Suppose the c-selection is for just AP; the fact that the whole complement must have type <t> will force there to be an adjoined DP to serve as external argument to the predicate AP. This is on the unmarked (and correct) assumption that *consider* does not transmit θ-roles, which we must register somehow. However, if the AP has no external θ-role, and so is of type <t>, we cannot have

10   *John considers [$_{AP}$ – [ridiculous that the sky is blue]]

despite the satisfaction of s-selection and c-selection requirements. Rather we must have

11   John considers [$_{AP}$ [it] [$_{AP}$ – [ridiculous that the sky is blue]]]

There are several possible moves to account for the ungrammaticality of (10). First, we might invoke a 'nil' θ-role, requiring to be discharged onto an expletive. Secondly, we might attempt to utilize D-structure predicate-argument requirements. Thirdly, we might suppose that available Case had to be discharged. Fourthly, we might stipulate a subject DP by means of a feature on the c-selected AP. Fifthly, we might follow Chomsky's suggestion (Chomsky 1986a, 133 ff.) that argument clauses must have something like Case, which they may obtain by coindexing to expletive *it*. Any of these can be made to produce a subject for the AP in (10), with a little effort.[36] But we must also account for cases where the head of the SC is canonically an argument rather than a predicate:

12   *I consider [$_{DP}$ [[t]$_k$ [a pity]] [that John is away]$_k$]

13   *I deplore [$_{CP}$ that John is away]

(I take it that [*a pity*] is the predicate head of a SC, with argument the CP.[37] Extraposition of the clause is, let us assume, a PF phenomenon). Both these require expletive *it* SC subjects.[38] In neither case can we appeal to a 'nil' θ-role. Nor can we appeal to D-structure canonic predicate requirements. With (13), we could set a feature [*it*] on the c-selection for CP, which would have to be realized in an adjoined position. But for (12), just this is not appropriate, since we need other DP subjects for other SC complements. The 'assign Case if it is available' option requires that Case-assignment is permitted to be constructive, a fairly radical move (that is, one might expect rather that if Case-assigning is obligatory, and no DP is available to receive it, then the construction is ungrammatical). It seems more natural to have a limited range of constructive principles. Besides, the idea will fail for (12), since we have a potential DP Case-bearer already. Chomsky's suggestion will fail for (13), since presumably the Case that can be assigned to a Small clause subject *it* could just as well be assigned directly to the CP (but I will consider the idea in its own right below).[39]

This suggests that we should force the DP of the SC directly; and then after this account for the *it* (see section 4.2.5). We may assume that a SC construction head may c-select with a feature [+DP], to be realized as usual on the Spec of the c-selected category. This will effectively prevent transmission. When we have c-selection for DP, as in (12), we still obtain a SC structure, given the feature realization principles. This has the further advantage of forcing the head DP into predicate position, so that its θ-type <e,t> can be derived from that fact. The conclusion in relation to θ-types is that these cannot be the sole constructive device here. We may ask if we need to use them constructively at all.

Within the geometric framework, we do not actually require that all 'potential' SC constructions DO have subjects. That is, if *be* is subcategorized for AP, and permits transmission, which is the reflex of a 'Raising' verb that we required for our definitions, the AP need not be expanded to SC construction:

14   i   John [$_{VP}$ – [is [$_{AP}\theta$ [tall]]]

    ii   John$_i$ [$_{VP}$ θ_i [is [$_{AP}$ t_i [tall]]]

Syntax

The fact that [*It is* [*John tall*]] is ungrammatical follows from the failure of predicational *be* to assign Case. If the c-selection is simply for AP, we will not exclude SC constructions except on some grounds, perhaps, of economy of derivation (Chomsky 1991) (see further in sections 4.2.4 and 4.2.5 for c-selection specification). However, if we look at the full range of 'predicational *be*' complements, we find that the Raising option IS necessary in addition to transmission, and that the θ-types must be capable of being used constructively. The evidence comes from presentational *there* clauses.

4.2.4 Expletive 'there'

> One could at most have said to us: 'Your fillips are doubtless legitimate, but you abuse them; why move the exterior objects so often?'
>
> Poincaré, *The Value of Science*

It is well-known that there is in Modern English a limited range of verbs that admit *there* subjects. One way to capture this fact is to have the *there* stipulated as an option somehow in the subcategorization for the head verb. This is not hard, given the feature system suggested. Suppose we have a subcategorization option for 'predicational' *be* of AP[$_{DP}$there], with the requirement of a θ-type <t>. This will give us a D-structure.[40] of at least

15   – is [$_{AP}$ [there] AP]

But unless the lower AP is already propositional in θ-type (as for instance *certain to be a storm*), the type-condition cannot be met without another role-bearing DP being introduced, again adjoined to the head AP. This might give us a D-structure like

16 i   – is [$_{AP}$ [there] [$_{AP}$ [someone] [$_{AP}$ willing to stay]]]

ii

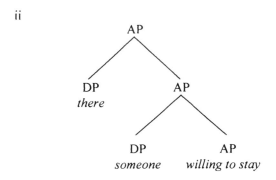

17   [There]$_k$ [is [$_{AP}$ [t]$_k$ [$_{AP}$ [someone] [$_{AP}$ willing to stay]]]

In order to get Case, the DP [*there*] moves to subject position, as in (17). Hence this DP must be an argument by virtue of its structural position in (16), for the purposes of Case theory. How does the other DP, [*someone*] get Case? I assume that something like the standard story is correct (Chomsky 1986a, 131 ff.). The predication relations set up by the adjunction structures will give rise to predication coindexing. So we will have [*there*] and its sister AP coindexed in (16ii), and [*someone*] and the head AP. Further, we expect coindexing of a category and its Head, and hence of all the AP nodes (or of all the AP nodes because of the adjunction structure—in some sense they are the same node). The upshot will be that [*there*] and [*someone*] receive the same index. Of course, this would be disastrous if it were not that *there* is expletive. The generalized AP (the set of projections) is to be predicated of only one proper argument. Principle C of the Binding Theory will ensure this. But *there* is a DP outside the <e>, <t> scheme of things (and indifferent to Principle C), and hence with respect to the θ-theory I have been constructing, expletive.[41] It is in fact a locative, and it is possible that the theory could be extended to cover these, perhaps with the introduction of a new type. But expletives may receive Case, and so the chain <*there, someone*> in (17) satisfies the visibility condition relating to the assignment of the θ-role from the head AP. We obtain expletive-argument coindexing 'free', under this story. We also see that our idea that the notion of 'argument' was relative to modules or principles is needed again. Here (for *there*), we have Case theory needing the D-structure idea of an argument—one that is indifferent to anything but the category and the structure, rather than the θ-module version (at least if all movement is forced item by item). Given that the Case to be assigned is structural, this is perhaps natural.

If this story is right, then we must have provision for SC and movement, as well as direct predication, for this *be*.[42] We need at least the first and the third of the subcategorization possibilities

18   *be*   (i) —AP;   (ii) —AP[+DP] ;   (iii) —AP[$_{DP}$ *there*]

The first and second ones will produce alternative parses with identical meaning for some strings, and so there cannot be direct evidence for the second in the presence of the first. We may assume that for such a string, the first would be postulated; so the middle one is not correct.[43]

We still need the type-theory to be constructive, in the sense that it is the choice of the AP [willing to stay], of type <e,t>, which forces the construction of the other DP, [someone], rather than categorial selection. Type-theory (θ-theory) is in this way a part of the grammar, in the same way as it is for Rothstein, and indeed for Combinatory grammar. This view contrasts with the use of types in the interpretive semantics of say GPSG. It differs also apparently from that of Higginbotham, who is concerned with very much the same problems as I am here (Higginbotham 1985, 1989). Higginbotham is concerned to point out that semantic interpretation of a string should not depend on the prior grammaticality of that string; and hence sees the combinatory rules for types as being independent of the grammar. But if the grammar is modular, then a string may satisfy θ-theory and yet fail to satisfy some other module. In addition, I am treating the relation to 'real' semantics as less direct than Higginbotham does, since I am taking it that it is the expressions in the language of thought for which a model may be sought.

4.2.5   Expletive 'it'

because thus the number of fillips is reduced to a minimum.
Poincaré, *The Value of Science*

Chomsky (1986a, 133) suggests that expletive *it* has much the same function as expletive *there*, but with respect to clauses rather than NPs. I have been ignoring any possible Case requirements for clauses, until now. But we might expect to produce a story for expletive *it* parallel to my one for *there*. Suppose that the S-structure of the DP small clause in (19) is (following (12) too) as in (20):

19   I consider it a pity that John is away

20   I consider [$_{DP}$ it [[that John is away] [$_{DP}$ O_k [$_{D'}$ a [pity t_k]]]]]

We might obtain this by giving *consider* a subcategorization '—DP[$O_{<t>}$][*it*]', where the subscript <t> gives the type of the operator (*i.e.* it binds and discharges its role to an item of type <t>).[44] As with *there* above, this will induce coindexing on the CP SPEC and the *it*, so the CP appears in a Case-marked chain. Hence, if argument clauses must be Case-marked, the [*it*] feature may be optional—it will be invoked just when it is needed. Subcategorization for all the SC complements need only mention the Head and this optional feature. It is then the verb *deplore* in (13) that is exceptional: it must be that with c-selection of CP, it selects for the feature [+DP] or [+*it*] as a lexical property.[45]

The *it* clauses that I have been treating as containing Adjectives followed directly by CP complements can equally be considered to be small clause structures parallel to (20). For instance, instead of (21), we may instead postulate an S-structure as in (22):

21   It is [$_{AP}$ absurd [that the sky is blue]]

22   It is [$_{AP}$ [that the sky is blue] [O_k [absurd t_k]]

Rhetorically, this is plausible, in that there is now a subject–predicate assertion, with the proposition about the sky as the subject.[46] And now it is simple to put the *it* into the complement at D-structure, so we have rather (23), entirely parallel to (20):

23   – is [$_{AP}$ *it* [$_{AP}$ [that the sky is blue] [O_k [absurd t_k]]

The AP '[$_{AP}$ O_k [absurd t_k]]' has the operator in its SPEC position. The relevant subcategorization for *be* will need to be (iv):

24   *be*   (iv)   — AP[$O_{<t>}$][*it*]

Given that *be* is expecting a complement of type <t>, there is only one (correct) way of fulfilling the feature requirements. This will replace the simple subcategorization (i) given in (18) above in just those structures where we have no external θ-role given by the adjective, and hence by Burzio's generalization, no Case assigned to the complement clause.

If instead of (21) we have

25   It is absurd for [a solid to be transparent]

then a structure parallel to (23) must still be needed. The *for* is assigned as a c-selection feature by the head adjective, and Case-marks the internal subject DP. But the clause must need to get its Case from *it*. Since it is arguments which need Case, and the IP is the argument, we must assume that the *for* does not Case-mark IP, or that the CP is derivatively an argument requiring Case. The structure will include:

25 i   – [$_{AP}$ [for [$_{IP}$ a solid to be transparent] [$_{AP}$ O_k[absurd t_k]]]]

Note that the IP must have all the features assigned to the complement, (I″[+*for*]) presumably through predication from the operator, which originated as an internal argument of the head. External roles do not carry such information. Here, we must have [$_{I″[+for]}$ O_k].

If we stipulate that *there* and *it* are both expletives (with respect to the <e>,<t> type-system), and both DPs, differing just in that at LF, *there* may be coindexed only to an NP, and *it* only to a CP.[47], we can eliminate reference to the particular expletive. Thus the expletive Adjectival c-selection for 'predicational' *be* is simply

26   *be*   (v) — AP[exp.]

It seems possible that all other expletive constructions can be treated similarly. If so, we obtain most of the effects of Chomsky's story, and in particular the symmetry between the two expletives. It is then explanatory (as well as tidy) to extend the visibility condition to all arguments. If we do, then we seem to need to assume that Burzio's generalization holds of adjectives with respect to CP (which does not show overt Case-marking), so that it is immediately known from the s-selection frame whether an internal CP argument is Case-marked.[48] Then the feature [exp.] is required in (v) of (26) either because that will be the only grammatical structure, or else whenever it is wished (presumably for pragmatic reasons) to retain the canonic structure of the complement of *be* (when Raising or transmission would be possible). If the AP head does have an external role to assign, but heads a non-raising structure, it can only be because there is a small clause, which will necessarily have an external argument needing Case. If the AP does not have an external role to assign, and does not assign Case, we can have movement of an empty operator to the vacant Specifier position. Its trace functions like an NP trace, so needs no Case (it is the argument to which the θ-role is given that does need Case).[49] It is also possible to have Adjective heads with no external argument, but with the capacity to assign *for*-Case to IP. We need merely to stipulate for *be*, then, that the feature [exp.] is an option.

4.2.6 Chains and θ-roles

> On the other hand, the series θ appears to us to leave nothing to be desired ...
>
> Poincaré, *Science and Method*

These θ-roles enter into various relations: in particular, predication, adjunction and compositional transmission. Since I am assuming the same coindexing as usual, it is necessary to redefine positions and chains to accommodate the newcomers. We now have two kinds of positions to which θ-roles are directly assigned: internal, and external. Let these be 'role-positions', and let us call the positions of SPEC of AP, N″, VP and PP 'x-role-positions'. They are not A-positions (but are A-bar-positions). The internal A-positions are as usual sister positions of X under X′, for the major categories. External A-positions include SPEC of I″ and E″ and subjects of small clauses.[50] Suppose we generalize the notion of specifier position, so that it includes any category on the left branch under XP, where the right branch dominates X. Then in all these cases, the subject A position is some SPEC position next above a role position (which itself is a SPEC position).

27

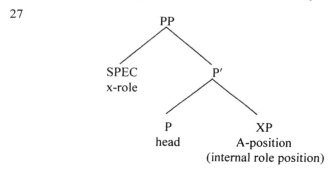

28 i

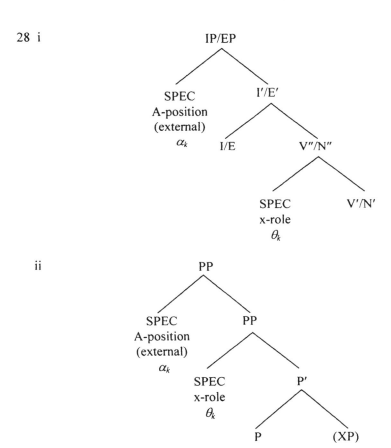

The other SPEC positions, SPEC of CP and perhaps of DP, will be A-bar operator positions. These definitions are neither elegant nor exhaustive, but will suffice (for English, and for my present purposes).

Let us call a chain linking an x-role-position to an A-position a predication chain. Such chains are shown in (27) above, where α is a role-bearer (*i.e.* CP or DP) and θ is some role assigned by the predicating head. The relation should probably be mediated by the maximal projection above the x-role-position, so that V″/N″ (in (28i)) and the lower PP (in (28ii)) are also indexed with k. This is the predication visible at D-structure, being just a relation between maximal projections; I appealed to this in my account of the indexing on expletive *there*. We can consider it to be realized by SPEC to SPEC coindexing at least by the time we reach LF (and this too was used above). So the external A-positions in (27) and (28) are θ-positions if there is a θ-role present in the SPEC of the predicating head, and are not θ-positions if there is no such role present (note that θ-positions are related to actual roles; whereas role positions and A-positions describe potential). In as much as the coindexing in the diagrams represents the assignment of the role by predication, it is only licit if the category α (as a chain, if appropriate) is visible.

We may define a chain as usual, as a sequence of categories chained by c-command and coindexing. We may classify chains according to the positions of their heads (leftmost category) into A-bar-chains, A-chains and what I shall call role-chains, where these have heads which are in A-bar operator positions, A-positions and x-role-positions respectively. A chain linking an x-role position containing a role to an external A-position (working right to left) is a predication chain. It will be argued that predication is obligatory if a potential θ-position is in the SPEC immediately above a filled x-role position.[51] This gives primary predication; secondary predication arguably may take place at a distance, as in

29   John$_{i,j}$ [[θ_i [left the room] [θ_j [angry]]

The θ-criterion (Chomsky 1986a) is ordinarily applied to A-chains: we need to consider whether the criterion applies as before.

30   i   Every argument must appear in a chain containing a unique visible θ-position

    ii   Every θ-position is visible in a chain containing a unique argument

In the discussion of adjectives above, θ-transmission was invoked in four kinds of structures; all involve chains of a new kind, or new links in old chains. I will discuss each in turn, and then compare them with VP constructions. For concreteness, let us suppose that in each case the AP is predicated of an adjacent NP, as in a small clause construction (with the NP receiving Case from outside), though the predicate must also be coherent if it stands alone. The four relevant examples adjectival phrases are as in 31:

31 i apt to feel gloomy
    ii ready to show off
    iii easy to see
    iv ready to eat *e*

32 i [[$_{NP}$ Ted] [– [apt [$_{VP}$ θ [to feel gloomy]]]]]
    ii [[$_{NP}$ Ted]$_i$ [θ_i [apt [$_{VP}$ t$_i$ [to feel gloomy]]]]]

Here, the θ-role is transmitted from its D-structure position in (i) to the position in (ii) from which it can be predicated of the NP. How should we say the θ-criterion is met for the argument *Ted*? The NP is in an A-position, receives Case by assumption, and receives its θ-role by predication. So <*Ted*> is a licensed A-chain. We may assume that <θ> and <θ_i, t_i> are licensed role-chains, with the latter arising from SPEC to SPEC movement.

33 i [[$_{NP}$ Ted] [θ_1 [ready [$_{VP}$ θ_2 [to show off]]]]]
    ii [[$_{NP}$ Ted]$_{1,2}$ [$\theta_{1,2}$ [ready [$_{VP}$ t$_2$ [to show off]]]]]

In (33), the pattern is much the same, except that we have a θ-position in the SPEC of the AP at D-structure. We need to assume that θ-roles can be 'added', giving us '$\theta_{1,2}$'. Strictly speaking, there is probably adjunction of one DP to another inside the SPEC of *ready*. We still have SPEC to SPEC movement for the role-chain.

However, we may then ask why the structure in (34) is ill-formed

34 [[$_{NP}$ Ted]$_i$ [θ_1 [ready [$_{VP}$ – [to seem that Mary is silly]]]]]

We cannot invoke any kind of uniformity condition, because in (32), the role present in the SPEC of the AP at LF arose from one nil θ-role and one real one. A lexical requirement on *ready*, to the effect that it must find [+θ] in V″ seems possible, and will be explored in the discussion of (36) below.

35 i [[$_{NP}$ Ted] [– [easy [$_{CP}$ [PRO to see *O*]]]]]
    ii [[$_{NP}$ Ted] [– [easy [$_{CP}$ *O$_i$* [PRO to see *t$_i$*]]]]]

iii   [[$_{NP}$ Ted]$_i$ [O_i [easy [$_{CP}$ e_i [PRO to see t_i]]]]]

We may suppose that the empty operator is freely generated in a non-subject NP position at D-structure.[52] The adjective *easy* c-selects an IP complement (we will come back to the operator). It is the level of (35iii) at which the θ-criterion must be checked, since only here can *Ted* receive any θ-marking. In (35iii), <t> is in a Case-marked A-position, and so must (as standardly) be a variable, an r-expression. Condition C of the Binding Theory requires that *t* is A-free (in the domain of the head of its maximal chain if it has one), (Chomsky 1986, 98). O_i is the head of the maximal chain if this is defined in terms of maximal movement, so coindexing with [Ted] is permitted. In (35ii), <O_i, t_i> is an operator chain, consisting as is proper of an operator and the head of an A-chain. In (35iii), we have a role-chain, consisting of the consecutive SPECs <O_i, e_i>, and an operator chain <e_i, t_i>.

We need to exclude examples exactly like (35) but with an adjective which does not allow the empty operator—adjectives such as *necessary*:

36 i   [[$_{NP}$ Ted] [– [necessary [PRO to see O]]]]

    ii [[$_{NP}$ Ted] [– [necessary [O_i [PRO to see t_i]]]]]

    iii [[$_{NP}$ Ted]$_i$ [O_i [necessary [e_i [PRO to see t_i]]]]]

It is clear that we need to appeal to subcategorization (or some similarly local constraint). The natural expectation is that we use a feature [+O] on the c-selection category, as indeed I assumed without argument earlier. If so, this cannot be checked either at the D-structure (i) or apparently at the LF (iii), but may be checked in (35ii). Since we must exclude *necessary*, it is not sufficient to ask for the presence of O for *easy* at SOME level—and in any case, *easy* does not require raising. It looks as if we must either ensure that there is a specific level at which such an operator is forced to be present in the complement SPEC; or we must have *necessary* perpetually on the lookout for unwanted operators. However, the empty operator may at least pass across an AP boundary in a WH-movement structure such as

37   a man [O_i you thought it necessary (for Mary) to please t_i]

and subjacency will require that it has a landing site associated with the embedded *please* clause. If it moved initially straight to SPEC of *necessary*, then there would be obligatory role-assignment to *it*, which is incorrect. There must then be a landing site in operator position (SPEC of C″) immediately between *necessary* and the I″:

37 i a man [O_i you thought it necessary [t [$_{I''}$ PRO to please t_i]]]

In either case, *necessary* will at some stage be able to see this O in an apparent c-selection-feature position. Possibly since the gross subcategorization for *necessary* is I″, the item in SPEC of CP is not visible. Otherwise, it follows that we must identify some particular level at which the conditions are met, or that passing elements destined for SPEC[+WH] positions are to be excluded somehow. It is not in fact possible to find a level at which all SPEC-feature conditions are met simultaneously. This is because it is (perhaps surprisingly) possible for a single element to satisfy the requirements of two heads. Consider

38 John is apt to be hard to find

The derivation from (38i) includes (38ii) and (iii):

38 i John is apt to be hard PRO to find O
    ii John is apt to be hard [O [$_{I''}$ PRO to find t]]
    iii John is apt [$_{V''}$ O [to be hard [t [PRO to find t]]]]
    iv John is [$_{A''}$ O apt [t to be hard [t [PRO to find t]]]]

We see here that the operator has moved into a x-role-position (in (38iii, 38iv), and loses its operator status (counting just as any other θ-role). And it is clearly impossible for one single level to satisfy the requirements of both *apt* (looking for a [+θ] in its V″) and *hard* (looking for [+O] in C″), at least directly. We need to look at traces; and we need to see what they are traces OF. Further, unless the empty operator of relative clauses is actually distinct from our operator here, we need distinguish one from the other by whether or not they enter into predication at the end of the chain: the subcategorized operator does (unless the XP stands as an isolated predicate); the operator in restrictive relative clauses is discharged by adjunction and determiner-binding. It is not adjunction structures as such that we must look for, because a conjunction of VP predicates will function just like a single one. So suppose we look at whether or not the role- or operator-chain is predicated of an argument. Fortunately, and presumably not fortuitously, there are no empty operators nor x-role-initial categories in non-restrictive relative clauses.[53] Role-chains must always enter predication, then; operator chains may not.

It seems then that the SPEC-content part of subcategorization must be checked on chains where movement has gone as far as possible (which may still be S-structure, perhaps). So in (35iii) for instance, *easy* has in its complement-SPEC part of a maximal chain terminating in an empty operator, which is in a role position: this licenses *easy*. In (37i), there is also an operator headed maximal chain in relation to *necessary*: this time it is licit, because it terminates in an position which is bound in an adjunction structure. In (34), the SPEC-of-complement expectations of *ready* are not met. For (38iv), the checking is carried out with respect to each of the heads *hard* and *apt*: *apt* requires that the chain terminate in some role-bearer, and the operator is such; *hard* actually requires that the role-bearer be the empty operator. But in checking the requirements of *hard* in (38iv), we do not need to know that the maximal chain terminates in an operator: this is ensured by the imposition of the CP in the subcategorization—any θ-role in the SPEC of the complement has to be an operator.[54]

The final kind of example, using the other *ready*, is unproblematic:

39 i   [[$_{NP}$ the food]   [θ [ready [$_{CP}$ [$_{IP}$ PRO to eat O]]]]]

   ii   [[$_{NP}$ the food]$_{i-j}$ [$_{A''}\theta_j + O_i$ [ready [e$_i$ [$_{IP}$ PRO to eat t$_i$]]]]]

This example will have just the same properties as the last, (35), except that there is a θ-role present in the SPEC of the AP at D-structure, so that it is similar to (33) in this respect. We see that it is necessary to keep the several roles and their indexings distinct in the AP SPEC, so that it can be checked that the chain with index *i*, relevant to *ready*, terminates in a suitable role.

The ungrammaticality of sentences like (40) is predicted correctly:

40   * John would be easy to be hard to find

   i   * John would be easy [$_{VP}$ O_i [to be hard [e [$_{IP}$ to find t]]]]

   ii   * John would be easy
         [O_i PRO [$_{VP}$ t$_i$ [to be hard [e [$_{IP}$ to find t]]]]]

In (40i), the subcategorization for *easy* is incorrect; in (40ii), the operator would have discharged its role onto PRO at t_i.

Syntax

The proposals above suggest that the categorial selection given in Table II needs additional interpretation. We need to assume that in this table, whenever there is c-selection for V″, this is to mean that we have a V″ of the canonic type <e,t>, so we obtain [$_{V''}$ θ [...]]. Every I″ is of type <t>, though if we have an operator specified ([+WH] or [+O]), the CP induced will itself have type <e,t>.

We have seen that the operator behaves just like a role generated in x-role-position, with respect to satisfying selection features and type checking. For types, the origin of the empty category is irrelevant. For features, we simply check the discharging at the head of the chain and the complement category. Consequently, it is not actually necessary to distinguish the empty operator from any other θ-role. If the empty operator at D-structure is simply a θ-role in an internal argument position, then the generalization is that "empty" θ-roles can be allocated to both internal and external role-positions, provided they can be discharged.[55] On moving to an operator position, a variable remains behind and the moved element acquires operator status (in the same way as QNPs subject to QR must do). Alternatively, it can move to a role-position. We may classify the 'empty role' intrinsically as an operator: it clearly is not capable of being a logical argument. We will expect that it can only move to A-bar positions: both operator positions and role positions are A-bar, but subject positions of course are not.[56] The surmise that the empty operator does not appear in subject position is supported—there is no way it could get there.[57]

4.2.7 Passives and anaphors

> that it is necessary to advance step by step, neglecting no intermediary; that our fathers were wrong in wishing to skip stations ...
>
> Poincaré, *The Value of Science*

Categories may c-select for complements other than those belonging to the N or V extended projections. There can be small clauses, and in principle transmission from other predicate categories, if the s-selection type is <t>. Small clauses are fairly common as complements to verbs, and arguably exist as Prepositional complements as in

41 [with [John drunk]]

We have demonstrated that such categories need to c-select for the head category of the SC, rather than for 'SC'. Transmission would be exhibited in a non-Raising derivation from

42   Ted is [$_{AP}$ θ [happy]]

This would have *be* c-select for an AP, and this has type <e*,t>, where the verb *be* is expecting type <t>. Such structures appear to be rare, though not unique to *be*—there is *seems*. But we do not need to accept the analysis of (42). The integrity of the AP is not violated by any assumption of Raising, here, so we may just as well have

43   Ted$_k$ is [$_{AP}$ t_k [$_{AP}$ θ [happy]]]

where the complement type is <t>, and the subcategorization would be AP[DP]. However, I argued above that this should be rejected. And we may find plenty of other verbs with the same simple structure as (42) if we consider passives. For example, we might derive (44) by transmission from (45):

44   Ted is considered kind

45   Ted is considered [θ [kind]]

I now want to consider passives. I argued that we needed these, like AP phrases, to be capable of standing as syntactically and semantically self-contained units, so that just NP movement is not a possible explanation for their occurrence. Problem cases for 'movement only', apart from stand-alone definitions, are secondary predication and conjunction of an active and a passive VP:

46   John went on his way [encouraged by their kindness]

47   John [[jumped] or [was pushed]]

What we need in at least some cases of passives is analogous to the AP case for adjectives such as *easy*: the role normally associated with an internal argument becomes available to be assigned to an external argument. This suggests that we should have the empty operator (where this is used now just for convenience to indicate a role originating in an internal position):

48 i   [$_{V''}$ *(θ)* [$_{V'}$ seen O]]

ii   [$_{V''}$ O_i+*(θ)* [$_{V'}$ seen t_i]]

Such a suggestion opens the way for the treatment of passive *be* as identical to the ordinary 'predicational' *be*.[58] The normal external θ-role of the verb becomes an implicit role, so I have bracketed a 'θ' in (48) (i) and (ii). The accusative-Case-assigning property of the verb is also lost, for familiar reasons.

It is clear that for active verbs, a configuration like that in (49) is to be ungrammatical:

49   [$_{V''}$ O_i+θ [$_{V'}$ see t_i]]

However, this should follow from Binding Theory. The empty category. t_i has Case, and is in a θ-position; hence <t_i> is an A-chain, t is a variable and an R-expression. If it moves to the SPEC, it will become predicated of and hence coindexed to some A-position NP, and hence there will be a violation of Principle C. Can we rule out the coindexing in (49) directly? If SPEC of V" is not an operator position, this will follow from Principle C as it stands, since <t_i> must not be bound (in the domain of the head of its chain if it has one). If the verb is passive, and t_i has no Case, it is not an argument, so principle C does not apply. In the passive, as in (48ii), <t_i> is to be an anaphor. In order to obtain obligatory coindexing to the SPEC positions, suppose we require *tout court* that an anaphor is to be bound in its governing category, where this is to be understood simply as the maximal projection of its governor.

We will thus expect that reflexives too will be bound to the θ-role in the x-role position, rather than directly to the external argument. This will among other things allow for a free-standing definition of the form, say *'to betake oneself'* (I do not have any from the dictionaries I used; this is from Liddell and Scott 1963, which uses such reflexives regularly).

The stipulation predicts correctly that reflexives cannot find their antecedents outside small clauses:

50 i   * [Mary$_k$ doesn't consider [$_{AP}$ John [$_{AP}$ fond of herself$_k$]]

ii   Mary doesn't consider [$_{AP}$ John [$_{AP}$ θ_{O+j} [fond [of herself$_j$]]]

Here 'θ_O' is the external role assigned by *fond*, and the dependency of *herself* on this role is shown with the '*j*'. The preposition *of* is a Case-marker, and presumably is not visible as a governor of *herself*. The structure (50ii) is ruled out when gender features are checked (on the predication).

We can still account for ditransitives:

51   Mary [$_{VP}$ θ [showed [John] [himself] (in the picture)]

Both [John] and [θ] are available in the governing category. For picture noun phrases, we need to show why there can be escape from the initial governing category just when there is no explicit subject of *picture*. Let us assume that if there is no explicit subject, the external role must be implicit, so that "coindexing" to the SPEC does not imply dependency on that role. The anaphor-index must find a host in the governing category of its new position:

52   Mary [θ [showed [everyone]] [$_{DP}$[$_{NP}$(α)\{k\} [pictures [of himself$_k$]]]]

Here, either [everyone] or [Mary] is available in principle as antecedent. I take it that either \{k\} moves to the next SPEC, in IP, (leaving a trace), and is associated with [Mary], or it remains where it is and is associated with [everyone] (apparently under the illusion that that DP is the subject of a DP small clause).[59] The association is not of course predication, so I have used curly brackets to identify the anaphoric index. Possibly it is in fact the NP [himself] that is to move at LF, so that what we have is a more normal movement chain.[60] This would be plausible, given that it is essential to ensure that the anaphor and its antecedent are together at LF, since under interpretation, the variables associated with each after QR will be treated as identical. We might expect that we should be able to interpret the LF as something like:

52 i   Everyone$_x$–himself$_x$ [Mary showed [[x] [pictures of x]]]

By the treatment above, we have excluded the possibility that a verb like *shave* could involve role-movement as in say

53   John$_{i+j}$ [$O_i+\theta_j$ [shaves t_i]]

There may however be verbs which are like *stupid*₂ in having an external and a transmitted role available for predication: *try* is a natural candidate, as in (54).[61]

54   John [$_{VP}$ $O_1+\theta_2$ [tried [$_{VP}$ t_2 to swim]]]

The other operator structure we might expect will be like (55), parallel to *ready*₂, with both an external and an operator-transferred internal role available for predication:

55   [$_{V''}$ $O_i+\theta$ [$_{V'}$ V [$_{CP}$ e_i [$_{C'}$ for [$_{IP}$ Sue to like t_i]]]]

As far as I can tell, this never happens. We do not even get the version without any external θ-role assigned by V. The reason seems to be to do with the Case assigning properties of verbs, in contrast to adjectives. It is probable that verbs assign accusative Structural Case to CP complements (and if these surface as 'higher type' DPs it is visibly so). We may suppose that as well, the verb may assign Intrinsic *for*-Case to the IP, and hence to its SPEC. But in the structure above, although there will be a CP to contain the putative subcategorized operator, the CP is not c-selected, and not visible for Case assignment; so the item <e_i> if it appeared would be assigned accusative Case. But operators cannot receive Case; and the structure would be rejected for other reasons. An IP alone without the operator would not run into trouble—there are verbs like *to long*. If the verb has no external role, then it will not assign Structural accusative. We must assume that (unlike adjectives) it will be incapable of assigning *for* Case via a feature, as well. Hence no verb c-selects I"[O], and no verb of type <t,t> selects I".

If there are no verbs subcategorized for I"[O], then (as usual) we need make no stipulation as to the difference between active and passive other than that in the passive, the external role becomes implicit, and (for English) that there must be Case marking lost. This latter in itself will ensure that the θ-role of object if licensed must form part of a chain Case-marked elsewhere, and hence that it move to the SPEC position; further movement will depend on how the role is to be discharged. A verb that has a passive form then must allow transmission; since this is not available in the active of passivizable verbs, we may assume that as suggested for (10) and (11) above, Case assignment must be projected (at least for the relevant subcategorization). Passivizable verbs are, then, like Raising verbs in permitting transmission; the difference is just that passivizable verbs also assign Case in the active.

The characterization of expletive *it* given above ensures that even in

56   It is thought [that the match will be lost]

we must have an operator-headed passive. The D-structure will be

56 i   – is [$_{VP}$ it [$_{VP}$[that the match will be lost][$_{VP}$(θ)[thought O]]]]

Verbs which may take *for* clauses may have passive forms; if as I suggested, the *for* is a Case-marker, we may expect it to be unavailable with passives. This is possible:

57 i   I hoped [for John to be sent instead]

   ii   * It was hoped [for John to be sent instead]

The passive is fine with a *that* clause instead of the *for* clause in (57ii). The *it* can successfully Case mark the clause, but *hope* cannot Case-mark the subject of the IP. But the verb *arrange* does not lose its capacity to transmit the feature [*for*], so that we can have

58   It was arranged for John to be sent instead

The [*for*] is available with the adjective *absurd* (example (25) above), too. The variability is compatible with Belletti and Rizzi's version of Burzio's Generalization (see footnote 48).

We also obtain passives with ECM verbs:

59   John was told [to leave]

(I assume that this *tell* is distinct from that in *tell John that...*). It is clear that a consistent story must have *tell* c-selecting a VP in the passive; and hence in the active too. The upshot will be that in the active, since the verb (obligatorily) assigns accusative Case, the complement must be a small clause headed by VP, as in (60).

60   Jake told [$_{VP}$ [John] [$_{VP}$ θ [to leave]]]

The typical SC intonation pattern has a pause between head and subject; such a pattern is common with sentences like (60). Perhaps all ECM clauses are in fact VP small clauses? It does not seem to me that this is a necessary consequence, since we have assumed that a head may assign Case both to a clausal complement and to its specifier. This would be no help with (57), since the Case comes only from predication coindexing.

4.2.8 Theta theory and chains

> Since some time, however, one of these explanations seems to be getting the upper hand ...
> Poincaré, *The Value of Science*

In the structure of (49), repeated here as (61),

61 $[_{V''} O_i + (\theta) [_{V'} \text{seen } t_i]]$

we will have the SPEC as a θ-position and role-position (NOT an operator position), and the trace will be an anaphor (NP-trace), a non-argument, as it is standardly. As usual, the whole may be predicated of a Case-marked NP. This structure is unlike the four for adjectives in that it contains an internal A-position which is not Case-marked. The other four LFs are repeated below, and a passive added:

62 $[[_{NP} \text{Ted}]_i [_{AP} \theta_i [\text{apt } [_{VP} t_i [\text{to feel gloomy}]]]]]$

63 $[[_{NP} \text{Ted}]_{1 \cdot 2} [_{AP} \theta_{1 \cdot 2} [\text{ready } [_{VP} t_2 [\text{to show off}]]]]]$

64 $[[_{NP} \text{Ted}]_i [_{AP} O_i [\text{easy } [_{CP} e_i [\text{PRO to see } t_i]]]]]$

65 $[[_{NP} \text{the food}]_{i+j} [_{AP} \theta_j + O_i [\text{ready } [e_i [_{IP} \text{PRO to eat } t_i]]]]]$

66 $[[_{NP} \text{the food}]_i [_{VP} O_i + (\theta) [\text{covered } t_i \text{ with mould}]]]$

The question is whether the θ-criterion needs any restatement, given the classification of positions and categories indicated above. In (62), (63), and (65), there are two role-positions associated with a single θ-position. In (64) and (66), there are two A-chains, but the inner one supplies a role for the outer one. Certainly, an argument must head a chain (including the unit chain) containing a filled role-position *i.e.* an argument must receive a θ-role. If there is no NP movement, we can simply say that an argument must be in a θ-position (it is the expletives that need a further account). Otherwise, the θ-criterion as stated in (30) above is required.

The θ-criterion is about A-chains. Theta theory must also set conditions on other chains. Operator chains are very simple: an operator must immediately bind a trace in another operator position or at the head of an A-chain. What we do need in addition is some statement about role-chains, since these are new. It appears that an anaphoric-index chain behaves much like the role-chain of an explicit role.

Role-chains involve just SPEC to SPEC movement; nothing else need be said, so that a role-position may immediately bind either another role position or an operator position. We may possibly need to count an empty category in operator position which binds a trace in a role position as a role-chain (see footnote 49). In contrast to the other chains, there may be addition of roles (*i.e.* we permit adjunction in a role-position). We may also have anaphoric indices in these position; when such an index coincides with an explicit role, the two thereafter must move together. Furthermore, we can have both implicit andexplicit θ-roles in some role position. It is an empirical question whether these ever move. The answer appears to be positive. Consider

67   * John was promised to leave

68   John was promised to be allowed to leave

The examples are based on Bresnan 1982; see also Farkas 1988. We suppose as usual that *promise* s-selects for an entity and a proposition, realized as DP and IP here. Omitting some complications, we have

67 i   John [$_{VP}$ – [was [$_{VP}$ (α)+θ_k [promised [$_{NP}$ t$_k$]
       [$_{IP}$ PRO [$_{VP}$ λ [to leave]]]]]]]

What must happen is that the role marked with 'λ' moves to the next SPEC, that of *promised*. But this contains a sum of θ-roles, with one implicit. Let us stipulate that in this situation, we cannot add λ to the explicit θ unless we have an implicit role to add to α. This is exactly what we would have in (68), where the IP will be as in (68i):

68 i   [$_{IP}$ PRO [$_{VP}$ (ϵ)+λ_j [to be allowed [$_{VP}$ t_j [to leave]]]]]

From this we may conclude that implicit roles must move if attached to an explicit role which does so, as anaphoric and other explicit indices do. The equivalent of this explanation in more standard formulations would be that where there is a controlled PRO, if the antecedent surface subject is paired with an implicit subject (arising from a D-structure subject in that position), then the controlled subject must also consist of an explicit (PRO) subject paired with an implicit one. Explicit subjects and implicit subjects are subject to the same control relationship. The explanation given forces it to be the same person who does the promising and the allowing in (68), which does seem to be correct. We must also conclude that the idea put forward by Baker and others (Baker, Johnson and Roberts 1989), is unlikely to be correct. They argue that the passive participle morpheme (*-en*) is the external argument of the verb. Much of the same data is accounted for under the 'subject in SPEC' story I have told here, but the parametrization for different languages has received no account from me.

In section 4.1.3, I suggested that some adjectives like *able* were capable of becoming 'passive'. What this is intended to mean is that the external role assigned by the head becomes implicit. Following the lines of the explanation just given for *promise*, we may suppose that when a V″ complement is passive, the PAIR consisting of the explicit and implicit external θ-roles of the V″ is moved to the SPEC of the AP. Suppose an active sentence is

69 $[_{AP}\ \theta_1+\theta_2\ [\text{able}\ [_{V''}\ t_2\ [\text{to see John}]]]]$

Then in the 'passive', the explicit roles become implicit, giving

70 $[_{AP}\ \theta_3\ (\theta_1+\theta_2)\ [\text{able}\ [_{V''}\ t_3\ (t_2)\ [\text{to be seen}\ t_3]]]]$

This has the required effect of imputing the ability to the one who does the seeing. What is required is that an implicit role must be moved with the explicit one, and that it must be added to an implicit one, as with *promise*.

It is clear that the suggestions above need further specification, and more support. The notion of these role-chains will be justified largely by whether their introduction enables us to give elegant formulations of conditions which will characterize proper chains other than just the ones discussed above. We need to characterize 'multiple chains' arising from conjunction, adjunction, and 'Right Node Raising', and to account for those of parasitic gaps. The first two are straightforward, and only lack of space forced their omission. The last two I have not attacked. Also, the effects of changing the status and part of the function of PRO needs following up. In addition, the exact nature of c-selection and feature selection needs more discussion.

Outside what may fall directly within the domain of the devices as sketched here, are a number of areas. Parametrization is one. The possible need for an extension of the type system to treat locatives properly has been indicated. I am also aware that operators of all kinds other than binding operators have been neglected.

Notes

1. In this sense, A-bar chains may represent NPs, otherwise we have binding operators as well as arguments, so that constituency would not be constant.

2. The fact that it is the complements only that are traditionally given as the syntactic content of the lexicon is interesting. The apparent implication is that failures of canonic correspondence between c-selection and s-selection requirements never extend to the subject or external argument position. However, if the external role is compositionally mediated, then the lack of specification has another explanation: it could not be guaranteed to survive the compositional process. An example is provided by

fill   [— NP P″[*with*]]

If the object NP is taken as a physical entity, then we expect the subject to be also a physical entity, realized as an NP. If the object NP is understood as a mental entity, then the subject will be propositional, and hence CP or a suitable NP.

   i   The aqueduct filled the cisterns with water

       *That it had rained a lot filled the cisterns with water

   ii The doctors filled Mary with drugs

   iii The doctors/that she was pregnant filled Mary with hope

In (i) and (ii), the subject must be a physical agent; the canonic realization will be an NP of type <e>. In (iii) the NP subject has at some level of representation to be augmented to a propositional content ("what the doctors said to Mary"), matching the availability of a type <t> clausal argument; a mental agent to a mental outcome. In order to avoid the ever-present option of postulating ambiguity, we would need to allow external roles to be undetermined with respect to type, in relation to the lexical item. However, I shall continue to specify the external argument.

3. It would be nice if this correspondence was necessary. That is, if it could be shown that taking say proposition and property as the basic types led to an inadequate type-theory as far as syntax was concerned, then we might suppose that the adequate types were given as corresponding to the syntax of the language of thought fairly directly.

4. The relation between the generalized V projection and the generalized N projection is not, on my present analysis, a simple correspondence. V and N are the basic heads. I″ holds temporal information, and subjects: I suggest later (4.2.1) that there may be a similar projection (E) inside DP. The head of C or D may hold a binary operator (*if, every*), or a unary operator (*that, the*). C may hold a Case-marking item (*for*), and for DP, we may go outside, with the equivalent (*of*), heading a PP. Possibly POSS (*'s*) is a Case marking head in DP (Abney 1987). The generalized projections of V are IP and CP; of N they are perhaps EP, DP, and under some circumstances, PP.

5. It might appear that *whether* could be omitted here, but it is more likely that it is *that* which is omitted. In general, except where noted, *that* is optional, and *whether* is obligatory.

6. The construction with *it* has a similar meaning to what one would expect if there was PRO_{arb} in the subject position—an impersonalized evaluation. It contrasts with *seems*, or *obvious*, where the personal view has to be added by means of a *to* phrase. The *to* for *seems* and *obvious* is probably the ordinary marker of the recipient (of a vision of reality, here) in relation to a head.

7. In a tensed clause, the subject cannot be an anaphor (as is required for A-chains) because the domain for finding the antecedent will be the embedded clause. If θ-transmission is invoked, we similarly need to have some device which produces a barrier for transmission just when tense is present. This information again cannot be used by the child learner unless the principles involved are known.

8. Though see below, footnote 20 examples (i) and (ii).

9. As usual, θ-transmission will have to be blocked or free under the same condition.

10. For verbs, the fact that ECM is indeed exceptional will be used.

11. There is again something missing in this. Intuition says—possibly unreliably or *post hoc*—that the conceptual differences between *necessary* and *easy* on the one hand, and *likely* on the other, account for the c-selection differences. There is a sense in which likelihood is impersonal, where ease clearly is relative to someone. Necessity (other than logical necessity) is related to someone's needs. Suppose then we took as frames representing the full conceptual structures for these as not just those in (9) or (10), but rather

i   It is necessary   [for/to us]   [that Mary doesn't come]
ii It is likely   *[for us]   [that the earth is round]

Intuitively, the *it* version of *certain* patterns with (ii). The introduction of the human view is discussed further below.

12. See Chomsky 1986 (p. 168).

13. Note that I have taken *wh*-complement clauses to be of type <t> here, still. Probably this cannot be done consistently, and below I introduce a type <q> for questions. Possibly the consequent type <e*,q> is simply impossible. I do not *a priori* rule out John's having two θ-roles.

14. We will then have to have an empty *that* complement as the head of every tensed root clause. This in turn ensures that the SPEC and Head positions are available as landing sites for movement.

15. Adjunction of *wh*-elements to IP is excluded in Chomsky 1986b (p. 5 and footnote 6).

16. There are a number of other ways that the effect might be accounted for, but the ones I have considered raise other problems. Note that Chomsky's example 144(i) (Chomsky 1986a)

John announced the decision [PRO to feed himself]

cannot be construed as John's announcing someone else's decision that John should feed himself (a perfectly plausible message in appropriate context); hence even here we seem to need control of PRO by the agent of the deciding—and some further mechanism ensuring that this role is identified with *John* (since we cannot mean that John announced someone else's decision to feed himself, either).

17. See discussion in 4.2.7 relating to verbs. There do seem to be nouns which take empty operator headed complements:

i   It is a pleasure PRO to read your work

ii Your work is a pleasure [O_k [PRO to read t_k]]

18. *If* and *whether* may be construed as one-place clausal operators (like *that*) in this context *i.e.* where their function is to produce a suitable argument to a head. But in some of these cases, we seem to have a variant of the ordinary two-place *if*, and a similarly connective *whether (or not)*. There is a contrast between (i) and (ii) in this respect:

i   I am not certain if she came

ii I asked if she would come

In the former case, we can and probably in some sense must construe this as 'if she came, I am not certain that she came—and if she didn't come, I am not certain that she didn't come'. The contrast is clearer with a factive like *know*. For *whether*, see Larson 1985.

19. There are a few cases where phonologically realized *that* is obligatory: in my dialect this is so with *eager* if it is followed by what I take to be a subjunctive as in (2) of Table 1.

20. That the subject of the embedded clause may be involved causally in the ease is certainly true. With sentences like "It is easy for clever children to do arithmetic," this is the natural interpretation. There is evidence that there used to be a subject-focused option available for adjectives like *easy*. The OED has examples such as

i   He is a very subtle fish, and hard to be caught.   (1653)

ii I am difficult to believe that ...   (1691)

These should be analyzed (superficially) as having <t,t> adjectives subcategorizing for V[*to*] complements, so that the external θ-role of the embedded verb is transmitted to the matrix subject. This is a combination which an adjective like *certain* has; but this is intuitively somewhat different, essentially in being more impersonal. A possible answer lies in supposing that *hard* and the others have in addition an implicit argument relating to the person who finds it hard, difficult, easy and so on. Like the implicit argument of a passive, this may (at least now) be linked to a designated PP, as we see in the *for*–NP of example (36). It is also capable of being associated with other subject roles (as in control of PRO in the case of passive): in (i), the implicit argument of *hard* is associated with the implicit external agent argument of *catch*, and in (ii) it is associated with the external argument of *believe*. If this assumption about an implicit argument is correct, then a sentence like

iv The fish is hard for me to catch

will have two possible analyses with identical meaning:

v   The fish is hard [for me to catch *e*]

vi The fish is hard [for me] [PRO to catch *e*]

In the case of

vii Fish are hard PRO to catch

we expect controlled PRO (with the normal implicit argument existential reading, possibly generic) rather than PRO_{arb}. We should also note that the syntactic rules are in fact incapable of referring to what I have suggested might motivate them—the agent and patient roles—but perforce work with subjects and non-subjects (taking advantage of any canonic correspondences to the roles).

21. Foldvik (1989) gives an analysis of *easy* under which similarly the adjective has the same thematic and syntactic subcategorization in its occurrence in sentences like my (9a) and (5), with the *tough*-movement one distinguished by selecting an empty operator in SPEC of CP. She does not however extend the analysis to occurrences as in my (12a). She analyses the constructions in terms of (non-standard) chains, in a way somewhat different from what I suggest in the next section.

22. There is discussion of this in Chomsky 1981 (p. 310), 1986a (p. 130).

23. I discuss below the possibility that the *of John* phrase is associated not with an internal but with an implicit external argument, as suggested in the discussion in footnote 20. We cannot get rid of all double arguments this way of course, since verbs like *persuade* have visible external arguments and N" and C" internal arguments; and the *of* Case suggests a regular external argument. Other factors, like the control of PRO, will be involved in the decision here. The participants introduced with prepositions mentioned in footnote 6 also need to be accounted for.

24. Of course, adjectives of type <t,t> frequently occur with NP complements moved into the subject position. However, in all these cases the NP in question is semantically (at some level) of the type of a proposition, rather than of an entity:

  i The answer was apt

  ii The recurrence of the problem is likely/certain/probable

25. For instance, in *The city's destruction* there is no passive morphology on *destruction* (though an agent will have a *by* phrase linked to an implicit external role).

26. Ingham (1989) argues that for English it is in fact necessary to learn whether or not an internal NP argument may be phonologically null, and if so, what the associated interpretation is, citing *eat*, *devour*, *fight* and *follow* as contrasting.

27. More properly, the *it* might be considered to be a pro-form for the sort of abstract noun-phrase which can routinely substitute for a clause. These should have type <t>, rather than type <e>, at least at some level.

28. We might suppose that the extra meaning postulate is reliably predictable from the syntactic structure. We would be asking, then, that ALL the adjectives in (6) gave rise to the same assumptions about causal involvement. This is not so, since John is in no way responsible for the fact that

   i John is certain to die before he is two hundred years old

is true. Given that the two are different, then, it looks as if we have *stupid*$_2$ being more or less *stupid*$_1$ with some extra concern for the NP subject of the proposition, as I suggested above.

29. Some comparatives may follow the same rule: we presumably have a displaced complement to the adjective in

   i a larger cat [than O_k/?what$_k$ I have t_k]

30. I think that sentences such as

   i John is a likely man [to vote for Nixon]

are ungrammatical. This will be because the versions with adjective and complement adjacent have V″[*to*] complements, rather than C″[*to*]. The alternative with the empty operator binding a subject position will be precluded by the Case filter, even if the empty operator bound a subject, since the adjective as putative Case-assigner is no longer adjacent to the clause.

31. It may also be correct to add V″ to the c-selection options, if the suggestions made in section 5.4 concerning *want* and similar verbs are correct. This would necessitate the addition of the θ-roles, as is required for *ready*$_2$.

32. In some dialects, we may have such sentences as

   i The bath is ready to overflow

For this, we need a V″ c-selection, with the subject being assigned both the external role of *ready*$_2$ and the external one of the VP.

33. The details here need a proper syntactic investigation, but it does seem clear that some extra structure is needed.

34. Enç (1986) has argued that only nouns and verbs (and possibly some adjectives) need any record of tense information (*i.e.* that scope of tense over clauses is unnecessary). This would give us a further parallel: the other information under E will be analogous to [*past*],

35. Generalized composition of functions is to include the combinators necessary for the summed θ-roles of *ready*$_1$ and *ready*$_2$.

36. The D-structure requirement that predicates have arguments would have to be constructive, and apply once only, otherwise the outer AP would again be visible as a canonic predicate, requiring another argument.

37. *c.f.*

    i   I consider it absurd/pathetic [that John is ignored]

But it makes intuitively no sense to suppose we have

    ii   I consider [it [$_{DP}$ a [pity [that John is ignored]]]]

even if *pity* unusually has type <t,t>). This casts doubt on the analysis of (i) as [$_{AP}$ A CP]—a matter discussed under expletive *it* below.

38. This is not to say that all such surface constructions are SC: but for verbs like these which take other type <t> complements, it would be surprising if they were not. See Postal and Pullum 1988.

39. I assume from the regularity of DP realizations of type <t> complements that the verb assigns accusative Case to CPs, in general. We can conjoin CP and DP complements, which supports this suggestion:

    i   Have you considered [how he is to get in, and the other problems]?

If this is not correct, then there will be possible Case assigning rather than feature assigning explanations for instances like (13).

40. The idea that this or (16) is an initial D-structure forced by the various requirements is apparently incompatible with some of the suggestions I have made. But if as I shall argue, the expletive appears as a feature, and if type-theory and c-selection for categories and features are all permitted to be constructive, then we can indeed still construct D-structure properly. Alternatively, we take D-structure to be a particular way of looking at S-structure (though it is harder to see how principles like 'all movement is forced' should be understood).

41. The weather-*it* on the other hand must count as being of type <e>, along with the DP *the weather*.

42. If we were to move to a more elaborated type system, we should probably obtain *there* and *it* as semantically related (as operators or predicates) to the clauses concerned; in this case, possibly no NP movement would be required. But the semantics of the chains would change.

43. There is some possibility of confusion with equative *be*, which does Case-mark. I take it that in (i), we have equative *be*, and non-expletive *it*. The PP is an obligatorily postposed restrictive modifier of *it*.

i [[It t_k] is milk] [on the doorstep]$_k$

In (ii) we have 'predicational' *be*:

ii [There]$_k$ is [t_k [milk [on the doorstep]]]

This gives a satisfactory account of the meaning difference here.

44. All the c-selected features will appear on *O*, too, and hence will be required of the external argument. It does not seem that we want QR of the DP *a pity* (see section 1.2).

45. Guéron 1981 (p. 103), citing Safir, points out that with some verbs there is a meaning contrast between alternants with and without an expletive *it*; so we expect a lexical idiosyncrasy.

46. See Burzio 1986 (p. 177 footnote 73), for the same suggestion (and also p. 226, footnote 1).

47. Or possibly, as we shall see below, to a c-selected IP in a CP. In the case of (12) and (20), we have available Case-marking, so why do we not get Case-marking of the CP across the SC boundary without the intermediary *it*? The answer (unless the assumption of footnote 39 is wrong) must be that if a head Case-marks a category of the right kind and type to be its argument, then that category must BE its argument. This will permit Case marking of NP into clauses, including NP-headed SC, while excluding the cases noted. It is a natural stipulation.

48. See Belletti and Rizzi (1988), who argue that the principle applies only to structural Case. Note that if this story about *it* is correct, then there must be no external argument in the *stupid of* constructions, since these have an expletive—presumably to Case-mark the VP argument.

49. We might suppose for (12), that the head DP has internal structure [$_{DP}$ O_k [$_{D'}$ a [$_{N''}$ t_k [pity t_k]]]]. If the SPEC of DP is an operator position, this will be ill-formed. I had assumed that it was an operator position because it held exclamative phrases as in

i I saw [[$_{DP}$ [how tall]$_k$ [$_{D'}$ a t_k girl]] she was]

We might investigate whether an <operator position, x-role position> chain could be a legitimate role chain rather than an illicit operator chain. We need more information about the structure of DP.

50. An A-position then appears to be some position capable of receiving Case and capable of receiving a θ-role directly or by predication.

51. If we need *wh*-movement to adjoin to VP, then a more complex formulation, referring to the chain of the SPEC, will be needed (along the lines suggested below for (36)).

52. It seems that subject binding by the empty operator is ruled out by some sort of 'minimal structure' principle: if O_k [t_k VP] or just [VP] are possible parses of a string, then the first is not a visible option. But for a chain condition version, see below.

53. A non-restrictive relative clause is probably something rather like a secondary predicate on its head NP, but unlike the standard secondary predication of (29) above, it does not appear to be amenable to treatment as an adjunction-of-predicates structure.

54. We might alternatively suggest that what should be checked is the ability of the SPEC of the adjective to hold the operator. But the problems turn out to be the same. I shall assume that checking of the SPEC of the subcategorized category is the correct move.

55. There are interesting questions here about how—or perhaps, whether—the θ-role associated with a null object which behaves like an empty operator is discharged. See for instance Authier 1988 for discussion. It may turn out that more than one kind of operator must be recognized—for example distinguishing definite from indefinite construal. It is unlikely that the required operators have a construal parallel to the lambda operator (as the [+WH] and my empty operator do).

56. We might then wonder if [+WH] elements can occupy x-role-positions. The answer must be negative if we want to preserve their usual behavior. Probably no x-role-position can contain phonological material. There is doubtless some explanation missing.

57. A possible counter example is

 i ??John is easy [PRO to imagine [t doing very well]]

This I predict to be ungrammatical, and find dubious. Certainly (ii)

 ii Fred is the man [O_i [PRO to hope [t will come]]

is bad (example after Wilder 1989).

58. As argued in Burzio 1986 (p. 148 ff.)

59. Longer distance movements as required in

i They [θ – [thought [it [– [likely
    [that [(α) – [pictures of each other$_k$]] would be on sale]]]]]

are unproblematic, if we assume that the index {k} will move through the SPEC positions marked with '–'. Association with [it] would be possible in principle, from the middle position, but it will be ruled out by feature checking or type-checking. In many languages, only subject antecedents are available to reflexives—the index must move until it is in a filled x-role position.

60. This notion arose from discussion with Rita Manzini.

61. For lack of a suitable theory of θ-roles, Burzio 1986 (p. 331) has to reject such an analysis for 'restructuring' verbs.

CHAPTER FIVE

The Language of Thought: Findings, Problems, and Speculations

> An explanation was necessary, and was forthcoming; they always are; hypotheses are what we lack the least.
>
> Poincaré, *Science and Hypothesis*

5.0 Points of departure

In chapter 1, section 1.5, there were set out the possible interpretations of a written natural language definition with respect to a representation of it in the language of thought. Throughout chapters 2 and 3, it was assumed that a definition could be processed as such, in one of the ways set out. In the course of attempting to spell out how the appropriate language of thought representation is obtained, various hypotheses about the internal language and its relation to natural language were made. Chapter 4 was largely concerned with the relation between s-selection and c-selection, but considerations of learnability relate these to the language of thought.

This chapter will collect together and briefly reconsider the various findings and suggestions concerning the language of thought that are scattered through the earlier chapters. These fall into three main groups:

  i properties of the language of thought itself

  ii relations between linguistic representations and corresponding representations in the language of thought

  iii considerations relating to the use made of the representations—how a definition is interpreted, and how it may be used inferentially, in particular

I shall try to bring some order to the miscellaneous collection of suggestions, and to draw out the underlying assumptions a little more explicitly, pointing out some of the gaps, and adding further speculations.

In what follows, I shall generally abbreviate 'natural language' to 'NL', which should cover whatever natural language a particular individual knows, not just English, and 'the language of thought', which will be that individual's internal language, to 'LoT'.

5.1 Variables

It probably looks as though I am committed to an 'operator–variable' vocabulary for the language of thought, where the variables range over role-types. I have used variables freely, in both NL levels and in LoT expressions. However, it is quite probable that all the conditions on some level of representation which can be stated using variables spread out over the geometry of a representation can equally well be stated in a combinatorial algebra over structures without these elements. Similarly, we can have variable-free quantification, and even variable-free scope specification (Cormack 1984a, Williams 1986). If this is so, we may be able to regard the variables as a notational convenience: it is easier to have pictures. The same probably applies to some other empty categories—trace of a moved role (NP-movement trace) and the empty operator, and intermediate movement traces. (PRO is a different matter—it is an argument, but not a variable, and there seems no reason to suppose it corresponds to an 'empty category' in the language of thought—or indeed that such a notion makes sense).[1]

I shall continue to talk about variables, and to assume that QR is a legitimate movement, so that the combinatorial rules are relatively simple. The combinatorial rules, as I have it, are not part of our knowledge, but they give the logical structure which must be respected by the inference rules which ARE part of our procedural knowledge. In as much as they give well-formedness conditions, they have been replaced by the chain-conditions on θ-roles, and by the feature satisfaction connected to subcategorization.[2]

The construal of all text definitions except the limited range available with *call* required that we use variables which were common to NL and LoT. For example, in (1i), from (37) of 3.2.2, the variables are derived directly from those given by QR and predication in (1ii); the latter belong to NL, and the former to LoT.

1 i $\lambda{<}x,y{>}\ (x{\in}\text{set}\ \&\ y{\in}\text{set}\ \&\ \exists z\ (z{\in}x\ \&\ z{\in}y))$
       $= \lambda{<}x,y{>}(x\ \text{intersects}\ y)$

   ii   A set which has some members in common with another set is said to intersect it

The variables were needed essentially to saturate a predicate that was being defined, and to fill the equivalent argument places in the definiens. The type-system itself, then, with respect to predicates and arguments and their compositionality, must be common to NL and LoT. However, it does not follow that it is identical in the two cases: in particular, the internal versus external distinction does not necessarily hold in the language of thought just because it does in NL. Suppose translation takes LF' onto LR. It is possible that the former does and the latter does not have an internal/external distinction as such, or that there is some inconsistency with respect to assignments for particular lexical items.[3] The discussion in section 2.4.3.1 tended to suggest that there IS something comparable to an internal/external distinction in LoT, but the arguments were slight. The leverage we have depends on cases where the definiendum in a dictionary definition has internal and external arguments: the two gaps must not get confused. But if it is true, then we might expect all NLs to preserve this format.

Most of the variables that have occurred have been of type <e>. This is partly because movement of NPs has been most exhaustively studied within the theory. But we have had a number of instances of movement of a category of type <t>, leaving a trace of type <t> (as in extraposition, for instance). The language of thought needs to record movement just in order to identify the generalized argument, so the type here is redundant. In the small clause analyses of *it* sentences, however, we had predicates with passive-like movement of the role:

2   – is [it [[that John is not here] [$_{AP}$ θ_k [regrettable t_k]]]]

Here it is essential that the role and variable have type <t>, in order that a θ-role of the correct type is offered to the proposition represented by the subject clause [that John is not here].

In the analysis of the definition of *putative* (2.4.2, example (2), given below as (3)), a variable over predicates was introduced.

3   *putative*   commonly supposed to be   C20

Opacity (intensionality) will be introduced by virtue of the matrix "commonly supposed to be ...." It is possible that all that is needed to achieve this is appropriate inference rules (or lack of these). The treatment of a putative text-definition of *fake* suggested in section 1.5.3 introduced a variable over an NL word, instead. This is probably required for *putative* too. We need variables over words for the translation procedures proposed in 1.5.3 and used for definitions with *call* in 3.2.1. For instance (from 3.2.1 (6)) the compositional LICENCE to move from (4i) to (4ii), (where (in LoT), F is the name of the translation function, NL is in quotes, and T names triangles)

4 i F 'equilateral triangle'

4 ii F 'equilateral' & T

can only be expressed using such variables, if this licence is to be in propositional rather than procedural form. A restriction of variables to the argument types would be desirable; we may take NL words as a kind of entity so far as LoT is concerned. Whether this restriction is possible for all cases depends not just on translations of NL strings, but on how the axioms and meaning postulates are formulated (e.g. for opacity and transparency). Further, I have not investigated the syntax of operators, so the matter must be left open.

Recent work in formal semantics has argued that NL uses generalized quantifiers. But if we follow some of the accounts of 'donkey' sentences, we need not just QR of the whole NP (the generalized quantifier), but 'OR' (Operator Raising of DET). I used this to account for examples like (1) above. However, for example (53) of 3.3.2, it appeared to be necessary that the restrictive term be outside the quantifying term. The logical representation needed seemed to be:

5    $X \in$ [two sets], $e \in$ [X have no members in common]
     [many <X,e> (e happens) & EVERY <X,e>
     (e happens $\Rightarrow X$ are disjoint)]

This suggests that perhaps the restrictive term is not part of a generalized quantifier, but rather to be construed as restrictive quantification originally was, as determining the domain of the variable. The notion that LoT used restriction on the domain of a variable independently of its expression in a particular sentence was put forward

The Language of Thought

in 3.2.2, in relation to 'filing' a definition under a particular concept. For the example (14), given here as (6i),

6 i   A triangle with all its sides equal is said to be *equilateral*

6 ii $T(x)$ & $S(x)$ then $(F\text{ 'equilateral'})x$

it was suggested that we obtain the effect of a conditional definition by filing the whole under T (LoT), and taking the unbound variables of the interpretation (ii) to range over triangles. It would be nice to have some more data bearing on this.

5.2   The expressive power and the syntax of the language of thought

The conclusion of section 2.3.2 was that elimination of an adjective could only take place at a level of representation where some NL ordering and many NL category distinctions were neutralized. On the assumption that the definition was to provide a 'word–word' translation, it was suggested that this could be a 'stripped down' LF, LF'; the categories then cannot be needed for LR. If on the other hand, the definiens is taken to indicate the equivalent language of thought expression, then it will equally follow that the language of thought cannot have in it categories differentiated as our AP, PP, VP etc. The required equivalence class is just that of predicate, defined as a maximal projection of type $<e,t>$ (or $<e^*,t>$ depending on whether or not there is an internal/external distinction). It does not follow that this class is undifferentiated in LoT—we might want to postulate subclasses to account for logico–inferential matters.

In section 2.4, I argued that LoT used a structural rather than a role-labeling identification of the arguments corresponding to the external and internal arguments of a head. I raised the question of the applicability of the ECP to LoT. For the example given, only a system with SPEC and internal argument on opposite sides of the head in LoT will allow the ECP satisfaction in NL to be preserved after translation.

If the ECP is, as Chomsky's characterization quoted in 1.1.7 suggests, an aid to the identification of chains in natural language, then provided the notation of the language of thought has something like explicit variables, we would not expect it to hold. But if chains are introduced into the LoT representations only at the point where the simple proposition is being reorganized for pragmatic and communicative purposes, we might expect it to hold.

The central question here is whether the possibility of more than one truth-conditionally equivalent form in LoT is useful for our own internal processing, perhaps to constrain the direction of hypothesis introduction, in ways comparable to the guidance of context construction by surface form. This does seem likely: after all, if I am attempting to solve a problem, I do have some idea as to relevant 'aboutness', for instance. I do not (perhaps) pursue all possible lines. Besides, the fact that NL processing is possible under the pragmatic guidance of the surface form suggests that reduction to canonic form is not necessary. The natural assumption is that non-canonic form is the norm for processing. If we take this to mean that the non-canonic structures should be comparable to those of NL (at LF'), then we might expect that some constraints applying to LF and not lost at LF' would apply to LoT.

It is certainly true that many LF ECP violations are unprocessable—but others are not. Consider (7i) and (7ii) from Chomsky 1986b:

7 i How did you leave [before fixing the car *t*]?

ii Who left [before fixing the car how]?

On my judgment, the first is hopeless, even after I have worked out what it would have to mean; but the second is not. Since the theory is still in flux, one cannot place too much reliance on any particular examples. And as far as I know, ECP violations do not turn up as production errors, whereas for instance I frequently find myself with a *wh*-island violation. I have to conclude, all the same, that there is insufficient evidence that the ECP does hold in LoT—and hence we can deduce nothing about the relative positions of SPEC and complement relative to a head.

If the type system is close to the category system of the syntax of the language of thought, which we expect now, then what happens to those cases where NL gave say V" complements, but s-selected for type <t> and transmitted roles? What will be needed is for LoT to see the transmitted role-holder as part of the 'generalized representation' of the propositional argument, in the manner I suggested for the generalized adjunct of (14) in section 2.3.2—see discussion of (16) below.

The requirement that the language of thought has logical predicates (*i.e.* heads) and arguments as its primary categories is hardly surprising. We need only add the variables and binding operators to obtain a simple predicate calculus, which we are accustomed to using for the display of uncomplicated truth-conditional meanings. The syntax has also to accommodate restrictive quantification, as noted above. In addition, it is apparent that we need to allow for operators (which I have discussed sporadically),[4] and for predicate-type adjuncts, which have entered in more systematically. The natural assumption appears to be that the s-selection system and the types carry over directly from LF to the language of thought, and that the syntax of the latter allows us to identify categories such as head, operator, argument, and so on. Exactly what falls under this 'and so on' is in need of further investigation.

Given appropriate types for binding and other operators, the algebra imposed on the types ensures that the stipulations that predicates have arguments, and so on, are met. We can take the Principle of Full Interpretation as the natural requirement that such an algebra exists, and that it is 'non-trivial' in some sense. An algebra of combinations would be trivial if it combined a with b in such a way that the result was independent of the value of b. This will correctly rule out Chomsky's example (1986a, 91)

8 Who did John see Bill

But it will correctly permit there to be verbs such as the 'predicational' *be* whose semantic value is such that its effect is frequently negligible. This is no more trivial than is the number one (which has no effect under multiplication).

There are some potentially serious objections to this happy picture. One can be dealt with reasonably quickly, although I am aware that further work is needed. This is the objection that it looks as if I have set up the language of thought to look rather like English. My defense is three fold. First, it has been argued independently that this should be so (Smith 1983; and see footnote 15 in Dowty 1987 for reasons to suppose this is possible). Second, it has been suggested (1.5.4, and at the end of 2.4.3) that one of the functions of definitions may be the construction of new items of vocabulary in the language of thought; naturally the effect of exposure to a lot of learning of this kind would be to make one's internal language more like one's native language in the concepts it coded directly. This feels right. In addition, LoT may be flexible enough to mimic some grammatical properties of NL. Third, it MUST be that the language of thought has sufficient structure to carry inference. And the elaboration of that structure must be adequate to the tasks that can be posed using natural language. Syntactic notations carry information; very roughly, we must expect comparable information to be carried in the language of thought, somehow. The assumption that it is carried structurally is perhaps arbitrary, but it is convenient, and it is not clear that we are yet in any position to decide between alternatives. Given this, the definitions themselves force us to accept correspondences between various parts of the structures of NL and the language of thought. Another indication that the language of thought needs to be like the user's natural language is the problem of using PF information, which is discussed in section 5.3 below..

The two other possible objections relate to the use of the language of thought as a medium for pragmatic processing. First, if the type system is common to NL and to the language of thought, with fully well-formed formulae in each, then what drives the enrichment procedures which produce elaborated forms from the supposedly underdetermined ones of natural language? In some cases the answer is straightforward: we have some item which is like a pronoun *sans* antecedent, and we must find an antecedent, or we have ellipsis, so that content but not type is missing. We may postulate, for instance for the missing comparison class of adjectives like *big*, that some such items are introduced in the translation from LF' to LR (see footnote 39 of chapter 2).

Sentences like *Johnny is being difficult today* pose a slightly different problem. If we want to keep the type system AND minimize lexical ambiguity, then there is an operator-headed clause missing in the NL syntax after *difficult* (in line with the complete structures in 2.2.2 for *hard*, and the subcategorization 'J' given for *easy* in 4.1.3).

9 Johnny is being [$_{AP}$ − [difficult [O_k [$_{IP}$ e] [for e]] today

This will avoid, in this case, the infinity of types that Chierchia (1982, 1984) argues that preserving the type system will lead to. But nominalizations need more discussion than I can give here. Consider

10 Multiplication is difficult

11 Multiplication is commutative

For (10), we could adopt the same strategy as with (9), or take *multiplication* itself to have inherently the type <t> (or at least, to give this type when saturated by its arguments). For (11), it is at present an open question as to whether the adjective is of type <p> or <t*,t>; in this particular case I think that Chierchia's notion of associating higher order entities with "abstract" entities of the ordinary type is the right move; but it is clear that it remains to be demonstrated that this is possible and appropriate within the framework I have been suggesting.

The other problem concerns the input to pragmatic processing. Why, we might ask, is natural language apparently so much richer in its syntax than the language of thought? Why is there c-selection as well as s-selection? Why does S-structure produce such variety, instead of just the canonic forms permitted? Why is there the intonation and stress (or variation in printing style and punctuation), and perhaps further stylistic movement at PF? The answer surely must be that the interpretation of utterances needs more than the bare representation of some proposition. Within the Sperber and Wilson theory, the hearer needs the speaker to guide him in the accessing of items, and in the retrieval or construction of the correct context against which to process the utterance. It is to achieve this end that the variety of language is necessary, and exploited. Then the question is, why is LF', distanced from this, the input to semantic interpretation? How can all this be exploited if it is NOT input to the language of thought?

It is not within the remit of this work to even begin to answer such questions—but having thrown them into relief, I think I must indicate that they might have satisfactory answers compatible with what I have been suggesting. This is the purpose of the next section (5.3).

The final comment in this section relates to the possibility that the language of thought is required to have sufficient expressive power that it can contemplate and give a formal semantics for natural language. That is, it can serve as a metalanguage for natural languages and their 'semantics' (in LoT translation). This was one of the possibilities I examined in chapter 1 (1.5.3). In chapter 3 (3.4.1), we did indeed find definitions that required processing relying on such properties. That there was not more evidence of this is due to the fact that in many cases, I simply have not spelt out how the translations are obtained; my discussion stopped short of that much detail.

5.3 LF as the sole input to interpretation?

Suppose for some linguistic utterance, syntactic processing supplies LF, and LF leads to the stripped down form LF', and this by translation to what I have called LR (logical representation). This latter is to lead to UR (utterance interpretation) via enrichment, reference assignment, and so on. The question is, have we lost too much of the information supplied by the original utterance?

Let me start with the easy bits. First, there is no reason to suppose that there will be any loss of how the information was packaged with respect to lexical items: I have been supposing for some time now that the language of thought was capable of having an item to correspond to every NL word. (If an item like *small* in NL has a more elaborate translation in LoT, this may simply involve a designated 'pronoun' at an extra argument place, to accommodate the comparison class—much more than that and my statement would be false). Second, LF itself preserves all the information of S-structure, albeit in what might not seem to be the most convenient form. Suppose that translation from LF or LF' to LR preserves structure and chains (modulo alternative notations). Provided we have some sort of "compositional" inference system, that is, provided we can run inference off such forms as they stand, without reducing them to a canonic form, we can still allow the inference to be guided by the particulars of S-structure. (See further example (16) of 5.4 below). Thirdly, we can if we are careful preserve the 'head versus adjunct' distinction, even when we lose category labels. We need to do this if there are pragmatic expectations set up by the distinction, as suggested in section 2.2.7.

Preserving the distinction depends on the detail of the structure of adjunction.

The Language of Thought

12 i

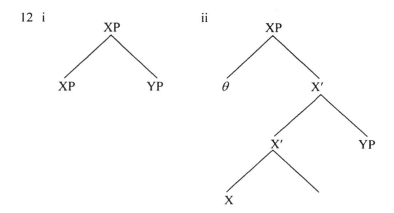

If we assume that the structure for the adjunction of predicates is as in (12i), and if $X = Y$, then the adjunct and the adjoinee can only be distinguished if adjunction is always to the right (or left). But it seems likely that at least some APs in English are base generated to the left within DP, and other predicates to the right. And in some languages (such as French), it appears that the base-generated position is lexically specified. If the structure is as in (12ii), there is no problem in distinguishing the head and its modifier, whether it is adjoined to the left or the right. But it is essential that in (ii), we keep the bar-level labels (or some equivalent), so we have X' distinct in kind from YP. It should be noted that algebraically, (i) is simpler and more natural than (ii), allowing just the generalized conjunction I have been assuming throughout (although we could interpret (ii)). However, the θ-role movement suggested in chapter 4 will take to (ii) better than to (i), since there is in (ii) a possibility of simply exploiting SPEC to SPEC movement to add the θ-role from YP to that already in SPEC of XP. This will give conjunction, effectively.[5] This might suggest that the geometric metaphor rather than the algebraic one is the best one, for NL and the language of thought.

That was an argument that NL categories are not needed in LoT. But then, why do they exist? A possible answer is that the imposition of a second tier of lexical properties, Categories and Case assigning potential, on lexical items permits a rather free use of 'move α' in the NL syntax, despite the inaudibility of the empty categories.

Paradoxically, this is because the categories and Cases permit the imposition of sufficient constraints to ensure that chains can be identified (*i.e.* that the correct relations between heads and arguments are retrievable despite the displacements from canonic positions). In LoT, if there are variables, then we may assume that they have 'phonological' realizations, so the same problems do not arise.[6] A subsidiary consequence of the dual system (of categories and types) in NL is that it is possible to introduce words into an utterance which have category but no type. Plausible examples are phrases like *Anyway...*, *Well...* (see Blakemore 1987), and perhaps expletive *it*, and *the*.[7]

The obvious remaining problem is PF. The simple answer would be to suppose that any PF information not coded in any way in S-structure could be used only in manipulating the accessibility of concepts, but not in any part of the processing dependent on the language of thought representation of the utterance. In fact it seems incoherent to suppose otherwise. If this claim turns out to be untenable (which is quite likely), then I can only suppose that S-structure is capable of holding all pertinent information relating to PF. That is, we might suppose that the processing permitted relevant parts of PF to be superimposed on S-structure, and hence onto LF. (This of course would not affect the logical dependencies between the levels). In this manner we might be able to account for guiding access to complex concepts, and in particular to the sorts of partially specified propositions that we need to make up background assumptions, for instance (see Smith and Wilson 1979, Sperber and Wilson 1983). The potential difficulties here might persuade one that it was worth attempting to do without LF itself—perhaps by turning it into a set of well-formedness conditions on the distribution of scope-marking devices at S-structure. Further investigation of VP anaphora, and the scope of tense and negation might be enlightening. In any case, it is hard to see how phonological information can be used unless the language of thought representation bears a rather direct relation to the natural language input. One small suggestion is made in relation to (17) below, utilizing Smith and Wilson's "focal scale."

5.4 Conceptual adicity, s-selection and c-selection

On the simplest story, conceptual types, s-selection, and c-selection would be in one to one (to one) correspondence. The simple story is not correct. Within the language of thought, we may assume a correspondence between syntactic and semantic types. In the NL syntax, we have c-selection, and no direct correspondence between this and s-selection. We require that s-selection[8] and the associated well-formedness conditions on θ-roles mediate conceptual and natural language structures, in the translation from LF' to LR. It is possible, however, that some of the argument roles represented in the conceptual structures may not appear as such in the s-selection for the 'nearest' NL word, but are introduced in the translation. Whether this is so, and if so, for which items and under what constraints is an empirical question.[9]

Two kinds of problem arise: one of learnability, and one of the interpretation of the various well-formedness conditions, given the possible lack of correspondence between c-selection and s-selection. I have argued for a variety of c-selection options, including features, in contrast to a very limited range of permitted s-selection types. Argument types must be saturated. Since I have introduced only two types, this reduces here to <t> or <e>. It is unlikely that this fact reduces learning in any way: it is more likely that LoT is literally incapable of processing any part of a representation not conforming to this. It is not clear whether for internal arguments, the existence of Canonic Structural Realizations is of any help; in section 4.1.2 it seemed that no subcategorization should be assumed unless there was positive evidence for it. For external arguments, the c-selection appears to be severely restricted, to just the canonic categories (4.1.3).

The assumption that s-selection relates directly to conceptual structure means that it is essential that all θ-roles are projected. Thus in nominalizations, we must always have PRO if no overt subject is present:

13   The [PRO's destruction of the city]

(This entails that something like the EPP operates to produce subject positions). However, we have seen that subjects of adjectives (4.1.3, 4.2.8, *able*) and nouns (2.5, 4.2.8 footnote 25, for *destruction*; footnote 40 from 2.4.2) can be implicit, like subjects of passives. We will have to have internal arguments of nouns and other heads syntactically present too, even when they are phonologically unrealized. At LR they must have appropriate representations (as anaphors, existentials or pronominals, for instance); at UR (utterance interpretation) anaphora and reference should be resolved. We saw the need for this in the *subject to V* constructions noted in 2.2.2.

One of the questions I have not addressed is the proper type for abstract nouns like *destruction*. Learning will be reduced by predictability. But there are several possibilities. In general, I have been assuming that we may expect morphologically related items to have at least some argument structures in common (as with the two *certain*s in 4.1.2).[10] But we may still have morphologically derived forms with adicity differing from the root. So for instance (considering again (10) and (11) from 5.2 above), I think it can be shown that in (14i) there is, and in (14ii) there is not, a role assigned to a person (PRO) by the language of thought item corresponding to *multiplication*:

14 i   Multiplication is difficult

    ii Multiplication is commutative

There are two related language of thought items involved. The first relates directly to *multiply*, and has its type, so that when saturated it gives type <t>.[11] In section 4.1.3, footnote 24, it was suggested that the NPs *the answer* and *the recurrence of the problem* could have type <t>. Perhaps all nouns with both subjects and external roles head DPs of type <t>. The second is more abstract, as noted in the discussion of (11). Of other nouns with internal NP arguments, some are abstract like the noun in (14ii), and others are operators. And I doubt if that is all that needs to be said. There are too nouns with just an internal clausal argument, like *fact* and *pity*. The former presumably has type <t,t>, like the adjective *certain*. The latter I find puzzling.

The fact that θ-roles must be projected (at every level) does not mean that the θ-criterion can be met at every level.

15   [The cat] is easy [[PRO$_{arb}$ to please O_k]]

It has been noted that examples like this show that the θ-criterion cannot be met at D-structure. Here, *easy* assigns its only, internal, θ-role (and Case) to the IP/CP which follows it. It has nothing to assign to the subject NP. At LF, after movement, a θ-role can be properly assigned by predication to the NP [the cat]. But at LR, logical representation in the language of thought, we need to preserve the elaboration of this structure, and yet we have stipulated that *easy* has an argument of type <t>.

We have postulated that forms like (16) are produced at LR.

16   [The salad]$_{1,2}$ [$\theta_{1,2}$ is [$t_{1\ 2}$ ready [t_2[PRO$_{arb}$ to eat e_2]]

Then such forms must be capable of entering in to whatever processes are needed to determine UR, in the usual case that LR is underdetermined. It does not follow that UR has to have all the elaboration of the NL structures: at least, when the discourse processing is finished, and the contextual effects arrived at, then the linguistic form is not needed. For long term storage, a neutral, canonic form may be preferred. There is some experimental evidence that normalization of form takes place within a short time during narrative, for instance (see references in Clark and Clark 1977, 138 ff.). But during the pragmatic processing, we need to preserve the forms.

Suppose we assume that pragmatic processes over the language of thought (such as inference) are capable of working directly on the representation as in (16). This has the advantage that forms such as (16) in LoT would (presumably) have proprietary inference rules and other pragmatic directives which would serve as motivation for the speaker's constructing the NL utterance in this sort of shape. But if the internal language works directly on forms such as (16), then we can apparently no longer assert that what we have in the language of thought (at LR) is a very simple categorial grammar. We have algebraic (combinatorial) or geometric (role-movement) complexity. The type system will serve as a well-formedness condition on representations. But the fact that arguments are saturated, only of type <e> or <t>, must have consequences at some level, if it is not trivial. If we allow what I have been suggesting here, we might as well have a GPSG-style grammar throughout, with the syntactic devices which have enabled us to limit lexical ambiguity being rather statements about possible relations between items in the lexicon.

We can retrieve our position if we allow the whole of the chain consisting of the predication chain and the related role chain to count as the generalized representation of the argument at t_k. If we consider (16) again,

16   [The salad]$_{1\ 2}$ [$\theta_{1\ 2}$ is [t_1 $_2$ ready [t_2 [PRO to eat e_2]]

we see that we have to untangle the contributions of [the salad] to the two arguments of *ready*: [the salad]$_1$ is part of the extended chain supplying the external role for the adjective, while [the salad]$_2$ is part of the generalized argument of the object in the propositional internal role for the adjective. If the argument types are given in the conceptual lexicon just in the simple forms (*i.e.* <e>, or <t>), then the axioms (meaning postulates) attached to the concepts will be stated just over these simple arguments. That is, we could suppose that any inferences drawn from (16) will be drawn by virtue of axioms concerning a type <t> argument to *ready*, and a general scheme relating to the retrieval of arguments from the structure of (16), rather than by virtue of a particular scheme concerning the type <e,t> argument that actually follows *ready* in (16). The NL c-selection option can be seen simply as a device for ensuring that an item (*the salad*, here) which occurs in both the external and the internal arguments of the LoT *ready* can be identified.

If we knew more about axioms in general, we might know whether the learnability problem would be reduced by their existence. I suggested for instance that for *easy*, some expectation of inferences commonly associated with the external argument or subject position might motivate the raising, and hence help in the acquisition of the c-selection for I″[O] (section 4.1.3). This seems to be in direct contradiction to what I have just suggested about the indifference of the axioms of an item to the surface positions of the heads of its arguments. However, we can introduce the effect we want, which is of a tendency rather than a truth condition, by allowing the elaborated configuration to generate pragmatic 'hypotheses'. So in (17) (i) but not (ii)

17 i   Mrs. Bloggs isn't easy for my children to please

    ii   It isn't easy for my children to please Mrs. Bloggs

the hypothesis that Mrs. Bloggs is causally responsible for this state of affairs will be generated (perhaps to be abandoned). This hypothesis, I envisage, will be triggered as part of the response to the 'grammatically specified entailment' (18):

18   [[$_{NP}$ X] [O_k [isn't easy for the children to please e_k]]

The Language of Thought

The idea is that focus on *Mrs. Bloggs* is recorded by the pair (17i) and (18). But this latter in turn might NOT be accessed if there is marked stress in the sentence (see Smith and Wilson 1979, 158–171.; Sperber and Wilson 1983 and 1986). Or perhaps more plausibly, it would fail to be reinforced if the focused constituent does not contain the stressed item, and so would tend to drop out. So if for instance *my* is stressed, the implication is rather that it is my children who are responsible for the problems.

It has been suggested by John Perry that when someone (say) wants to eat, they usually do not entertain a proposition of the form "I want to eat," but rather a desire relating to "eat," not explicitly including the "I".[12] If something like this is correct, there may be conceptual motivation for the c-selection option of V‴, allowing

19   Minerva [θ_{1+2} [wants [$_{V''}$ t_2 [to eat]]]]

This particular case would apparently demand that elaborated forms should be accessible to the axioms: how can we encode the suggestion just made except by reference to forms like (19)?[13] In this case, it is probable that the linguistic content of what appears after the propositional attitude verb is indeed processed in some special way—that is, not solely as if the argument of *want* is of type <t>. The same should be true of adjectives like *ready* with VP in

20   Minerva [θ_{1+2} [is ready [$_{V''}$ t_2 [to eat]]]]

If, as argued by Sperber and Wilson (1986), reports of propositional attitudes are to be taken as Interpretive Use, then an effect somewhat like mention, in addition to use, of the string after the relevant attitudinal would not be surprising, nor contrary to the limitations suggested for axioms in the ordinary non-intensional case. Again, without an attempt to spell out appropriate axioms and pragmatic processes in detail, these remarks represent hopes.

5.5   How are definitions interpreted and used?

5.5.1   Learning or identifying concepts

If a word is new, it does not follow that the concept is new. So although a definition may be put to use in constructing a new concept, as I have argued (1.5.4, 2.4.3), it may also be put to use simply in identifying a connection between a lexical item and an existing concept. This will perhaps be the norm in using a foreign language dictionary. But this process itself is not just an association, on account of the syntax of the two languages involved (*i.e.* those of definiendum and LoT). If the function is identification, rather than construction, it can be the case that the 'definition' consists entirely of encyclopedic information. This is how so-called ostensive definitions should normally be construed. Below, I am concerned only with the properly definitional uses of definitions—those where something new is constructed.

5.5.2 Dictionary definitions

Given such properties of NL and LoT as I have attempted to establish, the form and function of dictionary definitions is unsurprising. The oddities can be blamed more on the intrinsic limitations of the format, and on lexicographical problems, than on anything more interesting. (They did however provide evidence as to the relations between NL and LoT). The remaining uncertainty is as to the level of elimination of the defined term. On one story, we have elimination at an LF' level, followed by translation to LR and the derivation of UR as usual. On the other story, we take the definition to require the construction of a new LoT term to match the NL one, allowing translation of the defined term to proceed. Processing depending on the content of the definition is carried out at a later level over LoT representations.

There are good reasons for supposing that the second story is the correct one. First, elimination at LF' would be a procedure peculiar to the use of definitions. It would be using logical or encyclopedic knowledge to process NL strings WITHIN the syntactic levels. This should not be possible, because of the two languages involved. It is, of course, possible for a reader, say, faced with an unknown word in a sentence, deliberately to consider the surface string, and substitute a definition in place of the unknown term. My son used this procedure when he was small, and was indignant to find it frequently useless.[14] This is not what we normally do with a definition. Second, the requirement that the definiens is opaque to normal syntactic procedures (such as QR and negative scope fixing) is more naturally accounted for if there is just the single item at any time in the relevant NL syntactic representations. An alternative is possible, but again it requires the intrusion of pragmatic processes into the processing of linguistic levels (see Carston 1989 for discussion of this issue).

The adoption of the second story supports the idea that the LoT may come to have a vocabulary which is in part in one to one correspondence with the vocabulary of NL, for a particular speaker. Some of the translation from LF' to LR can be rather simple; and there is no question of 'decomposition of meaning' at this level. Just how simple the translation will be depends on what syntactic differences there are between LF' and LR. But it is not the case that there could ever be a total one-one correspondence, even leaving aside questions like the representation of variables and other phonologically null categories of NL. Between LR and UR, the items which are in part or in whole directives to pragmatic processing must be changed or eliminated, and (by assumption) a fully propositional form produced. In particular, items like *the* or *here* will require (in general) that reference is assigned, and the names of the referents are most probably not available in NL at all (see Carston 1988). LoT may not have names as such (*i.e.* within its "phonological" representations), but it must at least have procedural equivalents.

There were a few definitions which required special processing—those which I characterized somewhat vaguely as being couched in metalanguage ((6), (7) and (8) of 2.5). I suspect that it is in fact only possible to process these on a conscious level—that is, by taking the definition and the NL string as objects to be thought about.

If we adopt the 'meaning–meaning' approach, then it is natural to suppose that the definition itself is not used in a special way (for elimination by substitution), but in the ordinary way—that is, the biconditional is to be taken as a pair of meaning postulates or axioms, either of which may be used when it would be useful. In general, one will be useful in downward-entailing environments, and the other in upward-entailing environments. Suppose we have

21   $A \Leftrightarrow B \& C$

where the '&' and '$\Leftrightarrow$' are generalized to conjoin any type. Then in a positive (downward entailing) environment P, we will usefully (and validly) replace 'A' by 'B & C' and this in turn by 'B' (or 'C')—that is, we will exploit some inference rules which gives us just this when given as input 'P' and 'A $\Rightarrow$ B & C'.

The other half of the biconditional has potentially two uses. The first possible use is directly associated with the concept A. In a negative (upward entailing) environment, we can validly replace 'A' by 'B & C' —that is, we will exploit some inference rule which gives us just this when given as input 'P' and 'A $\Leftarrow$ B & C'. Given the notorious difficulty we have in adequate reasoning in negative environments, we must regard the existence of such an inference rule as doubtful. This is an empirical question. But it may be that it is not the lack of such an inference rule that causes problems, but what happens next in the inferential processing. We cannot, this time, proceed to replace 'B & C' by 'B' (or 'C'). If this is the problem, then maybe the biconditional IS what is stored at A, and maybe this DOES license (possibly as a consequence of where it is stored as the logical entry) simple substitution. Then another interpretation of this pair of processes would be that there is an 'A elimination' inference rule, since that is exactly what would happen. The issue is not entirely terminological; and in as much as it is not, the simplest solution on this evidence would be to assume the pair of processes.

The second potential use is less straightforward. Sperber and Wilson in the process of restricting the logic, ban '*and* introduction'. This leads to the suggestion that any proposition of the form 'B & C $\Rightarrow$ A' will be reformulated for use as 'B $\Rightarrow$ (C $\Rightarrow$ A)' and 'C $\Rightarrow$ (B $\Rightarrow$ A)'. This would suggest that the second half of the biconditional should be stored in these forms under the concepts B and C respectively. I have an unsupported suspicion that such a reorganization of information does not take place automatically. On the other hand, if it does not, there seem to be other problems. Suppose for a moment that B and C are in some sense primitive concepts corresponding to properties. How am I supposed to identify something as an instance of A, without identifying it first as an instance of B and then of C, using the reformulation above? Possibly there are processes whereby I can perceive this (say, using associative networks of some kind) without actually having to formulate it propositionally. One or other of these two sorts of ways of introducing A into my thoughts on the basis of the evidence of 'B' and 'C' must surely be valid; the

The Language of Thought 321

intuition that a definition enables me to use the new term and the new idea is extremely strong (and I have been assuming it throughout).

We know as teachers that 'learning a new concept' can be slow, even when adequate definitions are supplied; this suggests that there has to be a certain amount of reorganization of knowledge, and that at least not all of this is automatic. But it may be that the initial move IS automatic, if the learner can be persuaded to set up the new concept at all. The slowness might be in organizing its exploitation. So for instance, suppose we already have 'B $\Rightarrow$ (C $\Rightarrow$ D)'. If (improbably, but the argument could be amended) only one inferential step can be guaranteed in pragmatic processing, then we will not get from the new A to D reliably unless somehow laboriously tracing from A to D via B and C eventually induces the filing under A of '$A \Rightarrow D$'. This suggests that we cannot use intuitions about availability of efficient processing very directly; we need detailed hypotheses about inference rules, filing, and accessibility before we can determine whether there are any grounds here for assuming particular non-inferential (e.g. associative) ways of changing the state of knowledge organization.

5.5.3   Text definitions

Text definitions do not have the definiendum in isolation. In section 1.5, explicit definitions were distinguished from implicit ones. Text definitions look as if they will produce implicit definitions, so that the question of whether these must be converted via lambda abstraction to explicit ones was raised. For the text definitions in general, the conditional effects were obtained via a 'universal' instead of an 'existential' interpretation of the indefinite NPs of the definition. But given the Barwise and Cooper (1981) style of interpretation of generalized quantifiers, this is even more naturally seen as an inclusion relation between N' denotation and VP denotation, complete with lambdas. In our cases, (for example in 3.2.2), following Heim, we did not have overt quantification anyway, but just the expressions with variables resulting from QR and some version of OR. If we assume that this sort of structure is given by LF', then it will be preserved (to syntactic equivalence) at LR. At UR, we need to disambiguate. Should we bind with lambda or the generalized universal quantifier? The answer would seem to be the latter, since indefinites in NL do not ever get interpreted like WH-words—generalized lambda gives the wrong answer, and we would need to stipulate the set-inclusion. So whatever has to be done to make the definition usable must be done by the inference rules, rather than by the translation. If the inference rules are more economical WITH some sort of lambda abstraction, this is a general matter, nothing to do with definitions as such.

What is most striking about text definitions is the variety of linguistic and pragmatic structures and procedures which are exploited in their construction. Typical here is the deployment of anaphoric and quantificational devices which permit the expression of facts which would in standard logical notation require identical variables in structurally distant positions. It is also noteworthy that in definitions with *if* (or *when*), which are interpreted as conditional definitions, the *if* supplies the main implication of the definition, while the conditional part comes from the interpretation of an indefinite NP (3.3.1 (5), 3.3.2).

Text definitions are not uniform in even the outline of how they should be interpreted. Those with *call* must be taken to refer to a word or phrase of NL, the definiendum. This does not of course prevent their use as instructions to construct a new LoT item—though if this IS done, perhaps it is because such a process is inevitable. Definitions with *say* (3.2.2), on the other hand, could only be taken to be entirely couched within a uniform level of language—the definiendum was to be treated as used, not mentioned. This forces the construction of the LoT item to correspond to the definiendum.

In section 3.2.2, I suggested that the biconditional effect of a definition might be obtained simply as a by-product of the information's being stored in the 'logical entry' part of a concept. The idea is that this inherently has a 'bottom line' saying, in effect "and nothing else is an X," for some property X.[15] But this idea raises even more acutely the problem of how the information is to be put to use. This time I am not even going to speculate (here).

This particular strategy is available only for items having sets as denotations.[16] If we take just simple sets of entities here, we will find that a large proportion consist of just the sorts of things for which definitions seem least suitable: natural kind terms, qualities, and so on. There are probably special systems in operation in relation to these terms.

For a word like *red*, an elucidation of meaning is possibly to be construed as consisting entirely of encyclopedic information, whose function is to identify, not define, the relevant innate concept. I suppose that there is an innate structuring for color concepts, set up with the expectation of prototypes and a metric. For a color term like *puce*, a 'definition' could supply a prototype. A prototype gives a member of the set: let us suppose this is stated as a proposition within the logical entry. Then the 'bottom line' for color terms will read something like "and no color not sufficiently like one of the prototypes is ... puce," and so on.

In the case of natural kind terms, there does seem to be logical as opposed to merely encyclopedic information—that a cat is an animal, that a domestic pussy is a cat, for instance. But there is no expectation that a definition could be exhaustive. A simple way of avoiding contradiction here if there is necessarily a bottom line of the ordinary sort is to assume that under every natural kind concept there is entered a proposition amounting to "$x \in cat' \Rightarrow x \in cat'$," and so on. This will effectively render the bottom line unusable: it amounts to stipulating that the essence of cat-ness is primitive. I do not know how we identify items as natural kind terms, but I assume that this is what we do do, rather than having each one innately specified.

It should be noted that logical information which is conditional but not definitional will not cause problems. In particular, it is only the propositions giving (partial) membership of the set being defined that would interact with the bottom line: domestic pussies are cats, for instance. The proposition that cats are animals is independent of this.

There has been no direct or even indirect suggestion that definitions introduce inference rules. Certainly the suggestions above concerning the biconditional interpretation cannot simply be reformulated in inference rule format. It seems simpler to suppose that all information is in conditional rather than inference rule format, given that propositions anyway are held with varying degrees of certainty. But I have argued above and for the interpretation of conditional definitions that there are structures available such that filing a proposition in one place rather than another affects its interpretation. There is thus support for a clear 'encyclopedic' versus 'logical' filing, and for a number of distinct ready-made patterns which can be accessed for logical entries.[17]

It is possible that it would be more appropriate for the information of these patterns to be in inference rule format, so that my 'bottom line' is procedural rather than propositional. We might attempt to cast all innate LoT 'knowledge' in procedural form, and only learnable and forgettable LoT information in propositional form.

If logical entries are what drives inference, and if they are not in general formulated as inference rules, two things follow. One is that there is so far no reason to suppose that there is more than one inference rule (*modus ponens*, say, for '⇒'). The procedural patterns postulated might need more, and so might the metalanguage functions considered in earlier chapters, among other matters. The second is that there must be an adequate number of propositions containing '⇒' under any conceptual entry to ensure that the concept will enter into the inference chains it should, with the appropriate degree of processing cost. To offer an ordinary definition for an item is to ensure that there is at least a logical entry there. In the simplest sort of *genus et differentiae* definition, this merely points elsewhere; so what is the virtue of the new concept?

Half the answer is to do with natural language; NL is in need of economy of packaging, so it needs words for complex concepts; this in turn requires that there is a translation equivalent in LoT. Furthermore, as we have seen, packaging eases interpretation with respect to potential NL ambiguities. Is there an equivalent need in the language of thought? Intuitively, the answer is yes. There are limits on memory, space, and time in any processing, even if removing defined terms would not in principle limit what can be expressed. That means that I can get around to thinking things that I could not have thought without the words. But this is going to work only if there is a real saving in time or space; and this implies that the definiendum in some occurrence does not function just as its definiens would logically.[18] But if the logical entry consists solely (as it might initially) of the definiens, there seems little possibility of any economy—rather the reverse. Economy in a true 'filing' model can only derive from the additional filing of logical or encyclopedic material under the concept itself, information which would be slower to derive via the definiens.[19] But in a more abstract model, we can see a derived concept as reorganizing the inferential-effort metric across the space of accessible propositions. Perhaps we can set up a model where this is accomplished directly, *rather than by filing or re-filing information*. Even for simple *genus et differentiae* definitions, the possibilities seem worth exploring. More elaborately derived terms, such as *multiplication*, would probably give more leverage on the required properties of the inferential system as a whole. That was what I had hoped to explore: but it turned out that there were too many preliminaries.

5.6 Conclusions

> *Conclusions.* —In the preceding lines I have set several problems, and have given no solution. I do not regret this, for perhaps they will invite the reader to reflect on these delicate questions.
>
> However that may be, there are certain points which seem to be well established.
>
> Poincaré, Science and Hypothesis

Notes

1. I have asserted that there is an equivalent of a phonological realization for the language of thought (1.3.1, footnote 18), and a syntax, so the notion of an empty category is possibly not incoherent. However, if we want strict compositionality at UR, we certainly do not want categories whose content is determined by general principles applying to the local or larger context. This would entail that NP-trace and *wh*-trace were distinguished in UR, should such structures appear at all. We might want to eliminate empty categories at UR but not at LR.

2. There is a possibility that syntactically ill-formed representations in LoT might occur. Then there is also the possibility that the well-formedness conditions could act on these—to modify or filter out—in which case they would count as procedural knowledge.

3. A reasonably clear instance is *strike*. In *The ball struck me*, there is no reason to doubt the normal correspondence. But in [John$_k$ strikes us [t_k as suitable]] or [It struck him [that Mary was angry]], we seem to have what should be the external argument as a second internal one. Translation from LF' to LR can put it back where it belongs (not that this is the only solution). Note that if external arguments in NL must have canonic category (see 4.1.3), the SC structure could not have the proposition as external argument.

4. The possible operators mentioned or discussed are:

    i   nouns such as *king* (1.5.2), *sentence* (3.3.1);

    ii adjuncts to adjectives: adverbs (2.2.2), and the PP headed by *for* in *hinged for drawing up* (2.1);

    iii adjectives like *putative* (2.4.2) and *fake* (1.5.3);

    iv adjectives like *former* (2.1.3 and footnote 12);

    v   *and* (1.1.2)

    vi It was noted that semantically, items of categories C and D were unary or binary operators (4.2.1); and I is a natural candidate at least as a semantic operator

5. This in turn suggests that where the adjective is an operator, the structure is not as in (ii). Possibly the operator-adjectives like *former* are adjoined to N″ or E″. They may even form quasi-projections (like *and* in 1.1.2).

6. They should also bear some equivalent of coindexing.

7. At least, these should have no type corresponding to what is in the model. Whether we need another set of types for the language of processing directives, I do not know. But anyway, the items do not correspond to typed items at UR. For *the*, see 2.1.3 (26–28).

8. What I say here is as usual related only to the <e>,<t> system. My neglect of intensionality, operators, tense, locatives, and possibly other such things must be borne in mind. But I think the comments I make are applicable in a more complex system; and things are complicated enough as it is.

9. This was one of the questions I had thought this thesis might answer. As it has turned out, only preliminaries have materialized.

10. Note also the common meaning postulates permitted by the ergative analysis of verbs such as *lean* in its two uses (footnote 45 of chapter 2).

11. But in line with the suggestion for *attempt* (4.2.1), there will be an external role to be bound by a DET, as well as a PRO subject.

12. Lecture given to the Joint Session of the Aristotelian Society and the Mind Association, London, July 1986. See Perry 1986.

13. Within the framework I am assuming, that is, where lexical ambiguity is minimized and s-selection of arguments restricted.

14. For example, most definitions of simple adjectives, such as

　　perissodactyl　　having an odd number of toes　　　　　　　C20

will cause problems at surface (see 2.3.2).

15. Note that we cannot use this notion to rescue dictionary definitions of the kind

　　i　　*elm*　　a tree　　　　　　　　　　　　　　　　　　C20

We get quite the wrong interpretation if we take this to license "an elm is a tree and nothing else is a tree."

16. I have not investigated whether it could be extended to items with complements, where X' rather than X is of type <p>.

17. The patterns noted related just to type <e,t>, but it would be surprising if the notion did not extend to other types. We might then attempt to account for instance for recurring structures such as source–path–goal (Lakoff 1989), and ordering relations, or for the limits on possible determiner meanings. See also Chomsky 1990 in relation to lexical acquisition.

18. See also the arguments of Fodor *et al.* 1975, and Fodor *et al.* 1980.

19. Typically, such information will be derived from the totality of the definition rather from one of its parts. For example, under square, I might store its symmetries. These do not follow from any one or even necessarily from any two of four primitive properties we can use to define it.

Bibliography

Note: the dictionaries and mathematics text books used as sources of definitions are listed at the end of the bibliography, with their abbreviations. Other books from which examples of definitions are taken are marked with an asterisk in the list below.

Abney, S.E. 1987. The English noun phrase in its sentential aspect. Ph.D. dissertation, MIT.

Ades, A.E. and M.J. Steedman. 1982. On the order of words. *Linguistics and Philosophy* 4: 517–558.

Alston, W.P. 1968. Meaning and use. In *The theory of meaning*, edited by G.H.R. Parkinson. Oxford: Oxford University Press.

Authier, J-M.P. 1988. Null object constructions in Ki-Nande. *Natural Language and Linguistic Theory* 6: 19–37.

Baker, M., K. Johnson and I. Roberts. 1989. Passive arguments raised. *Linguistic Inquiry* 20: 219–251.

Barwise, J. and R. Cooper. 1981. Generalized quantifiers and natural language. *Linguistics and Philosophy* 4: 159–219.

Belletti, A. and L. Rizzi. 1988. Psych-verbs and θ-theory. *Natural Language and Linguistic Theory* 6: 291–352.

Bergmann, M. 1982. Cross-categorial semantics for conjoined noun-phrases. *Linguistics and Philosophy* 5: 399–401.

Bierwisch, M. and F. Kiefer. 1970. Remarks on definitions in natural language. In *Studies in syntax and semantics*, edited by F. Kiefer. Dordrecht: Reidel.

Blakemore, D. 1987. *Semantic constraints on relevance*. Oxford: Blackwell.

────── 1989. Denial and contrast: a relevance theoretic analysis of *BUT*. *Linguistics and Philosophy* 12: 15–37.

Boguraev, B. and T. Briscoe, eds. 1989. *Computational lexicography for natural language processing*. London: Longman.

Bošković, Z. 1994. D-structure, theta-criterion, and movement into theta-positions. *Linguistic Analysis* 24: 247–286.

Bresnan, J. 1982. Control and complementation. *Linguistic Inquiry* 13: 343–434.

Bridge, J. 1977. *Beginning model theory*. Oxford: Clarendon Press.

Brody, M. and M.R. Manzini. 1988. On implicit arguments. In Kempson, ed. 1988.

Burzio, L. 1986. *Italian syntax*. Dordrecht: Reidel.

Carnap, R. 1942. *Introduction to semantics*. Cambridge, Mass.: Harvard University Press.

——— 1958. *Introduction to symbolic logic and its applications*. New York: Dover.

Carruthers, P. 1996. *Language, thought, and consciousness; an essay in philosophical psychology*. Cambridge: Cambridge University Press.

Carston, R. 1988. Implicature, explicature, and truth-theoretic semantics. In Kempson, ed. 1988.

——— 1989. Modularity and linguistic ambiguity. *University College London Working Papers in Linguistics* 1: 340–351.

Chierchia, G. 1982. Nominalization and Montague grammar: a semantics without types for natural language. *Linguistics and Philosophy* 5: 303–354.

——— 1984. Topics in the syntax and semantics of infinitives and gerunds. Ph.D. dissertation, University of Massachusetts.

Chomsky, N. 1981. *Lectures on government and binding*. Dordrecht: Foris.

——— 1982. *Some concepts and consequences of the theory of government and binding*. Cambridge, Mass.: MIT Press.

——— 1986a. *Knowledge of language: its nature, origin, and use*. New York: Praeger.

——— 1986b. *Barriers*. Cambridge, Mass.: MIT Press.

——— 1987. Reply. *Mind and Language* 2: 178–197.

——— 1990. Language and mind. In *Ways of communicating: The Darwin College lectures*, edited by D.H. Mellor. Cambridge: Cambridge University Press.

——— 1991. Some notes on economy of derivation and representation. In *Principles and parameters of comparative grammar*, edited by R. Freidin. Cambridge, Mass.: MIT Press.

——— 1995. *The minimalist program*. Cambridge, Mass.: MIT Press.

Chomsky, N. and H. Lasnik. 1993. The theory of principles and parameters. In *Syntax: an international handbook of contemporary research*, edited by J. Jacobs, A. von Stechow, W. Sternefeld, and T. Vennemann. Berlin: de Gruyter.

Cinque, G. 1990. Ergative adjectives and the lexicalist hypothesis. *Natural Language and Linguistic Theory* 8: 1–39.

Clark, H.H. and E.V. Clark. 1977. *Psychology and language*. New York: Harcourt, Brace, Jovanovich.

Cole, P. 1987. Null objects in universal grammar. *Linguistic Inquiry* 18: 597–612.

Cormack, A. 1984a. VP Anaphora, variables, and scope. In *Varieties of formal semantics*, edited by F. Landman and F. Veltman. Dordrecht: Foris.

——— 1984b. Plural indefinites as variables. University College London. Photocopy.

——— 1985. *Inference and meaning: mostly about 'most'*. Paper read at the September meeting of the Linguistics Association of Great Britain.

——— 1986a. *Concepts and the language of thought*. Paper read at the April meeting of the Linguistics Association of Great Britain.

——— 1986b. *Questions about arguments*. Paper read at the September meeting of the Linguistics Association of Great Britain.

——— 1987. *Quantification structure in noun phrases*. Paper read at the September meeting of the Linguistics Association of Great Britain.

——— 1995. The semantics of Case. *UCL Working Papers in Linguistics 7*: 234–276, Phonetics and Linguistics, University College London.

——— forthcoming. Without Specifiers. In *Specifiers: Minimalist approaches*, edited by D. Adger, S. Pintzuk, B. Plunkett, and G. Tsoulas. Oxford: Oxford University Press.

Cormack, A. and R. Breheny. 1994. Projections for functional categories. *UCL Working Papers in Linguistics 6*: 35–61, Phonetics and Linguistics, University College London.

Cormack, A. and N. Smith. 1994. Serial verbs. *UCL Working Papers in Linguistics 6*: 63–88, Phonetics and Linguistics, University College London.

Cormack, A. and R.M. Kempson. 1991. On specificity. In *Essential readings in modern semantics*, edited by J. Garfield and M. Kitely. New York: Paragon House.

Cromer, R.F. 1987. Word knowledge acquisition in retarded children: a longitudinal study of a complex linguistic structure. *Journal of Speech and Hearing Disorders* 52: 324–334.

Davidson, D. 1967. Truth and meaning. *Synthese* 17: 304–323.

Dowty, D.R. 1987. Quantification and the lexicon. In *The scope of lexical rules*, edited by M. Moortgat *et al*. Dordrecht: Foris.

——— 1988. Type raising, functional composition, and non-constituent conjunction. In Oehrle *et al*., eds. 1988.

——— 1991. Thematic proto-roles and argument selection. *Language* 67: 547–619.

Dowty, D.R., R.E. Wall, and S. Peters. 1981. *Introduction to Montague semantics*. Dordrecht: Reidel.

Emonds, J.E. 1976. *A transformational approach to English syntax: root, structure-preserving and local transformations*. New York: Academic Press.

Enç, M. 1986. Towards a referential analysis of temporal expressions. *Linguistics and Philosophy* 9: 405–426.

Farkas, D. 1988. On obligatory control. *Linguistics and Philosophy* 11: 27–58.

Fine, K. 1985. *Reasoning with arbitrary objects*. Oxford: Blackwell.

Fillmore, C.J. 1968. The case for case. In *Universals in linguistic theory*, edited by E. Bach and R.T. Harms. London: Holt, Rinehart and Winston.

Fodor, J.A. 1975. *The language of thought*. Cambridge, Mass.: Harvard University Press.

Fodor J.A. and J.D. Fodor. 1980. Functional structure, quantifiers, and meaning postulates. *Linguistic Inquiry* 11: 759–770.

Fodor, J.A., M. Garrett, E. Walker, and C. Parkes. 1980. Against definitions. *Cognition* 8: 263–367.

Fodor, J.D., J.A. Fodor and M.F. Garrett. 1975. The psychological unreality of semantic representations. *Linguistic Inquiry* 6: 515–531.

Foldvik, S. 1989. Easy-adjectives, tough-movement. *Trondheim Working Papers in Linguistics* 8: 1–96.

Gazdar, G. 1980. A cross-categorial semantics for coordination. *Linguistics and Philosophy* 3: 407–409.

Gazdar, G., E. Klein, G.K. Pullum and I.A. Sag. 1985. *Generalized phrase structure grammar*. Oxford: Blackwell.

Geach, P. 1962. *Reference and generality*. Ithaca, N.Y.: Cornell University Press.

Giorgi, A. 1991. Prepositional phrases, binding, and theta marking. In *Long distance anaphora*, edited by J. Koster and E. Reuland. Cambridge: Cambridge University Press.

Grimshaw, J. 1979. Complement selection and the lexicon. *Linguistic Inquiry* 10: 279–326.

——— 1990. *Argument structure*. Cambridge, Mass.: MIT Press.

Guéron, J. 1981. Logical operators, complete constituents, and extraction transformations. In May and Koster, eds. 1981.

Haack, S. 1978. *Philosophy of logics*. Cambridge: Cambridge University Press.

Haïk, I. 1985. The syntax of operators. Ph.D. dissertation, MIT.

Heim, I.R. 1982. The semantics of definite and indefinite noun phrases. Ph.D. dissertation, University of Massachusetts.

Heim, I. and A. Kratzer. 1998. *Semantics in generative grammar*. Oxford: Blackwell.

Heny, F. and B. Richards, eds. 1983. *Linguistic categories: Auxiliaries and related puzzles*. Dordrecht: Reidel.

Higginbotham, J. 1985. On semantics. *Linguistic Inquiry* 16: 547–593.

——— 1987. Indefiniteness and predication. In Reuland and ter Meulen, eds. 1987.

——— 1989. Elucidations of meaning. *Linguistics and Philosophy* 12: 465–517.

* Hodges, W. 1977. *Logic*. Harmondsworth, England: Penguin.

Hornstein, N. 1996. On control. University of Maryland, College Park. Photocopy.

Horrocks, G. 1987. *Generative grammar*. London: Longman.

Ingham, R. 1989. Verb subcategorization in children's language. Ph.D. thesis, University of Reading.

Jackendoff, R.S. 1972. *Semantic interpretation in generative grammar*. Cambridge, Mass.: MIT Press.

——— 1990. *Semantic structures*. Cambridge, Mass.: MIT Press.

——— 1992. *Languages of the mind: Essays on mental representation*. Cambridge, Mass.: MIT Press.

Jacobson, P. 1990. Raising as function composition. *Linguistics and Philosophy* 13: 423–476.

Kamp, H. 1981. A theory of truth and semantic representation. In *Formal methods in the study of language*, Part 1, edited by J. Groenendijk et al. Mathematisch Centrum Amsterdam.

Kayne, R. 1981. Unambiguous paths. In May and Koster 1981.

Keenan, E.L. and L.M. Faltz. 1985. *Boolean semantics for natural language*. Dordrecht: Reidel.

Kempson, R.M. 1986. Definite NPs and context-dependence: a unified theory of anaphora. In *Reasoning and discourse processes*, edited by T. Myers, K. Brown and B. McGonigle. New York: Academic Press.

——— 1988, ed. *Mental representations*. Cambridge: Cambridge University Press.

Koopman, H. and D. Sportiche. 1985. θ-theory and extraction. *GLOW Newsletter* 14: 57–58.

Ladusaw, W.A. 1980. *Polarity sensitivity as inherent scope relations*. New York: Garland.

Lakoff, G. 1989. Some empirical results about the nature of concepts. *Mind and Language* 4: 103–129.

Larson, R.K. 1985. On the syntax of disjunction scope. *Natural Language and Linguistic Theory* 3: 217–264.

Larson, R. and G. Segal. 1995. *Knowledge of meaning*. Cambridge, Mass.: MIT Press.

* Leech, G.N. 1969. *Towards a semantic description of English*. London: Longman.

Levin, B. 1993. *English verb classes and alternations*. Chicago, Ill.: University of Chicago Press.

Lewis, D 1975. Adverbs of quantification. In *Formal semantics of natural language*, edited by E.L. Keenan. Cambridge: Cambridge University Press.

* Lyons, J. 1968. *Introduction to theoretical linguistics*. Cambridge: Cambridge University Press.

McCawley, J.D. 1981. *Everything that linguists have always wanted to know about logic—but were ashamed to ask*. Oxford: Blackwell.

Maling, J. 1983. Transitive adjectives: a case of categorial reanalysis. In *Linguistic categories: auxiliaries and related puzzles*, edited by F. Heny and B. Richards. Dordrecht: Reidel.

Manzini, R.M. 1989. Categories and acquisition in the parameters perspective. *University College London Working Papers in Linguistics* 1: 181–191.

Manzini, M.R. and A. Roussou. 1997. A minimalist theory of A-movement and control. University College London. Photocopy.

May, R. 1985. *Logical form: Its structure and derivation*. Cambridge, Mass.: MIT Press.

May, R. and J. Koster, eds. 1981. *Levels of syntactic representation*. Dordrecht: Foris.

Montague, R. 1974a. The proper treatment of quantification in ordinary English. In Thomason, ed. 1974.

——— 1974b. English as a formal language. In Thomason, ed. 1974.

Oehrle, R.T., E. Bach and D. Wheeler, eds. 1988. *Categorial grammars and natural language structures*. Dordrecht: Reidel.

Partee, B. H. 1986. Noun phrase interpretation and type-shifting principles. In *Studies in discourse representation theory and the theory of generalized quantifiers*, edited by J.Groenendijk, D.de Jongh, and M.Stokhof. Dordrecht: Foris.

Partee, B. and M.Rooth. 1983. Generalized conjunction and type ambiguity. In *Meaning, use and interpretation of language*, edited by R.Bäuerle, C.Schwarze and A.von Stechow. Berlin: de Gruyter.

Perry, J. 1986. Thought without representation. *The Aristotelian Society* Supplementary volume LX: 137–151.

* Poincaré, H. n.d. *Science and method*. New York: Dover.
* ——— 1952. *Science and hypothesis*. New York: Dover.
* ——— 1958. *The value of science*. New York: Dover.

Postal, P. 1974. *On raising*. Cambridge, Mass.: MIT Press.

Postal, P.M. and G.K.Pullum. 1988. Expletive noun phrases in subcategorized positions. *Linguistic Inquiry* 19: 635–670.

Pustejovsky, J. 1995. *The generative lexicon*. Cambridge, Mass.: MIT Press.

Radford, A. 1981. *Transformational syntax*. Cambridge: Cambridge University Press.

——— 1988. *Transformational grammar*. Cambridge: Cambridge University Press.

Rappaport, G.C. 1987. Syntactic binding into adjuncts in Russian. *Linguistics and Philosophy* 10: 475–501.

Reinhart, T. 1976. The syntactic domain of anaphora. Ph.D. dissertation, MIT.

——— 1983. *Anaphora and semantic interpretation*. London: Croom Helm.

——— 1987. Specifier and operator binding. In Reuland and ter Meulen, eds. 1987.

Reuland, E.J. and A.ter Meulen, eds. 1987. *The representation of indefiniteness*. Cambridge, Mass.: MIT Press.

Robinson, R. 1954. *Definition*. Oxford: Oxford University Press.

Roeper, T. 1987. Implicit arguments and the head-complement relation. *Linguistic Inquiry* 18: 267–310.

Rothstein, S. 1984. On the conceptual link between clauses I and II of the extended projection principle. *Proceedings of the Tenth Annual Meeting of the Berkeley Linguistics Society*: 266–273.

——— 1989. Degree phrases. Bar-Ilan University. Photocopy.

——— 1991. Heads, projections and category determination. In *Views on phrase structure*, edited by K.Leffel and D.Bouchard. Dordrecht: Kluwer Academic Publishers.

Rumelhart, D.E., J.L. McClelland and the PDP research group. 1986. *Parallel distributed processing.* 2 vols. Cambridge, Mass.: MIT Press.

Russell, B. 1903. *The principles of mathematics.* London: Allen and Unwin.

Sag, I.A, G. Gazdar, T. Wasow and S. Weisler. 1985. Coordination and how to distinguish categories. *Natural Language and Linguistic Theory* 3: 117–171.

Schiffer, S. 1987. *Remnants of meaning.* Cambridge, Mass.: MIT Press.

Smith, N.V. 1975. On generics. *Transactions of the Philological Society*: 27–48.

———— 1983. Speculative linguistics: An inaugural lecture delivered at University College London. London: University College London.

———— 1989. Can pragmatics fix parameters? in *University College London Working Papers in Linguistics* 1: 169–179.

* Smith, N. and D. Wilson. 1979. *Modern linguistics.* Harmondsworth, Middlesex: Penguin.

Sperber, D. and D. Wilson. 1983. The effects of linguistic form on pragmatic interpretation. University College London. Photocopy.

———— 1986. *Relevance: communication and cognition.* Oxford: Blackwell.

Sportiche, D. 1988. A theory of floating quantifiers. *Linguistic Inquiry* 19: 425–449.

Steedman, M. 1988. Combinators and grammars. In Oehrle *et al.* 1988.

Stowell, T. 1991. Alignment of arguments in adjective phrases. In *Syntax and Semantics Volume 25*, edited by S. Rothstein. New York: Academic Press.

Suppes, P. 1957. *Introduction to logic.* New York: von Nostrand.

Takami, K. 1988. The syntax of *if*-clauses: three types of *if*-clauses and X'-theory. *Lingua* 74: 263–281.

Tarski, A. 1931. *Logic, semantics, metamathematics.* Oxford: Oxford University Press.

Thomason, R.H. 1974. ed. *Formal philosophy: Selected papers of Richard Montague.* New Haven, Conn.: Yale University Press.

Vikner, S. 1988. Modals in Danish and event expressions. *Working Papers in Scandinavian Syntax* 39: 1–33.

Wilder, C. 1989. *Predication, null operator infinitives and for-deletion.* University College London. Photocopy.

Williams, E. 1980. Predication. *Linguistic Inquiry* 11: 203–238.

———— 1986. A reassignment of the functions of LF. *Linguistic Inquiry* 17: 265–299.

——— 1987. NP trace in theta theory. *Linguistics and Philosophy* 10: 433–477.
——— 1994. *Thematic structure in syntax.* Cambridge, Mass.: MIT Press.
Zwarts, J. and H. Verkuyl. 1994. An algebra of conceptual structure: an investigation into Jackendoff's conceptual semantics. *Linguistics and Philosophy* 17: 1–28.

Dictionaries

C20   *Chambers's twentieth century dictionary.* Ed. W. Geddie. 1959. Edinburgh: Chambers.

Chambers's twentieth century dictionary. Ed. W. Geddie. 1983. Edinburgh: Chambers.

OED   *Oxford English dictionary.* 1971, compact edition. Oxford: Oxford University Press.

SOED   *Shorter Oxford English dictionary.* Ed. C. T. Onions. 1970, third edition. Oxford: Oxford University Press.

LOD   *Little Oxford dictionary of current English.* Compiled by G. Ostler. 1941. Oxford: Oxford University Press.

LDEL   *Longman dictionary of the English language.* 1984. London: Longman.

A lexicon. Abridged from Liddell and Scott's *Greek-English lexicon.* 1963. Oxford: Oxford University Press.

Mathematics texts

A   *School mathematics project.* Book A metric. 1970. Cambridge: Cambridge University Press.

SMP   *School mathematics project.* Book 1 metric. 1971. Cambridge: Cambridge University Press.

MME   *Midlands mathematical experiment.* Volume 1, Part A. 1967. London: Harrap.

Sh   *Learning mathematics.* Book 1. R. S. Heritage, 1966. Harmondsworth, Middlesex: Penguin.

Sk   *Understanding mathematics.* Book 1, second edition. R. R. Skemp, 1970. London: University of London Press.

Index

a, 187. *See also* article
abbreviatory conveniences, 57
able, 101, 102, 103, 115, 236, 240, 259–60, 261, 313
Abney, 16, 292
absurd, 286, 297
accessibility, 312, 321, 324
A-chain, 96, 98, 99
acquisition, 58, 79
act, 162
addle, 170, 222
Ades, 55, 157
adicity, 313
　of derived forms, 314
adjective, 231–35, 236–61
　and tense, 296
　category of definiens, 109
　definition of, 83, 94, 192
　elimination from attributive position, 114
　non-intersective, 83, 134
　operator, 326
　predicative use, 170
　propositional attitude, 247
　small clause complement of, 261
　target, 169–74
adjunct, 26, 55, 83, 248, 307
　generalized representation of, 117
　linear ordering, 118
　to adjective, 91, 326
　to noun, 86, 109
　to VP, 124
　vs. head, 310

adjunction, 10, 14, 19, 156, 198, 200, 201, 214, 228, 274, 289, 311
　base-generated, 214
　by movement, 214
　interpretation of, as generalized conjunction, 92, 93, 111, 257
　left and right, 114
　licensing, 93
　successive, 86
adverbs
　modifying adjectives, 95
agent, 103, 295
airplane, 39, 43
Alston, 81
ambiguity, 30, 74, 150, 152, 161, 183, 184, 185, 187, 188, 204, 234, 253, 255, 308, 315, 324, 327
analyticity, 36, 42
anaphor, 21, 206, 281–87
anaphora, 163, 189, 197, 210, 212, 213, 218, 314, 322. *See* ellipsis: VP. *See also* dependency
　device for, 204
　discourse, 218
　in definition, 155, 174
and, 198, 320, 326
angry, 88, 124, 276
antecedent, 189, 204, 308
antinomy, 81
any, 93, 168

339

AP
  distribution, 113
  modifier generated to right of NP, 159
apple, 111
application, 55, 131, 266
  function–argument, 48, 118
apt, 101, 102, 103, 115, 149, 150, 236, 239, 245, 277, 279, 295
apt_1, 239, 240, 242, 245, 260
apt_2, 236, 240, 242, 260
arbitrary object, 184, 185
argument, 5, 10, 11, 13, 14, 17, 18, 23–26, 48, 54, 86, 209. *See also* subcategorization
  amalgamated, 149
  and complement, 10
  external, 24, 55, 83
    canonic category, 261
    two, 327
  extra in LoT, 310
  generalized, 303, 316
  generalized representation of, 306, 315
  identification of, 305
  implicit, 27, 28, 204, 211, 229, 251, 313
  internal, 23, 83
  missing, 153
  phonologically null, 295
  propositional, 29, 236–61
  saturated, 235
  set-argument, 149
  type, saturated, 313
  unordered set of, 141
argument structure, 231–35
  conceptual, 235

article, 86, 108, 191, 210, 229
  definite, 108, 151
  heading noun definition, 93
  modifier not binder, 93
as, 147
assignment function, 46, 57
association, 31
associative network, 320, 321
attempt, 327
Authier, 299
auxiliary, as operator, 123
axiom, 34, 39, 56, 57, 58, 74–76, 182, 316, 317, 319
axiomatic logic, 34

backwoods, 85
bacon, 85
Baker, 289
bar notation, 78
bare plural, 92, 107
bare singular, 92
barrier, 241
Barwise, 52, 158, 321
be, 106, 121, 123, 167, 173, 182, 186, 269, 272, 282, 274–90
  ambiguous, 192
  auxiliary, 160
  equative, 160, 223, 298
  identity, 183
  interpretations of sentences with, 184
  passive, 133
  predicational, 183, 307
believe, 147, 150, 233
Belletti, 286, 298
Bergman, 79

biconditional, 196, 203, 319, 320, 322, 323. *See* implication, two-way
  generalized, 319
Bierwisch, viii
Bimbo, 161
binder, 18, 53
  generalized, 53
binding, 20
  by lambda operator, 51
  by quantifier, 51
  by quantifier of pronoun, 217
  unselective, 206, 207, 212, 218, 221
  unselective, 208
  vertical, 97, 98
binding theory, 18, 20–22, 99
binocular, 108
binomial equation, 185
bisector, 191
Boguraev, ix
bogus, 82
Bošcović ix
bottom line, 211, 322, 323
  procedural, 324
bound variable pronoun. *See* pronoun
bounding theory, 20–22
brackets, 130
brain, 100
branching
  binary, 48, 131
  multiple, 86
Breheny, ix
Bresnan, 252, 288
Bridge, 79
bridging cross reference, 120
Briscoe, ix
Brody, 158, 229

Burzio, 111, 121, 161, 273, 286, 298, 299, 300

calculus, 38
  internal, 38
call, 166, 167, 173, 174–80, 181, 191, 302, 304, 322
canine, 112
canonic correspondence, 131, 232, 233, 291, 295
canonic form, 310, 315
  for proposition, 306
canonic structural realization, 28, 122, 313
Carnap, 34, 39, 57, 63, 64, 81
Carruthers, viii
Carston, 319
Cartesian, 169–71
Case, 7, 22–23, 99, 134, 144, 148, 233, 267–69, 273, 287, 298, 311
  assigned to clause, 271, 297
  inherent, 242, 250
  optional, 249
  theory of, 77
  weak, for PRO, 242, 244
Case-marking, 83, 298
  of VP, 298
  optionality, 250
cat, 202, 216, 323
catchword, 130, 169
categorial grammar, 47, 55, 78, 97, 98, 131, 315
category, 84
  A/B, 47
  at LF or LR, 130
  defective, 200, 215
  in NL and LoT, 209

category (cont'd)
  label in LoT, 83, 311
  minor, ix, 14
  of external argument, 261
  operator, 235
causal responsibility. *See* subject
c-command, 19, 189, 197
certain, 238, 243, 245, 295, 296, 314
  attributive, 205
certain₁, 236, 240, 244, 245, 260
certain₂, 236, 245, 260
ceteris paribus clause, 223
chain, 7, 18, 24, 88, 96, 106, 116, 154, 158, 274–90, 295, 302, 305, 310, 316
  identification, 312
  logic for, 77
  semantics, 297
  type <t>, 303
chair leg, 111
Chaucer, 215
Chierchia, 308, 309
child learner, 258, 292
Chomsky, vii, viii, ix, 4, 5, 6, 7, 8, 9, 10, 15, 16, 17, 18, 19, 20, 21, 22, 23, 24, 25, 26, 27, 28, 29, 55, 77, 79, 86, 88, 89, 98, 100, 105, 111, 122, 152, 153, 157, 158, 161, 199, 232, 233, 245, 249, 250, 253, 265, 267, 268, 269, 270, 271, 273, 276, 278, 293, 295, 305, 306, 307, 327
Cinque, ix
circularity, 58
citation. *See* mention
citation form, 161

Clark, E.V., 315
Clark, H.H., 315
clausal complement, 236–61
clause
  adjunct, within VP, 198
  and Case, 23
  category of, 123
  null, 250
  purpose, 91, 258
  type for, 303
coindexing, ix, 18, 97, 218, 269–71, 274–90, 327
Cole, 153, 158, 229
collocation, 112, 171, 178, 222
combinator, ix, 55, 297, 315
combinatorial grammar, 55, 98, 265
combinatorial operations, 39, 302
comparative, 296
comparison class, 138, 161, 308, 310
complement. *See* argument, *and* subcategorization
complementizer, 78, 244
  doubly filled COMP filter, 244
completeness, 45
complexity, 315
composition, 101, 129, 245
  process, 291
  rules for, 118, 183
composition of functions, ix, 56, 97, 98, 266
  generalized, 297
compositional assignment of θ-role. *See* θ-role
compositional semantics. *See* semantics
compositionality, 5, 47, 48, 89, 127, 172, 178, 180, 189, 232, 304, 326

Index

of metalanguage, 71, 72
of object language, 72
with respect to inference rules, 72
comprehension, 28
computation, 37, 42
concept, 4, 30, 39, 209, 239, 305, 307, 316, 320. *See also* logical entry, lexical entry
  accessibility, 312
  adicity, 313–17
  and accessiblity, 324
  blank, 43
  combinatorial operations on, 39
  complex, 42, 144, 324
  formation, 58
  innate, 323
  internal structure, 43
  learning of, 41
  new, 43, 144, 180, 317, 321, 324
  node for filing, 193, 194
  primitive, 39, 42, 43, 320, 323
  selection, 253, 258, 259
  storage, 322
conceptual entry, 36
conceptual lexicon, 35
conditional, 195–221, 225, 228
  counterfactual, 45
  question, 227
conditional definition. *See* definition
conjunction, 110, 112, 118, 158, 289, 311
  covert, ix
  generalized, 53, 78, 92, 319
  interpretation of adjunction as, 92
  of active and passive, 282
  of constituents, 50
  of NP and CP, 297
connectionism, 37

connective, 221, 228
  propositional, 188
consider, 267, 272
constituent, 84, 86, 203
constituent negation, 126, 128, 129
constraint satisfaction, 78
constraints
  on s-selection and c-selection, 104
construal, 30
constructivity, 232, 268, 269, 297
context, 155
  negative, 179
  null, 185
context construction, 306
contextual effects, 30, 315
contextual implication, 32, 33
control, ix, 20, 21, 293
convention, 192, 193
convex, 163
Cooper, 52, 158, 321
coordination, 12. *See also* conjunction
copula, 106, 113
Cormack, ix, 55, 77, 80, 93, 118, 161, 162, 185, 186, 190, 223, 224, 225, 302
cornflakes, 158
correspondence
  c-selection and s-selection, 313
  NL and LoT, 308
counterfactual conditional, 45
CP. *See* C″
creativity, 66
crystalline, 112
c-selection, 28, 102, 145, 217, 233, 297, 309
  and s-selection, 103, 313
  conceptual motivation, 317

c-selection (cont'd)
 of VP, 102
 positive evidence for, 239
CSR. *See* canonic structural
 realization
cubical, 112
Curried term, 78

dainty, 100, 115, 132
dark, 3, 94, 107, 114, 125, 126, 127, 129
Davidson, 40
deaf, 94, 115, 116
debateable, 104
decadent, 94, 105, 122
decanal, 94, 107
decent, 94, 115
deceptive, 100, 101
decided, 49, 94, 106, 136
decisive, 94, 106
decomposition, 42, 180, 319
deductive rules, 32
defaults, 27
defective category, 200, 215
defective projection, 14
definiendum, viii, 58, 83, 164, 167, 189, 195, 321, 322, 324
 in dictionary, phrasal, 169
definiens, 58, 83, 85, 164, 189, 195, 324
 coherent LF of, 96
 opacity, 318
 unknown words in, 75
definites, 162
definition, 195, 282, 317–25
 'in use', 40, 60
 "and nothing else" clause, 192, 195, 225, 322, 327
 and axiom, 74
 and inference rule, 74, 323
 by abstraction, 63
 by listing, 63, 192, 225
 complex, 164, 174, 195–221
 conditional, 59, 62, 63, 167, 171, 180, 191, 192, 193, 194, 196, 210, 220, 221, 224, 305, 321, 322, 323
 conventional format in texts, 163
 dictionary, 64, 82–155, 176
 eliminative, 188
 exhaustive, 323
 explicit, 44, 60, 64, 180, 188
 formal, 58, 164, 174, 181, 213
 formal interpretation of, 56–76, 57
 function of, 75, 83, 307, 318, 321
 generalization of, 194
 identification of, 165, 168, 180
 idiosyncratic, 166
 implicit, 44, 155, 164, 180, 192, 193, 211, 321
 improper, 57
 in language of thought, 39
 interpretation as, 192
 interpretation of, 322
 introductory, 163, 181, 196, 213
 meaning–meaning, 130, 180, 192, 209, 319
 metalinguistic comment in, 93
 naive idea of, 3
 object-language statement, 58
 of adjective, 83, 94
 of noun, 83, 85–94
 of transitive verb, 138
 of true sentence, 82
 ostensive, 64, 318
 phoric, 164, 175, 221

problem, 151–55
proper, viii, 60, 113, 176, 222
recursive, 63, 70, 171
reflexive in, 283
roundabout, 112
simple, 174–95
text, viii, 321–25
translation into language of thought, 66
usability, 322
utilization of, 176
well-formed. *See* proper.
word–meaning, 114, 120, 130, 192, 209
word–word, 114, 130
degenerate case, 223
degree phrase, 101, 137–38
denial, 127
denotation, 46, 48, 92, 322
denotation operator | |, 48, 80
denotes, 67, 69
dependency, 18
  anaphoric, 190, 197, 207, 218, 221
descendant, 203
desire, 317
destruction, 65, 151, 153, 295, 313, 314
  optionally passive, 153
  type for, 162
determiner, 52, 78, 92, 93, 108, 109, 197, 203, 262–65
  binding two variables, 190
  meaning, 327
  stray, 154
determiner-phrase. *See* DP
devour, 295
dictionary, 82–155, 172, 222
  argument structure in entry, 144–50
  maker, 144
  use, 155
dictionaryese, 142
difficult, 308
disambiguation, 33, 321
disjoint, 218
disput, 104
disputable, 100
disunite, 149
do, dummy, 147
dog, 67
dominance, 228
domination, 19
donkey, 18, 52, 189, 191, 205, 212, 224, 225, 304
downward entailing context, 179, 223, 319
Dowty, ix, 80, 162, 307
DP, 297, 298. *See* NP
DP hypothesis, 12, 16, 78, 111
dramatist, 85
drawbridge, 85
D-structure, 6–10, 87, 88, 90, 114, 116, 124, 129, 158, 182, 232, 297, 314
dude, 85
dummy variable. *See* variable

e, 246. *See* empty category
eager, 147, 148, 236, 238, 242, 245, 248, 260
easy, 236, 240, 241, 246–60, 247, 248, 249, 255, 258, 259, 260, 277, 278, 280, 292, 294, 299, 314, 316
eat, 119, 120, 295

echo-questions, 77
ECM, 28, 142, 250, 261, 286
economy, 324
  of packaging in NL, 324
ECP, 20–22, 143, 144, 159, 197, 306
  in LoT, 305
-*ed* phrase, 92, 105–6, 157
effective, 84
effort, 32, 78
egg, 84, 140
egret, 154
eliminability, 58, 60, 62, 63, 83, 113, 114, 179, 189, 241
elimination, 34, 83, 99, 135, 143, 152, 154, 164, 176, 179, 222, 318
  at D-structure, 114
  at LF, 117, 136
  from canonic predicate position, 121–25
  of noun and adjective, 113
  word–word elimination, 130
elimination rule, 34, 320
ellipsis, 27, 195, 252, 308
elm, 327
Emonds, 16
empty category, 211, 238, 239, 243, 274–90, 302
  designated, 252
  determination of content, 326
  in LoT, 302, 326
  inaudibility of, 311
  new, 83
  principle. *See* ECP
empty object. *See* object gap
empty operator, 27, 78, 81, 88, 97, 100, 118, 132, 134, 243, 246–60, 255, 278, 299, 302
  and lambda operator, 53
  feature, 298
  for external theta-role, 133
  in 'deviant relative clause', 254
  in AP, 96
  rhetorical purpose, 247
  role transmitter, 91
encyclopedic entry. *See* lexicon
encyclopedic information, 36, 113, 120, 155, 318, 323
  use in syntax, 318
Enç, 158, 296
English, 66, 209, 295, 307, 311
English', 66, 67, 68, 69, 71, 73, 82
entail, 147, 148
entailment
  grammatically specified, 316
entailment. *See* downward, upward
entity, 28, 233
  type <e>, 49
EPP, 25, 156, 313
EQU, 188, 189, 190, 191, 192, 195, 203, 223
equality, 188
equilateral, 163, 164, 177, 179, 182, 194, 195
equivalence, 188. *See* biconditional logical connective, 178
ergativity, 327
event, 191, 265
event variable, 202
EVERY, 187, 188, 190, 191, 196, 203, 210, 221, 262, 265
evidence
  positive, for c-selection, 239
Exceptional Case Marking. *See* ECM
exclamative, 77, 298
exclusion, 20

EXIST, 187, 195
existential, 185. *See* indefinite, *and* quantification
explanation, 37, 110
expletive, 21, 77, 87, 101, 147, 271–74
   feature, 297
   it, 268, 271–74, 286, 298, 312
   there, 269–71
explicature, 30, 31, 32, 78
explicitness, 33
expressive power, 52, 53, 75
extended projection principle. *See* EPP
external θ-role. *See* θ-role
external argument. *See* argument
external world. *See* world
extraposition, 217

F, 177, 222, 304
fact, 314
factor, 155
fail, 265
fake, 73, 304
Faltz, 47, 79, 80, 160
Farkas, 253, 288
feature, 13, 14, 17, 29, 234, 302
   [+DP], 268
   [+O], 278
   [+WH], 244, 246
   checking, 299, 300
   lexical item as, 17
   passing, 159
   realised on complement, 239
feline, 112
fight, 295
filing, 39, 193, 194, 195, 209, 305, 321, 324
   logical vs. encyclopedic information, 323
   reorganization, 320
fill, 291
Fillmore, 139
filter, 124, 130
Fine, 184, 185
fish, 294
fish, subtle, 294
flow diagram, 171
focal scale, 36, 312
focus, 128, 247, 294, 317
Fodor, vii, viii, 4, 5, 33, 35, 37, 38, 39, 40, 42, 43, 119, 120, 142, 327
Fodor, J.D., 119, 120, 327
Foldvik, 295
follow, 295
fool, 138
foppish, 85, 88
for, 91, 292, 326
   beneficiary, 249
   complementizer, 238–46
for clause, passive, 286
for-Case, 285, 286, 292
   to IP, 274, 285
form, 173
former, 157, 326
for–NP, 253, 255, 259
French, 177, 311
fro, 222
Full Interpretation, 26, 119
function, 46. *See* translation function
   type-name for, 48
function composition. *See* composition of functions
functionality, 6, 77

function–argument application. *See* application
functor category, 48

garden party, 111
Garrett, 327
Gazdar, 12, 13, 14, 17, 80
Geach, 52, 189
generalizations, 168, 190, 206, 228
generalized projection. *See* projection
generalized quantifier. *See* quantifier
generic, 186, 187, 192, 205, 223, 225, 228, 295
generic interpretation, 183, 185, 186
genus, 85
genus et differentiae, 83, 84, 113, 178, 324
German, 144, 175
gerund, 152, 248
Giorgi, 156, 157
giraffe, 35, 79
giraffe-elimination rule, 34
government, 20, 29
  antecedent-government, 22
GPSG, 13, 14, 17, 158, 271, 315
grammar. *See also* categorial grammar, *and* GPSG.
  monostratal, 158
graze, 138
Greeks, 113
Grimshaw, viii, 236
grind, 138
guard, 138
Guéron, 298

Haack, 79
hard, 98, 100, 115, 132, 279, 280
  implicit argument for, 294

hard$_1$, 258
hard$_2$, 258
hatch, 138
hearer, 120, 156
heaviness, 118
Heim, viii, 189, 191, 202, 205, 206, 224, 228, 229, 321
help, 225
here, 319
hierarchy, in lexicon, 85
Higginbotham, 82, 93, 102, 106, 264, 271
hinged, 85, 90, 91, 326
hit, 233
hope, 286
Hornstein, ix
Horrocks, 203, 204, 210
hyponymy, 85

idealization, 81
identity, 112, 184, 188, 191, 222
idiom, 24, 29, 40, 112, 172
idiot, 177
if, 195–212, 215, 228, 247, 262, 293, 322
  cross-categorial, 226
  operator on VP, 226
  with complementizer, 215
if-clause
  adjoined to CP, 227
  varieties of, 225
iff, 203
ignorance, 36
IL, 44, 47, 74
imitate, 141
impersonalization, 292, 294
implication
  generalized, 178

logical, 179, 183, 203, 204, 220, 324
material, 202
one-way, 183, 188, 192, 222
two-way, 180, 182, 183, 192 *See also* biconditional
implicit argument. *See* argument
implicit role. *See* θ-role
impute, 145
in free variation, 172
inalienable possession, 108
indefinite, 188, 191, 196, 205, 207, 195–212, 220, 223, 224, 321
  generic, 205
  readings of, 224
inference, 31, 34, 80, 131, 170, 178, 201, 225, 305, 308, 316, 324
  compositionality, 310
inference rule, 27, 34, 36, 39, 57, 74–76, 75, 81, 223, 228, 259, 302, 304, 315, 320, 321, 323, 324
inferential effort, metric, 324
inferential system, 325
infinitival phrase
  as definition, 124, 161
  as SC head, 122
  in definition of adjective, 100
information, 144, 167, 175, 180, 308, 310. *See* filing
  conditional, 323
  innate vs. learnable, 324
  logical vs. encyclopedic, 323
  reorganization, 321
information processing. *See* processing

-ing phrase, 92, 105–6, 122, 248
Ingham, 295
innateness, 47
inside, 148
Intensional Logic, 44, 47
intensionality, 51, 72, 203, 304, 317, 327
intermediate trace, 302
internal language, 301. *See* language of thought
interpretation, 30, 84, 119, 309
  constraining, 56–76
  input to, 310–12
  non-decomposed, 171
  relative to a model, 54
interpretive use, 36, 127, 128, 317
intersect, 182, 190, 192
IP. *See* I″, clause
irrealis interpretation, 91
isle, 93
ism, 93, 154
isobare, 154
isosceles, 61, 62, 195
it, 297, 298, 303
  clausal antecedent for, 225
  pro-form of type <t>, 296
  weather-*it*, 297
ivory, 93

J, 93
J, defective category, 13, 200
Jackendoff, viii, ix
Jacobson, ix
Johnson, 289
Juggernaut, 155

Kamp, 190, 191, 202, 206, 229
Kayne, 131, 161

Keenan, 47, 79, 80, 160
keep tabs on, 29
Kempson, 162, 185, 205
Kiefer, viii
king, 61, 326
Klein, 12, 13, 17
knowledge. *See* information
  procedural, 326
  procedural vs. propositional, 324
Koopman, 11, 156
Kratzer, viii

label
  for bar-level, 311
  for Case, 149
  for categories, 83
  for roles, 149
Ladusaw, 35
Lakoff, 327
lambda abstraction, 88, 97, 144, 321, 322
lambda operator, 50, 51, 52, 56, 65, 81, 106
  binary, 53
  type for, 51
lament, 139
landing site, 217
language, 44, 318
language of thought, vii, viii, 36–44, 37, 39, 47, 61, 78, 81, 111, 119, 120, 130, 141, 143, 161, 176, 177, 183, 187, 209, 220, 221, 259, 271, 300–325
  NL word in, 304
  'logical' term, 57
  ambiguity in, 187
  and ECP, 144
  as metalanguage for semantics of NL, 309
  categories in, 305
  expressive power, 309, 324
  internal vs. external selection, 130–50, 131, 303
  logic for, 39
  new item in, 75, 180
  packaging, 324
  primitive term, 57
  realization of, 79
  semantics, viii, 47
  s-selection, 307
  syntax, viii, 235, 291, 305–12
  truth-conditionally equivalent forms, 306
  vocabulary, 39, 57, 75, 180
lap, 140
Larson, viii, 294
Lasnik, ix, 157
launch, 141
lawn mower, 111
lean, 141, 146, 327
leap, 140
learnability, 47, 231, 236–61, 252, 301, 313, 316
learner, using dictionary, 179
learning, 317, 321
leave, 141
leptokurtic, 170, 222
leptokurtic distribution, 169
Lesniewski, 58
less, 137–38
level, 302, 312, 315, 318
  for elimination, 123
level of representation, 6–10, 55, 86, 114, 231, 291
Levin, ix

Index

Lewis, 80, 202
lexical entry, 4, 5, 27, 252
  for related items, 150, 152
lexical head. *See* logical predicate
lexical item, 176, 209, 310
lexicography, 3, 64, 84, 318
lexicon, viii, ix, 4, 24, 26–29, 38, 85, 103, 124, 128, 161, 211, 231, 232, 234, 315. *See* lexical entry
  acquisition, 79
  economy in, 169
  encyclopedic entry, 35
  hierarchy in, 85
  learning of, 234
  non-canonic entry, 235
  organisation of, 34–36
  regularities over, 27
  related items in, 28
  storage of information in, 36
LF, 6–10, 51, 54, 77, 78, 83, 107, 114, 116, 148, 177, 187, 218, 220, 310
  categories at, 136, 161
  elimination of, 312
  non-standard, 117
  well-formedness conditions on, 117, 136
LF', 119, 143, 305, 308, 309, 310, 319, 321
library ticket, 31
licence, 304
licensing
  of maximal projections, 86
  of predicate, 88
light, 106, 129
like, 107, 158

likely, 95, 96, 97, 98, 100, 102, 129, 158, 236, 240, 241, 238–46, 245, 260, 292, 295, 296, 300
literal meaning, 30, 192, 203
locative, 327
logic, 44, 47
  contribution to survival, 45
  elimination rule, 34, 320
  for the language of thought, 39
  intensional, 44
  internal, 38
  introduction rule, 34, 179, 320
  natural vs. axiomatic, 34
logical closure, 32
logical entry, 192, 322, 323, 324
logical from. *See* LF
logical positivist, 169
logical predicate, 307
logical representation. *See* LR
LoT. *See* language of thought
LR, 78, 83, 84, 119, 124, 143, 148, 188, 305, 308, 310, 315, 319, 321

Maling, 158
mammal, 167
Manzini, ix, 11, 156, 158, 229, 300
mass term, 107
material implication, 202
matrix
  of definiens or definiendum, 167
  of target in text definition, 172–74
maximal projection, 156
May, 20, 77, 89, 123, 224
McCawley, 80, 228
McClelland, 79
m-command, 19

m-denotes, 70
mean, 165
meaning, viii, 167, 177, 182, 258, 323
  extensions of, 193
  inferred, 170
  relational, 155
  representation of, 176
  truth-conditional, 307
meaning postulate, 5, 34, 35, 39, 40, 42, 46, 57, 74, 80, 120, 162, 180, 182, 223, 250, 253, 259, 296, 316, 319, 327
  default, 247
means, 67
memory, working, 32
mental computation, 37
mention, 36, 57, 165, 175, 176, 177, 317
  vs. use, viii, 322
metalanguage, viii, 39, 40, 51, 57, 66, 67, 81, 93, 127, 172, 174, 176, 177, 188, 192, 319, 324
  compositionality of, 71, 72
  richness of, 41
meta-level, 183
metalinguistic term, in definition, 165, 168
metalinguistic use, 93, 127, 151, 154
meta-statement, 195
metric
  for likeness, 323
mini-model, 45
Minimalist program, viii
mislead, 158
modal, ix

in definition, 166
model, 5, 42, 44–51, 75, 81, 82, 233, 271, 327
  abstract mathematical structure, 44
  consistent, 72
  for natural language, 44–51
  intended, 45
  realization of, 45
  representational, 79
model theoretic interpretation, 57
model theoretic semantics, vii, viii, 4, 44–51, 66
  for language of thought, 47
modification, 10, 172
modifier, 26, 83, 86, 88, 92, 111
  categories, 94
  discontinuous, 114
  non-restrictive, 113
modify, 138, 140
modus ponens, 324
moist, 121
monetize, 140
monopolize, 140
monotonicity, 179, 222
Montague, 5, 44, 47, 57, 68, 80, 81, 95, 134, 157, 160, 183, 223
moribund, 94, 96, 99, 121
morpheme, 27
morphological default, 161
mortal, 94, 98, 99, 105, 115
most, 52, 53, 108, 109, 224
mouldy, 94, 105, 122, 123, 124
move, 140
move-α, 6–10, 116, 234
movement, 17–18, 17, 18, 297, 300, 311
  geometric vs. algebraic interpretation, 311

of adjunct, 218
of NP, vii, ix, 282
of theta role, 266
operator, 118
optional, 115
rightward, 143, 159, 215
much, 108
muffle, 140
multiplication, 309, 314, 325
multiply, 314

name, 319
names
  for phrases, 68
naming, 181
natural, 168
natural kind term, 322, 323
natural language, 61, 74, 158, 187, 235
  economy of packaging, 324
  types in, 131, 135
natural language utterances, 47
natural logic, 34, 35
necessary, 236, 240, 241, 242, 260, 261, 278, 279, 280, 292
necessary truth, 45
necessitate, 138, 140
negation, 125–30, 312. *See also* '*not*'
  cross-categorial, 125–30, 160
  of constituent, 126, 128
negative environments, 320
neg-raising, 128
neuter, 155
NL. *See* natural language
nominalization, 147, 295, 308, 313
non-argument, 23
non-compositional semantics, 172
non-compositionality, 172

non-creativity, 58, 65
non-intersective adjective, 134
non-primitive terms
  constraining interpretation of, 57
non-truth-conditional use, 126
not, 129, 157
  metalinguistic, 127
  modifier of adjective in definition, 125–30
  'search and replace', 127
  type for, 129
  with non-standard scope, 128
notation, 223
notational variant, 99, 119
noun
  abstract, 105
  and *genus*, 85
  and tense, 296
  definition of, 83, 85–94, 192
  modifier, 92
  relational, 111, 148
  target, 169–74
  type for, 162, 314
noun phrase
  as definition of adjective, 108
  quantified, 21, 54, 108, 109
noun–noun compound, 92, 111
NP, 16
  attributive, 109
  determinerless, 108
  function of, 54
  generic, 186
  movement, vii, ix, 297
  of type <t>, 314
  parenthetical, 109
  predicate, 24, 109, 156
  propositional, 251, 295
  restrictive modifier, 110

NP (cont'd)
  subject in, 161
  type <t>, 297
null object, 299

O. *See* empty operator
object gap, 100, 102, 120, 140, 142, 151, 158
object language, viii
object language, viii, 57, 82, 93, 127, 176, 177, 188
obvious, 261, 292
of, 105, 107, 140, 148, 172, 249, 250, 259, 295
  Case marker, 107
ontology, 46, 73
opacity, 84, 304. *See* intensionality
open class category, 172
open sentence, 25, 51
operator, 18, 21, 50, 61, 83, 86, 302, 307. *See* empty operator *and* lambda operator
  adjoined to right, 135
  adjunct as, 95
  binary, 197
  binding, 86
  definition of, 60
  lexical, 326
  movement, 118
  position, 244, 275, 298
  scope-inducing, 119
  semantic, 14, 129
  set-abstraction, 50
  unary vs. binary, 326
  vs. operand, 228
  with two complements, 262
operator raising, 197, 304, 321
optional movement, 77

optionality, 152, 155, 211, 251, 252
OR. *See* operator raising
ordered entailments, 36
ordering, 119, 149, 159
  exploitation of, 158
ordering relation, 327
other, 204
Oxford English Dictionary, 150

pair-quantification, 52, 80, 206, 207, 208, 195–212, 221, 224, 228, 229
parallel, 195, 203, 208, 209, 212, 235
parallel distributed processing, 37, 79
parallel processing, 78
parasitic gap, 257, 289
Parkes, 327
parsing, 103, 130
Partee, 80
partially-specified lexical item, 129
participial phrase, 123, 157, 248
  in SC, 122
participle, 105–6
  passive, 28
  past, 122
passive, 33, 153, 281–87
  no A-chain for, 106
  of adjective, 259
passivization, 28
patient, 295
pattern matching, 31
Peano, 63
penniless, 108
perissodactyl, 4, 327
Perry, 317, 327
Peters, 80
PF, 6–10, 114, 118, 308, 309, 312

information, 312
phonologically null elements, 27
phony, 160
phoric, 213. *See also* definition
picture, 284
picture noun phrase, 284
pidgin-logic, 61, 81
pidgin-semantics, 177
piebald, 168
pity, 268, 297, 298, 314
place-holder, 51, 147
plurals, 186
polyhedra, 175
positive context, 179
possible worlds, 45
Postal, ix, 297
PP
 locative, 157
 predicational, adjoined to VP, 140
 target, 172
pragmatic directive, 315, 319
pragmatic hypothesis, 316
pragmatic processes, 131, 183, 188, 192, 203, 220, 221, 308, 309, 315, 321
 and linguistic processing, 319
pragmatic purposes, 306
pragmatics, vii, 47, 84, 110, 113, 151, 185, 223
precatory, 112
precede, 204, 208
predicate, 23–26, 24, 51, 54, 86, 103, 265–66
 generalized representation of, 270
 licensing of, 88
 logical, 55, 262
 of the language of thought, 39
 one-place
 definition of, 132
 polyadic, 138, 144
 set-taking, 222
 syntactic, 55
 type for, 305
predicate calculus, 23, 34, 223, 307
predication, 10, 97, 99, 234, 270, 274
 by NP, 54
predictability, 45
preposition
 default, 140
 designated, 105, 145, 149
prepositional phrase
 complement of verb, 138
 as definition of adjective, 107
presuppositional effects, 110
prince-bishop, 112
Principle of Full Interpretation, 136, 307
Principle of Relevance, 32, 120
PRO, ix, 21, 27, 105, 123, 152, 211, 239, 242, 245, 253, 289, 295, 302, 313
 coindexation, 152
PRO$_{arb}$, 153, 184
probable, 236, 240, 242, 260, 295
procedural knowledge, 302
processing, 30, 120, 128, 129, 163, 165, 177, 183, 194, 224, 291, 309, 312, 318. *See also* pragmatic processes
 conscious, 319
 cost, 33, 324
 directive, 327
 left to right, 157, 159
 limitations, 324
 syntactic vs. pragmatic, 221

production, 155
  errors, 306
projection
  defective, 14
  generalized, 234, 270, 292
projection principle, 7, 8, 9, 25, 86, 88, 89, 123, 132, 161, 231
pronominal, 21
pronoun
  'avoid pronoun', 249, 253
  bound variable, 77, 192, 196, 197, 200, 216
pronunciation, 84
proper name, 54, 228
property, 87
  coded as noun or adjective, 110
  predicated of set, 186
  primitive, 328
proposition, 28, 30, 87, 233. *See* filing
  accessibility, 324
  analytic, 36
  as argument, 236–61
  degree of certainty, 323
  hypothesized, 31, 32
  s-selection for, 146
  synthetic, 36
  type <t>, 49
  underdetermined, 33
propositional attitude, 38, 239, 247, 317
prototype, 323
psycholinguistics, 42
psychological reality, 46
puce, 43, 323
Pullum, 12, 13, 17, 297
Pustejovsky, ix
putative, 132, 303, 304, 326

QNP. *See* quantified noun phrase
QR, 18, 51, 54, 107, 116, 128, 155, 177, 194, 196, 197, 200, 220, 298, 302, 321
qualities, 322
QUANT, 187
quantification, 180, 186, 192, 206, 322
  binary, 158
  existential, 205, 206, 224, 228, 229, 295
  generalized, 186
  generic, 186
  substitutional, 72
  universal, 186, 188, 189, 190, 206, 224
  unselective, 203
  variable-free, 302
quantifier, 51–53, 54, 197, 224
  binary, 52
  binding pair of variables, 52
  generalized, 52, 78, 80, 158, 304
  non-standard, 52
  restrictive term, 53, 304
  standard vs. generalised, 52
  type for, 51
  variable-free, 51
  variables, 51
quantifier-raising. *See* QR
quasi-projection, ix, 14, 16, 17, 198, 326
quasi-referential item, 233
question, 246
  echo, 77
quotation, 173, 177
  in text definition, 175
  quoted item, as NP, 173

quotation marks, 81, 165, 168, 176, 209, 210, 304
  in definition, 67, 69
quoted phrase, 78

Radford, 95, 229
Raising, ix, 268, 285
range, 193
Rappaport, 157
ready, viii, 90, 104, 236, 255–59, 258, 277, 280, 296, 316, 317
ready$_1$, 255–59, 260
ready$_2$, 255–59, 260, 261, 285, 296
realization, 38
  phonological, 151
reasoning. *See* inference
Recoverability of Deletion, 252
rectangle number, 168, 171
rectangular number, 4, 169, 171
recurrence, 314
recursion, 46
  in definition, 63
recursive, 210, 211
red, 111, 323
redundancy, 45, 78, 232
reference, 314, 319
reflexive, 283, 300
regard, 147
Reinhart, 19, 186, 190, 191, 197, 198, 199, 206, 226
relation, 46, 59
  between person and predicate, 103
  definition of, 59
Relative Clause, 247
  as definition of adjective, 106
  non-restrictive, 299
  predicate, 88

relevance, 156, 168, 306
Relevance theory, vii, 30–36, 37
repose, 139
representation, 36, 37, 183, 220
  abstract, 118, 231
  ill-formed, 326
  of argument
    generalized, 117
  procedural equivalent, 319
  subsymbolic, 37
  variable-free, 51, 52, 302
r-expression, 21
rickety, 94, 107
right node raising, 56, 289
Rizzi, 286, 298
Roberts, 289
Roeper, 229
role. *See* θ-role
role-position, 274
Rooth, 80
Rothstein, ix, 101, 156, 271
Roussou, ix
ruin, 142
rule. *See* logic
Rumelhart, 79
Russell, 25, 60, 63

Safir, 298
Sag, 12, 13, 14, 17, 80
saturation, 232, 303
  of arguments, 102, 103
say, 166, 167, 173, 180–95, 191
SC. *See* small clause
scope, 108, 119, 120, 190, 197, 201, 202, 207, 208, 219, 224, 228, 312
  and c-command, 19
scope-sensitive elements, 119

secondary predicate, 87, 282, 299
seek, 141
seem, 233
seems, 87, 122, 126, 160, 261, 282, 292
Segal, viii
segment, 20, 199, 200, 201
selection, 211
semantics, viii, 23, 38, 182, 203, 219
   compositional, 47, 117
   Conceptual, viii
   cross-categorial
      for negation, 160
      for indefinite NP, 187
   formal, 309
   model theoretic, vii, viii, 4, 44–51, 66
      for language of thought, 47
   non-compositional, 172
   of function composition, 56
   of natural language, 47
   real, 42, 44, 271
   real vs. translational, 38
   recipe for, 66
   translational, 47, 82
   truth rule, 40
   type-driven, 184
semiquotation, 120, 127, 128, 129, 130, 160, 177
sentence, 326
   open, 25, 51
   type for, 229
separate, 149
set, 46, 49, 87
   denotation for noun, 92
   identity, 184, 191
   inclusion, 183, 184, 191
   intersection, 183
   membership, 184, 191
set abstraction operator, 50, 137
set intersection
   interpretation of adjunction, 92
shave, 284
Shelley, 107
silly, 254
sink, 124
sleeps, 131
small, 161
small clause, 10, 29, 54, 55, 93, 101, 114, 121–25, 121–25, 122, 133, 157, 161, 184, 257, 267–69, 271–74, 303, 326
   reflexive in, 283
Smith, ix, 36, 166, 185, 186, 250, 307, 312, 317
something
   variable, 151–55
soundness, 45
souwester, 85
speaker, 120, 129, 315
SPEC, 152, 262–65. *See also* specifier
SPEC-head construction, 112
specific reading, 185
specificity, 168
specifier, 10, 11, 78, 96, 105, 111, 274–90
   murky status of, ix, 11
   positions, 262–65
Sperber, vii, 4, 30, 32, 33, 34, 36, 127, 168, 309, 312, 317, 320
spleen, 85
Sportiche, 11, 26, 156
square, 328
SR, 96, 114

Index

s-selection, 27, 28, 102, 122, 145, 150, 233, 236
  and conceptual adicity, 313
  and c-selection, 103, 313
  compositional, 265
  intuitive notion of, 91
  of unsaturated argument, 102
S-structure, 6–10, 6–10, 116, 118, 124, 310, 312
  and PF information, 312
statement
  construed as definition, 30
  particular or general, 168
Steedman, 55, 157, 265
stipulation, 182, 208
storage. *See* filing
Stowell, ix
strike, 326
structure, 149, 310
  flat, 156
  postulation of, 103
structure preserving principle, 16
stupid, ix, 236, 239, 240, 247, 251, 259
stupid$_1$, 240, 242, 249, 250, 251, 254, 260, 296
stupid$_2$, 240, 249–55, 250, 254, 259, 260, 261, 285, 296
stupid$_3$, 252
style, 189
subcategorization, 17, 25, 122, 123, 124, 146, 231–35. *See also* feature
  at LF, 124
  C″[O], 246–60
  C″[*that*], 238–46, 247
  C″[WH], 238–46
  for clause, 236–61

I″[O], 255
I″[*to*], 238–46
  non-canonic, 232
  syntactic promiscuity, 127
  V″, 25, 156
  V″[*to*], 238–46
subject, 11, 83, 107, 151, 156, 197, 262–65, 313
  bound by empty operator, 299
  causal responsibility, 247, 294, 296
subjunctive, 294
subordination, 12, 14, 15, 198
substitution, 121, 126
  of definition, 99
Suppes, 58, 59, 60, 61, 62, 81, 171
suppose, 133
symbol, as target, 173
syntactic variable, 77
syntax, vii, viii, 38, 46
  information in, 308
  of LoT, 39
  richer in NL than LoT, 309
synthetic proposition, 36

Takami, 225
target, 169–74, 181, 192, 195
  adjective–noun phrase, 169
  adverb–adjective, 171
  non-compositionality in, 172
  noun–noun, 171
  of definition, 74, 167
Tarski, 25, 57, 69, 71, 80, 81
tautologically equivalent, 171
temporal phrases, 223
tense, 158, 312, 327
textbooks, 163
that, 244

the, 151, 312, 319. *See also* article
metalinguistic, 93
thematic role. *See* θ-role
θ-criterion, 257, 276, 287, 314
θ-grid, 232
θ-role, 6
  added, 246–60, 277, 311
  and A-chain, 96
  assignment
    geometric vs. algebraic, 265–66
    site of, 154
  binding of, 264
  canonic, 141
  chain, 289, 298
  compositional assignment, 97, 98, 101, 106
  discharging, 136
  external, 92, 95, 262
    compositional assignment, 24
    multiple, 160
  implicit, 288, 289
  implicit, 283
  indicator of classes of inference rule, 27
  internal vs. external, 130–50
  kinds of, 141
  movement, 311, 315
  nil, 267, 268, 277
  optionality, 152
  position in specifier, 265–66, 274
  projection, 313, 314
  roles per head, 130–50
  transmission. *See* transmission
θ-theory, 56, 77, 231–35, 262–90
θ-type. *See* type
then, 215
theory of mind, 36
there, 297

expletive, 142
thought
  subsymbolic, 37
threshold
  for gradable noun, 138
tigers, 198
timelessness, 185
to, 105, 107, 154, 160, 239, 292
too, 157
topic, 181
topicalization, 54, 77, 218
topic-comment structure, 181
totally redundant, 164
tough-movement, viii, 295. *See* '*easy*'
trace, 18, 243
  intermediate, 119
  of NP, 302
  type <t>, 303
tractability, 57
transitive verb, 48
  defnition of, 138
translating, 130
translation, 74, 176, 183, 189, 211, 223, 304, 313, 318, 322, 324
  'translates into' relation, 68
  definition as, 66
  procedure, 143, 309
translation function, 304
  from English to LoT, 177
transmission, of θ-role, vii, 98, 99, 101, 136, 147, 234, 243, 245, 253, 267, 274–90, 274–90, 292
  prevented, 268
triangle, 195
triggering, 79

Index

triviality, 26, 45, 66, 144, 202, 307
true, 81, 147
truth, 223
  with respect to a model, 57
truth rule, 40
truth values, 48
truth-condition, 183, 187, 190, 223
try, 285
two, 186, 196
  adjective, 108
type, 124, 201, 231–35, 327
  <p>, 109
  algebra, 307
  and θ-theory, 49
  and well-formedness condition, 49
  changing, 80, 81, 157, 183
  checking, 232, 252, 300
  constructivity, 267–69, 271
  for adjective, 92
  for entity, <e>, 233
  for external argument, <e*>, 55
  for function, 48
  for lambda operator, 51
  for predicate, 48
    <p>, 55, 233
  for preposition, 92
  for proposition, <t>, 233
  for question, <q>, 244, 246
  for transitive verb, 48
  for truth value, 48
  higher order, 309
  name, 48
  system, 303, 306, 308, 315
  theory, 297
  word without type, 312
type changing, 54–56
type lifting. *See* type changing
type shifting. *See* type changing

typographical devices, 167

UG, 27
unbound variable, 193
uncertain, 243
uncertain$_1$, 236, 244, 260
uncertain$_2$, 236, 244, 245, 247, 260
underdetermination, 75, 170, 308, 315
understand, 167
undetermination, 291
unicorn, 156
uniformity condition, 277
uniqueness condition, 88
universals, 47
unlikely, 236, 242, 260
upward entailing context, 35, 179, 223, 319, 320
UR, 84, 114, 120, 129, 314, 315, 319, 321, 326
urge on, 157
use, viii, 165, 175, 177, 209, 317. *See also* interpretive use
  metalinguistic, 93, 127, 151, 154
  non-literal, 113

vacillating, 106
valency, 130
variable, ix, 21, 40, 80, 180, 189, 195–212, 204, 209, 218, 322
  bound, 193, 196, 204, 195–212
  strongly, 100
  common to NL and LoT, 302
  constraints on types, 144
  domain of, 304
  dummy, 51
  free, 203

variable (cont'd)
  in definition, 58, 189
  introduced by NP, 189
  phonologically realized in LoT, 312
  place-holder, 25
  range for, 302
  restricted, 193, 194, 202, 219, 220, 221, 224
    outside quantifier, 219, 220
  Tarskian style, 25
  type, 51, 303
    for clause, 303
    for event, 265
    for predicate, 133
    for values or measures, 137
    for word, 304
  unbound, 96, 189, 191, 210
variable-free notation, ix, 51, 52, 302
verb
  definition, 192
  restructuring, 300
  target, 169–74
  valency alternants, 139
Verkuyl, ix
vertical binding, 97, 98
Vikner, ix
visibility, 10, 23, 77, 90, 151, 242, 270, 273
  for Case, 285
VP complement, non-canonic, 156

Walker, 327
Wall, 80
want, 317
washer-dryer, 112

Wasow, 12, 14, 80
weather, 297
weather-*it*, 297
Weisler, 12, 14, 80
well-formedness conditions, 7, 8, 9, 20, 21, 117, 130, 136, 151, 232, 302, 312, 313, 326
wh-determiner, 53
when, 212–21, 322
  temporal use in definiton, 213
whether, 215, 293
wh-island effects, 243
wh-item, 53, 81, 88
  status of, 243
wh-relative, 106
Wilder, 299
Williams, viii, 26, 97, 98, 106, 157, 302
Wilson, vii, 4, 30, 32, 33, 34, 36, 127, 166, 168, 309, 312, 317, 320
wonder, 157
word, 313
  for complex concept, 324
  NL
    entity in LoT, 304
  typeless, 312
world
  real, 46
  real, as model, 42, 82
worth, 248

X-bar theory, 8, 10–17, 311
x-role position, 274–90, 299

Zwarts, viii